BATTLEFIELD TOURISM: HISTORY, PLACE AND INTERPRETATION

ADVANCES IN TOURISM RESEARCH

Series Editor: **Professor Stephen J. Page**
University of Stirling, UK
s.j.page@stir.ac.uk

Advances in Tourism Research series publishes monographs and edited volumes that comprise state-of-the-art research findings, written and edited by leading researchers working in the wider field of tourism studies. The series has been designed to provide a cutting edge focus for researchers interested in tourism, particularly the management issues now facing decision-makers, policy analysts and the public sector. The audience is much wider than just academics and each book seeks to make a significant contribution to the literature in the field of study by not only reviewing the state of knowledge relating to each topic but also questioning some of the prevailing assumptions and research paradigms which currently exist in tourism research. The series also aims to provide a platform for further studies in each area by highlighting key research agendas, which will stimulate further debate and interest in the expanding area of tourism research. The series is always willing to consider new ideas for innovative and scholarly books, inquiries should be made directly to the Series Editor.

Published:

Tourism Local Systems and Networking
LAZZERETTI & PETRILLO

Progress in Tourism Marketing
KOZAK & ANDREU

Extreme Tourism: Lessons from the World's Cold Water Islands
BALDACCHINO

Benchmarking National Tourism Organisations and Agencies
LENNON, SMITH, COCKEREL & TREW

Tourism and Social Identities
BURNS & NOVELLI

Micro-clusters & Networks – The Growth of Tourism
MICHAEL

Tourism in the New Europe
THOMAS & AUGUSTYN

Hospitality: A Social Lens
LASHLEY, LYNCH & MORRISON

Tourism and Politics
BURNS & NOVELLI

The Critical Turn in Tourism Studies
ATELJEVIC, MORGAN & PRITCHARD

Travel Medicine
TALES BEHIND THE SCIENCE

Forthcoming:

Tourism Research
AIREY & TRIBE

New Frontiers in Marine Tourism
GARROD & GÖSSLING

Asian Tourism
COCHRANE

Tomorrow's Tourist: Scenarios & Trends
YEOMAN

For other titles in the series visit: www.elsevier.com/locate/series/aitr

Related Elsevier Journals — sample copies available on request
Annals of Tourism Research
International Journal of Hospitality Management
Tourism Management

BATTLEFIELD TOURISM: HISTORY, PLACE AND INTERPRETATION

EDITED BY

CHRIS RYAN

University of Waikato, New Zealand

ELSEVIER

Amsterdam • Boston • Heidelberg • London • New York • Oxford
Paris • San Diego • San Francisco • Singapore • Sydney • Tokyo

Elsevier
Linacre House, Jordan Hill, Oxford OX2 8DP, UK
Radarweg 29, PO Box 211, 1000 AE Amsterdam, The Netherlands

First edition 2007

British Library Cataloguing in Publication Data
A catalogue record for this book is available from the British Library

Library of Congress Cataloging-in-Publication Data
A catalog record for this book is available from the Library of Congress

ISBN: 978-0-08-045362-0

For information on all Elsevier publications
visit our website at books.elsevier.com

Printed and bound in The Netherlands

07 08 09 10 11 10 9 8 7 6 5 4 3 2 1

To Mr Charles Perkins — history teacher, St Joseph's College, Beulah Hill, London, SE19, in the 1960s — the late Peter Heron, Anca, and Mark.

Contents

Acts of Remembrance

List of Figures

List of Photographs

List of Maps

List of Diagrams

List of Tables

The Contributors

Jenny Cave's qualifications include a masters degree in museum studies from the University of Toronto, Canada; a B.A. honours (Otago) in oceanic prehistory; an open fellowship (Toronto); and extensive training in programme evaluation, comprehensive audit, marketing and ISO 9000. Her research experience ranges from academic studies in prehistory and communication through design (Otago and Toronto) to applied research projects investigating audience development techniques and an extensive range of market research, effectiveness and management issues from 1981 to 1991 for the Canadian government. She now lectures in special interest and cultural tourism at the University of Waikato, New Zealand. Her current research interests are in the arena of cultural tourism, adventure and backpacker tourism, and she has published in journals that include *Tourism Management* and the *Journal of Travel Research*. She is currently completing her doctorate at the University of Waikato into the development of small business enterprises among the South Pacific Peoples now resident in Auckland, New Zealand, with emphasis on cultural product and its tourism associations.

Li-Hui Chang a native of the Kinmen, is an assistant professor in the Department of Tourism Management at National Kinmen Institute of Technology (Taiwan), where she has been teaching for nine years. She holds a masters degree in park, recreation and tourism from the University of Missouri-Columbia (USA), and is currently completing her doctoral studies at the Graduate Institute of Building and Planning at the National Taiwan University. Li-Hui's research interests are tourism planning and development. She has published several academic papers and conducted numerous studies in tourism planning and development for Kinmen local government. She is currently completing work on an undergraduate textbook on interpretation for park visitors.

Malcolm Cooper has had a long career as an academic, town planner, and consultant in the tourism industry, and subsequently became a professor of Tourism to establish the degree of tourism at Wairiki Institute, New Zealand. He subsequently moved to the University of Southern Queensland, Australia, and then to his present post as professor and Vice president of Research at Ritsumeikan Asia Pacific University, Japan. Malcolm has a long history of publication, but in recent years has published in *Current Issues in Tourism* on State intervention in tourism planning and 'top down' intervention in local affairs, *Tourism Review International* on Japanese tourism and the *ASEAN Journal on Hospitality and Tourism* on issues of tourism strategy. His research interests include the impacts of the ageing of the Japanese population on future patterns of tourism in, and out of Japan, and on issues pertaining to Japanese culture and world perceptions.

Warwick Frost obtained his doctorate from La Trobe University, Australia, and lectures at Monash University, Australia. He is the author of *Travel and Tour Management* and has research published in journals that include *Tourism Management, The International Journal of Heritage Studies*, and was co-editor of a special issue of *Tourism, Culture and Communication* on tourism and the media. His current research interests relate to the tourism implications of the Australian Gold Rush and their interpretation, and his chapter on the Eureka Stockade forms part of a current research project. At the time of writing, his other major projects include the origins of the National parks concept, changing interpretations of intangible heritage and the imagining of villages as rustic tourist destinations.

Mary-Catherine Garden is a lecturer in heritage studies and associate director of the Heritage Futures Network at Glasgow Caledonian University, with responsibilities for local/community history. Her wider research interests include the investigation of the perception and use of past places, in particular, heritage sites and other heritage landscapes with a particular focus on the exploration of heritage as a social construct. She is interested in the interface between history, heritage and archaeology as specific ways of interpreting the past and, in turn, how each is used and understood both by individuals and by groups. Specifically, she is interested in exploring the process whereby elements of history and 'the past' are selected out and/or celebrated by society in both tangible and intangible ways.

Huimin Gu is professor and deputy dean of the School of Tourism Management and Vice President of the Beijing Hotel Institute at Beijing International Studies University. She has been commissioned to undertake research by the China National Tourism Administration (CNTA), Beijing Tourism Bureau and the China Hotel Corporation among others. In 1998 she won an award for work completed on the Chinese domestic market. Professor Gu has been the sole or co-author of five books, a sixth being completed in 2007 and she is currently working as co-author on a book on research methods applied to tourism for publication in 2007. She has published research in both Chinese and English in Chinese tourism journals, and has forthcoming work to be published in UK/USA-based journals having already published in the *Cornell Quarterly, Journal of Vacation Marketing* and *Tourism Recreation Review*. She has been a visiting scholar at the Conrad Hilton College at the University of Houston, USA, and has a doctoral degree from Renmin University's Management School in economics.

Teresa Leopold is completing her PhD in tourism at the Department of Tourism, University of Otago, New Zealand. Her research looks at internal and external community issues involved in the disaster recovery process of a destination. She has a first-class honours degree in Tourism Management from the University of Brighton, UK and a masters in tourism from the University of Otago, for which she was awarded a postgraduate scholarship.

Additional to her teaching responsibilities, her particular research interests are the ethical presentation of and visitor behaviour at war heritage sites, destination development and recovery, event and convention management as well as wine tourism. She is particularly interested in the development of Southeast Asia and the Pacific, where most of her research is based.

Fiona McLean is a professor in heritage management at Glasgow Caledonian University. Fiona has attracted research grants and published widely in the heritage field, most notably on the negotiation and construction of identity at heritage sites. Fiona is currently the editor of the *International Journal of Heritage Studies*, published by Routledge. Her publications include articles in the *International Journal of Cultural Studies*, the *International Journal of Cultural Policy* and *Tourism Culture and Communication*. She has gained ESRC research grants, including one for work on the contributions made by museums to the inclusive community. Her research interests include the social role of heritage and negotiation and construction of identities through heritage. Fiona is currently working on a number of research projects on museums and national identity; museums and the audience; the role of museums in an inclusive society; issues of identity, place and policy in battlefield sites; and was appointed to evaluate the V&A Image and Identity project in 2005.

Charlie Panakera was a former resort owner in the Solomon Islands and retains close connections with his birth place. Charlie came to New Zealand in 1988 and taught at Massey University in the Department of Accounting, School of Business Studies. In 1990 he moved to Waikato Management School as a lecturer in the Department of Accounting, and from 1995 to 1997 was the founding director of the Tourism Programme at the Business School. From 1997 to 1998 he was an Assistant Director of the Executive Education (International MBA) within the Waikato Management School and currently teaches in its Diploma Program. He is currently a Visiting Professor at the University of the South Pacific, Suva, Fiji. He also conducts research through AUSAID programmes, and advises on Pacific Affairs for the New Zealand Ministry of Foreign Affairs.

Mark Piekarz lectures at the University of Worcester and holds degrees in political theory and institutions from the University of Liverpool, UK, and a masters degree in leisure management from the University of Sheffield. He is currently undertaking doctoral studies into issues of political risk assessments for sports, tourism and adventure organisations. His research interests lie in risk management, environmental scanning and sports and adventure tourism. Mark is also a member of the Institute of Leisure and Amenity Management in the United Kingdom.

Bruce Prideaux is a professor of Marketing and Tourism Management at James Cook University, Australia, having previously held a professorial post at the University of Queensland. Bruce has published widely in all of the leading tourism journals including *Annals of Tourism Research, Tourism Management* and *International Journal of Tourism Research*. He has been guest editor for a number of journals including the *Asia Pacific Journal of Tourism Research* and *The Journal of Vacation Marketing*. His research interests include transport and tourism (which was the subject of his doctoral degree obtained from the University of Queensland), destination development and life cycles and crisis management. Bruce was a joint leader of a Co-operative Research Centre for Sustainable Tourism Research project into transport, tourism and sustainability. His interest in military issues and tourism is also deep seated, Bruce having been an active reservist in the Australian armed forces for twenty eight years. He also helped edit a special issue on tourism and warfare published in the *International Journal of Tourism Research.*

Chris Ryan is a professor of tourism at the University of Waikato, editor of the journal, *Tourism Management*, and an elected fellow of the International Academy for the Study of Tourism. He has acted in an advisory capacity for meetings of the APEC Tourism Ministers, has been a part of the Special Projects Committee of the New Zealand Ministry of Tourism and is responsible for that ministry's Research Index. He has published widely in major journals and has contributed to, edited and authored several books including *Researching Tourist Satisfaction* and *Recreational Tourism*. With a background in economics and psychology, he is interested in tourist behaviours and their impacts on tourists themselves, communities and environments; and in the political ramifications of those impacts. His current research includes projects with colleagues from China, USA and the UK. In China, he has been a keynote speaker at several conferences; he was a visiting professor at the College of Charleston in 2006, and is an honorary Professor of the University of Wales at the Welsh Centre for Tourism and Hospitality Management, UWIC.

Hugh Smith is a lecturer in tourism and travel at Glasgow Caledonian University, having previously worked in the finance sector, travel sector and as a business development consultant in the Moffat Centre for Travel and Tourism Business Development at the University. His research interests include the challenges and politics of managing and interpreting tourism heritage sites that remain following conflicts, and he has conducted research on such sites in the Czech Republic and Spain. His other research interests include business tourism and small- and medium-sized enterprises.

Gordon Urquhart works in heritage development in the Highlands of Scotland. He is currently developing a web site for the heritage industry (www.heritagenorth.org.uk), but has also published on social inclusion and museums, built populist soundscapes for Inverness City and curated an exhibition of 1,476 thimbles. Among his roles has been that of assistant director of the Glasgow Conservation Trust West, his book *Along Great Western Road* has been well received and shows both his enthusiasm and knowledge of Glasgow's and Scottish heritage. It comprises a collection of over 300 photographs, complete with text, and portrays the architecture, residents, institutions, and the development, and later destruction, of parts of Glasgow West's picturesque townscape.

Craig Wight is a business development consultant in the Moffat Centre, Glasgow Caledonian University undertaking commercial project work for a range of public and private tourism organisations. Craig has undertaken academic research into visitor attraction management, the discourses of remembering human tragedy and war crimes, national icons in tourism interpretation, war museum interpretation and 'culinary tourism'. Recently, Craig has carried out research into Lithuanian Soviet and Jewish tragedy in the context of museum interpretation, and such research continues to underpin his evolving PhD work.

Vivian Zhang is currently engaged in PhD research in the field of 'Destination Choice of Chinese Outbound Tourists' at the University of Waikato, New Zealand. In 2004 she obtained her masters degree in tourism management from Beijing International Studies University, China. During her postgraduate study, she published papers with the main topics of strategic alliance of travel agencies, hotel employee turnover and tourism crisis management in the journals, *Tourism Science*, *Hotel Modernization* and *China Tourist Hotels*. Back in 2002, she attended the First Asia Pacific Forum for Graduate Students in Macau and presented the working paper of 'Tourism Marketing Strategies in Beijing Suburbs'. From 2004 to 2006 Vivian taught at Beijing City University before moving to New Zealand. She was a lecturer in management, hotel business and English for hotel service. Her current research interests include tourism and hospitality education and teaching methods, reducing employee turnover in the hospitality industry, tourist behaviours and motivation and destination marketing.

Preface

This book has had a long gestation. I think it was initially prompted by my interest in history and visits that were made to various castles commencing from holidays spent in my childhood home of Wales. How could I not be so interested? The place of my early youth, the Mumbles on the Gower Peninsula, nestles at the foot of Oystermouth Castle, built by the Normans in the 13th and 14th centuries. I can also remember visiting Scotland as a student, and still have my photographs of the Monument at Glenfinnan, where Bonnie Prince Charlie raised his standard, and of Culloden, where the adventure ended and the 'butcher', Cumberland, maintained the house of Hanover. The opportunity to actually write this book came in the early part of 2006 when I was on sabbatical at The College of Charleston in South Carolina, USA. Again, my lay interest in history was prompted as of course South Carolina was the state that first seceded from the Union in 1861. As a school pupil, I had read Winston Churchill's *History of the English-Speaking Peoples*, and had read his descriptions of the battles of the American Civil War. Here, I was at the heart of these events, and it was but a matter of time before I visited Fort Sumter and began a more detailed reading of the American Civil War. However, I quickly realised if I was to write a book that was to appeal to people in several parts of the world it was necessary not only to consider the places with which I had familiarity, but also to draw upon the experiences, enthusiasm and knowledge of others, who could then write about other sites that possessed importance. I am therefore very grateful to my colleagues who have contributed their chapters to this book.

It will be noted that these chapters represent in many ways a hegemony of an English-speaking university world and its tradition where tourism is either an established or emerging area of academic importance. It can be objected that the examples from China are an exception to this observation but, as I observed at both the conferences in Hualien and Beijing in 2006 (Ryan, 2006a, 2006b), given the stage of evolution of tourism studies in the Chinese-speaking world, the influence of the English speakers is still strong inasmuch as many of the first generation of Chinese academics in tourism have studied for doctoral degrees in either the United States, United Kingdom, or other countries such as Australia, Canada and New Zealand. One consequence for this book is the presence of silences. There are no contributions from India, the African continent or Latin America. In that sense, many of the observations made in this book may not have global significance, but I would like to think that the issues raised, and the commonality of the human experience of warfare, means the contributions would be of some help to scholars from these parts of the world, if only to help them begin to shape their thinking. I also take solace in the view that knowledge can advance by acts of rejection, as much as by acts of acceptance, and thus any disagreement with the contents of this book is also a contribution on the part of the authors in as much as disagreement is recognition of a given discourse.

Of course any editor performs acts of selection, and this editor in particular has not only made such selective acts, but has also imposed patterns of order through style of editing and by contribution of much of the material. These acts have been born of necessity and choice. Necessity in the sense that while a request for contributions over Trinet elicited high initial levels of interest, few actual contributions (some of which were 'culled') eventuated. Choice as much as this eventuality provided an excuse for the editor to insert more of his own material! With such actions and choice comes the responsibility that the faults are more my own than those of any other contributor — and so while I would wish they should take credit for their contributions, any brickbats and negative comments that might emerge need to be directed at myself as the contributors became prisoners of my own interpretations.

Equally, I must protect my publishers even while I thank them. I would wish to acknowledge the contribution made by my colleague Steve Page, who as book series editor articulated a belief in this text by ably persuading Pergamon-Elsevier to publish the book. I would also wish to thank Mary Malin, Tony Roche and Jo Scott at Elsevier for their support at different stages and equally for scheduling the book into the production schedule even though I signed no contract — the contract only being delivered with the manuscript. Thank you for being patient with my idiosyncrasies.

Finally, it is the custom of an author to indicate the place of writing. This has been a book developed over time and in different places. Indeed this preface is being written in a hotel bedroom in Bolzano. It is evident from the contents that I have visited locations in different parts of the world. Thus I must thank not only the colleagues who directly contributed chapters but also my colleagues at the Waikato University's Department of Tourism and Hospitality Management: namely Jenny Cave, Asad Mohsin, Christine Lim, Tim Lockyer, Alison McIntosh, Charlie Panakera and Anne Zahra — who covered my teaching while I was absent from the University — John Crotts and Steven Litvin in particular at the College of Charleston, but also to Bob Frash Jr, Heather Goldman and Barbara Green, Harold Pechlaner and Barbara Klingsbigl at the University of Salzburg who unknowingly provided the wherewithal for me to complete the first chapter, Wihu Bu at Peking University and Zhang Wen at Beijing International Studies University, and again particularly 'TC' Huan at National Chiayi University, Taiwan, and Gu Huimin at Beijing International Studies University for their friendship and providing a means to obtain some insight into Chinese culture, and Zhang (Vivian) Wei, one of my doctoral students, for again aiding me by not only contributing to a chapter and undertaking translations from Chinese, but also by covering some of my classes during my absence. To all these colleagues, thank you.

Chris Ryan
Hamilton, Charleston, Beijing and Bolzano.

Chapter 1

Introduction

Chris Ryan

As is noted in the preface, the antecedents of this book and its actual gestation are long. I noted that as a child enjoying long summers in the Mumbles on the Gower Peninsular, I did so under the shadow of the Norman Castle of Oystermouth. Indeed, in those days it was not open to the public, but what boy could resist slipping through inefficient fences to play at laying ambush upon a misplaced Sheriff of Nottingham, or aiding Walter Scott's hero, Ivanhoe, to lay siege to the castle. And scattered around the peninsular lie other remnants of Norman castles and keeps, while on forays then and later into the heartlands of Wales one could not but be aware of the presence of military fortifications. Later, I became interested in history more formally, and indeed my original intention was to read history at university but, through what proved to be a lucky chance (although that was not my feeling at the time), I ended taking an economics degree. Nonetheless, I have long retained a personal interest in history, and have taken many opportunities to visit different places of historical interest across Europe, North and South America, Asia and Australasia. Increasingly, over the past two to three decades those visits have become aligned with other interests related to tourism. I have become interested in how places are presented and managed, what is said and what is not said; how views are directed and gazes structured through the placement of notices, the spiel of guides, the writing of brochures and the very goods sold in souvenir shops. Such things are themselves acts of interpretation, acts that are not neutral, but constructed with an alignment to (a) what is perceived as professional good practice, and (b) the reinforcement, modification or rebellion against cultural *mores* and values — which acts are political and in recognition of nodes of differing structures of power. In some instances, the power and the interpretation is open and quite naked, as is evidenced to some degree by the concept of Red Tourism that is explored in this book by Gu, Ryan and Zhang. In other instances, it is complex hearkening back to important events based upon and still shaping a sense of difference, as is evident in the chapters in this book relating to the American Civil War sites in the state of South Carolina. Thus, for example, references to the Northern War of Aggression are readily evident in histories that inform the continuing debate in the United States of the relationship between Federal and State government. At other times, as in the chapter on the Eureka Stockade authored by Warwick

Frost, places are not only sites of disputed facts but also of the making of myths that become important in shaping how societies (or the governments of those societies) like to see themselves — which myth making is turned to economic advantage.

The economics of battlefields is also a continuing theme that runs within many of the chapters. There is the obvious commercial gain that can result from visitation, and thus Mark Piekarz in his chapter on the identification of English Battlefields notes not only how a battlefield can create employment, but also their importance in contributing to a portfolio of tourist attractions to support a tourism industry in places devoid of iconic attractions. Yet the issues of economics possess their own inconsistencies. It is perhaps an irony that one of the strongest motives for the development of Red Tourism is not simply a confirmation of the heroic status of the founders of modern China, but a wish to develop the economies of rural areas. In an intriguing interweaving of tourism and the construction of major transport networks, Red Tourism sites are being developed to give reason for the usage of new transport systems that also bring regions and peoples into the mainstream of Chinese economic development. However, in the most capitalist of all countries, the United States, the development of the significant re-enactment movement is almost wholly motivated by a wish to better understand the conflicts of a past that shaped America, to use the re-enactments of engagements to inform a current generation of a history that some argue is in danger of being forgotten in an emergent popular culture of sound bites, of transitory moments of attention and the dominance of perception rather than reality. In the Bush years, after 11 September 2001, one can argue that public reaction to perceived threat has become a significant influence in American decision taking, and perhaps this was best exemplified in the debate of potential Dubai management of US ports in the first part of 2006 when the view was expressed on more than one talk back radio show that the facts did not matter, it was sufficient that the potential management company was Arab. It is perhaps an irony that it is a Bush presidency that exemplifies the post-modern importance of signage over reality.

For her part, Teresa Leopold in her chapter argues that one of the functions of battlefields is to serve as reminders of the past in order to create a better future. If only it could be so! My own belief is that these are complex phenomena located in the cultural politics of silence and absence as much as articulation and presence. References to silences, and to discourse, and the nature of that discourse, and the relationship between agreement, disagreement, presence and absence reflects an underlying philosophical paradigm that helped shape this book. It seems to me that much of the content concerns itself with four related things or processes. First, there is the question of how a culture is made, of how, in this instance, an interpretation of events is created so as to contribute to an understanding of the present. Second, there is a need to analyse the text of such interpretations. The researcher needs to question that which is taken for granted. There is a need to search for the silence and the alternatives that such silences may represent. There is in the academic debate about tourism, a longstanding concern and questioning about what is and what constitutes 'the authentic'. I have long come to the conclusion that that is the wrong question. What we should be concerned about is the 'authorisation' of stories that are constructed about events, about interpretation and about culture. In a sense, who authorises the authentication? Who authorises the story telling, and for what purpose is the authorisation given? The issue possesses importance because the authorisation helps shape the experience of place. Therefore, third, it seems to me, especially given the nature of the tourism, we must look at the 'lived in experience' of the place. There is, of course, the experience of the tourist, who comes to the place with a set of mental constructions, born of their own past experience, and of expectations filtered through the presence or absence of significant other people. We know that an experience of any place is never the same, no matter how many times it is visited. As I said in Peking (Ryan, 2006), to visit a place alone, to visit with family, to visit with friends, to visit with lovers, to visit with students — all of these companions make differences even though the landscape and the physical constructions and professional interpretations and representations of any given place remain the same. Tourism is about relativities of lived in spaces — or perhaps that should be of visited places — and these relativities are never the same. But in addition to the visitor there is also the host. The visitor's place of difference is the host's place of everyday work. In the case of battlefield sites and other commemorations of war, they are also living reminders of a past, which form part of the host's daily social ambience and to which, by their functions and perhaps personal interests, they contribute and possibly identify with. Fourth, there is the presence of another significant influence — the managers of the sites. Not only do the managers of sites impact upon interpretation of place by what they choose to say, and not to say, they also impact upon that experience of place by the construction and non-construction of paths, viewing sites and the other means of destination management. It is they who literally direct the tourist gaze, informing what there is to see, how to see and thereby framing sight — and it is for the visitor to question or not to question the framing. In this they react to and with the political hegemonies and sites of resistance that shape the culture of their society. Consequently much of this book might be said to be informed by a sense of symbolic interactionism (e.g. see Goffman, 1959; Clough, 1991), albeit with full recognition of post-modernistic interpretations of signage, and the consumption of signs as a means of self-definition. Indeed, given the importance of communication within symbolic interactionism, it seems to me totally in accordance with the pragmatism of the Chicago school that in the early part of the twenty-first century the role of media in both form and content in determining self-concept based on consumption of signs and not possible 'reality' must be recognised. In adopting this perspective the nature of messages and their omissions become important in understanding the construction of signage, which in turn impacts upon the 'lived in experience'.

Symbolic interactionism has been defined as 'a down-to-earth approach to the scientific study of human group life and human conduct' (Blumer, 1969, p. 47). Denzin (1989, 1992) argues that its data are the voices, emotions and actions of those studied, of the life experiences to which people attribute importance and which shape their personal meanings and understandings of the world in which they live. It is therefore a means of looking at and examining battlefield sites that accepts definitions of heroism; that individuals can face dangers knowing that the days of their own mortality are indeed numbered, and that in turn, these stories can emotionally impact upon the visitor, as described in the chapter on the aircraft carrier *Yorktown*. In short, while histories and battles are the outcomes of significant social forces as, for example, described by Hugh Smith in his contribution on the Spanish Civil War and its comparative lack of interpretation at Belchite, these forces result in selections of actions and behaviours by individuals. Equally, while tourism is a social and economic force of significance, it is as individuals that we stand and stare at sites, listen to and read interpretations and incorporate them into our own neural networks of understanding — which understandings are affective as well as cognitive. Emotional responses to places of conflict, injury and death are thus to my mind an appropriate subject for description and analysis.

Thus, in the past as I have gazed upon battlefield sites, I have experienced a mixture of emotions, which the research for this book has intensified. People died at these sites, and these deaths become the subject of our gaze. Not all, indeed one suspects most, of the dead wanted to be at these sites. Some died as cowards, others as heroes. Some died with fear, others with hate, and others perhaps almost unaware, victims of an unseen bomb or a sniper's bullet. Some will have believed in the cause in which they served, others were present through a sense of responsibility even while entertaining doubts, and others were present through conscription or ill-luck. Some hated their military service, while for others it provided companionship and sense of purpose. And what of the survivors of battle? Some survived the immediate aftermath of conflict as either being wounded or as a prisoner, only subsequently to die of poor or no care. Some survived periods of internment, while others survived as 'victors', to continue their lives as witnesses to horrors or, in more modern periods, encased in the isolation of a distant strike but perhaps victim to an imagination of what befell their victims. Given these multiplicities of experiences, it is no wonder that battlefield sites possess multiple 'truths'. They are the constructions of reactions to individual stories, wider social constructs and ideologies that formed our past and inform our present and future.

Having stated my own perspectives, it should be noted that they are not necessarily the perspectives of other contributors to this book. As noted in the preface, as editor I have sought to create an ordered text. In doing so it is more than possible that I have imposed interpretations that are not perhaps wholly consistent with the intent of the original contributors, and as noted in the introduction to the 'act of resource management' it is recognised that a spirit of positivism does inform some of the contributions. However, it must also be recognised that regardless of any intent on the part of either author or editor, the final constructions will be those of the readers, who will bring to the subject their own perspectives. It is hoped however, that the following chapters will help inform those perspectives.

While battlefields possess multiple truths, Bruce Prideaux points out that they increasingly possess multiple categories of locations. In the Second World War, the battlefield could range several miles as demonstrated by Prideaux's own analysis in this book, and the chapters on the *Yorktown* and Solomon Islands by Ryan and Panakera, respectively. Today, argues Prideaux, war could be in cyber space, or a viral warfare, while what is one to make of a 'War on Terror' which is waged by Bush not only in the lands of Afghanistan and Iraq, but through the monitoring of phone calls in the United States and prison camps and 'holding areas' in countries not otherwise involved in the 'hot' war zones. The implication is that the battlefield is not geographically bound to a specific place, but becomes free of geography; or rather it is bound by the geography of the location of the enemy who is outside of any given entity known as a state or country. In a world or society of 'war against drugs' or a 'war against terror' where the enemy is defined as a 'drug baron' or terrorist who is often embedded in more than one society, the definition of the battlefield as previously understood becomes either incomplete or is redefined in terms of a pre-modern or modern world only and hence, by definition, is incompatible with a post-modern world where war is constructed by engagements over media, hostage takings, non-declaration of hostilities, cyber space, eaves-dropping on one's own citizens and the surrounding of houses in one's own country. These new realities are recognised by Bruce Prideax in his chapter, and by Mark Piekarz in his chapter on 'hot' and 'cold' war but, for the most part, being concerned with tourism, the main part of the text concentrates upon specific destinations or artefacts of war that can be visited by the tourist.

One problem with the approach of adopting multiplicities of definitions, 'truths' and experiences of sites in tourism is that identified by positivists such as Huber (1974) and McPhail (1991) who argue that it is all very well creating contextualised stories of specific places at specific times for specific actors, but such an approach becomes atheoretical, does not permit generalisation and lacks the rigour of scientific enquiry. It also becomes a concentration upon reaction to events, writings and presentations rather than an enquiry into the 'why' of events, writings and presentations. From another perspective it begins to omit an analysis of power and politics. However, it can be objected that of necessity in order to communicate there must be shared understandings, and the specificities of given places and times are transferable to illuminate other places and times — and it is in the aggregation of constructed stories that themes emerge, which are testable in the ways required of post-postivisitic enquiry. Already in this chapter opposites have been posed that represent an initial framework of enquiry. These are shown in Figure 1.1.

Therefore, the site might have varying degrees of being 'hot' or 'cold'. Piekarz in his chapter on hot war tourists thus writes of tourists attracted to current rather than past conflict and includes in his analysis the peacekeepers and others who have differing degrees of interaction with combatants. However, such sites become less hot as hostilities cease, time passes, and eventually the direct combatants die and pass away. The events then pass into history and subsequent generations interpret them in terms of their own needs. Such interpretations can range between the poly-vocal and the uni-vocal as those subsequent generations seek to either confirm their own status and homogeneity by perceiving others through a gaze of 'otherness' or alternatively embrace more inclusive interpretations. The nature of this voice in terms of whether it embraces or is silent about

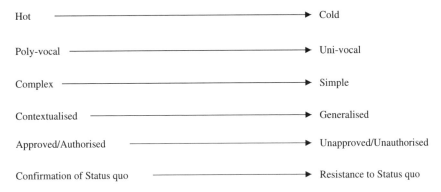

Figure 1.1: Continuums of battlefield interpretation.

others is not necessarily a precursor to the complexity of the interpretation. While there is a correlation between a poly-vocal voice and complexity, this need not necessarily be the case. The interpretations of 'the other' may be comparatively simple, and divisions within one's own society may be glossed over. The interpretations that are on offer may be confined to a contextualisation confined within the chronology of a given battle without reference to wider social significance or, alternatively, they are generalised in terms of what lessons might be thought to exist for a contemporary society and its future. Both interpretative alternatives represent a judgement and thus imply the existence of an autho-rised perspective, which of course raises the interesting question of who authorises and for what purpose? However, in some circumstances, where commemoration has emerged from a bottom-up rather than a top-down drive for recognition, then the interpretations may well be sites of resistance to the dominant myths and structures of a society. This is perhaps particularly true of sites that relate to indigenous people, who had hitherto been margin-alised and in part silenced by incomplete representations of their perspective. The chapter by Ryan that compares Rangiriri and Batoche touches upon such issues. These different perspectives of interpretation are possibly tied to two ways of viewing the battlefield, and these are suggested not as metanarratives but as constructs to help inform perceptions of battlefields and their functions as tourist sites. The first arises from the above continua and the second adopts Weaver's (2000) own adoption of Butler's (1980) life cycle to the site of war.

Figure 1.2 represents four possible patterns of interpretation and management of battlefield sites based upon two dimensions of the mythic vs. factual adherence in inter-pretation, and the concern to tell a story specific to the events of a site as against a concern to contextualise interpretation within a wider setting of social, economic and political forces. A subset of this second dimension is the issue of justification of events as against

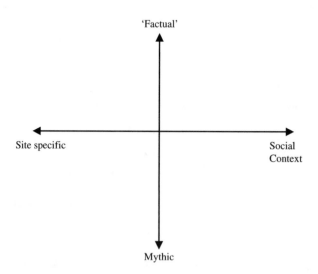

Figure 1.2: Patterns of interpretation.

a vilification of parties to a conflict. Four possible scenarios thus arise, but they are not mutually exclusive and a site can occupy more than one space on the grid. These spaces are shown in Figure 1.2.

The Factual-Site Specific

This relates to an adherence to historical 'objective' fact in the sense that it depends upon scholarship and enquiry and seeks to 'explain' a sequence of events at a given site. It might be characterised at an extreme as a narrow perspective of military history, which traces the movements of troops and is concerned with the tactics and strategy of war and a particular engagement. In some instances, it may deliberately silence the reasons for conflict but particularly articulate the emotions of those engaged in conflict, and in this book possible examples of such an articulation are the interpretations offered at the *USS Yorktown* and to some extent at the re-enactment of the Battle of Aiken.

The Mythic-Site Specific

The mythic can be interpreted in many different ways. Arguably, early interpretations of Red Tourism sites existed to explain and enhance the role of early Chinese Communist leaders and their involvement at specific sites. The articulation of the experience of those engaged in battle, especially if perceived as undertaking a defence of freedom or engaged in acts of patriotism or heroism, might mean interpretation risks not being confined in the factual-site specific domain, but strays into the territory of the mythic-site specific. The passing of time and incomplete records might reinforce the mythic, or the wish to engender interpretations of what it means to be a member of a particular society and the defining role of the site might move a place into this cell. Thus Warwick Frost's chapter on the *Eureka Stockade* or Ryan's chapter on the *Yorktown* may fit, at least in part, within this cell. Certainly, Ryan's chapter implies that the visitor may experience a sense of the mythic through attributing his or her own thoughts on what it meant to be in such circumstances — yet arguably one message of the *Yorktown* was that these were ordinary people in extraordinary circumstances.

The Factual — Socially Contextualised

Here interpretation uses the site to better explain not only what happened, but also to offer a scholarly interpretation that seeks to be inclusive in as far as it can. Examples from this book that might fit into this quadrant are the chapters on Fort Sumter, the description of the site of the Battle of Batoche in Canada and the wider considerations of Mark Piekarz's chapter on English battlefield sites.

 The role of sites changing from hot to cool and in consequence their changing interpretations and usages are demonstrated in the chapter on Xiamen and Kinmen, as what were once points of an artillery exchange between mainland China and islands within the control of the Kuomintang (KMT) have now become shopping excursions and places of business amid the remains of tunnels and barracks that add to the visitors experience.

The Mythic — Socially Contextualised

There are circumstances where societies or ruling cliques may wish to sustain a myth about the past, which myth is socially sanctioned to justify the *status quo*. Possibly Hugh Smith's chapter on the Spanish Civil War sites and comparative lack of narrative at those sites fits within this domain. A similar chapter is that of Malcolm Cooper's on Japanese interest in the sites of the Second World War. Of specific interest is where the mythic becomes displaced from the original site, and this is demonstrated by Ryan and Cave's chapter on Armistice Day celebrations in the small New Zealand town of Cambridge.

It is to be noted that in the above conceptualisations the attribution of importance to the social context implies that the destination life cycle of the battlefield site is not solely one to be measured by visitor numbers alone, but also it is one surrounded by a changing pattern of interpretation. Weaver (2000) suggests the existence of a war-distorted destination life cycle building upon Smith's (1996) five-fold typology of battle- and war-related attractions; namely 'the heroic phase', 'remembrance of the fallen', 'lest we forget', 'when we were young' and 'reliving the past'. Like Prideaux, Weaver also notes the role of personnel associated with war as explorers of a destination and acting as tourists and purchasers of locally made items — again noted by Panakera in this collection of texts. Although Weaver is not specifically concerned with issues of interpretation, it is implicit in the scenarios that he develops. Sites visited by past participants may well have roles as being memorials to the recent dead being honoured by those who knew them. The example of the *USS Yorktown* discussed later in this book is one such example. Such sites speak at a strong emotional level to visitors who have shared sets of reference and experiences, and what must be left unstated because visitors are able to provide their own inputs of meaning. But, as again demonstrated by the *Yorktown* example, passing time and the death of survivors mean that subsequent generations have different needs to both recall the nature of the past and the meanings for their present periods. Interpretation then begins to differ, for a failure to offer a new perspective means that which sufficed in the past no longer appears relevant — as again is illustrated by the *Yorktown*. For the future, Weaver draws attention to the changing nature of battles fought over large distances within brief periods of time as in the 1991 Gulf War, where he suggests the future places of visitation are to be found in virtual reality recreations and the meetings occur through the hyperreality of the internet.

It is evident though, that however classified, battlefield sites fit but comparatively poorly within any given categorisation as suggested above because changing times and needs require new interpretations, and indeed at any one time on-site interpretation may fit into any one of the real-mythic site-specific social contextualisation frameworks. Being potentially multi-vocal, the sites may offer ambiguities and contradictions in interpretations. It may be said that interpretations are acts, and acts are staged stories: they are the performance of wisdoms, cultures, perceived truths; they are selections from stories, for some stories are not performed; they are silenced, but their very non-statement is a legitimisation of that which is articulated. The denial of one story is the justification of the other. In turn, what are the characteristics of the stories that are told? What genre forms are being used — documentary as is traditional in museums, or the more melodramatic as in battle re-enactments; what narrative traditions do they draw upon and to what contextualisations do they appeal; to what extent do they purely draw upon regimes of presumed factual detachment or do they seek to engage the emotions, thereby drawing upon the personal, popular as well as the scholarly (Ulmer, 1989)? Accordingly, the remainder of the book is divided into various sections described as 'acts' — these being:

Acts of resource management
Acts of silence
Acts of discovery and rediscovery
Acts of imagination
Acts of remembrance

In Neil Leiper's much cited model of the tourism system, tourism is divided into a tourism-generating and a tourism-receiving system. Ryan and Trauer (2005) amended that model, as demonstrated in Figure 1.3, where the tourism-generating zone is replaced by tourism demand, which is viewed as divisible into the intra- and inter-personal. The first, with reference to battlefield sites, could be related to motives of remembrance, acquisition of knowledge, fulfilment of curiosity, while the latter relate to bonding with survivors, establishing senses of belonging with comrades or significant others for whom the site has meaning (e.g. for young Australians and New Zealanders attending Gallipoli on ANZAC (Australian and New Zealand Army Corps) day). The tourism-receiving zone is replaced by the tourism industry, which in this specific instance relates to the given site and its associated museum and interpretative services, but also including access, transport, car parking and the like. In their model Ryan and Trauer (2005) argue that much of the tourism experience is shaped and filtered through the role of the media in the ways in

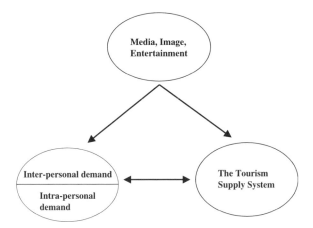

Figure 1.3: A modified tourism system.

which it generates images of what are the appropriate forms of behaviour and experience. It might be said that the same exists with battlefield sites, where from a number of different sources (e.g. books, television documentaries, war films, and computer games) the visitor will have obtained sets of information and images about the site, its meaning and resonance through time. That such reference sets are important is clearly shown in various chapters in the book. For example, McLean, Garden and Urquhart clearly show how visitors derive a sense of meaning and history from both the nature of the site and images obtained from a history of 'Bonnie Prince Charlie' in their experience of Culloden. In short, patterns of interpretation and images created round the cultural significance of these sites are important determinants of the visitor experience.

ACTS OF RESOURCE MANAGEMENT

Introduction

Chris Ryan

This section comprises four chapters. As becomes evident in these and other chapters, battlefield sites attract several hundreds of thousands of visitors each year. Like other destinations, they need to be managed, and many of the issues of flow management that are found in case of the natural environment apply to these sites. There is a need to identify the appropriate location for a car park; calculate the number of car parking spaces required; identify and signpost the location of the entry; indicate entry prices when required; establish means of collecting entry fees; provide information; and then, establish routes around sites with reference to points of interest, interpretation, sight lines and carrying capacities. Are people able to wander at will, or are conducted tours required? Where is there a need to protect artefacts? Should some parts of the battlefield be placed under cover? Where might a visitor centre be established, how large should it be, where should the toilets be, what souvenirs and merchandise might be stocked, how should sewage be treated, is the site connected to water and electricity mains? These and many similar questions need to be answered, and thus many books on site management can relate to battlefields.

But first, there is a need to identify the battlefield, and that is not always as simple as it first sounds. In his chapter Bruce Prideaux raises the issue — where does the battlefield exist? He notes the changing patterns of war and how, over time, war involves civilian populations and the conflict is fought over cyber networks as much as in the field, and where strikes are initiated, several hundreds if not thousands of miles away from where the final weapon lands. And what of wars fought many miles away from the places of residence of those often intimately affected? He then highlights the role of museums as places of commemoration of conflict, and also shows how places associated with the military, which perhaps were fortunate not to have become directly involved in battles, can nonetheless serve as a focus of attention and memory. These considerations are particularly pertinent for Professor Prideaux's own country of Australia, whose troops have partaken in some of the major conflicts of the twentieth and twenty-first centuries, and who have served different causes in theatres fortunately, for the most part, well removed from what Australians call 'The Lucky Country'.

Battlefield Tourism: History, Place and Interpretation
Copyright © 2007 by Elsevier Ltd.
All rights of reproduction in any form reserved.
ISBN: 0-08-045362-7

The next chapter by Mark Piekarz comes from a different perspective of both country and length of history. Located in the United Kingdom, Piekarz also identifies problems in the identification of sites. What constitutes a battle as distinct from a skirmish? And how does one literally find the site of a battle that had significance, but from a time several hundreds of years ago, where records are incomplete, and passing economic conditions have changed the nature of the landscape? Additionally, like Prideaux, Piekarz also has to note the changing pattern of warfare. How, he asks, does one commemorate a battle such as the aerial Battle of Britain as a key turning point of the Second World War? So, again like Prideaux, Piekarz has to consider sites of commemoration and their visitor centres that may well be divorced from the actual location of battle in so far as they can be ascertained.

In the third chapter, Teresa Leopold adopts a critical analysis perspective inasmuch as she is of the opinion that battlefield sites exist not simply as a memory or a commemoration of the past when drawing upon her experiences and research of the battlefields of countries like Laos and Cambodia. She also argues that among the multiple truths of what is remembered and the different motives for visitation: 'One important meaning of these sites is the promotion of peace through the commemoration of the past and education of future generations' (Leopold, 2007, p. 49). Therefore, sites must be managed to ensure that this purpose is also explained within the context of site interpretation. Certainly, it can be recognised that where sites relate to conflicts within living memory, such messages of reconciliation and the need to avoid future loss of life are possibly much more pertinent than those sites that in the language of Piekarz (2007) are cooler by reason of time and perhaps distance. Yet, it can be argued equally that any site that records the loss of life in war represents a human tragedy as fathers, sons, husbands, wives, mothers and daughters are sacrificed in the name of various ideologies and ambitions — each death representing a disruption of family life and the loss of someone loved and cared for. In that sense, every site should call forth the reflection that battles and warfare should only be a last resort, if justified at all. Consequently, Leopold calls for a code of ethics in interpretation that requires recognition of multiple voices and respect for those that visit, and their own perspectives on past conflict.

All three of the above mentioned authors note the economic significance of battlefield tourism — in that sense, this form of tourism is no different from other forms for attractions that bring out-of-region visitors, and also attract revenues and possible job creation that might not otherwise exist. The economic possibilities created by such tourism are also one of the key themes of the final chapter in this sequence of 'acts' — and that is the chapter by Gu, Ryan and Zhang. This chapter considers the current emergence in China of 'Red Tourism' or, in this case, of 'red-green' tourism as the China National Tourism Association promotes a revolutionary past in rural parts of China to not only develop visitor flows but also to link the historic product with eco-tourism opportunities. In many ways, this represents an interesting phenomenon as from the one perspective, given the cultural and political setting, it differs from the other chapters in this collection of texts. Consequently, given the discussion in Chapter 1 about the nature of cultural background and its communication through media, and the wish to secure (as is discussed in the final part of this specific chapter) economic change within a managed political structure and adherence to the power centres of the China Communist Party, then the importance of a certain approved story becomes paramount. However, the planning and management of 'Red Tourism' is seen to be pragmatic in this chapter. The improvement of the economic wellbeing of rural China is fully consistent with the ideals of the Chinese communist revolution, and the use of tourism to achieve this is thus understandable. Yet in this instance it is noted that tourism is fully incorporated into a wider framework of planning. The importance of improvements in transport networks to create accessible tourist sites is evident — equally evident is the fact that people use such networks only if they have reasons to do so — and thus 'red-green' tourism creates such a reason. Additionally, transport networks are not wholly neutral, in that their very existence opens up parts of China previously more difficult to access, and thus the rural parts are brought into mainstream of economic life. While the modes of planning normally adhered to here are more subject to 'top down' processes than is common in the western democracies, the chapter provides evidence of how participation in the benefits being created by these developments is evident among the rural lower income groups, and at least some of these gains are directly attributable to tourism.

Each of the chapters that form this 'act' is to a large extent based on a detached, scientific orientation. The stance is that of the researcher observing and using their frameworks of expertise to offer an interpretation of what is being offered. Pierkarz draws upon definition and existent documentation to define problems with the management of English battlefield sites. Gu, Ryan and Zhang adopt a macro-perspective to indicate problems with an arguably deficient resource but show how the story telling links into and is a driver of significant tourism and transport developments. Prideaux also initially adopts a macro-perspective, querying the nature of the battlefield to finally discuss the military site as the site of interpretation, even when the site itself has little history of direct conflict. Leopold offers a more specific focus, it is true, based upon a wish to achieve a given end of not simply recording, remembering or seeking historical accuracy, but based upon a perceived ethical end to aid the achievement of promotion of peace. Yet, nonetheless, the code of ethics being proposed is one based upon a scientific detachment, in that the stories to be told are premised upon scholarship to achieve an educative aim. In that sense, all the chapters have linkages based upon an underlying positivism, and thus they together form a coherent 'act'.

Chapter 2

Echoes of War: Battlefield Tourism

Bruce Prideaux

Introduction

War is a uniquely human institution, frequently lacking logic but always characterised by paradox. Often, the violence and bloodshed of war is a precondition for peace and harmony, with the ultimate sacrifice of the few required for the comfort and prosperity of the many. During the periods of war, the sanctity of life, enshrined by the national laws and protected by the courts in times of peace, is replaced for a time by the exhortation to kill and maim one's fellow human beings on the battlefield. Yet amidst the terror of the expectant death, individuals engaged in the enterprise of killing often show great compassion to fellow comrades, placing themselves in danger to save, for even a short while, the lives of their fellow combatants. At other times nations once locked in combat become peaceful partners, but may once again become mortal enemies in a future conflict. And out of the brokenness of war there often arises the prosperity of peace. To these many layered paradoxes of war is added the human urge to visit the battlefield: to remember comrades; to rekindle memories of loved ones who fell in battle; to ponder on the feats of those who they will never know; and to gloat on victory or lament over defeat. For whatever reason they come, visiting battlefields has emerged as a growing subsector of the tourism industry.

The ultimate paradox of the battlefield is the freedom of the tourist to wander through a once dangerous place where the agony of the combat has given way to the tranquillity of peace. Where combatants once fell, visitors now reflect, question, experience sadness or even express gladness. This chapter draws on some of these themes to examine one small aspect of battlefield tourism: the military site that was designed for war, never became a battlefield and instead houses a military museum that encourages reflection on a nation's military past.

The constant search by the tourism industry for new attractions, allied with the interest in visiting battlefields has created a new, a somewhat minor tourism phenomenon centred around battlefield tourism. Nested within the larger grouping of touristic experiences described by the term Dark Tourism (Lennon & Foley, 2000), battlefield tourism has emerged as an important form of tourist activity that has expanded beyond the parameters

Battlefield Tourism: History, Place and Interpretation
Copyright © 2007 by Elsevier Ltd.
All rights of reproduction in any form reserved.
ISBN: 0-08-045362-7

of former battlefields and museums to include new experiences such as re-enactments, alternative histories, and the addition of sites that have an association with military activity.

Military heritage and its role in tourism have received increased attention from researchers in recent years. In a special issue of the *International Journal of Tourism Research* (2006), a number of authors examined the role of war as a tourism attraction. Knox (2006) examined the attractions of the Glencoe battlefields in Scotland, and found that the massacre that took place there in 1692 continues to stir Scottish nationalism and is an example of dark tourism. From a different perspective, Hannam (2006) discussed the contested nature of the Indian Mutiny of 1857, where the views of the protagonists present quite different views of the battle. From an Indian perspective the battle is known as the First War of Indian Independence, while from the British perspective it was a mutiny that when resolved, allowed Great Britain to secure its hold over the subcontinent. Other investigations by Lee (2006), Cooper (2006) and Agrusa (2006) provide examples of the significance of battlefields as a tourism attraction. From a different perspective, Ospina (2006) examined the impact that narco wars in Columbia's national parks' system have had on tourism.

Commemorating Battlefields

Battlefields, more than almost any other form of touristic experience, create deep emotional feelings. Battlefields are poignant reminders of humanity's inability to live at peace with neighbours and a statement of the selfishness of individuals and nations who seek to take what is not theirs through aggression. Moreover, they are also a testimony to those who make a stand against tyranny and injustice, sometimes at the expense of their own lives. Battlefields are also reminders of the past and for some are the places where national pride was born or national disgrace was suffered. The significance of battlefields is multi-natured and often measured against scales, such as national identity, political maturity, the quest for freedom and remembrance of defeat. Battlefields also exhibit a number of dimensions including the battlefield itself, measurement of the outcomes on the victor and the vanquished, the impact on participants and the consequences on their family and friends.

The impact of war on nations either within national borders or on foreign battlefields has a meaning that may be expressed within the context of national identity. For Australians and New Zealanders, past wars are powerful reminders of the passage from colony to independence and nationhood, not through revolt against the mother country, but through demonstration of national maturity on the battlefield. Each year both Australia and New Zealand celebrates the 1915-Gallipoli campaign fought in Turkey. While only a part of a much larger allied force and a battle that ended in allied defeat and Turkish victory, the Gallipoli campaign created a powerful legacy of national self-identity in each of the three nations and continues to be widely celebrated in New Zealand and Australia as an important national holiday. For Australians and New Zealanders, the Gallipoli campaign has become the focus for annual national remembrance of the nation's fallen soldiers and celebration of the birth of nationhood. Each year large numbers of Australians and New Zealanders converge on Gallipoli to commemorate the event, a tradition that started soon after the end of the First World War (Scates, 2006). For Turkey, Gallipoli is also significant as a battlefield where Turkish troops defeated the Western powers. Moreover, Turkish General Mustafa Kemal emerged as a hero of the campaign and later led Turkey into the modern era after overthrowing the last Sultan of the Empire Ottoman.

Museums have an important role in reminding nations and their citizens of their past. In Australia, the National War Memorial has emerged as the most significant repository of the nation's military history (*Australian War Memorial*, 2006) and annually attracts about 900,000 visitors. Aside from the National War Memorial, there are a large number of publicly and privately funded museums that reflect on the nation's past military activities. The Australian Defence Force maintains an extensive network of specialist museums that exhibit aspects of the nation's land, air and sea military heritage. Recognition of the importance of the military history, both to the nation and to the military formations that participated in past battles, is a major theme of these museums. The Army in particular has developed a series of 39 museums with two specific purposes in mind. From a military perspective, these museums, administrated by the Military History Unit, remind serving service personnel of the strong military traditions of the Army, its units and formations, and assists in the development of strong unit loyalty and *esprit de corp*. For the nation, the Army museum network is a tangible reminder of the role of the Army in defending the nation's independence in times of external military threat and in a sense, a celebration of the sacrifice of soldiers for the common good. On a smaller scale, museums are also operated by the Air Force and the Navy and by a number of private organisations.

Battlefields evoke many emotions and are remembered in a variety of ways ranging from preservation as a national park to simpler expressions, such as monuments or naming of geographic features. The American Civil War of 1860–1865 left approximately 10,000 battlefields (Goodheart, 2005) ranging from the sites of minor infantry clashes between platoons of the Union and Confederate armies to the battlefields of Spotsylvania County, where 108,000 soldiers were killed, wounded or captured during the course of the conflict. Today, many of these battlefields have been lost to the encroachment of urbanisation. Spotsylvania County has become an outer suburb of Washington with its Civil War heritage barely acknowledged and then only by names, such as Artillery Ridge and Lee's Park, conferred on the site of old battlefields by their developers (Goodheart, 2005). According to Goodheart (2005), of the 400 battlefields deemed worthy of protection by the US Government Commission in 1993, only 50 have been preserved to some degree; 65 have been fragmented or lost; and many of the remainder are being threatened. Of the 200,000 acres of privately owned Civil War battlefields, approximately 10,000 acres is being lost each year to redevelopment (Goodheart, 2005). This is despite the enormous popularity of Civil War re-enactments and the large numbers of people who visit Civil War battlefields. One battlefield, the site of the three-day Battle of Gettysburg, which cost 40,000 troops killed or wounded, receives two million visitors each year (Goodheart, 2005).

More recent battlefields, particularly where the original combatants or their relatives are able to revisit in the quiet of peace, have also become popular tourism attractions (Newark, 2001). Second World War battlefields such as Normandy in France and Stalingrad in Russia; the battlefields of Korea and Vietnam; and the many smaller and more recent battlefields that hold significance to the citizens of countries fighting for independence from colonial masters or from dictatorial regimes, attract numerous visitors either on independent journeys or as members of organised tours, such as those promoted by the

Australian War Memorial (2006). Even ancient battlefields, such as Troy, Roman battle-fields in Europe, and numerous sites in Japan, China, India and elsewhere continue to attract visitors.

Changing Shape of War

In the contemporary era, the form of war itself has changed as new technologies have shifted the place and altered the form of warfare. In the past, the battlefield was symbolised by a physical site either on the land or on the surface of the sea, where opposing forces clashed. In the 20th century, the places where battles occurred grew to include both under-water and in-air. Moreover, the form of battles changed with horses giving way to tanks, and submarines and airpower reshaping maritime warfare. German Blitzkrieg tactics in France and Russia in World War II, the Battle of Britain waged between the air forces of Britain and Germany, and the World War Two Battle of the Atlantic using submarines are examples of the manner in which warfare evolved in the 20th century. The growth of terrorism and insurgency as forms of warfare in the late 20th century has forced a further redefinition of the concept of the battlefield.

In the future, it is entirely possible that new forms of battlefields will emerge, echoing the advances in technologies that are available for waging war. Space has already experi-enced some degree of militarization with the placement of military reconnaissance satel-lites in orbit by a number of nations, the development of anti-ballistic missiles that intercept incoming nuclear warheads while still in space and the use of space for the deliv-ery of intercontinental ballistic nuclear missiles. The space wars that are the subject of speculation by science fiction writers and movie producers are yet to occur, but given the history of humanity's ability to develop or adapt technology to find new methods of attack-ing an opponent, battles of this nature are almost inevitable. Other future battlefields that may emerge (if they have not already) include the biological battlefield where various forms of biological agents, such as infectious diseases, will be used to wage battles, and cyberbattles where computer networks are attacked by opponents using hackers and computer viruses.

One aspect of war that is rarely considered is the 'battleless' battlefield that in some respects achieves almost the same outcome as a physical battle, but without the damage that symbolises the usual concept of a battlefield. The deterrent value of a strategic fortification or the presence of an overwhelming force in the vicinity of a potential hotspot or a point of tension between nations may be sufficient to prevent a physical battle. In serving this purpose, these sites have some claim for acknowledgement of their role as places where battles may have been contemplated or even planned by an adversary, but where deterrence prevented active conflict. The Cold War is the most recent example of this form of 'battleless' battlefield. Waged over a period of 45 years between the Warsaw Pact lead by the USSR, and NATO led by the USA, the Cold War was an era of high mil-itary tension that fortunately never crossed the threshold to an actual battle, except in proxy wars located far away from the potential European theatre. Although the Cold War never produced actual battlefields in Europe, the many sites associated with this era arguably deserve attention in much the same way as the actual battlefields of earlier conflicts.

Missile silos, military fortifications, military barracks and the equipments potentially used to wage war are all significant elements of the 'battleless' battlefield. While the understanding of battlefield visitation usually evokes images of visiting sites and structures now free from the terror of the past, contemporary forms of warfare have forced a redefinition and expansion of the concept of war. Under a revised interpretation of battle, the site of the September 11, 2001 aerial attack on the New York World Trade Centre, other sites of terrorist attack and the South American sites where the militarised forces funded by narcotic warlords clashed with opposing narcotics warlords or the national police and the military forces (McGahey, 2006), must now be regarded as legitimate battlefields. As a consequence of new forms of conflict including insurgency, guerrilla activities and terrorism, many civilian communities have now become the sites of battles waged between terrorists and governments. The front line that once formed a physical boundary between opposing armies has dissolved and the concept of battle and battlefield has again been redefined. An entire nation may now become an active battlefield with battles being fought wherever a target of interest is attacked. Citizens of nations enduring this form of warfare have limited ability to flee to areas of safety in the type of refugee movements that typified the past, and instead are forced to endure the uncertainty of battle and attempt to live as normal a life as possible. Surprisingly, nations suffering this form of warfare continue to attract tourists. Although virtually a nationwide battlefield during the Palestinian Intifada from 2000 to 2005 where insurgent attacks could occur without warning and in almost any location, Israel continued to attract tourists, though in much smaller numbers than during the previous period of peace. London at the height of the Irish Republican Army (IRA) bombing campaigns of the 1980s, and Nepal locked in a nationwide Maoist insurgency campaign for several years prior to the start of 2007, are further illustrations of nations where the site of a 'battlefield' is determined by an engagement of civil authorities and armed resistance and which, in spite of the conflict, continue to attract tourists.

In Iraq, during the height of the anti-Government and anti-US insurgency campaign in 2005, domestic tourism still took place. McGahey (2006) observed that in parts of Iraq including the northern Kurdish provinces, domestic tourism was flourishing with university level tourism courses being offered, regular trade shows being organised and academic tourism conferences being conducted.

The preparation for war as well as the prosecution of war has left many sites that are remembered long after their abandonment and continue to attract the interest of nearby residents and visitors. Some of these have been identified previously as 'battleless' battlefields, others may be as mundane as the site of a military barracks, prisoner of war facilities, war cemeteries or logistical installations. On the Atherton Tablelands, west of Cairns in North Queensland, the sites of numerous Australian and US military installations are remembered by simple signs that indicate the name of the military unit previously based there, such as the 2/164 Australian General Transport Company illustrated in Figure 2.1. Collectively, the military history of the region, which lasted only for a short period prior of the Second World War, is remembered in the form of a stone garden at Rocky Creek, formerly the site of a large World War II-military hospital. Figure 2.2 illustrates the entrance to the Memorial Park created to remember this aspect of the military heritage of the region.

Wars are also remembered through monuments, and objects and displays found in museums. In Nagasaki, the 1945 US aerial attack on the city with an atomic bomb is

Figure 2.1: Small memorial erected to commemorate the location of the 2/164 Australian
General Transport Company on the Atherton Tablelands, Australia (Photo courtesy of
Bruce Prideaux).

Figure 2.2: The entrance to the Memorial Park created to remember this aspect of the military
heritage of the Atherton Tablelands region Australia (Photo courtesy of Bruce Prideaux).

remembered by a museum built in a peace park located next to ground zero. Nations commonly remember war and its participants in specialised national museums or in designated areas of national museums. In Australia, UK, South Korea and many other nations, war is remembered in specialised National War Museums. On a local scale regional museums may also remember specific campaigns or battles by housing the memorabilia of the military activity or by marking the site of a 'battleless' battlefield installation.

The hunger of the tourism industry for new sites to attract visitor interest has led to a new understanding of the concept of the battlefield that encompasses the 'real' and increasingly the 'play'. The 'real' refers to the actual place of battle previously described while the 'play' is a new form of battle that involves re-enactment of past battles and, more recently, battle scenarios based on alternative histories. Alternative history builds on the 'what if' factor of an unfolding of events in a manner that differs from the actual, to create an alternative view of the past.

This new dimension to tourism interest in battlefields and battlefield re-enactment where participants relive battles of the past have become a major attraction in a number of countries. The US Civil War battlefield re-enactment movement has encouraged similar activities in other nations. In New Zealand, the small village of Cambridge celebrates Armistices Day with a range of activities including re-enactments of actual battles and others that are scripted to achieve a favourable outcome for the New Zealand re-enactment troops. In Australia, the passion for battlefield re-enactment has taken a new direction. Lacking a history of major battles fought on Australian soil re-enactment now encompasses alternative histories. In Victoria, the 19th century fear that Napoleonic France could invade the colony is acted out through the formation of the 21éme Regiment de Infanterie to clash with British Regiments (Powell, 2001) in simulated battle in an alternative history of war.

As just mentioned, Australia has few battlefields on its home soil and most of the battles in which Australians served were fought offshore. The minor uprising of Irish convict rebellion in the one-sided battle of Vinegar Hill, in 1804 (Battle of Vinegar Hill, 2006; Silver, 1989); a rebellion by gold miners in 1854 at Eureka in Victoria; and the World War II bombing of Darwin and Broome by Imperial Japanese Forces are the only nationally recognised battlefields. In contrast, the numerous skirmishes between European settlers and Aboriginals, defending their tribal lands are largely forgotten and the sites rarely visited or even acknowledged. Not surprisingly the level of recognition given to the Australian battlefield sites compared to overseas battlefield field sites where Australians died is small. Thus, recognition of the nation's military history occurs primarily through museums, memorials and monuments rather than through battlefield visitation.

Australian Army Museum Network

In Australia, each arm of the military has established military museums. For example, the Australian Army supports a network of museums based on three categories of collections: Regional Museums (7), Corps Museums (10) and Unit Historical Collections (22). Regional and Corps Museums are usually open to the public, while Unit Historical Collections are not always publicly accessible. An interesting aspect of the museums is that many are located in former military installations that have been replaced by newer installations that conform to contemporary military requirements. In this sense, the museums reflect the changing role of technology in warfare. Museums such as the Army Museum of NSW located in Victoria Barracks, Sydney and the Fort Queenscliff Army Museum near Melbourne, occupy buildings that once housed significant military command centres. Fort Queenscliff for example, once housed the command staff who issued the orders to fire Australia's first shots in both the First and the Second World Wars. In the contemporary era the technology of command has changed, making older sites obsolete and available for other uses such as museums. Similarly, a number of redundant coastal forts have been converted into museums. The following case study illustrates how one obsolete coastal fort has been converted into a regional Army museum.

The Kissing Point Military Museum

Townsville, located in North Queensland, was established as a port city in the 1860s to service hinterland mining and pastoral activities, and later became the northern administrative centre of the Queensland Colonial Government. The withdrawal of the British military detachments forced the Colonial Government to establish its own defence force. Events in Europe, including the Crimean War, alarmed many citizens in the Australian colonies and most Colonial governments responded by constructing a series of coastal forts to defend key ports. Townsville and other ports in Queensland were considered as potential targets and in need of protection by coastal forts.

In 1884, a report on the defence of the Colony recommended that a coastal fort be built on a low rocky outcrop near the city (locally known as Kissing Point). Work on the fort commenced in 1888, in parallel with similar work on coastal forts at Lytton, to guard the Port of Brisbane and at Thursday Island to protect the coastal shipping passage to Darwin. By 1891 the Kissing Point fort was completed along with an adjoining barracks and a training area. This part of the military complex continues to be used as a military base and is currently occupied by Army Reserve units.

In the early part of the 20th century the threat changed and Russia was replaced by Germany as a possible aggressor. During the First World War the fort was manned, but never came under attack. After the defeat of Germany, the Fort was used by militia forces but with the emergence of the Japanese threat in the 1930s, new concerns were raised over the need to protect the port. Prior to the Second World War, the firepower of the fort was upgraded in anticipation of a possible attack. Following the defeat of Japanese naval forces at the Battle of Coral Sea and the Battle of Midway, and halting the Japanese Army advance in New Guinea by Australian forces, the role of the Fort was downgraded and in 1943 the coastal guns were moved. The site remained as part of the militia barracks and in the 1960s, the World War II additions were dismantled, causing some damage to the original 1890s structure.

A revival of interest in military heritage in the 1970s resulted in restoration work on the site being undertaken by the Army Engineer Corps. On completion of the restoration program and the recovery of one of the former guns from the nearby ocean, the Fort became the North Queensland Military Museum and was opened to the public in June 1980. Figure 2.3 illustrates one of the original guns installed at the fort and in the background the city it was

Figure 2.3: Gun emplacement Kissing Point Military Museum (Photo courtesy of Dr Murray Prideaux).

designed to protect. The Museum was given a charter by the Military History Unit to display military memorabilia in the period 1890–1946, paralleling the years during which the Fort was an active military establishment. While the fort never fired a shot in anger, despite threats from three nations, its presence arguably had a deterring effect justifying its classification as a 'battleless' battlefield.

Operation of the Museum

Compared to civilian museums, Army museums operate on a different management and governance model that includes utilising serving-military personnel as well as volunteers. Similarly, the financial model used by Army museums differs from civilian museums. While oversight of the museum network is entrusted to the Army History Unit, the museum is run by the Kissing Point Military Foundation (KPMF), a registered non-profit company. The Foundation has a board of six persons drawn from the local community. The management structure comprises the KPMF Chairman and board, and a serving Army Reserve Officer who is also the Army History Units representative.

Apart from the part time Army Reserve Manager and two non-commissioned officers, the museum is staffed by volunteers. Many of the volunteers are past regular and reserve Army members who served with units stationed at Jezzine Barracks, which includes the site of the fort. At the time of writing, the museum had 26 volunteers who are treated as unpaid contractors to the Department of Defence. Under this arrangement, volunteers are covered for Workers Compensation insurance including travel to and from the museum. Volunteers are organized into four teams responsible for gardening and mainte-nance, tour guiding, curating and archiving and administration. The Army History Unit provides courses for volunteers in curating and museum ethics, with each course being of one-week in duration.

Funding is obtained from a number of sources including the Army History Unit, dona-tions from the public, and support from the Army's logistics system for maintenance, com-munications, consumables, office equipment and minor works. While there is no entrance fee, visitors are encouraged to make a small donation. This system works well and the manager indicated that the support from the Army and public donations is sufficient to operate the museum. The museum is open on four mornings each week, although it opens at other times by appointment. In the calendar year 2005 the museum attracted 3000 visi-tors. In the near future the museum will be expanded and the coverage of conflicts will expand beyond the current 1890–1946 time frame to include more recent conflicts, such as Iraq and Afghanistan. As part of the expansion project, the library space will be increased and additional public access computers will be installed. Currently, marketing can be described as ad hoc and relies on the goodwill of the local media.

As with numerous other regional museums, the Kissing Point Museum provides a tan-gible link with the city's military past. It is also a site that attracts some tourist interest, though not on the scale of museums that either have a more imposing physical presence or a collection that has national significance. The museum is also an excellent example of the type of military installation that may be found in many 'battleless' battlefields and which, on the cessation of their military function, are available for new roles, such as museums.

Conclusion

War is a uniquely human institution, unremarkable in that it has been a common theme throughout human history, but remarkable in that preparation for war continues to con-sume considerable national resources even in the poorest countries and continues to occur despite the suffering that it brings. Perhaps it is the inevitability of war, but also the wish that there were no such institution, that continues to fascinate tourists and draws them to the many sites associated with the battlefield. This chapter commenced with the observa-tion that war had many paradoxes. A final paradox focusing on the rebuilding of lives shat-tered by the loss of loved ones, is found in the observations of General Mustafa Kemal who, after his victory over allied forces at the battle of Gallipoli, wrote of the allied sol-diers killed in the conflict, "Those heroes that shed their blood and lost their lives ... you are now lying in the soil of a friendly country. Therefore rest in peace. There is no differ-ence between the Johnnies (allied) and the Mehmets (Turkish) where they lie side by side here in this country of ours…You the mothers who sent your sons from far away countries wipe your tears. Your sons are now lying in our bosom and are in peace. Having lost their lives on this land they have become our sons as well". (Ersavic, 2006)

Echoing Kemal's words, an estimated 10,000 Australian and New Zealand tourists gath-ered at, or as some commentators observed, invaded Gallipoli on 25 April 2006 to celebrate the original landing date of the campaign. Armed Turkish soldiers were present in large numbers, as on 25 April 1915 not to repel, but to protect the descendents of the original invaders from terrorist attack. While foes in the past, Turkey, Australia and New Zealand are now friendly nations, each celebrating the significance of the Gallipoli battlefield in terms that are unique to each nation.

Military history occupies an important place in the heritage of many nations and is celebrated in many ways including memorials, ceremonies, monuments, museums, re-enactments and by preservation of battlefields. Within this broad field of military heritage, battlefields occupy an important place and arouse within visitors a range of emotions. However, as discussed previously in this chapter, battlefields can be defined in several ways including those where actual combat occurred and others that had a deterrent value. Interest in battlefield tourism is increasing in line with other forms of tourism experience and it can be expected that in the future, military heritage will continue to be an important touristic activity.

The diversity of battlefields explored in this chapter indicates that there remains considerable scope for incorporating new forms of battlefield tourism into the current catalogue of sites and places that are recognised as being of interest to the tourist. Unfortunately, it is highly likely that in the future, as in the past, humanity's inability to live in peace will add to the already extensive list of battlefield sites. It is also likely that future battlefields will continue to change in form and in location, adding further sites to the already long list of battlefields visited by tourists

Acknowledgements

I wish to thank Captain David Soper, an Army Reserve mate, for providing details of The Kissing Point Military Museum and my brother and fellow officer, Major Murray Prideaux PhD for the photographs he kindly provided.

Chapter 3

It's Just a Bloody Field! Approaches, Opportunities and Dilemmas of Interpreting English Battlefields

Mark Piekarz

Introduction

Not all battles take place in fields. Indeed, modern warfare is often characterised by its urban setting. For England, however, where the last pitched battle to take place on English soil was the 1685 Battle of Sedgemoor, one can say that using the term 'battlefield' is a reasonably accurate description of the many conflicts that have taken place. Yet these fields are often viewed in contradictory ways. To many, when looking at these places, they appear empty and devoid of interest. The relative lack of built structures, their inert appearance and the empty open space can mean that the significance of the site can be difficult to appreciate, and so remains to observers as just a vacant space, lacking any specific focus. But it is only one viewpoint. To others, the lack of a built environment can allow for the field to act as a canvas on which one's imagination can play, visualising past events, which can then instil a sense of resonance, further intensified by the peculiar effect of 'being there' has on the visitor experience. To these people, the significance of the place is grounded in the fact that it was once a 'bloody' field that helps provoke cognition and generates a feeling of satisfaction from understanding how the past events fit into the observed landscape.

It has been within these contradictory attitudes that the debate about English battlefield preservation and interpretation has been framed. Throughout the 1990s there was a growing recognition that the battlefields of Britain had a potential to be used as a recreational and educational resource. This has been reflected by the growing interest in academic research, interpretation initiatives, historical re-enactments, organisations concerned with their preservation and even TV programmes. It was a recognition that was relatively slow to develop, particularly when contrasted with other countries, such as America's development of battlefield attractions.

This chapter examines how the use of battlefields as a tourism resource has developed in England. This focus on English battlefields permits sharper comparison with Scotland's battlefield utilisation, thereby highlighting some of the more unique developments that have occurred in English battlefield preservation. It pays particular attention to why there is so much variation in their preservation and use as a recreational and tourism resource (if at all), together with some of the current key issues and challenges facing English battlefield utilisation. Comparative country analysis is used throughout the discussion in order to provide more insights into the English experience; an approach that ultimately allows for the development of a framework, which others can use to further evaluate battlefield utilisation in their countries.

English Battlefields as a Resource

To some, reducing battlefields and sites of conflict to a notion of being a 'resource' can diminish and distract from the tragic events that took place there. The problem, however, is that pressures from modernity are constantly forcing the measurement and categorisation of the world in order to help inform and justify decisions, particularly in the context of land-use planning decisions. Thus, for those who have been drawn to preserving English battlefields, the arguments of desecration and respecting the sites for those who died has not been sufficient to help ensure their protection: to these moral and emotive arguments, more rational constructs and language have had to be developed, particularly in terms of their educational, recreational and touristic potential.[1] As Griffiths (1993) stated bluntly, "it is far easier to bulldoze an empty field, than a flourishing visitor centre". Battlefields, rightly or wrongly, being presented and articulated as a resource has become a fact, with their recreational and tourism utilisation offering an important quantifiable measure to help gauge their value.

Whilst this chapter is primarily concerned with battlefields used as a recreational and tourism resource, it is important to appreciate how this use relates to other resource functions, which include:

- *Hallowed ground/memorial function.* This role primarily relates to the notion that the ground where people died is deemed as somehow sacred and should therefore be revered, respected and used as a place for remembrance. This function tends to be much stronger in other countries, particularly in relation to some sites of the American Civil War, many World War I battlefields in Belgium and France, or even the Battle of

---

[1] This not to say that these more emotive arguments are not unimportant as the objection by the Battlefield Trust to English Heritage's proposal to expand the café facilities at Battle Abbey illustrate, whereby it was deemed as insensitive to build the café on the actual battlefield itself where people had (possibly) died (the media certainly like the more emotive, provocative headlines). Eventually, the café proposal was abandoned for a new site after the debate went on for number of years.

Culloden in Scotland. In England, battlefields do not tend to have a strong sense of the sacred, with only a minimal use for remembrance.[2]

- *Educational function and archaeological resource.* For the few battlefields that do have a dedicated visitor centre in both England and Scotland, a core visitor market relates to school groups. In addition, there has been an increase in battlefield research in relation to history and archaeology, which can take place in both a formal context, such as university-related research, and in an informal, recreational context, such as the non-professional, lay person developing an interest in the battlefield. One of the critical elements of this function is the need to preserve the archaeological deposits that can help tell a story of the battle.

- *Land-base function.* This function can relate to a number of roles, ranging from farming, or preserving a green space for wildlife. The battlefield may, or may not be given formal recognition as a site of conflict, but some use patterns represent a more harmonious use of a battlefield than alternative forms in retaining some meaning. Such usage, however, does not necessarily prevent damage to the archaeological resource.

- *Recreational/tourism function.* This function can relate to various direct uses, such as establishing a visitor centre, developing themed trails, TV programmes,[3] and their use by tour operators specialising in history and battlefield tours. Indirect uses, whereby the space, rather than the history are used for the basis of the attraction, can range from parks to golf courses. As with the land-base function, whilst initially some of these functions can seem to represent a sensitive use of the site, they can, in fact, still damage the archaeological resource and distort the battlefield landscape.

- *Cultural function.* The final key resource element relates to a more esoteric concept of a cultural asset, which can be intimately entwined with notions of national and regional identity. For many nations around the world, battles are woven into the cultural fabric, often providing key cultural marker points in state and nation development, and so can be deemed as important and worthy of preservation.

These functions vary considerably as to which are given primacy, not just in England, but for all battlefields around the world. What should be appreciated is that the differences between the functions can be opaque, together with having many inherent contradictions. This is particularly true in relation to the tourism/preservation dilemma, whereby tourists are encouraged to visit historical locations in order to generate revenue and support, yet in doing so can end up damaging the site, both in terms of atmosphere and physical conditions. The possible consequence is a failure to provide satisfactory visitor experiences, which in turn threatens financial and interpretative viability and potentially long-term preservation goals.

How have English Battlefields been Used as a Resource?

In order to conduct a proper audit of English battlefield recreational and tourism utilisation, one first needs to identify the number (the supply) of English battlefields. Whilst the

---

[2] With the latter, examples of commemorative services at English battlefield tend to be rare and low key, such as the annual service held by the Richard III Society at the Battle of Bosworth.

[3] Examples include 'War Walks', 'Two Men in a Trench' and 'Battlefield Britain'.

logic of this is easy to appreciate, the practicality of actually arriving at an exact number of battlefields in England is fraught with difficulties. These relate to (a) what is defined and included as a battlefield and (b) to what extent can the battles be verified from historical records and actually be located in landscapes with a reasonable degree of accuracy? The result is that one can find numerous variations in the literature as to how many battlefields are identified and discussed. Smurthwaite's (1984) work has been an influential text on British battlefields, discussing battles from the Roman invasion of 44 BC to the Battle of Britain in 1939–1940. In his work he identifies a total of 61 English battlefields. Comparing books on British or English battlefields, one can find many variations in the number of battles included, with no clear rationale as to why some books cover certain battles, but not others. Seymour (1997), for example, only examines 19 English battlefields, but is useful for the many aerial shots of present-day landscapes, with superimposed illustrations of the battlefield formations in the pictures. Kinross (1988) on the other hand identifies 46 English battlefields or conflicts, but includes a number of interesting sites not identified by Smurthwaite, such as the 1460 Battle of Wakefield, where the father of King Edward IV and Richard III was killed, and the April 1944 action off Slapton Sands, where 787 American soldiers died when a German E-boat sank a number of landing craft, which were in operations rehearsing for the Normandy Landing in June later that year.[4]

Raynor (2004) produces by far the most comprehensive work on English battlefields. His authoritative and exhaustive study of English battlefields makes reference to over 500 sites of conflict (the broader term increasingly used in literature, but one not always clearly defined), locating approximately 384 as land-based battlefields. His definition of a battlefield includes many major sieges on castles and towns, and a personally selected number of key skirmishes, such as the 1642 Powick Bridge skirmish outside Worcester, which marked the beginning of the English Civil War. In addition to these land battles, he also includes naval actions that involved more than one ship, and the aerial Battle of Britain (but excluding the many cities, which were bombed during the war, even though as he himself recognises, one can put forward an argument for their inclusion and being understood as a battle location).[5]

These variations of what can be included as a battlefield, together with the problems of locating the sites, were high in the mind of English Heritage – the organisation with the responsibility for conserving, educating and increasing public access to the historic environment, and which reports back to government. The 1990 Government White Paper, *This Common Inheritance,* stipulated that a register of English battlefields needed to be drawn up to help in their preservation. This register was published in 1995, identifying 43 English battlefields, the names of which appear in Table 3.1. Battlefields were included on the

---

[4] It is also worthwhile highlighting that Kinross is one of the few writers who includes examples of Welsh battlefields, such as the 1402 Battle of Pilleth (which is of real Welsh cultural significance as it was where Owen Glendower inflicted a significant defeat on an English army), and the action in Fishguard in 1787(which can be deemed as the last official invasion of Britain, with a approximately a thousand French soldiers landing in Wales, but resulted in their surrender three days later, with only three people being killed). The reason these are highlighted is because Welsh battlefields tend to receive little or no recognition in books, which purport to cover British battlefields.

[5] In Richard Holmes's book, *War Walks* (1997), he does include the Blitz, which further illustrates the problem of deciding what can be included as a battlefield or a field of conflict.

Table 3.1: English battlefields included in English heritage's Battlefield Register.

Name	Date	Description	Name	Date	Description
Adwalton	1643	M, PL, P *Secure*	Nantwich	1644	OS *Secure*
Barnet	1471	M, OS, P *Secure*	Naseby	1645	P, M, OS *Exact*
Blore Heath	1459	M[a]	Neville	1346	M, P, WT *Accurate*
Boroughbridge	1322	M, PL *Approximate*	Newburn	1640	P, OS *Secure*
Bosworth	1485	M, VC, P, WT *Disputed*	Newbury	1643	M, PL *Accurate*
Braddock Down	1643	*Alternative site*	Northalerton	1138	M, PL *Probably accurate*
Chalgrove	1643	M, P, PL *Accurate*	Northhamtpon	1460	PL *Secure*
Cheriton	1644	Pl *Alternative*	Otterburn	1388	M, P[a]
Cropredy Bridge	1644	M, P, PL *Secure*	Roundway Down	1643	P, WT[a]
Edgehill	1642	M, P, OS *Accurate*	Rowton	1645	*Secure*
Evesham	1265	M, PL, OS *Approximate*	Sedgemoor	1685	M, P, T *Very Accurate*
Flodden	1513	M, P, l, OS *Secure*	Stamford Bridge	1066	M, P, OS, PL *Secure*
Halidon Hill	1333	M[a]	Shrewsbury	1403	M, P, WT *Secure*
Hastings	1066	M, VC, P, WT, A *Probably accurate*	Solway	1542	P *Secure*
Homildon Hill	1402	[a]	Stoke Field	1487	M, OS, WT (Defunct) *Approximate*
Hopton	1643	PL *Accurate*	Stow	1646	M, PL *Secure*
Langport	1645	OS *Alternative*	Stratton	1643	P, PL, M, OS *Secure*
Lansdown	1643	M, WT, P *Accurate*	Tewkesbury	1471	PL, M, P, OS, WT *Secure*
Lewes	1264	M, PL, OS *Secure*	Towton	1461	M, OS, P[a]
Marston Moor	1644	P, M, PL *Secure*	Winciby	1463	M, PL *Approximate*
Maldon	991	PL, OS *Probable*	Worcester (with 1642 Powick Bridge)	1651	VC, P *Secure*
Myton	1319	*Approximate*			

Source: English Heritage Battlefield Register and the Battlefield Trust.

Key: M – Monument/memorial; VC – Visitor centre; M – Museum; OS – Off-site interpretation, such as in a church or a museum; P – Interpretive panel; WT – Way marked trail; Pl – Plaque or inscription; A – Audio.

[a] Indicates that the battlefield is not currently on the Battlefields Trust Resource Database.

Note: In addition to the Battlefield Register, The Battlefield Resource Centre also includes the following battles: Fulford, 1066; Mortimers Cross, 1461; Edgecote Field, 1469, and Brentford, 1642. Battlefields, which receive some recognition, such as a panel or monument, but do not appear in the Register or Database includes Albans, 1455; Wakefield, 1460; Preston, 1648. There is also the Battle of Torrington, which falls somewhere between a siege and a battlefield, but does have a visitor centre dedicated to interpreting the historical time period of the English Civil War and the battle itself.

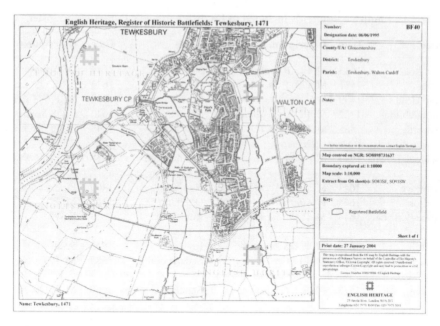

Figure 3.1: Map outlining the area of action for the Battle of Tewkesbury from the *English Heritage Battlefield Register*.

basis that they could be located with a degree of accuracy and had significant remains, in the sense of the remaining open space, original buildings, monuments and graves (see Figure 3.1 for an example of the useful maps produced). The number of 43 battles appears as a strikingly small figure in comparison with Raynor's work, which not only reflects the tighter conceptual parameters of what constitutes a battlefield, but also the fact that many locations have been lost to development, such as the Battle of Leeds, or cannot be accurately located to the landscape, such as the many battles associated with Alfred the Great, even though these have undoubted historical significance.

The establishment of the Battlefield Trust in 1992 has also been a crucial development in relation to the preservation, research and interpretation of British battlefields. It was established when the battlefield of Naseby, the decisive battle of the English Civil War, was to be bisected by a motorway link. It threw into focus the need for greater research and coordination if battlefields were to be preserved and utilised more effectively as a resource. The Trust has continued to build on the *Battlefield Register*, having secured funding for a two-year research project running from 2006 to 2008, with the results being found on the very useful *Fields of Conflict Online Database* (see recommended websites at the end of this chapter for more details).

In relation to releasing the recreational and tourism resource potential of a battlefield, one of the critical factors is the development of some form of interpretation. In the context of the battlefields identified by the *Battlefield Register* and the Battlefield Trust, one can identify the following key methods that have been used to interpret English battlefields:

• *Dedicated visitor centre.* This is the most sophisticated interpretive approach, which uses many interpretive techniques and has the most extensive visitor amenities. In England there are, in 2006, only two dedicated, high-quality attractions, which are for the battles of Hastings and Bosworth.

- *Off-site museum/interpretation*. Many battlefields are interpreted off the battlefield site, often as part of a museum, such as in Tewkesbury, Evesham or Barnet, or as part of a wider interpretation of a building, such as at Elsdon Castle, which offers some interpretation for the Battle of Otterburn. For the battles of Naseby and Edgehill, these each have small-scale museums, with limited opening times and fall somewhere between an off-site museum and dedicated visitor centre.

- *Interpretation panels*. Interpretation panels seem to have become the contemporary memorial structures to English battlefields, with their growth in the number having echoes to the Victorian period and the penchant for erecting monuments to battles and historical figures. Most battlefields only have one dedicated panel, but in the instance of Bosworth and Hastings, these are used as part of a battlefield trail. For the English battlefields cited in Table 3.1, approximately 22 sites now have an interpretive panel of some form, with more planned by the Battlefield Trust, often in conjunction with various local authorities. There are also some battlefields not in the list, having problems in their physical location to the landscape, but which still have an interpretation panel, such as the Battle of Heavenfield in 633, in Northumberland.

- *Monuments*. Whilst many monuments were built as memorials, they can also serve as a form of interpretation, acting as a physical reminder of the events that took place, or marking a particular event in the battle itself. Monuments having significant pulling power on visitors can end up as the key focal point on a battlefield, even though many are critical of such structures, saying that they can distract the visitor from the battlefield itself, or even be misleading as they may be placed in the wrong location, as some argue with the Battle of Cheriton monument. Of the battlefields cited in Table 3.1, approximately 29 have monuments of variable size, quality and accessibility.

- *Plaques*. These tend to be an older form of interpretation, whereby a short description is given of the battle, often attached to a monument, or on a built feature, such as a bridge. As with monuments, plaques vary in quality and can sometimes give misleading information, as some argue with the 1643 Battle of Landsown.

- *Self-guided trails*. These have grown in popularity, which can be designed for a walking or driving tour. Identifying a walking route is one of the key ways a battlefield can be used as a recreational resource, which is why the Battlefield Trust and the *Battlefield Register* were keen to identify possible, circular walking trails. Identifying a trail, which some local authorities have waymarked with distinct signs, such as with the Battle of Tewkesbury, can also be a very cost effective way of opening up the battlefield as a recreational resource, particularly if it is complemented with leaflets or guidebooks. For some battlefields, however, there are no public rights of way or natural trails and so they remain inaccessible, apart from a fleeting glance from a roadside.

- *Guided trail*. This is done in a variety of ways, whether by volunteers, or as part of a commercial package tour. Guided trails can also form the focus of special events and can mean that the stories from the past can be told, even in landscapes, which have been lost to development.

- *Books and maps*. For many years, books were at the heart of so much battlefield interpretation. In addition to the more scholarly works, one should also note the various fictional books that can also help interpret a place. In relation to maps, it is of interest that not only do many battlefields receive recognition on the more detailed Ordinance Survey maps, but also increasingly in many road atlases, where they are given a red symbol indicating a place of interest.

- *TV, films and plays*. Battles have long history in live entertainment, as Shakespeare's history plays illustrate. Films[6] and many TV programmes also offer an excellent means of interpretation and have encouraged greater interest in many battlefields, although their impact tends to be more short term.
- *Leaflets*. Leaflets are a simple and straightforward way by which battles can be interpreted, together with offering wider themed touristic trails, such as a drive tour that links locations associated with the battle, characters and historical time period.
- *Re-enactments*. These range from small living history demonstrations, to full-scale battle re-enactments. In relation to the actual battle re-enactments, it can be a source of controversy as to whether they should occur on the actual battlefield itself. Whilst for Culloden in Scotland, or the many American Battlefields enactment is not allowed or encouraged, as it is deemed insensitive, for the various English battlefields it has not been such a provocative issue.

What is vital to appreciate is that whilst on first appearances, English battlefields can seem to be quite well served by various forms of interpretation, there are considerable variations in their range, quality and accessibility, with the general consensus being one where English battlefields are believed to be under-utilised and under-valued as a resource. The factors that can help explain why this may be the case are examined next.

Why are not More English Battlefields Used as Visitor Attractions?

Although it is possible to present an alternative view for English battlefields being well preserved and presented, for the purposes of this discussion, the more critical premise of under-utilisation is assumed. The prime reason is that this view propels a more thorough examination of the topic, leading to an identification of the factors which influence the attractiveness of English battlefields to tourists, which in turn helps gauge their viability as possible larger-scale attractions. The different factors advanced by various writers as determining the attractiveness of English battlefields are based around the following themes: the difficulty in securing the locations of battlefields; the paucity of tangible remains; temporal distance of the conflict; the scale of the conflict; comparative lack of emotional appeal due to the passing of time; and the cultural significance attached to the site. Throughout this discussion, comparative analysis is used to help put the factors into some form of perspective and importance.

Degree of Confidence in Locating Battlefields and Extent of Remains

Modern warfare tends to leave marked evidence of battles on the landscape, ranging from pocked-marked landscapes and damaged buildings, to the later additions of memorials

---

[6] Many of which adapt Shakespeare's plays, such as Lawrence Olivier's *Richard III*, or Orsen Well's *Chimes of Midnight*, which has a particularly vivid and original approach to the Battle of Shrewsbury.

and wargraves. For English battlefields, the passing of time since the conflicts often means that there tends to be less physical evidence remaining, and the landscapes themselves have often changed significantly over the years.[7] Furthermore, the very nature of early warfare required relatively open spaces, often with some high ground, but with the result that the actual topography itself can initially appear unremarkable, which only serves to compound the problems. The result is that English battlefields can easily slip out of people's consciousness because of the lack of visual clues and reminders of the conflict so that, as Kinross (1979) noted, they can appear rather dull on first examination. Monuments are one way of helping to prevent this 'memory slippage', although as Tunbridge and Ashworth (1998, p. 118) note, "the very ubiquity of many war memorials", particularly in relation to the First World War, can mean they too can become invisible and ignored by most people. Interpretive facilities and centres are a more contemporary way of avoiding this 'slippage' but, as will be noted later, these can also have a number of problems.

The *Battlefield Register* of 43 sites, or the slightly greater number included by the Battlefield Trust, indicates that many battlefields cannot be properly located, or have been lost to development. Looking at Table 3.1, descriptors are given of the relative accuracy of the battlefields' physical location, which are drawn from the Battlefields Trust *Fields of Conflict Database*. It is of interest that only 17 were deemed as having a 'secure' location, 8 as having an 'accurate' location and only 1 battlefield, Naseby, having an 'exact' location, which partly reflects the amount of work done on examining the archaeological evidence, such as the distribution of musket balls. For the rest of the battlefields, they tend to receive the descriptors of 'approximate', 'probable', 'alternative site' or 'disputed'.

Although there is an inherent logic of the need to locate a battlefield to an actual physical landscape for effective interpretation and visitor utilisation, if one cannot do this, it does not mean that the site cannot be used as a tourism resource, as the Battle of Bosworth site illustrates, which, despite all its sophisticated visitor interpretation, is now regarded as a 'disputed' site in terms of its location.

The Temporal Distance of the Conflict

One of the factors that can affect battlefield utilisation relates to the length of time that has passed since the actual battle took place. In England (excluding the Battle of Britain), the last pitched battle was over 300 years ago, so the events are no longer vivid in peoples' minds. In Europe, after the two world wars, the changed economic and social figurations allowed for more people to visit the battlefields than was previously possible. For the First World War, the peak in visitor numbers to the actual battlefields themselves in France and Belgium was in the few years after the war had ended, with numbers steadily dwindling as time went on and the sites became more "cold" (Lloyd, 1998); the legacy, however, was that it created a tourism infrastructure, which gave an impetus for further tourist attractions for subsequent generations. A similar life cycle may also be evident in countries with more recent conflicts, such as in Vietnam.

---

[7] One of the advantages of many English battlefields is that they tended to be on a smaller scale in comparison with many later battles and so easier to appreciate.

The temporal time element, whilst important, is not sufficient in itself to explain why conflicts may be forgotten. There are many battlefields from around the world, which can attract thousands of visitors, despite having taken place long before living memory, as the 718 Battle of Covodonga in Spain,[8] the 1030 Battle of Sticklestad in Norway,[9] or the 1746 Battle of Culloden in Scotland all illustrate.

The Scale of the Conflict

The larger the conflict, the more who are affected by the war, which in turn can influence the number of people who may have some interest or connection to the battles. In the instance of the American Civil War, it was estimated that 620,000 people were killed — more than all the American losses in any subsequent war. If one was to multiply the number of people who would be touched by each death, then it is hardly surprising that it became so ingrained in the cultural identity of the country.[10] In the context of English battlefields, the number of casualties can seem very small when compared with more contemporary conflicts and so can seem to have less impact on the population. Yet even a cursory examination of the battlefield attractions of Scotland (particularly Culloden, where casualties were relatively modest), demonstrates the potential of battles involving relatively few casualities yet nonetheless still possessing huge cultural significance that influences their ability to act as a visitor attraction.

Therefore the scale of the conflict not only relates to the actual numbers fighting and the casualties, but also to the impacts it has on wider society. In this instance, the impression can sometimes be given that the nature of English wars and battles were limited. Smurthwaite (1984), for example, makes the comment that many of the conflicts could be relatively self-contained, with instances of farmers continuing to plough only a few fields away from the actual battle itself. This idea of minimal impacts, or even a notion of an 'English' approach to war, which is used as a synonym for 'gentlemanly', can, however, be strongly contested. Carlton (1992), for example, in his work on the English Civil War, gives numerous vivid accounts of the many atrocities and racial killings which took place during the conflict, as illustrated by the majority of Irish prisoners dying in captivity, or the instances of Scottish and Welsh prisoners sold into slavery to work on the sugar plantations in the Caribbean. Past wars in England do not seem to have immunity from being any less brutish or violent in comparison with other conflicts from around the world, so

---

[8] Which, strictly speaking, seems to have been more of a skirmish, where the Visigoth King defeated the moors, thus preventing the final conquest of all of Spain, meaning that a pocketful of resistance could grow in what is now present-day region of Asturias. It is an event that is given great cultural significance as it is seen as the turning point for the Christian reconquest of Spain.

[9] This was where the Christian Viking Olav II was defeated, later becoming a place of pilgrimage for Christians.

[10] The America Civil War, which in relation to its scale, symbolism and the residual bitterness it left behind, affected the political and cultural landscape for generations. Indeed, it was not really until the election of President Reagan in the 1980s, that this legacy was broken. Before this time, one would have the anomalous situation (to an outsider at least) whereby one would see a pattern of the South voting predominantly for the Democratic party, even though this tended to be seen as the liberal, reforming party, which would be out of synch with many of the more conservative views held by Southern voters. Differences were vividly illustrated during the 1960s and the civil rights reforms initiated by Democratic presidents, with the strongest opposition emanating from the many Southern Democrats.

one must continue to explore other factors that help explain the relative lack of interest in English battlefields.

The Cultural Significance and Emotional Appeal of the Battle

At the first English Battlefield conference held in 1991, Rhona Moir, the then custodian of the Culloden visitor centre, gave a particularly useful insight into explaining some of the differences in battlefield utilisation between England and Scotland, noting how a variety of factors, when combined, can help in battlefield utilisation and preservation. She said:

> The [battlefield] must have general appeal because of its historic context, historical impact, emotional appeal and the funeral profile. Culloden has that appeal — albeit, ironically, often as a complete misunderstanding of what it was about (the frequently mistaken notion that it was a fight between Scotland and England, for Scottish independence). It is, however, justified in being a watershed in history, with a direct link to subsequent emigration. It has the mass appeal of its part in the legend of the romanticised Charles Edward Stuart; it has a memorial cairn and the grave (a site of virtual pilgrimage); above all, it has pathos and tragedy. Even Bannockburn fails on these counts — and it shows in the figures (Moir, 1991).

In the context of the English experience, although there is little doubt that battles have shaped history, there does not seem to be the same strength of attachment to them as in Scotland. It seems that the many battles that have occurred on English soil do not seem to have sufficient resonance or symbolic power in relation to the contribution they can make to the English national psyche. What war and battles do so well is to focus attention on a sense of 'we' and belonging, in opposition to a notion of 'other' and an enemy to be fought against. They provide potent tools for weaving together a national consciousness and identity, where both losses and victories can be equally remembered. These events, quite simply, can shape how people view themselves and others. The 1690 Battle of the Boyne in Northern Ireland graphically illustrates these points, where it has come to symbolise Protestant 'togetherness' and Catholic 'otherness', and a highly emotive issue in terms of its commemoration and which, as Holmes noted, has "cut a far deeper groove in history than its military importance might suggest" (Holmes, 1997, p. 120). In this sense, for England, the conflicts that tend to be drawn upon — particularly when used as the basis of analogies for sporting contests by the tabloid newspapers — usually relate to battles that have not taken place on English soil, such as the Battle of Agincourt,[11] Rorke's Drift, Dunkirk, the Battle of Britain or the Blitz, all of which help illustrate a collective strength of spirit, or the overcoming of adversity, often against the odds. Quite simple, attempting to try and evoke, for example, a 'Battle of Naseby' spirit, does not really have the same

---

[11] It is of interest how English visitors to the little village of Agincourt — the battle where Henry V defeated the much larger French army — have helped sustain the visitor centre there; yet in terms of the cultural significance attached and attention received in history books or schooling, the differences could not be more marked. It is also of interest how the Battlefield Trust becomes involved in preventing the development of a wind farm near the battlefield.

emotional appeal, despite its undoubted historic significance in shaping English history, often being cited as the second most significant battlefield after Hastings (Raynor, 2004).

Another factor that Moir points out as being important in creating a sense of attachment and recognition relates to the stories that can be told. The Battle of Bosworth is one of the English battles that stand out in relation to the emotive issues it generates. As Shakespeare's play, *Richard III*, testifies, it is a story that can be set within certain parameters, which gives the story a coherence and tangibility and thus it becomes easier to relate to, albeit it towards a possible misdirected view as many would argue,[12] particularly in relation to Richard III as the 'evil' usurper of the crown, who is reputed to have murdered his brother, wife and his nephews (the two young princes in the Tower), in order to achieve power. Whatever the truth, there is no doubting that it is powerful material. Hastings also stands out in terms of the coherence and tangibility of the key events involved in the Battle. For most other English battlefields, it can be far more challenging to bring out some of these more intimate, powerful stories, and so part of the appeal will always be limited; this is not to say that that other battlefields do not have powerful stories to tell, just that they may not be as well known, or as easy to relate to.

Clearly, a vital ingredient in understanding how and why battlefields can be used as a resource relates to how they are woven into the cultural fabric of the society and the wider appeal the stories can have to people. In this sense, most English battles play a modest role, with the stories often remaining distant and impersonal to many people.

Location of Battlefields to Significant Population Centres

In the context of theme parks, a benchmark figure often touted is that in order to be viable attractions, they need to have a population of "over a million people within one-and-half hours drive time" (Yale, 1991, p. 3). Whilst a little simplistic, it does act as a reminder of the importance of distance, communications and the notion of 'pulling power' of an attraction. When examining travel patterns for the battlefield attractions at Bosworth and Hastings, a majority of visitors seem to travel from within 30 miles, or under an hour drive time, of which this can include tourists staying in the local area.

For most English battlefields, one would have to conclude that they do not have large enough local population centres from which to draw significant numbers of visitors. In instance of Culloden (the UK battlefield attraction with the highest numbers of visitors), it not only has the benefit of being located 6 miles from Inverness, which acts as a hub for visitors to the Scottish Highlands, but its cultural significance means it has a broader appeal to both the nation and a global diaspora as the event that precipitated the Highland clearances and emigration to the New World — factors which mean its pulling power is much stronger in comparison with many English battlefields. Equally the story of Culloden aids reinforcement of a sense of Scottish nationalism — which sense is absent from many English battlefields. This does not undermine the value or use of English battlefields as a recreational resource, rather it means that their utilisation often needs to be subtle and there exists a need to consider more cost-effective forms of interpretations as discussed in the next section.

---

[12] The Richard III Society was established in 1923, which strongly contests the evil, villainous image of Richard III.

Opportunities and Dilemmas of English Battlefield Utilisation

Despite the many factors that inhibit the viability of English battlefields as more signifi-cant visitor attractions, there are still many recreational opportunities that can be identified but which, in turn, also generate further problems or dilemmas. These opportunities and problems will be discussed around the themes of researching the location battlefields; the need for diversity in interpretation, managing dissonance, seeking wider appeal and interest, the need for organisational coordination; the importance of good quality research and understanding product life cycles.

Continued Research into Battlefield Locations and Events

From the discussion so far, it is clear that for many battlefields there are problems as to the actual locations of events within their physical landscapes. For some writers, such as Seymour (1997), this lack of knowledge is part of the enjoyment of battlefields, being viewed almost like puzzles whereby the past events are unlocked from the landscape through research. For most, the demand is for the battlefield location to be already processed in terms of research and interpretation. Added to this element is the importance that the 'being there' principle has on the visitor experience, even if it is based on subjec-tive perceived reality, rather than an objective truth.

The experience of the Battle of Bosworth attraction is instructive here. This is the English Battlefield with the most developed visitor amenities and interpretation; yet it is defined as a "disputed location" according to the Battlefield Trust *Fields of Conflict Database*. In all there are two other alternative locations to the battlefield within the nearby vicinity. Despite these problems, it has not prevented the site from undergoing a £2 million redevelopment, which has been spent on new interpretation, visitor amenities and further archaeological and historical research into the different possible battlefield locations. Interestingly, they have also blended the historical controversy into their interpretation in a manner that highlights adherence to, and the integrity of, their educational principles.

What one can conclude is that it is perhaps vital that there is *some* notion that the battle can be located in the landscape, but it is not necessarily essential to have *the* com-plete picture. Indeed, the elements of the unknown can be of interest in themselves, or else compensated for by the quality of visitor amenities and interpretive techniques used.[13]

Whilst having gaps in knowledge about battles and their location is not necessarily a deficiency, this should not mean that greater understanding and research is unnecessary and not strived for. What the English experience has illustrated since the 1990s, is the importance of research in relation to approximating battlefield locations through battle-field archaeology, conducting further research into archive materials and illustrating their

---

[13] If one thinks hard enough, or literally enough one can usually find something tangible with which to hang the interpretation of historical events from, so letting the story of the battle unfold in the persons mind. This is illus-trated with the Battle of Britain, which may seem to initially offer few opportunities for interpretation and a vis-itor attraction yet, as Raynor (2004) illustrates, there are numerous places on the ground where the important story of the Battle of Britain can be made more tangible, such as the many airfields and radar stations from which the battle was fought.

cultural significance. As the medieval battle of Evesham illustrates, new primary sources of data can be discovered and so transform the understanding of the past events.[14] It is from these scholarly foundations, conducted by both professional academics and from the hobbyist researcher,[15] that battlefields can be more clearly demarcated on land-use plans, which in turn helps in their preservation and in resisting new developments that could destroy the visual integrity of the field and the archaeological record. It is also from these research materials where the crucial ingredients for the interpretive materials are found, which are relevant for both directed educational groups or the more general recreational visitor.

Diversity in Interpretation

Although more understanding and knowledge about the battles should always be sought, this is not the same as saying there should be uniformity in their presentation and interpretation. The danger with interpretation is that there may be the temptation to simply replicate a formula that has worked elsewhere. Just as having a lack of interpretation and amenities can mean a battlefield location can appear uninteresting to many, paradoxically, having a similar approach to interpretation can also lead to boredom, which emanates from familiarity with the approach. It has been a long running debate in heritage tourism that the commodification or packaging of the past brings many problems, as illustrated by the provocative writings of Hewison (1989) and Lowenthal (1981). Lowenthal says:

> So we set out to attempt to attract more and more visitors, often in a spirit of evangelism as well as financial gain. Our anxiety to increase the general interest can result in an urge to 'make accessible' both physically and in terms of information. This includes the didactic attempt to interpret everything, to 'bring out its meaning' for the good of others. … Then everything tends to be 'on show' nothing is left to speak for itself or the chance of discovery; the whole country becomes an exhibition. Visitors numbers may rise, but atmosphere is irrevocably eroded. (Lowenthal, 1981, p. 195)

One of the reasons for highlighting different methods of interpretation for battlefields, is that they act as a reminder of the diverse ways in which meaning and significance of a place can be revealed. This is not presenting an argument that certain forms of interpretation, such as visitor centres or interpretive panels are wrong or bad, rather, it is an argument for seeing battlefields as a portfolio of resources which need to be managed and presented in diverse ways. Whilst for some locations they may be best served by more sophisticated interpretation and amenities, for others the sense of remoteness, solitude and lack of imposing monuments can add to their power and be of interest to different groups (market niches or segments if you like), who can use less intrusive

---

[14] Another example is in relation to the Battle of Marston Moor, where archaeological work and the discovery of musket balls has extended the range of the battlefield initially identified for the Battlefield Register.

[15] Who incidentally have played an absolutely vital role in the understanding of so many English battlefields, therefore the term 'hobbyist' is used in no way a lesser or derogatory sense.

methods of interpretation, such as guide books and maps. In this sense, the fact that some battlefields may not have wider appeal can in fact also be seen as an opportunity in terms of maintaining diversity.

A further important issue in relation to English battlefield interpretation relates to the notion of dissonance. This refers to the idea that a tension will almost inevitably be created with the presentation of the past, whereby stories or a peoples' heritage can be ignored or a community misrepresented. As already highlighted, wars and battles by their very nature possess an inherent element of division and violence that can be used to remind communities of their differences. Whilst in England, the divisionary power of the battlefields has been greatly dissipated, this does not mean that all issues of dissonance have disappeared. In particular, there is the difficulty of what aspects of the battle the interpretation should focus on. Uzzell, for example, offers a reminder of the different directions interpretation about war can take, saying:

> Why do interpreters ignore, or abandon the tragedy of war? Destruction, torture, the abuse of human rights, slaughter, death and inhumanity are all side-lined in favour of the power and the glory of conflict. (Uzzell, 1989, cited by Stevans, 1989.)

The issue here is the tightrope that must be walked between sanitizing war and battle, with sensationalism and gore. Whilst the means of fighting war and waging battles has changed, the fundamental human experience of war can remain remarkably similar, which can offer some important lessons when trying to understand today's conflicts, or using today's conflicts to help put a more intimate face on past battles.

Organisational Coordination

For the tourism resource of battlefields to be released they must first be secure. To achieve this, not only is it is necessary to have continuous research about the battles, their location and the events which took place, but it is also vital to have effective organisations who can utilise this data and coordinate actions to prevent battlefields being lost to development — the failure to prevent the road going through the Battle of Naseby site illustrated the importance of these factors: hence the establishment of the Battlefield Trust.

Since this second '1991 Battle of Naseby', as it became known, there have been some notable successes in battlefield preservation that illustrate the importance of effective organisation that can help coordinate actions. In the instance of the battlefield of Blore Heath, a proposal for gravel extraction in 1992 was rejected — thanks largely to the coordinated actions of different groups and the *Battlefield Register*, which at that time was still in its early stages of preparation. The Battle of Tewkesbury was a more drawn out affair, with the proposal for new housing on the site submitted in 1992, with the fight to preserve the battlefield space lasting until 1998, when planning permission was eventually refused by the Secretary of State, John Prescott. In both instances it illustrated the importance of organised bodies, good quality research and an appeal to the wider benefits that could be gained from their preservation as open spaces.

Product Life Cycles and Economic Viability

If one examines the visitor figures for the key battle-related visitor attractions, it is highly instructive to frame the demand patterns within the notion of a product life cycle. This basic marketing principle provides some useful imagery in terms of the pattern of usage that has occurred, not only for English battlefield attractions, but also for many of the Scottish ones, such as Culloden or Bannockburn. The pattern, which emerges over the past decade or more, is one where there was a steady increase in visitors during the take-off stage, seeming to reach the peak, or maturity in demand after two to three years, followed by a steady period of decline. The Battle of Hastings, which also has the advantage of the remains of Battle Abbey and a key focus for tourism, has gone from a peak of 109, 000 visitors, down to approximately 67,000 visitors in 2005. For the Battle of Bosworth, its peak usage of 37,000 paying visitors has declined to approximately 20,000 visitors. Even in Scotland the Battle of Culloden site, which always stood out in the UK because of its high visitor numbers, has seen demand decline from over 120,000 visitors in the early 1990s to around the 80,000 mark in 2004, which is still, it should be noted, a high number for a UK battlefield attraction. As response to declining visitor numbers, all the sites have secured funding for significant refurbishments of their facilities in the attempt to halt the decline in demand and rejuvenate the service and visitor experience.

There have also been some battlefield interpretative initiatives that have come and gone. The Battle of Stoke, for example, had a battlefield trail developed in the 1980s, replicating elements of the Bosworth battlefield trail, but this has now become defunct with the interpretation panels being placed in the local church. The Commandary in Worcester, a museum that was set up in 1991 to focus on the English Civil War and interpreting the Battle of Worcester, saw its demand reach a peak of 40,000,[16] but then steadily declined to around 20,000 visitors. In 2005 it closed for a major refurbishment to reopen in 2006, returning the interpretation to the history of the building, with the battle exhibit forming a subsidiary part of the storytelling.

What is the implication of these life cycle trends for existing battlefield attractions or future ones? In the first instance, they act as reminders of how a visitor attraction can be developed for historic events for which there may be few tangible remains. In the second instance, it shows how demand will almost inevitably fluctuate, perhaps eventually slipping into decline, unless there are constant attempts to revive or rejuvenate the product or service, something which can often cost significant amounts of money. Although educational-related groups — which often form around as much as a quarter of total visitors — tend to fluctuate far less in terms of demand in the short term, over longer periods, this group can also suffer serious decline, as changing demographic trends set in both nationally and locally. All of these things stress the importance of thinking strategically in relation to how to manage the demand changes over a three-year, five-year and ten-year period, together with the need for making realistic demand projections and considerations

---

[16] This peak was tied in with the significant amount of publicity the English Civil War received through the 350 anniversary of its start in 1992. This commemoration was used by many local authorities to organise numerous special events to help boost tourism to their local area, which illustrates another way to tap into the tourism potential.

of where the money will come from for future redevelopments. Quite simply, change is inevitable and so should be planned for, with considerations of fund raising a constant process.

Although the visitor figures cited for the various battlefield attractions do not give the true demand figure, as there are many more visitors who come to the sites, but do not pay to go into the visitor centres, in terms of economic viability it should be recognised that these attractions are hardly likely to be significant money spinners.[17] Most centres will aim to cover their operational costs with only facilities such as Culloden, with its higher visitor numbers, able to generate a small surplus. Does this, then, undermine their viability as a potential attraction? If taken in isolation it appears to do so, as for most English battlefields it would be difficult to make a profitable visitor attraction; something that many would perhaps be relieved about as somehow 'profit' seems an inappropriate motive for a battlefield attraction. If, however, the battlefield is a resource to be viewed in a more strategic manner whereby it is placed in the context of a portfolio of attractions in an area, or for the basis of developing themed historical trails or special events, then their value is far higher than the revenue generated from paying visitors would suggest. This is clearly demonstrated in parts of Leicestershire, where the landscape and villages can lack the dramatic landscapes and buildings in comparisons with other parts of the UK, but the attractions of the Battle of Bosworth, Twycross Zoo and the nearby restored Battlefield steam train line, all combine to help draw people to the area.

Bringing it all Together

What this audit of English battlefields allows for is the development of a framework with which battlefields from different countries can be compared and assessed with in relation to their resource viability. To help in this function the key elements from the different sections are presented in Figure 3.2. This diagram loosely adopts the basic checklist framework used in location theory (Smith, 1993). The method is a relatively straightforward technique, whereby the notions of identifying 'essential' and 'desirable' criteria (here adapted to 'vital' and 'influential' criteria) are used, by categorising the key variables that can affect the resource utilisation and viability. Underpinning all these things are the inherent tensions of battlefield resource utilisation, which creates a constant dynamic of threats and opportunities being generated, but which always needs to be managed.

---

[17] Something that many would feel relieved about. Disney found how vociferous a group this could be in 1996, where a proposed $500,000 to 1 billion battlefield theme park attraction at the bloody Battle of Bull Run site inflamed opinions and widespread distrust of the corporations suitability to develop such an attraction, even though it was estimated that it could potentially attract over 30,000 visitors a day. The proposal was described by many as a desecration, with one critic saying " how can we trust an organisation who would not draw bellybuttons on their cartoon characters to give us an authentic portrayal of our history", and another saying "Disney will do to American history what they have already done to the animal kingdom — sentimentalise it out of recognition" (Bates, 1994). Disney later dropped the proposal.

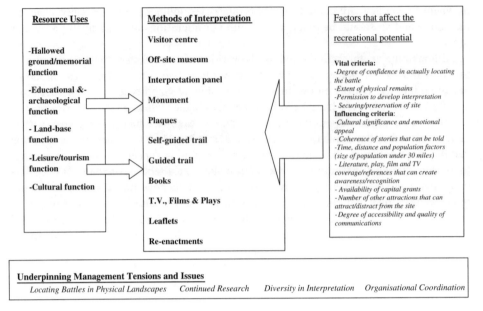

Figure 3.2: Developing a framework for battlefield resource assessment based on English battlefields.

Conclusions

This audit of English battlefield utilisation as a recreational and tourism resource reveals a number of issues. Of primary importance is the need to secure the sites from urban or industrial developments, for without the maintenance of the open space, it can mean interpretation is made difficult, archaeological records are lost and the quality of the visitor experience severely reduced. Yet if battlefield sites are to be secure from future land-use developments, they must draw on a mixture of qualitative and quantitative arguments that not only stress the morality of treating the sites where people have died with respect, but with also a notion that they are a cultural, educational and recreational resource from which people will benefit.

In the context of their recreational and tourism potential, this rationale for preservation has clearly grown in importance, having the ability to be used in a variety of ways, ranging from a fully developed visitor attraction, to more subtle walking trails, with the minimum of structural interpretation, apart from a leaflet or guidebook.

Care should, however, be taken, not to simply equate visitor numbers with profitable attractions. For most English battlefields, they simply lack the key locational factors, such as being near a sufficiently large density of population, to attract visitors in any significant numbers. Whilst for some battlefields around the world, unfavourable location factors can be compensated for by the strength of the cultural significance and their emotional appeal, for most English battlefields these factors are not strongly felt. A more effective way of understanding their tourism potential therefore is to understand how they can fit into a portfolio of tourism and recreational resources, whereby they can be used to help comple-ment demand for existing attractions, or providing an attractive park space.

It should also be appreciated that the preservation of battlefields is not the same as saying which ones can be turned into visitor attractions. Not only is this an unviable option for many battlefield sites, it is also undesirable. The key is in maintaining the diversity of battlefields and the interpretive techniques that can be used to reveal the meaning of a site.

Finally, a visit to the Anne Frank Museum in Amsterdam offers an important lesson that can be used to reflect upon English battlefields. Whilst the scale of the genocide on the Jews is shocking, what the story of Anne Frank does is put a single face on those millions who died, acting as a reminder that each person who was killed had their own story which will probably never be told: so too it is with each death that has occurred on the many English battlefields. This should be remembered, helping to ensure that battlefields as a resource should be approached with sensitivity and care.

Useful Websites

http://www.battlefieldstrust.com — The Battlefield Trust is a key organisation in battlefield preser-vation and interpretation. They provide a key database, which should be utilised when looking at UK battlefields, particularly their link to the Battlefield Resource Centre and the development of the *UK Fields of Conflict* database, which gives many maps, photographs and illustrations, together with some of the key issues around the battlefields themselves.

http://www.english-heritage.org — Through their site one can find the links to the detailed battle-field register, which is a very useful document in land-use planning.

http://www.britishbattles.com — This site provides many details on battles fought by Britain and its Empire forces from the 18th century to the end of the 19th century, with many illustrations and maps.

Chapter 4

A Proposed Code of Conduct for War Heritage Sites

Teresa Leopold

Displaying a country's war history in museums, through memorials, and even in the form of tourist attractions, are primarily attempts to find an appropriate language and instrument to remember and commemorate horrific events of the past. Development is taking place, which has to consider a country's need for protecting, remembering and presenting its culture and landscape. At the same time tourist demand, which ranges from pure entertainment to cultural education, has to be considered and satisfied. Whereas visitors are likely to attribute multiple meanings to war heritage sites, providers of war heritage sites may have one or more interpretations that they wish to privilege, and which inform the construction and management of the sites. One important concept is the promotion of peace through the commemoration of the past and education of future generations. It is argued that adherence to an agreed code of conduct would facilitate this meaning of a war heritage site. The objective of this polemic is to propose principles, which inform any such code. The suggested principles are based on research examining the main components of war heritage sites in Laos, Cambodia and Vietnam, how managers present and manage these war heritage sites by themselves and within a community setting, and what managerial problems exist with the presentation and preservation of the sites.

With the introduction of the Global Code of Ethics for Tourism in October 1999, attention was drawn to the need for guidelines for various tourism stakeholders (World Tourism Organisation (WTO), 1999a). Codes of conduct are designed to reflect today's intercultural society, prevent the destruction of people's cultural traditions and environment, create awareness of different norms of social interaction, ensure ethical norms and stimulate awareness of the socio-cultural costs communities can face as a result of tourism. Thus it is argued that a code of conduct for war heritage sites could act as a fundamental tool for maintaining a country's war heritage and presenting its meaning in an ethical and sustainable manner. The 11 key principles introduced in this chapter focus upon internal as well as external concerns of war heritage sites. It is argued that the acceptance of, commitment to, and further development of these principles would ensure a clear assertion of the facilitated meaning of a site.

War Heritage as Growth Industry

The existence and presentation of heritage, history and culture are key components in present-day tourism. War, tragic events and disasters are shaping and re-shaping the culture and heritage of countries by changing people's understanding, acceptance and comprehension of the world and their role within it (Merridale, 1999). Mihalic (1996, p. 234) described the connection between war and tourism as follows: "when the war is over, it becomes part of the historical memory of a certain destination and this memory becomes a tourist attraction". Selecting parts of history and converting them into products results in a transformation of some historical resources into recognised and managed heritage sites whereas other resources are simply being ignored.

Ironically, after the destruction of heritage, heritage itself is used as an essential tool to rebuild a torn country, often resulting in the emergence of new forms of tourism or tourist attractions. Smith (1996, p. 148) argues that "memorabilia of warfare and allied products probably constitutes the largest single category of tourist attractions in the world", thus identifying war heritage sites as important elements of the supply side of tourist attractions. The former war-torn countries of Vietnam, Laos and Cambodia particularly support this contention. Over the last century, several wars have been fought in Vietnam, Laos and Cambodia, often related to the colonial past of these countries and their struggle for independence. The most protracted of these wars was the Vietnam War, which destroyed the economic development of the region, caused numerous fatalities and injuries (both civilian and military) and removed Vietnam, Laos and Cambodia from the traveller's map. Even though the Vietnam War officially ended in 1975, it has been only during the last decade that tourist development, in terms of awareness creation and image recovery, has taken place. All three countries are currently rebuilding their destroyed infrastructure and are re-opening their borders to tourism, indicating that they are each at a similar stage of recovery and development. Applying Weaver's (2000) *War-distorted Destination Life Cycle* to these countries, facts regarding the positive economic- and tourist-related developments of Vietnam, Laos and Cambodia place them within stage *t6 development*. This stage is characterised by an increase in visitation by veterans and a growing attractiveness and number of war heritage sites. A total of 18 war heritage sites in Vietnam, Laos and Cambodia were researched. An initial case-study approach enabled the author to gain background information on the countries and sites, followed by a postal questionnaire survey sent to the site management.

The Influence of Managers upon the Presented Meanings of Sites

War heritage sites use various forms of interpretation to represent the past. Many "historians, curators, archaeologists, anthropologists, sociologists, and more recently marketing and management specialists" have had an ongoing discussion about how the past should best be presented (Goulding, 2000, p. 836). Generally speaking, representations should enable visitors to understand the relationship of past, present and future, and should increase their understanding through the resources presented (Hornstein, 2003; Timothy & Boyd, 2003). Explanations and interpretation have to be provided, and especially because some authentic sites and artefacts in particular do not speak for themselves and their meaning could often be hidden (Noakes, 1997). In other words, "representation refers to the process of producing meaning, not directly from an object but from the way in which its representation is created through classification and display" (Graham, Ashworth & Tunbridge, 2000, p. 33).

As Goulding (2000) observed, much discussion still remains about how and what is presented in historic sites. Simply being able to discuss certain ways of representation shows the power a certain society has over the presented meaning. Thus, constructing heritage sites results in an obvious selectivity of representation, with certain events and people being remembered, while others are ignored. Generally, the choice lies with the manager, with regard to which particular artefacts and knowledges should be elided, while "emphasising others through the same mirrors of gender, class, 'race' and nationalism" (Graham, Ashworth & Tunbridge, 2000, p. 32). This power of choice is one of the greatest difficulties many heritage managers are facing (Hall & McArthur, 1998).

Consequently, providers and managers of sites can have one or more particular readings they wish to privilege, and which inform the construction and management of the sites. Hornstein and Jacobowitz (2003, p. 5) argued that a memorial site "is never neutral and history and national agendas are at all times political". Foley and Lennon (1997, p. 159) went further and claimed that the representation of the past is not just manipulated and relabelled to promote a political message, but also "to convey a tourism/leisure orientation". Similarly, Swarbrooke (1994, p. 225) explained the exhibition of non-authentic artefacts, in order to "milk this lucrative cash cow" called heritage, pointing towards a certain exploitation of these sites. It is a truism that managers or providers of war heritage sites can privilege one or more meanings of the sites. But at the same time, a memorial has the responsibility towards society to present a socially acceptable and suitable meaning.

Commemoration and Education as Main Meanings

War heritage sites can present places for public and private reflection, where visitors can show individual respect to victims, their suffering and/or deaths (Hornstein & Jacobowitz, 2003). After a war or other tragic event, directly affected people such as victims and veterans often contribute to the social understanding of the past by presenting their unmediated, raw experiences. These memories, in the form of narratives, provide first-person testimonies for future generations. Simultaneously, a representation of history is connected with the ambition to teach new generations through past experiences. Research carried out by a number of authors (e.g. Foley & Lennon, 1996; Weaver, 2000; Leopold & Ritchie, 2003) showed that with a growing time difference, the interest in visits to commemorative sites expands to other visitor groups who are not only motivated out of commemorational reasons, but also by a wish to secure a better understanding of the past. Thus, there exists an argument to evolve from acts of commemoration to those of education. Research of war heritage sites in Vietnam, Laos and Cambodia identified commemoration and education as the two most important interpretative motives for visits. It is also suggested that commemorating and learning about the past through the visitation of war heritage sites can ultimately lead to the promotion of peace. However, using war heritage sites as educational mediums has to be carried out with caution. "In educational work it is important not to make excessive moral demands on learners. ... People must always have the possibility to remain detached or to withdraw themselves and educators must accept this" (Lutz, 1994, p. 23). It is argued that if the promotion of peace through commemoration of the past and education of future generations is to be effective, then adherence to an agreed code of conduct will facilitate this reading of battlefield sites.

The introduction of the Global Code of Ethics for Tourism in October 1999 drew attention to the desirability of providing clearly formulated guidelines for tourism stakeholders that reflect today's global society (World Tourism Organisation, 1999b; Frangialli, 2001). During the implementation of this global code of ethics, numerous set guidelines for different subsections of the tourism industry have been developed. Reisinger and Turner (2003, p. 145) refer to such codes as rules of social interaction, with their main function to "maintain harmonious interactions". However, codes of conduct are also self-regulatory as they set minimum behavioural standards and, at the same time, publicly attest to a certain commitment to a site (International Council of Museums, 2001). Thus codes can help prevent the loss and destruction of people's cultural traditions and environment by providing guidelines for visitors and tourists through creating awareness of the different norms of social interaction.

Provisional Code of Conduct

The importance of the development and introduction of key principles that underline a code of conduct is based on the need of war heritage sites to present a clear meaning. Thus, principles were formulated to ensure the recognition of the role commemoration and education plays at a war heritage site. At the same time, principles were developed to protect war heritage sites from misinterpretation, inappropriate redevelopment, unethical marketing and similar threats. The author identified the following 11 fundamental principles that could appropriately inform such a code of conduct for war heritage sites.

1. *Developing national and local government policies*

> The role of government has to be acknowledged and clearly identified in
> order to set standards regarding managerial bodies, influence on exhibition
> design and development, as well as financial matters.

Governmental policies would control the amount and nature of governmental involvement, especially with regards to their involvement in the development of sites. Research of managers identified that governments are expected to play an important role within heritage protection. This expectation was generally met with respect to all researched war heritage sites. Thus, national governments initiated the establishment of six researched war heritage sites, at all sites at least one governmental department or body was recognised as responsible for the day-to-day management of sites, and governments acted as an important information source for the creation of five war heritage sites and their exhibitions. To ensure consistency, but also to avoid over-dependence on governments, the actual level of involvement should be clearly defined. Previous research discovered that governments (national, or national and district) financed or subsidised six war heritage sites fully (one no-reply) pointing towards governments playing an important role with respect to the financing of war heritage sites, though an overall lack of sufficient governmental funding was noted. An appropriate financial commitment of governments would be manifested within this key principle.

Initiatives to protect a nation's heritage for future generations and to support the development of memorials or museums which are open for visitation could be proclaimed as minimum responsibilities for governments. Thus, this key principle calls for a clear policy that makes manifest the involvement of governments within the preservation, management and financing of war heritage sites.

2. *Representative role*

> The responsibility of war heritage sites to clearly portray one or more privileged meanings has to be encouraged and the important meaning of commemorating the past to be acknowledged.

This principle pursues the issue of complexity and diversity of portrayed meanings to visiting audiences. A need exists to clearly identify the representative role of each war heritage site. These roles are bound up with the functions of the sites, and with the multiple readings or meanings that may be inferred by different audiences from the interpretive material presented at the sites. The commemorative function performed by war sites is implicitly or explicitly political (Cole, 2003), and this principle is designed to ensure that the dominant voice that informed the design and function of the site is identified.

With the application of this key principle, unbiased exhibitions, visitor facilities and services would be ensured, which would transform war heritage sites into appropriate presentation platforms of a war-distorted past of a nation. With this key principle it could further be ensured that a clear understanding exists regarding the relationship of the presented meaning and the perceived meaning. Different motivational factors exist regarding various visitor groups (Cameron & Gatewood, 2000). Thus, the provision of particular services, such as brochures (available at five sites) and displays (available at six sites), even in different languages, should be aimed at privileging one or more meanings. This would enable war heritage sites to act as bridges between other nations and their own citizens (Clark, 1998), in other words to promote peace. Thus, this principle would ensure that particular attention is given to various visitor groups to war heritage sites and how their expectations of the sites are imbedded in the presented meaning.

Consideration should also be given to the information sources consulted during the development of war heritage sites. The results of this research clearly indicated the importance of consulting a number of different information sources when developing war heritage sites. It can be anticipated that this would enhance the commemorative aspect of war heritage sites.

3. *Commit to the role of an educator*

> The educational meaning and perception of war heritage sites has to be
> pursued and privileged.

The introduction of this key principle is based on a number of findings of this research. Replies received by managers and findings in the literature (e.g. Lutz, 1994; Foley and Lennon, 1997; Clark, 1998) identified education as the most important meaning of, and a very important motivation for, visiting war heritage sites. Further, educational groups were seen as the most important visitor group. Thus, special commitment should be shown towards the role of war heritage sites as an educator of war history and memory.

The war history of a nation can be analysed in terms of the presented meaning of each site, and also in terms of how well it is presented. Generally, the presentation of history can be done in verbal or written form. This research showed that all heritage sites offered either or both types of information sources. Thus, trained tour guides, printed material and explanatory displays were common features in the researched war heritage sites. As these presentation techniques enhance the educational experience of visits to war heritage sites, such methods should be recognised as a common standard at all sites.

Committing to the role of an educator aligns with a number of key principles identified in this provisional code of conduct. Thus, adequate leadership and guidance of visitors at sites can not only enhance the visitor experience but also prevent negative impacts upon a site (Lutz, 1994; Hornstein & Jacobowitz, 2003). In addition, regular monitoring of visitors, in terms of numbers and groups, would provide extra information vital to accentuate the educational aspect of the exhibition.

4. *Respect for other cultures*

> War heritage sites have to show respect for visitors from different cultures,
> be aware of their traditions and demonstrate tolerance towards international
> visitors, thus know who the visitors are.

Having local, national, as well as international visitors at war heritage sites leads to a clash of different cultures and traditions (Payne & Dimanche, 1996; Reisinger & Turner, 2003). For war heritage sites, this aspect is especially concerning with opposing histories or political ideologies of various nations, such as Americans visiting Vietnamese war heritage sites. Managers of these sites have to establish a clear profile of their visitors to show awareness of their culture and background. In general, this research showed that special development to accommodate international visitors has been carried out by various sites, which points towards a general awareness of knowing your visitor groups. It follows that especially historic events have to be displayed in an un-biased and ethical manner. The research identified that a change in explanation and description of war museums, war attractions and monuments is taking place over time (Leopold & Ritchie, 2003). These changes, in particular, should be carried out with awareness of visitors' expectations and cultures.

However, in the same way as host nations have to show respect to visitors' cultures, visitors have to behave in an acceptable and appropriate manner towards the host communities. Even though un-ethical behaviour from visitors has not been identified as a major problem in this research, behavioural guidelines, as provided by two research sites, would be one way to ensure respectful manners when visiting war heritage sites. Considering the expected increase of visitors to such sites in Southeast Asia (World Tourism Organisation, 1998), this point should be given special consideration.

Thus, knowing your visitors and being able to respect and fulfil their expectations and attitudes towards displayed messages in war heritage sites, represents a key principle within this provisional code of conduct.

5. *Minimise the impact of visitors on the local community*

> Local populations have to be aware of visitor activities within their community and should have the possibility to gain economic benefits through this visitor interaction; at the same time visitors have to be aware of local customs and traditions.

This research showed that the role of local communities is seen as quite diverse with some managers strongly agreeing and others disagreeing that local businesses and residents benefit economically from the site. This principle would contribute towards the minimisation of negative impacts to the local community through offering locals an opportunity to economically gain from the visitor arrivals in the area through employment at war heritage sites (Johnson & Sullivan, 1993). Research identified a direct link between visitor and employee numbers; thus employee numbers at war heritage sites are likely to increase in future. This principle would ensure that a preference should be given to the hiring of local people in these jobs. Further, certain financial benefits, such as free or reduced entrance fees for locals help improve the interaction with, and acceptance of, visitors within a community.

6. *Minimise the impact of visitors on the war heritage sites*

> Negative impacts of visitors to war heritage sites have to be kept as low as possible, especially with consideration of an expected future increase in visitor numbers to war heritage sites in Southeast Asia.

Information material, introductory films and tour guides are all methods that can be implemented to minimise the impact of visitors on sites and attractions (Lutz, 1994). The provision of these services enhances the knowledge base of visitors with regards to the history and behaviour expected at war heritage sites. Most researched sites identified the offer of information material in various languages to suit their known visitor profiles. These are responsible and necessary steps for the maintenance of sites. This is especially true for visitors who return to Southeast Asia for commemorative purposes. The provision of appropriate facilities, such as reflection rooms and comment books, could enhance the visitor experience and a site's attractiveness (Lutz, 1994). Nevertheless, the two most important methods to minimise the impact of visitors are the provision of informative printed material before the visit to establish a picture of what can be expected at a particular site; and behavioural guidelines for visitors to avoid inappropriate behaviour (Payne & Dimanche, 1996). This information should be provided through a variety of institutions and in a number of different languages to reach all visitor groups, for example, through regional tourist organisations or tourist information centres as well as other memorials and museums. In addition, regular monitoring of visitor numbers and behaviour would enhance managers' awareness of what is happening at the sites and thus encourage appropriate management techniques (Cameron & Gatewood, 2000; Graham, Ashworth & Tunbridge, 2000).

7. *Maintain accuracy*

> Truthful displays and an un-biased representation of artefacts have to be ensured to present an objective picture of war heritage sites.

Special consideration has to be given to government propaganda, which needs to be prevented in order to display a site that is detached of former prejudices. The marketing of war heritage sites, normally in the form of brochures, magazine and newspaper articles or advertisements, has to be carried out whilst still maintaining ethical standards. With regards to displays, more value is given to authenticity than reproduced artefacts (Richter, 1999) and the appropriateness of former soldiers and victims as information sources for developing war heritage sites was acknowledged. Further it should be considered that most war heritage sites, except monuments, develop over time and add to or change displays within their exhibition as well as the onsite facilities. Especially with these new developments, truthful presentation has to be ensured to keep an alteration of the sites' meanings to a minimum. This key principle should be given special attention as site degradation was clearly identified as a major concern among the sample war heritage sites. This degradation could also negatively impact upon the displays. Thus, applying this principle would attempt to interpret war histories in a more honest light, analysing the motives of all participants and the effects of their actions upon other people.

8. *Provide professional service*

> Commitment and support are key factors in the provision of professional services at war heritage sites.

Support given to the visitor includes specialised and trained tour guides, ethical and truthful displays, as well as professional and educational information material (Lutz, 1994). Considering the importance given to the aspect of commemoration and education, these services are considered as enhancing the visitor experience. Thus services offered should be in agreement with perceptions and expectations of visitors. Applying these principles within a provisional code of conduct to war heritage sites would ensure the successful implementation of these supporting factors. The commitment and attitude of employees to war heritage sites, to visitors and to presenting the message of the site, are also contributing factors to the provision of a professional service. Through their commitment employees ensure the maintenance of the site, the satisfaction of the visitor and their role as educators.

9. *Introduce adequate site policies*

> All sites have to ensure that company policies are in place, which guarantee rights of employees.

Employees should be treated with respect and management should be carried out with regards to applicable governmental policies. Considering the emphasis managers have given to tour guides, all tour guides should have the right for proper training and education that is related to their job. Further, local people should be employed within each workforce. Governments are playing a major role for war heritage sites, thus commitment should be shown to national laws and political concerns related to the sites. However, this commitment has to be carried out with care, as political propaganda within the exhibitions has to be avoided (Cole, 2003).

A set-operating budget should be allocated for marketing actions. This would help to implement key issues related to minimising the impact of visitors upon the local community and on the war site, as a financial share would ensure the publication of information material for visitors on a regular basis.

10. *Network with similar institutions*

> The need for a consistent network between similar institutions exists to
> ensure up-to-date development within the heritage and tourism industry.

This cooperation can also be used for combined marketing efforts, to design behavioural guidelines for visitors, to distribute information material in a less commercialised way, to design development plans and to ensure appropriate industry representation within governmental debates. Researched war heritage sites identified relatively little networking with other memorials and war museums. This can be explained by the large geographical spread of respondents. However, especially in major cities that have a number of war heritage sites, a combined network should be established.

11. *Secure health and safety*

> The health and safety of employees and visitors has to be ensured at the site.

Considering that a high demand exists compared to supply facilities and an increasing number of visitors are foretold for the coming years (World Tourism Organisation, 1998), regular safety check-ups of provided facilities and fire safety have to be carried out. Further, the site has to ensure the implementation of any health and safety policies required by the government, even if the site was not established through governmental initiative. This key principle plays an especially important role for war heritage sites that offer additional facilities, such as snack shops and restaurants.

Conclusion

One important meaning of war heritage sites is the promotion of peace through the commemoration of the past and education of future generations. Formulating a code of conduct based on the introduced principles would facilitate this reading of the sites. Even though more research regarding an official code of conduct has to be undertaken, the principles present a foundation for ensuring a clear portrayal of battlefield sites.

Previous research showed that development in war-distorted nations, and war heritage sites in particular, takes place over time. This inevitable development, which is influenced by and based upon the history of a nation, is often at whims of governmental authorities, financial contributions and visitor interest. War heritage sites have to be aware of the role they play within the image construction of a destination. With the acceptance of a final code of conduct, war heritage managers would not only show commitment to presenting a clear meaning, but also to acknowledge the sites' important moral values. This does not necessarily mean that all war heritage sites will have appropriate exhibitions and management schemes without any biases or stereotypes, but rather that a certain regulatory control and commitment to a high level of professional standard is prevalent. With these principles, the author wishes to lessen the negative impact misinterpretation and misrepresentation have upon visitation and to encourage development in a positive and responsive way that reflects the meaning of peace through commemoration and education.

Chapter 5

Jinggangshan Mountain: A Paradigm of China's Red Tourism

Gu Huimin, Chris Ryan and Zhang Wei

Introduction: China's Red Tourism

Red Tourism is based upon a revolutionary narrative weaved around memorials and places of history associated with the period from the birth of the Chinese Communist Party to the founding of New China. Like all forms of tourism, 'Red Tourism' is able to generate economic, social and ecological benefits. The attractions of 'Red Tourism' are also consistent with China's natural resources, its more general historical and human resources as well as drawing upon social and communal assets. It specialises in organizing tours whereby tourists can learn about this revolutionary period of Chinese history, gain insights into what were traditional revolutionary processes of education, as well as meet more generic needs of expanding tourist experiences and offer periods of escape, relaxation and socialisation amongst like-minded people.

This period of Chinese history covers the founding of the Chinese Communist Party, the Long March of the Red Army, the Anti-Japanese War and the period of the Liberation Wars. With the passing of time since these events took place, and given the considerable economic and social change that has occurred within the last few decades since the adoption of a more open-door policy, one of the purposes of this form of tourism is to allow people to learn about the revolutionary sentiments of their predecessors, which sentiments still possess importance as a spring of national and patriotic feeling that is instilled within the Chinese population. From the perspective of destination management, it is also an important means by which regional economies can be stimulated (Yao & Wang, 2005).

Today, tourism planning authorities seek ways in which the historic and tumultuous events of the early half of the twentieth century can be interpreted for a different, contemporary generation even while calling upon memories of those with direct knowledge and experience of some of that period. It can be said that in the first half of the twentieth

Battlefield Tourism: History, Place and Interpretation
Copyright © 2007 by Elsevier Ltd.
All rights of reproduction in any form reserved.
ISBN: 0-08-045362-7

century, the struggle of the Chinese people is a red (revolutionary) history book. In 2003, an educational campaign, themed as preserving the progressive nature of the Chinese Communist Party, was undertaken across the whole of China with much thinking and questioning about how this might be done while remaining true to the principles of the Chinese Communist Party and its more recent evolution. The planning also required the selection of key destinations, and consideration of how they might be presented and managed. Subject to approval by the central government, the China National Tourism Administration began to promote 'Red Tourism', which has now established a national presence within China's portfolio of tourism products. In January 2004, the Zhengzhou Declaration was initiated by Jiangxi Province and jointly signed by seven municipalities and provinces, an event that attracted significant attention and interest in the concept of 'Red Tourism'. In the latter half of 2004, at the 70th anniversary of the Long March of the Red Army, the China National Tourism Administration officially initiated Project 121 of Red Tourism, which plans to establish a 'backbone' of Red Tourism across China based upon 10 'Red Tourism Bases', 20 'Famed Red Tourist Cities' and 100 'Red Tourism Scenic Sites '(China Tourism Newspaper, 2004). The project thus identifies a series of priorities and objectives. The Red Tourist Base extends from the Soviet Region of the Chinese Communist Party, the cradle of the People's Republic of China, and comprises such red scenic sites as Jinggangshan City, Ruijin City, Yongxin County, Xingguo County and Yudu County in Jiangxi Province — all of which are listed among the top 10 key bases (Red Tourism Web, 2006). Of these it is suggested that Jinggangshan Mountain is the exemplar par excellence of Red Tourism and it is this that forms the main text of this chapter (Yu & Lu, 2005).

Jinggangshan Mountain: The Cradle of the Chinese Communist Party

Located in the southwest of Jiangxi Province, Jinggangshan Mountain lies in the middle section of Luoxiao Mountain at the border between Hunan and Jiangxi Provinces. Its strategic position based upon these borders and 'the abdomen of Luoxiao Mountain' has meant that it possessed military importance since ancient times. Before liberation, Jinggangshan was not an independent county, but a remote mountain village with a population of less than 2,000 people and a grain production of less than 10,000 piculs. After liberation, under the care of the Central Committee of the Chinese Communist Party and the State Council, Jinggangshan Special Region was established in Ciping in 1950. Then in 1959, Jinggangshan Administration under the jurisdiction of Jiangxi Province came into being. In 1981 it transformed into Jinggangshan County and then, in 1984, Jinggangshan City, through the approval of the State Council. In May 2000, again approved by the State Council, the former Jinggangshan City and Ninggang County were incorporated into a new Jinggangshan City. The city now has 21 townships, towns and sub-district offices under its jurisdiction, with a total population of over 149,700 people and a total area of 1,297.5 km^2. It is thus primarily rural in nature and readers need to be aware that the description of 'city' primarily relates to a form of administrative local government under the Chinese system rather than a description of an urban landscape.

The 'city's' contemporary historic and subsequently tourism importance lies in the fact that Jinggangshan Mountain is the cradle of the Chinese revolution. In October 1927, Mao Zedong, Zhu De, Chen Yi, Peng Dehuai and Teng Daiyuan led the Red Army of about 1,000 Chinese workers and farmers to Jinggangshan Mountain following the failure of the Autumn Uprising in Changsha. It was here he established his Chinese soviet as the first rural revolutionary base in China inaugurating a guerilla-based warfare by encircling the urban areas with the rural areas and using the rural base to harry the cities and seize the regime by force, thereby unveiling a new chapter in Chinese revolutionary history. It was also the base from which, in October 1934, the Long March commenced. Since then, Jinggangshan Mountain has been recorded in the annals of Chinese revolutionary history as the cradle of the Chinese revolution and the cornerstone of the People's Republic of China. The history of Jinggangshan and the difficulties endured by the fathers of the Chinese Revolution subsequently come to epitomise the spirit of the Chinese people (Dang, 2005).

There are over 100 well-preserved revolutionary sites and relics in Jinggangshan Mountain. Among them, 21 sites and relics are listed as the key cultural relics and preservation units at the provincial level, while 35 are designated as key cultural relics and preservation units at the municipal level (Lilong, Ligang & Shaohong, 2004). Since 1979, and the adoption of a more open-door policy and further social reform, it is estimated Jinggangshan Mountain has received more than 30 million international visitors including overseas Chinese from over 150 countries and regions including those of Hong Kong and Taiwan as well as mainland visitors. In 2005, the total number of tourist arrivals was 2,184,600 with the total revenue of RMB 1,128,000,000, an increase of 33.74 and 34.93%, respectively compared with that of 2004. The number of overseas arrivals in that same year was 32,000 with the revenue of US$ 6,500,000, an increase of 53.86 and 60.9%, respectively compared with that of 2004 (www.jgstour.com, 2006).

The mountain has long been visited by key Chinese leaders whose presence further legitimises and sustains the importance of the site. These include more than 100 communist party and state leaders such as Mao Zedong, Zhu De, Dong Biwu, Deng Xiaoping, Peng Zhen, Yang Shangkun, Guo Moruo, Hu Yaobang, Jiang Zemin, Li Peng, Qiao Shi, Li Ruihuan, Zhu Rongji, Hu Jintao, Wu Bangguo and Wen Jiabao. The towering Jinggangshan Mountain, with an area of 275 km², integrates the numerous revolutionary sites into a whole, and has become a museum without walls, a lively classroom for people offering not only the values of the mountain scenery with steep cliffs and deep valleys but a means by which to promote the education of patriotic and revolutionary traditions.

Educational Status of the Mountain

The site's educational importance has been well recognised by the Chinese government. It has been successively named by Jiangxi Provincial Committee of CPC as Jiangxi Social Educational Base, been listed by the Secretariat of the Central Committee of the Communist Youth League (CYL) as one of the First Ten Best Bases to Educate Chinese Teenagers about the Revolutionary Traditions, and been named by the State Cultural Relic Administration as one of the Excellent State Social Educational Bases. In 1996, Jinggangshan Mountain was again named as one of the 100 Exemplary Bases for the

Patriotic Education among the Elementary and Middle Schools in China by the six ministries and commissions: the Publicity Department of CPC Central Committee, State Educational Commission, State Cultural Relic Administration, Central Committee of the CYL, Ministry of Civil Affairs and General Political Department. And in 2004, Jinggangshan Revolutionary Place was assessed as one of the Excellent Exemplary Bases for the Patriotic Education in China.

The Natural Setting: Linking 'Green' with 'Red' Tourism

Reference has been made above to the natural beauty of the area, and this is an important component of the tourism mix, permitting the promotion of a 'green–red' tourism as described below. The region has an average height of 381 m, but extends as high as 1,841 m at the peak, Jianxi'ao. The climate is sub-tropical although the height means that cold winters are the norm with night temperatures below freezing, and winters are long, summers short, autumn is early and spring is late. Nonetheless, forest covers about 86% of the land area, and the landscape is characterised by waterfalls, sub-tropical virgin forest, dramatic ravines and a rich fauna and flora. Consequently, plans for the administration of the region recognise 11 scenic zones, 76 scenic sites and over 460 specified sights and scenes. In January 2001, China National Tourism Administration categorized the region as a National 4A Tourist Site in recognition of its clear air, lack of pollution and aesthetic values. Thus, like many mountainous areas in China, it appeals to the Chinese who wish to climb heights, enjoy fresh air and view spectacular sunsets and sunrises.

'Red Tourism': The History of Struggle and Patriotism.

The development of Jinggangshan Mountain as a tourist asset based upon its communist history can be traced back over four decades to some original initiatives in 1957, when groups of construction teams were joined by government officials, servicemen transferred to civilian work and students who commenced construction of pathways and other infrastructure work to improve accessibility. Initially however, the number of people visiting the region were small, other than in the period of the Cultural Revolution when, at its peak, as many as 30,000 Red Guards might arrive in a year, many on foot, to relive the Long March. Such numbers imposed a strain on local accommodation, water and food supplies, but with the end of the Cultural Revolution numbers fell away quickly. However, in 1988, the Jinggangshan Tourism Bureau was established and development commenced apace as described below. Today a combination of the private and public sectors have come together to develop products that range from exhortations to the patriotic, include eco- and cultural-tourism product and to some extent an uncontrolled private enterprise sector that is continually the subject of State checking. Commencing with the formal, the city has successively carried out a large-scale renovation of Xinghou Red Army Slogan Group, the Buxingyun Drill Ground, the Memorial of Joining Forces and Square of Joining Forces. A sculptural garden has been built with group images of revolutionary figures at the Jinggangshan Martyrs Cemetery. A 27-m high monument was built here in 1997 on the 80th anniversary to commemorate past events. Remnants of past fortification are being conserved such as the Huanyangjie Border with its trenches and crumbling walls, while planting of flowers help commemorate other locations such as the Red Army Sentry Post. Other sights include Jinggangshan Revolutionary Museum (Jinggangshan Geming Bowuguan), which used to house the Red Army Dormitory (Geming Jiuju), Mao's House (Mao Zedong Guju) and the Former Revolutionary Headquarters (Geming Jiuzhiqun), the communist command center in 1927–1928. Currently, the displays might be said to be comparatively Spartan, with much of the museum display being given over to maps showing battle sites and troop movements, and signs banning spitting, smoking and laughing! A small amusement park also exists where children may clamber around a real MiG-style fighter.

The revolutionary theme has been carried into a number of planned experiences for tourists under the auspices of the Chinese Communist Party. In addition to guided tours visitors are able to partake in various activities that include sewing Red Army shoes, weaving Red Army caps and bamboo hats, having a Red Army set meal, singing patriotic songs and having a classical red musical evening party, thereby gaining an insight into the pattern of life on the mountain as experienced by the founders of modern China.

In truth therefore, as discussed below, there exists a problem in generating tourist product in an area rich in symbolism and history, but because of the nature of that history and the realities of a guerilla-based army, the original remnants of that time tend to be few other than subsequent monuments constructed by a proud nation. Consequently, the tourist experience is often supplemented by 'green' tourist activities, which potentially can include bamboo raft drifting, touring lakes and rivers, exploring some aspects of Hakka culture or indeed going rock climbing.

From this brief description it thus becomes evident that private enterprise is also present in the region. Concern has emerged with issues pertaining to the degrees of professionalism existing within the local industry, and the Jinggangshan Tourist Bureau has undertaken a number of training and quality control initiatives. In 2004, it appears on evidence available to the authors, that the Bureau carried out over 2,000 spot checks, which revealed two illegal, unlicensed operations and three serious cases of 'violations of tourist rights' and a number of minor requests for help on the part of tourists.

Economic Impacts of the 'Red–Green' Tourism

The motives for developing 'Red Tourism' in this 'green' setting are primarily driven by a wish to record and recapture a patriotic history, but economic motives of rural regeneration are also of importance. This area of China is among the poorest and agricultural incomes are among the lowest. The nature of the region's rurality is perhaps best described by its population size, which numbers but 149,700 over the area of 1,297.5 km^2 that comprise the administrative region of Jingganshan City. Nonetheless there are signs of economic well-being beginning to emerge. An accommodation provision is fast growing. In 1997 there were but 3 star rated hotels offering 656 beds; by 2004 there were 29 such hotels offering 2,981 bed spaces. The increase in capacity owes much to improved accessibility with the development of highways such as the Ganyue Highway from Jiangxi Province to Guangdong Province (which opened in March 2005) and the Changtai

Highway being two examples. Of prime importance has been the construction and opening of Jinggangshan Airport at an expense of US$15.83 million in May 2004 (*People's Daily*, 2004). The airport is able to handle 280,000 passengers annually and is linked to improvements in rail networks. Domestic visitor numbers have thus accelerated from an estimated 400,000 in 1997 to over 1,550,000 in 2004. In the same period, international visitation rose from 2,679 to over 11,000 tourists and overcame a decline when Severe Acute Respiratory Syndrome (SARS) was an issue. Group tourism is now evident — in 2004, 20 chartered tourist planes landed at the airport with 58 groups.

That this is having an impact on income and job creation, at least in some small way, is evident. It is thought (Jia, Zhang, and Fang, 2005) that, in 2003, 14% of the local population owned cellphones — a statistic that might be thought unexceptional, but which means much in a previously very poor rural community with poor communications. Average farm incomes are increasing and average per capita income in 2004 was 2,184 Yuan. In the village of Dialing, where the Red Army Hospital used to be, a community of 39 households, some of whom sell souvenirs of arts and crafts, the income is more than twice this figure. Huang Quantico, a local farmer is quoted as now having a capital of several hundred thousand Yuan, which he attributes to the development of 'Red Tourism' (Jia, Zhang, and Fang, 2005).

Promotion of the Region

The development of new rail, air and road links has been accompanied by increased promotion of the administrative region. Advertising and public relations copy has been secured on CCTV, in the *People's Daily, Jiefang Daily* and other newspapers. The theme of Red Tourism with its historic and patriotic themes has secured coverage in special television programmes, while a Red Tourist Cultural Festival has been launched with growing success in recent years. In 2005, the 40th anniversary of Mao Zedong's revisit to the mountain became the focus of further special events and promotions, while a Sacred Torch Relay up the mountain has also been established. Emboldened by success, direct marketing in overseas markets has commenced and, in November 2005, a promotional visit was made to Nemaha-gun, South Korea, and other initiatives in Korea and Japan are envisaged.

Future Issues

For all of the promotional effort that has been undertaken, there is a need to recognise that this part of China is rural and relatively deprived of resources for all the progress that has been made. The pride and sense of history that motivates 'Red Tourism' is not without problems too. Comparison might be drawn with the issues associated with the *USS Yorktown*, USA, described in another chapter of this book. The old soldiers of the Red Army, the former enthusiasts of the Red Guard — these are a passing generation holding to sentiments increasingly no longer dominant in a rapidly changing world and, in China's case, an increasingly open world. There is a need to reorient the product and experiences on offer to a new generation, many of whom are computer literate. Reference has been made to the static displays of the museum, and while participative exercises are being developed of the nature described above, their associations with earnest, overlong lectures are increasingly at odds with a consumer-led market that, while interested in the past, is used to slick promotional marketing and participation that is fun-oriented (Yu & Lu, 2005; Yao & Wang, 2005).

Second, too much emphasis on a 'Red Tourism' — even while it is strongly state sponsored — creates a one-dimensional tourism product. As already described, the region has the advantages of scenic values and an indigenous component based on the Hakka people, but Chen, Lu and Lin (2004) indicate that effective packaging and integration of product has yet to be achieved.

Other chapters within this book draw attention to multiple truths, issues of interpretation, power structures and the silence of omission. It is true that similar issues can be raised not only of Jinggangshan itself, but of the concept of 'Red Tourism'. Yu and Lu (2005) allude to some of the problems referred to above with reference to changing generations, and it can be commented that silences can be noted. For example, one school of history notes that in the retreat to Jinggangshan, Mao Zedong allied himself with Wang Zoo and Yuan Wincey, who might be regarded as being local bandit chiefs, who nonetheless enjoyed a reputation for robbing the wealthy to help the poor much along the lines of the semi-mythical figure of 'Robin Hood' in western culture. Much of the early military survival of the communist forces owed much to their help; yet in 1930, in circumstances still not fully explained, both were shot by Communist forces, although it should be noted that Mao Zedong himself expressed criticism of officials of the Jiangxi soviet thought responsible for this action, and in the official histories of the Chinese Communist Party their role was restored after 1949. In a society where there is still a felt need for interpretations designed to encompass and create a developmental sense of nationhood, silences are, as elsewhere, important. Such stories as these reveal complexities not generally found in the little interpretation that is present. Indeed, it can be argued that silence has a function within a society that has yet to wholly come to terms with a turbulent and comparatively recent past; especially one having to cope with significant economic and social change. Given the predisposition of the Chinese Communist Party to permit economic change and a freeing of entrepreneurial activity within a stable political order, the myths of 'Red Tourism' perform an important role in ensuring social cohesion that, it can be argued, is of a long-term benefit to China and its people. Therefore, in contrast to the other chapters within this book, the example of 'Red Tourism' is one that to some extent is modernistic and predates the post-modern concerns of other examples, even while it too uses the techniques of omission and exaltation for creation of a smooth transition from a revolutionary past to a twenty-first century economy and society premised upon social harmony and order. Certainly, this transition and the mode of desired change has been well-explained on many occasions by Premier Wen Jiabao, who, for example, was quoted in an interview as noting that "Democracy and direct election in particular should develop in an orderly way in keeping with the particular condition of a country. ... China's development is a long-term and daunting task. To achieve development, we need peace, we need friends and we need time" (Landwehr, 2006).

ACTS OF SILENCE

Introduction

Chris Ryan

Four chapters form this section of the book, bound together by 'acts of silence' — but equally having identified silences, they, the silences, become subjected to articulation and discourse and so become problematic. The four chapters in this book are by Hugh Smith, Malcolm Cooper, Chris Ryan and Craig Wight. The military events with which each, in turn, deals with are, first, the Spanish Civil War with specific reference to the site at Belchite; second, Japanese visitation to the war sites of the Second World War; third, battles involving indigenous peoples in Canada and New Zealand; and finally, the recollection of aspects of Lithuanian history.

Hugh Smith provides first a context of the Spanish Civil War, noting that even as it was being waged, it was a site of 'hot war' tourism. However, by the second half of the 1940s Spain remained the only totalitarian fascist regime in Western Europe, having sustained neutrality during the Second World War despite Franco having achieved power with the help of Hitler and Mussolini. An argument can be made for the premise that, for much of the period from 1946 to 1975 when Franco eventually died, a key concern for Spanish politicians was to engineer a way by which Spain could again enter the mainstream of European economic and political life — a concern that arguably Franco himself began to increasingly recognise as the foundations for the constitutional monarchy were laid in the final years of his regime. Indeed, it can be said that the development of tourism that commenced in the 1960s with the construction of the resorts of the Spanish *costas* and the Balearics was a means by which northern Europeans could come to learn something of Spain, even if it were a Spain of mass tourism, hedonistic resorts and an appeal to flamenco. It is also meant that Spain became almost indispensable to a tour operator and airline industry based primarily in the United Kingdom, Germany and Scandinavia, and an economically mutual symbiosis developed whereby Spain came closer to the mainstream of European economic life, even allowing for the subsequent development of other Mediterranean resorts. With the subsequent discovery of the 'myths' of key market segments such as eco-tourists or cultural tourists, the Spanish marketing organisations sought to broaden the perceptions of Spain — but for the most part where it involved an appeal to culture or heritage, it was based primarily upon the artefacts and buildings of a 'golden

Battlefield Tourism: History, Place and Interpretation
Copyright © 2007 by Elsevier Ltd.
All rights of reproduction in any form reserved.
ISBN: 0-08-045362-7

period' prior to the early nineteenth century, or upon the *gitano* culture of Andalusia with its flamenco dance, guitar music and the tradition of the bull ring. However, it is now some seven decades since the end of the Civil War, and recognition is emerging that the War too represents a possible tourism asset, if only because it was an important contribution to the understanding of socialism and its own myths of the International Brigades caught in the still influential writings of authors such as George Orwell and, to a degree, Ernest Hemingway.

However, Smith also rightly points out that, at least domestically, there was interest in some aspects of the Civil War, and domestic tourists had, for some years, visited places such as the Valley of the Fallen. The issue then becomes one of how past civil conflict is to be (re-)interpreted. The social discourse within Spain today is a very different matter to that of only a quarter of a century ago. In the early twenty-first century, the monolith of a Madrid-centred government has been replaced by a model of high degree of autonomy so that Spain today comes to resemble, to some degree, a federal state with differing Castilian, Catalan, Andalucian, Mallorquin and Basque cultures evolving and diverging — and thus, the articulation of a Civil War past becomes both more difficult and arguably less pertinent to a contemporary society other than as an explanation of what should be avoided. Thus, as Smith demonstrates, the attempts to create interpretation and product development are hesitant, and as yet unsure, even as time 'cools' the passion of the past.

Cooper also has to deal with past conflicts, but one wherein passions are still aroused and which continue to have serious implications for Japanese relationships with neighbouring countries such as South Korea and the People's Republic of China. What is of interest in Cooper's chapter is how visitation on the part of Japanese people to various sites of the Second World War becomes not simply a means of education, but also a specific point of resistance and demonstration of personal disapproval of Japanese government policy in the early years of the twenty-first century. But there is also a further twist in this complex story for visits to the battlefields of the past are also a reminder of past military traditions at a time when, in 2006, Japanese government policy is beginning to erode the non-offensive role adopted by the Japanese armed forces since 1946 — a process that has been abetted in part by the Bush Presidency in the United States that became embroiled in military adventures of its own in parts of the world it has failed to understand. Cooper's chapter is thus interesting in several respects. Not only is it about visits that address deficiencies of past official Japanese government silences, but such visits also serve to remind tourists of a pre-pacifist era. Consequently, the sites may be shared by both those seeking to better understand and be sensitive about the past and what it means to Japan's neighbours, and those who may view such sites as statements about a more assertive Japan and indicative of a need for a more assertive stance consistent with Japan's contemporary economic importance. What Cooper also does is to illustrate specific biases within Japanese visitation patterns, interests and concerns by juxtapositioning different theatres of war with which the Japanese have been involved. Thus, the Peace Park of Nagasaki creates a sense of victimhood, while the strong interest in the Pacific area including the Solomon's (the subject of Charlie Panakera's subsequent chapter) avoids a need to address issues that arise on the Asian mainland. Silences exist, but are becoming, in the light of such biases, so marked that they can increasingly no longer be ignored — and thus these tensions are the subject of Cooper's chapter. Equally, he notes generational differences, and in some senses ends on a note that may promise a minimisation of future difference.

Ryan offers the reader a comparison between two battle sites: those of Batoche in Canada and Rangiriri in New Zealand. Initially he indicates the similarities. Both involved respective indigenous peoples, namely Métis people, then primarily residing in the Province of Saskatchewan; and Maori, living in the Waikato region of North Island, New Zealand. Both faced British Colonial governments, albeit both needed to consider the changing fortunes of their respective dominions. In the case of Canada, Batoche represented the last battle of any significance on Canadian soil, while in the case of the Battle of Rangiriri, hostilities continued until an uneasy peace ensued between the Maori Kingite movement and the colonial forces, north of what is now the King Country. Both were conflicts in which the native people sought to maintain and protect land rights in the face of encroachments by an expanding colonial population wishing to assert itself on what was perceived as virgin land waiting to be settled and farmed. Both dominion governments shared to a degree a late British Victorian certainty in being civilising forces, while both groups of indigenous people were about to commence a period of economic decline that was to threaten their well-being, culture and populations. However, what Ryan concentrates upon is the current differences in interpretation at these sites. At the one in New Zealand, commemoration is centred upon a tea shop while the battle field site itself has been split by past road construction. In Canada, a multi-million dollar Visitor Centre stands complete with museum and interpretative materials that place the battle within a context of the then current political forces. The obvious question is why the difference, and what does it say about the contemporary nature of the two former colonial countries? Yet the differences are complex, because it cannot be said that New Zealand is oblivious to the current needs of Maori, for the issues of Maori and their role in contemporary society is evident from even the briefest of news reviews. Nor might it be said that in Canada the role of Métis is fully determined as Ryan illustrates by reference to recent controversies over hunting rights. So the discourse between silence and articulation is complex. Both sites carry their respective signage, but the absence in the case of one does not necessarily imply a wish to hide the past, even while the reverberations of that past still cause unease for many on both sides of the racial divide in New Zealand. The signage of events in Canada does not imply any higher degree of comfort. The reader may conclude that tourism has its own role and its own imperatives. Saskatchewan is far distant from the population and political centres of Canada that lie in the west in Calgary or Vancouver, or in the east in Toronto and Ottawa. North Waikato is in danger of becoming an extension of Auckland as new motorway links speed the travel time between that city and Hamilton, some 90 minutes drive south. Arguably, Waikato has a number of tourist attractions and sustains a thriving tourism industry while large distances and sparse population require Saskatchewan to develop as best it can the few sites of culture and history that it possesses that date about 100 years or more. In short, the silences and articulations may need to be contextualised in a social setting within which tourism and the existence or non-existence of Park authorities create their own paradigms of actions.

The final chapter in this 'act' is that of Craig Wight who offers a reading of museum displays of Lithuania's past by also offering a juxtaposition — that of the Imperial War Museum in Manchester with the Lithuanian 'Genocide' Museum — the comparison being based upon the researcher's wish to compare differences of rhetoric inasmuch as the two obviously commemorate very different pasts — the one of the colonising country, the latter a country colonised by, most recently, the Russians. Wight concludes that the text of the Imperial War Museum becomes sanitised by its emphasis on the technology of war and utilises a meta-narrative of a past imperial age, whereas by comparison the interpretation offered in Lithuania is unorganised, but centred around a notion of heroic resistance and is even written in a sensationalist manner.

The four examples together provide evidence that writings are political acts. Language is either neutral, or gender based; it is hegemonic or a point of resistance; it is either a confirmation of dominant social *mores*, or an act of legitimisation of the marginalised; language may be exclusive, a means of developing difference, or inclusive seeking to create commonalities of feeling and yet language is changing, developing and is not consistent. Through this medium humans give expression to their understandings, their epiphanic acts and existence — through language both men and women create a sense of meaning of the world and their place within it — and through this medium and its uses and silences the tourist anticipates, reads about, articulates the experience of visiting sites of past conflict based upon ambition, hatred, wishes to dominate and where acts of great heroism and self-sacrifice — sometime on behalf of the indefensible occurred. Little wonder, therefore, that articulation and the wish to hide go hand in hand at such tourist destinations.

Chapter 6

Post-Colonial Representations of Japanese Military Heritage: Political and Social Aspects of Battlefield Tourism in the Pacific and East Asia

Malcolm Cooper

Introduction

The Pacific Theatre of the Second World War provides several important sites in the tourist geography of war and peace. These range from the Pearl Harbour, Hiroshima and Nagasaki Memorials to battlefield detritus throughout the Pacific and Asia, and to battlefield sites on Okinawa and Sakhalin, the Solomon Islands and the Northern Mariana Islands. As the war progressed, land, sea and air battles filled the jungles and lagoons of Southeast Asia, China, Micronesia and Melanesia with discarded equipment, war graves and fortifications. These are now sought as tourist attractions by visitors ranging from ex-combatants to scuba divers, and are on one level outstanding examples of the disaster of war turned to peace-time profit. On another, they are memorials to battlefield action and human suffering. As many authors have noted, nostalgia has long been a potent factor in tourism; the incorporation of the Second World War's legacy into Asia-Pacific tourism travel not only rekindled interest in some destinations, it was largely responsible for creating interest in others, like the Solomon Islands (Seaton & Bennett, 1996; Lennon & Foley, 2000; Douglas, Douglas & Derrett, 2001; Weaver & Lawton, 2002).

Asia-Pacific attractions, for which war is ultimately the prime source, have become part of the regional visitor experience, even if not as much for Japanese tourists as for those from other combatant countries and interested bystanders. Cemeteries or memorial parks celebrating war-dead feature prominently in the promotional literature and local tour itineraries of countries as disparate as New Caledonia, Papua New Guinea, Singapore, Vietnam, the Philippines, Cambodia, Burma, Guam, Saipan, China and the Russian Far East. More iconic remnants of the war have also been incorporated into the catalogue of visitor attractions — many of the region's major air and seaports were once bases of military operations in the Pacific War. Even if hurriedly constructed, with little respect for the landscape or forest that had to make way for them, they were easily converted to civilian use, and as international gateways they bear the names of their military founders to the present.

This chapter describes and attempts to understand the attitude of the Japanese towards the rising popularity of Asia-Pacific battlefield tourism in the early part of the 21st century. It therefore represents a case study of how one particular country is presenting its recent military and colonial heritage to its own people as tourists and general public, as well as to the world at large. In order to achieve this outcome it is necessary to distinguish between the experiences of areas originally subsumed within the League of Nations mandated Empire of Japan and those brought about by the addition of other areas to Japanese military control during the brief period of the late 1930s and mid-1940s. It is also necessary, given ongoing tensions between China, Japan and Korea, to compare and contrast Japanese responses towards the events of this period of recent history with those of their colonies and the former occupied territories. The difference between these sets of responses goes a considerable way towards explaining the apparently low level of interest in *battlefield* tourism currently exhibited by the Japanese. In examining these differences, the chapter centres discussion on the debates current in the early 2000s in the Japanese media and in government and scholarly circles on the nature and intent of the Pacific War, and the response of Korean and Chinese commentators in particular, although the range of responses from other affected countries is also identified. The efficacy of tourism as a vehicle for peace and the avoidance of war are also discussed in the context of the way in which the Japanese now see their role on the battlefields of the Pacific War and in China and Korea prior to 1941.

Background

The Pacific War from the Japanese perspective is described as *Diatowa Senso*, the Greater East Asian War, a war ostensibly entered into to liberate Asia and the Pacific from Bolshevism and white colonialism (Biao, 2005; Kibata, 2005), but in fact being more about trying to break America's stranglehold on essential resources (Buruma, 1994). Too short to effectively consolidate the resources of the Asia-Pacific region in Japanese hands, it nevertheless did contribute to breaking the European colonial hold in Asia, and helped pave the way for Japan's post-war economic success at the same time as it resulted in a humiliating national defeat for the Japanese and immense suffering for this country and the peoples of its former empire and Pacific War conquests. This dichotomy is important, as it goes some way towards explaining both the Japanese national and individual attitudes to battlefield tourism, and the reluctance on the part of former colonies and conquests to welcome Japanese veterans at those sites (Kibata, 2005).

·   The Japanese Empire is formally said to have begun in the late 19th century, although it had many antecedents in the Edo (1600–1868) and earlier periods (Toby, 1984; Hellyer, 2002). A relatively recent construction of conquest, trade and of a League of Nations Mandate (a process going on since approximately 1895), it centred on Korea and northeastern China on the Asian Mainland and a string of islands radiating out from the Japanese home islands, including Saipan, Sakahlin and Guam. Whatever modern analyses (Hellyer, 2002) suggest, it is not strictly true that Japan was isolated in Asia prior to this wave of imperial expansion as a result of the Shogunate of the Edo period (1600–1868) enforcing a 'closed' Japan, only to be broken by American intervention in the 1850s. Certainly the Meiji Restoration of the 1860s did see formerly restricted foreign trade develop with Europe and the America. Growing military power in a localised sense and revived imperial ambitions built upon this economic success brought wars with China and Russia resulting (a) in Asian mainland colonies, and (b) an economy tied to the outside world, while (c) certain former German colonies in the Pacific Islands were also mandated to Japan after the First World War (Young, 1998).

The intensifying adverse reaction of both the United States of America and the United Kingdom as the other imperial powers in the Asia Pacific in the 1930s to these developments is now recognised as one of the major reasons for the Pacific War of the 1940s (Buruma, 1994; Conrad, 2003). In that war the Japanese armed forces were initially successful, removing European colonial control over parts of the region and forever changing the political structure of much of Asia and the Pacific during their four years of occupation. However, the 'shame' of ultimate defeat and the impact of post-war American efforts to change Japanese social and political culture led to a curious paradox; on the one hand assiduous internal promotion of the idea that Japan was and had been all along in reality an isolated island nation, poor in natural resources, unable to understand the outside world and constantly struggling to break from Edo period shackles (Kawakatsu, 2000), but one which, on the other hand, was promoted to the outside world as a country now enjoying rapid economic development based solely on internationalisation and liberation from the past (Ellis, 2005). This dichotomy has in fact been very useful in avoiding discussion of the actual impact of Japan's imperial actions on its own veterans and on the subject peoples, as the new Japan could not be seen as being in any way responsible for the old Japan (Buruma, 1994; Yoneyama, 1999; Hellyer, 2002; Biao, 2005).

In the post-war period former western enemies also clamoured for involvement in the new Japanese economic miracle, as astute private investment in America and Europe (as well as in former conquered territories) created dynamic transnationals out of Japan-based conglomerates. However, at the same time references to the activities of the occupying forces in China, Korea and other parts of the Asia-Pacific Region during and before the war in Japanese school textbooks were censored (Buruma, 1994; see Kibata, 2005, pp. 104–107 for a description of how this is done). In fact, the ruling coalition in Japan has systematically promoted selective historical amnesia during the 50 years since the American occupation by in effect ceding sovereignty for extraterritorial matters through Article 9 of the Constitution to the Americans (thereby 'legalistically' escaping apparent responsibility for external relations), while at the same time focussing the minds of the Japanese people on such programs as 'double your income' (in the 1960s) rather than on the sort of soul-searching about past actions that occurred in Germany, for example (Buruma, 1994, p. 65; Ellis, 2005; Biao, 2005).

However, there have, it is true, been continual attempts to correct the official history texts seemingly used in schools to disinform new generations of Japanese about the nature of the Asia-Pacific War (Kibata, 2005, pp. 105–107), and individual Japanese visitors to such important battlefields as those of the Burma and Manchuria campaigns have noted that they came to correct the wrongs and learn more about their Country's war history (Kogure, 2004; Yoneyama, 1999). Moreover, recent media attention on the reaction of former foes and occupied peoples to the then current Prime Minister's regular visits to the Yasukuni National Shrine to the war-dead (see *Tokyo Shimbun*, April 8, 2004, for an example), on the government's treatment of claims for compensation by Korean 'comfort' women and others, on the visits by old soldiers to the battlefields of Saipan and Okinawa, on the Japanese view of the bombing of Hiroshima and Nagasaki, on the Ministry of Education's continued unwillingness to sponsor teaching about war atrocities, and on a comparison between recent American military abuses in Iraq and those of the Japanese occupying forces in World War II, has refocussed at least media attention on this period of Japan's history (Kogure, 2004).

The Economic Dimension

The Economics of (Re-)Involvement

A digression is necessary here, but one that may explain part of the dichotomy so far revealed between the Japanese national view of their recent military history and that of their former foes. As the then Imperial Government did during the mandate period, the post-war Japanese government has worked closely with Japanese business in pursuit of economic opportunity throughout the Asia-Pacific Region (Peattie, 1988; Poyer, Falgout & Carucci, 2000). The Japan–Micronesia Association, for example, established in 1974 as an affiliate of the Foreign Ministry, is a prime example of this cooperative effort. Founded by men of influence and position in Japanese politics and business, and supported by major shipping, construction, food and real estate interests, the association has helped to ease Japanese re-entry into the Pacific through a carefully modulated program of economic and cultural exchanges and a two-way dissemination of information in Japan and Micronesia.

In important respects, however, Japanese economic activity in the Asia-Pacific region since the Second World War has developed in a radically different way from that of a century ago: the expulsion of Japanese citizens from Micronesia, China and the Soviet Union, for example, required by American and other countries' deportation and repatriation policies, and the former host countries' reaction to wartime atrocities, made that certain. But most obviously it is no longer carried on within the sheltering protection of a colonial government, and depends on the tolerance of independent nations whose governments are sensitive to the merest hint of exploitation. It has been accompanied, moreover, by a Japanese program of overseas development economic assistance to many countries — extended mostly in the form of grants, low interest loans and technical assistance, as well as by private investment (Koppel & Orr, 1993). In contrast to its place in the old colonial setting, the Japanese economic presence in the Asia Pacific, while still directed from a distance, derives from the boardrooms and offices of giant companies in Tokyo and Osaka, not directly from government offices in Tokyo. The driver of Japanese economic interest in the Pacific in particular has also changed dramatically in the post-war era. Indeed, of the four principal industries of the colonial period — sugar, phosphate, copra and fishing — only the last retains an important place in the range of Japanese economic activities in the Pacific.

In the Pacific, for example, such trading patterns have been supplanted by tourism, specifically Japanese tourism, which is now often the greatest money-maker for both Japanese investors and the island peoples. This new bonanza has been stimulated by the ease of air travel, by the burgeoning prosperity of a post-war middle class now able to afford foreign travel on a scale previously unprecedented for Japan, and by the common migratory impulse of tourists from competitive industrialised societies of the north to seek the warmth of southern islands and seas, especially in winter. In the great cities of Japan, young office workers and newlyweds are bombarded with the natural splendours of the tropical Pacific. The beaches of Saipan, the rock islands of Palau or the waters off Rota and Guam, home to the colonial administration and the Japanese navy, army and air forces only 65 years ago, have seen Japanese luxury hotels, dive companies and resorts developed in their dozens, and thousands of young and middle-aged visitors every year.

The Political Dimension

Yoichi Kibata, in a perceptive essay entitled *Unfinished Decolonisation and Conflicts over Historical Memories* (Kibata, 2005), notes that Japan, like many countries in the modern world is experiencing the globalisation of national historical memories where hitherto these could be and often were confined to internal debate. Historical actions and their consequences are being played out in the press both inside and outside Japan almost irrespective of whether or not the Japanese people themselves wish to engage in such debate. As already noted, recent media attention on the reaction of former foes and occupied peoples to the former Prime Minister's regular visits to the Yasukuni Shrine, on the government's treatment of claims for compensation by Korean 'comfort' women and the Ministry of Education's continued unwillingness to correct textbooks about war atrocities, has generated internal and external discussion about the *Diatowa Senso* period of Japan's history (Figal, 2002).

There has been very strong external and some internal opposition to the 'rewriting of history' that has been going on in Japan since, at least, the 1980s, but considerable internal support from the long-time ruling party (undoubtedly abetted by the outspoken views on foreigners held by the then Governor of Tokyo, Mr Ishihara) exists in the political sphere (Morris-Suzuki, 1998). Politically, Japan has managed to alienate the rest of Asia in the late 20th century simply by not coming to terms with the reality of its World War II and earlier colonial past (Trefalt, 2002), and now runs a grave risk of "becoming diplomatically marginalised in its own region" (Restall, 2005, p. 8). Also, the concept of *Nihonjinron* (Cooper, Jankowska & Eades, 2006), or *Japaneseness*, is in this case used to marginalise internal debate. Kibata (2005, p. 107) notes that several authors and publishers of school textbooks who had openly discussed the above matters in earlier editions of their works, have voluntarily chosen to 'exercise restraint' and remove such discussions from their early 21st century editions, presumably on behalf of the wider society and its sensitivities. Added to this is an increasing tendency to see Japan as a victim (of American aggression through bombing) as much as an aggressor in the Pacific War, while the events of mid-August 1945 on Sakhalin and the Kurile Islands when Soviet troops moved south in an obscure coda to World War II have kept Japan and Russia from signing a peace treaty nearly six decades after the end of World War II — Japan still claims the islands, which Russia administers out of Sakhalin (Mason & Caiger, 1997).

Externally, Japan is projecting the image of a country coming to terms with its past, but essentially only that recent past, which was decreed by the Americans during their occupation of Japan (pacificism and no military) and which is now inconvenient for the self-same USA. Internally, there is little debate about how this will be done, but it certainly involves rewriting the constitution to allow the conversion of the already extremely powerful 'self-defence' force into a mainstream military machine in defiance of regional concerns about unresolved attitudes and actions of the past. In conjunction with the USA, that military force has already identified China as a potential threat and Taiwan as an area of 'common strategic concern' for Japan (Restall, 2005, pp. 10–11). Taiwan of course was a former colony of Japan.

Politically then, it is very likely that Japan as a nation will not now have to face the political impacts of 'decolonisation' in quite the same way as the Europeans had to in the 20th century, and it will do this by once again becoming a major military power in a *de jure* rather than in a *de facto* sense in conjunction with the USA. But what will this mean for continuing and/or developing tourism to former battlefields on the part of the individual Japanese tourist and their host nations or regions? The following sections of the chapter discuss this question in the light of the factors just outlined.

The Pattern of Japanese Battlefield Tourism

The dichotomies discussed in earlier sections of this paper, of original empire versus conquests, of Nihonjinron versus ownership of the actions of its military and colonial bureaucracy, and of the image of Japan still being poor, isolated and feudal versus the fact that its economy is the second largest on the planet, are evidenced in the way in which the existence of guilt and its repression are both part of the discourse on Japan's involvement in the Pacific War. For the Japanese, symbols of the war abound in the Asia-Pacific Region: the Saipan cliffs; the Soviet and Mongolian gulags for Japanese army prisoners; the battles of Midway; the Coral Sea; Savo Sound and Okinawa are particularly important. For the few remaining armed forces veterans the Malayan Campaign, Singapore; Burma, the much longer Sino-Japanese war and the Kwantung Army's experiences at the hands of the Soviet Union are just as important. However, their experiences of these theatres as soldiers are to a great extent overshadowed by external views of the Nanjing Massacre, the Sandakan track death march, the human costs of building the Burma railway and the Nagasaki/Hiroshima atomic bombs. The images of Japanese behaviour that are conjured up for an outside observer in certain parts of Asia and the Pacific evoke a corresponding embarrassment for would be Japanese battlefield tourists to these areas, and often hostility on the part of potential hosts to the desire to visit them, thus limiting the potential of tourism to heal the wounds of war between the former combatants (D'Amore, 1989; Butler & Mao, 1996; Glosserman, 2004). Nevertheless, Japanese tourism to overseas battlefields does exist and may be growing, as younger generations make the events of the past a concern. However, official statistics do not allow any reliable count to be made of these flows at the time of writing (February, 2006).

Veterans of both sides in the Pacific War now mingle mainly in private, as on Iwojima where a yearly meeting takes place between former adversaries on this largely uninhabited island — the 59th commemoration ceremony was held on 11 March 2004, for example, amicably bringing together veterans and relatives of war-dead of both sides in the conflict (Talmadge, 2004). Close to Pengkalan Chepa airport on Kelantan, Malaysia, is a Japanese war cemetery, typical of those across South East Asia. A local firm, Sampugita Holidays Sdn Bhd is one of the battlefield holiday tour operators in this part of Malaysia, and one of its specialities is covering the actions of 8 December 1941–15 February 1942 (the fall of Singapore). The company reports that Japanese war veterans are among Kelantan's regular visitors, along with British and Australian veterans (Ahmad, 2004). At Kuching in Malaysia (Batu Lintang) there is another cemetery, also host to many Japanese war veteran visitors, generally in groups of 10–12 people, throughout the year (Sakai Kazue, January, 2004, personal communication).

15 June 2004 marked 60 years from the day the United States invaded the Japanese League of Nations — mandated islands of Saipan and Tinian in the Northern Marianas. Nevertheless, in inviting veterans and their families to commemorate these events the Governor of the Marianas did *not* include former Japanese veterans except as the *enemy* from whom the invasion liberated his people (his comments may be found in 'to join the *American* family of peoples' — http://data.worldwarii.info/cftemplates/amp60th/index.cfm? pageID=17). However, tour operators such as Battlefield Expeditions to Saipan make no such distinction (http://www.battlefieldexpeditions.com/) between their clients, although it is unclear exactly how many Japanese veterans they attract on their tours. It is more likely that Japanese Veteran Associations run parallel tours to Saipan and other islands, although the extent of these is also unknown. Such firms specialise in offering an ongoing series of in-depth historical explorations of the battlefields of Saipan, Tinian, the Northern Marianas and other Pacific Islands. Each expedition provides a detailed examination of the battles from both the Japanese and American perspectives, and includes optional hiking and walking tours of these remote battlefields along the ridge-lines, hillsides, mountains and jungles of the Islands. Their clients include as many young people as veterans.

Okinawa

The involvement of Japanese forces in other imperial theatres such as China and Korea, and any subsequent (albeit limited) battlefield tourism is too big a subject to be covered here (there were 20 million dead in the Sino-Japanese war alone), but the example of Okinawa may be of some relevance to the central argument. Okinawa was formally made subject to Japan in the early Meiji period (although the Kingdom of the Ryukus had been tributary to the Satsuma Clan of Kagoshima under the Tokugawa Shoguns since the 1600s), and was as a result the only part of Japan proper to be actually invaded during the Second World War. Okinawa was the largest amphibious invasion of the Pacific campaign and the last major campaign of the Pacific War. More people died during the Battle of Okinawa than all those killed during the atomic bombings of Hiroshima and Nagasaki: casualties totalled more than 38,000 Americans wounded and 12,000 killed or missing, more than 107,000 Japanese and Okinawan conscripts killed and perhaps 140,000 Okinawan civilians who perished in the battle. American losses at Okinawa were so heavy as to bring Congressional calls for an investigation into the conduct of the American military commanders. Not surprisingly, the cost of this battle in terms of lives, time and material weighed heavily in the decision to use the atomic bomb against Japan just six weeks later (http://www.globalsecurity.org/military/facility/okinawa-battle.htm).

Touring sites related to the battle of Okinawa is an activity which attracts not only many US military personnel (the US maintains control over a significant proportion of Okinawan land to this day), but also some Okinawans, Japanese and other foreign tourists (Siddle & Hook, 2003). One of the most popular tours is that organised by the US Marine Corps Community Services every second week, which attracts tourists because it includes the battlefield perspectives of *all* participants. Again, though any discussion of Japanese battlefield tourism in the Okinawan context needs to take into account the tensions still evident between the record of the Japanese military's treatment of native Okinawans during the battle, the opposing fact that Okinawa is still occupied by American forces (though officially part of Japan from 1972), who control some of the best lands, and the desire of the Okinawans, the Americans and the Japanese to commemorate their war-dead as best as they can.

The Solomons

Guadalcanal in the Solomon Islands was the scene of some of the bloodiest fighting in the Pacific during World War II. From August 1942 to February 1943, thousands of American, Allied and Japanese troops engaged in a fight for the island, and some 7,000 Americans and 24,000 Japanese were killed. Six decades later the near-bankrupt Solomon Islands are emerging in 2006 from four years of chaos and civil war with the help of an Australian-led intervention force. Desperate for foreign cash, the Solomon Islands is pinning hopes of economic recovery on battlefield tourism, keen to attract Japanese and American tourists to the mountains and jungles where their "fathers and grandfathers fought" (Squires, 2003, p. 12).

Guadalcanal, one of the largest islands in the archipelago, is still littered with the by-products of war. Between Guadalcanal and the nearby island of Savo, so many US and Japanese war ships were sunk that the channel is known as Iron Bottom Sound (many visitors come to dive on the shipwrecks). The many battleships, cruisers and transport ships bombed or torpedoed during the war have become coral-encrusted artificial reefs, attracting schools of fish, sharks, manta rays and a multitude of other marine life. It is the excellent state of preservation of such remains that has led to hopes that battlefield tourism could inject much-needed revenue into the Solomon Islands' ailing economy. Before the country was plunged into ethnic conflict by a coup in June 2000, it was visited by about 15,000 foreign tourists a year, many from Japan. In 2002, with armed militants roaming the streets of the capital Honiara less than 3,000 tourists arrived. Now, with the restoration of law and order by police and soldiers from Australia, New Zealand and other Pacific states, locals want to cash in on the Islands' war history. At the time of writing AusAID, the Official Development Assistance arm of the Australian government, has called for a tender for a 'Profile and Marketing Plan for a Tourism Niche: the World War II History of the Solomon Islands' in recognition of the importance of the Islands to the Pacific War (*GRM International*, 3 April 2006). Presumably this study will include the reactions of Japanese tourists to this future opportunity.

The Philippines

An estimated one million Filipinos, of a wartime population of 17 million, were killed during the Pacific War. But for people affected by Japan, perhaps like no other in Southeast Asia, Filipinos are now very friendly towards that country, a phenomenon that appears to baffle many historians and sociologists considering that in countries like China and South Korea anti-Japanese sentiment still exists (Conde, 2005). Filipinos still suffer in the same way as do Korean women from the comfort woman label, and the war-time experiences of the whole country are partially obscured by the Japanese school textbook question discussed earlier. Nevertheless, the Philippines continues to try to develop Japanese tourism, including raising memorials to battlefields (for example, the Mabacalat, Pampanga, memorial to Japanese Kamikaze Pilots), and downplay the more painful (for Filipinos) aspects of the past.

In considerable part, this approach to Japan and Japanese battlefield tourism by the Philippines is due to economic factors (some 80,000 or more Filipinos are employed in Japan's entertainment industry alone (http://www.asahi.com/english/nation/TKY200412150155.html)). Japan has been, for many years, the Philippines' top foreign investor, educator of Filipino scholars and donor of official development assistance. While most of these investments were actually loans and were in fact linked to Japan's quest for export markets after the Pacific war, they were nevertheless important. The loans, which were mainly used for infrastructure like highways, were indeed tied to contracts with Japanese contractors and suppliers, but paved the way for further private investment by Japanese firms in the domestic Philippines economy. It is neither surprising therefore that another major Japanese industry, tourism, should be important to the Philippines, nor that one of the important links between the Philippines and Japan with respect to tourism is the Pacific War.

Japanese Domestic Military History as Tourism

Based on an earlier Supreme Court decision on the separation of religion and state, the Fukuoka District (Kyushu) Court ruled on 1 April 2003 that Prime Minister Koizumi's August 2001 visit to the Yasukuni Shrine violated Article 9 of the Japanese Constitution (Asahi Shimbun, 2004). Yasukuni is dedicated to not only the nation's 2.5 million war-dead but also enshrines former soldiers of the Japanese Imperial Army convicted of war crimes, and the political act of visitation encapsulates the ongoing debate on Japan's actions during the Imperial era and the level of recognition (if any) that these should receive. Both Asian nations and Japanese people alike are offended by these visits, but they continue to this day supported by groups representing 'families of the war dead', a powerful Liberal Democratic Party (LDP) (governing party) support base.

Other memorials to the conflict as it impacted on the home islands (apart from Okinawa); including those to the treatment of prisoners of war also exist throughout Japan, often on private lands. Evidence of brutality towards prisoners of war and suppression of information about war crimes and also of compassion and remorse abound and, since the death of the Showa Emperor in 1989, a greater openness about the past has begun to inform local Japanese on social and political debate in this era. New regional museums have been developed that tell of the reality of war, and Japanese domestic tourists are certainly visiting them 'in increasing numbers' (Buruma, 1994, p. 229). Both Japanese and their former prisoners visit the various war cemeteries around Japan, as well as the shrines set up at particular sites such as that on Mt. Hachimen (Sanko Peace Park, Oita Prefecture).

Hiroshima and Nagasaki

Apart from the significance of the Yasukuni Shrine for the Japanese Nation as a whole, perhaps the most important of the battlefield sites in Japan are the Peace Parks of Hiroshima and Nagasaki. The bombing of Hiroshima and Nagasaki is seen by the Japanese as the supreme symbol of absolute evil — as being equivalent to the European Holocaust (Buruma, 1994). That the use of the atomic bomb should have been treated as a crime against humanity was certainly a widely held view at the time (Yoneyama, 1999), and has continued to inform the discourses evident in the presentations at both the Peace Parks and in writings on these events to the present. At the particular sites, the events of August 1945 are, however, depicted as statements of fact with very little reference to the rest of the war or to politics, including very little acknowledgement of the deaths of the prisoners of war and many Korean 'slaves' also killed by the bombs. Thus the conflation of guilt (responsibility) and victim status, even at Hiroshima and Nagasaki, continues to obscure analysis of battlefield tourism in the Asia-Pacific context of the Second World War (Buruma, 1994; Yoneyama, 1999).

Other World War II Memorials in Japan

There are many more examples of domestic battlefield related tourism sites in the country. Fukuoka Camp No. 6, also known as Orio Camp, is a representative Prisoner of War (POW) camp from the Second World War. Most of the POWs were Dutch and a group of ex-POWs from the Netherlands set up a gravesite memorial several years ago. A monument also memorialising prisoners of war is at Soto Dam in Yunoki near Sasebo, Kyushu, and was set up in April 1956 by that city, which is now the base for a considerable American military presence. The POWs were from Fukuoka Camp #18, located about a quarter mile above the dam construction site. In the mere six months this camp was in operation, some 65 POWs lost their lives during the construction of the dam.

The Taketa 'Sky Martyrs' monument in Oita Prefecture, erected on 5 May 1977 commemorates the 11 airmen aboard a B-29 bomber as well as the Japanese pilot whose plane destroyed it. A memorial service is held each year at the monument on May 5. Sanko Peace Park, also in Oita, commemorates the destruction of another B-29. A peace monument was set up at the foot of Mt. Hachimen initially by the landowner, Masayoshi Kusunoki, in the early 1950s as a memorial to both the Americans and the young Japanese pilot who died attacking the B-29. A larger monument was completed in 1970 by a group of Japanese along with some US officers from nearby Itazuke Air Base. Yearly memorial services are held at this site on May 3rd and include representatives from all over Japan, including Iwakuni Marine Corps Air Station, making this site the most prominent in all of Kyushu.

Outside of Kyushu, another important site is the Naoetsu Peace Memorial Park in Niigata in central Japan, built on the former site of the Naoetsu POW Camp No. 4B (Niigata Prefectural Board of Education, 1997). Most of the POWs there were Australians. A book about the site and events leading up to its construction are recorded in *Preserving Peace: Beyond the Tragedy of Naoetsu POW Camp (Heiwa wo Mamoru: Naoetsu Horyo Shuyojo no Higeki wo Koete)* by the Niigata Prefectural Board of Education in 1997. The Japan–U.K. Friendship Monument, Mukaishima is located east of Hiroshima where mostly British POWs were interned at Hiroshima POW Camp No. 4B. Other memorial sites in Japan are

* Omori Peace Memorial, Tokyo: Tokyo POW Main Camp;
* Kanose, Niigata: Building at site of Tokyo POW Camp No. 16B;
* Mitsushima Memorial Monument, Nagano: Tokyo POW Camp No. 12B;
* Iruka British POW Memorial Monument, Mie: Nagoya POW Camp No. 4B;
* Oeyama British POW Memorial Monument, Kyoto: Osaka POW Camp No. 3B;
* Omine Memorial Monument, Ube-Sanyo, Yamaguchi: Hiroshima POW Camp No. 6B;
* Yokohama War Cemetery: more than 1,700 British Commonwealth POWs (United Kingdom, Australia, Canada, New Zealand, India, Pakistan) are buried here;
* Ryuhoji temple where five Americans and a Norwegian were buried (died in Ofuna Navy Interrogation Camp);
* Ishihara Sangyo factory in Yokkaichi, Mie Prefecture and
* Many other aircraft crash sites.

Many of these sites were jointly constructed by or were solely built by local people, and this shows that at least in some local communities in Japan the events of World War II are understood and commemorated in the same way as for many of those people (and tourism operators) who are involved in the other Pacific War battlefields described above.

Rekishi Trails

Battlefield tourism in Japan, as in Europe and other countries, has a wider context in history than the Second World War. For example, the Kansai Region (centred on Osaka and Kyoto) has sought to redevelop a sense of Japanese cultural history though the *Rekishi Kaido*, a Japanese version of Germany's famous Romantic Road. The Rekishi Kaido (historic route) Promotional Council, a semiprivate group, is pushing this 300-km long theme park of major shrines, battlefields and eras of historical Japan. Now in its fifth year, the main tour route and its eight theme routes run from Ise Shrine through Asuka (6–7th century capital), Nara (8th century capital), Kyoto, Osaka and Kobe, taking the traveller through a progression of historical eras (a map of these routes can be found at http://www.kiis.or.jp/rekishi/route-e.html). The Kansai area is the second largest economic zone in Japan but at the same time it has 60 per cent of Japan's national treasures and half of the country's important cultural treasures, and the project aims to group these historical and cultural assets into easily understood themes, all linked together by one route. At particular points along the trail are the sites of defining moments in Japanese military history, largely from the struggles that characterised dynastic change during the long rule of the Shoguns.

Two of the theme routes are the Omi Warring Period Route and the Echizen Warring Period Route. Both are essentially for domestic tourism. The Omi Warring Period Route, on the theme of the 16th century Warring Period, goes from Kyoto along the east coast of Lake Biwa and continues to Fukui. The route follows the physical manifestations of the ambitions of the warlords who dreamed of conquering the whole of Japan. This journey passes the ruins of Azuchi Castle where Oda Nobunaga gave the order to subjugate Japan by force of arms; Nagahama Castle, where Toyotomi Hideyoshi first became a feudal lord; and historic battlegrounds such as Shizuga-take. The Echizen Warring Period Route also crosses Fukui Prefecture, past historic battlefields such as Kanegasaki, Kinome-toge and the ruins of Somayama Castle on the way. Other famous places on the journey include Ichijo-dani, the power base of the Asakura clan; Maruoka Castle built by Shibata Katsutoyo and the Eihei-ji Temple, the head temple of the Soto Sect of Zen Buddhism (http://www.kiis.or.jp/rekishi/kaido-e.html).

Such domestic battlefield tourism sites are replicated throughout the country. Each has a particular period or set of events associated with it (such as the Satsuma Rebellion sites in Kagoshima Prefecture, which commemorate the civil wars that occurred at the time of the Meiji Restoration in the late 19th century), and each is progressively being opened up and promoted to wider groups of tourists.

Discussion

When understanding of the past has been so systematically impacted by the actions of the 'establishment' in post-Second World War Japan, it is not surprising that information on Japanese *Diatowa Senso* battlefield tourism is hard to come by, or only surfaces as a by-product of the broader debate on how to overcome such censorship. While the idea that silence on such matters as the actions of the Imperial Army and Colonial Bureaucracy during the 1930s and 1940s may be preferable to the embarrassing controversies that periodically erupt in the newspapers or that strain Japan's relations with regional countries, it has served to obfuscate and promote ignorance about the propensity of the Japanese to undertake battlefield tourism.

That it exists, along with a considerable interest in domestic battlefield tourism, is not in doubt, and that it can occur even with the controversies unresolved is also evident, especially in the attraction of visitors to the Peace Parks in Hiroshima and Nagasaki as well as to those memorials to World War II scattered around the country. But as this chapter has shown, even portraying the actuality of disasters such as the atom bomb to domestic tourists creates a contradiction — victim and aggressor are reversed and the broader questions that others in the Asia Pacific want addressed remain unanswered, even in relation to the atomic bomb sites and POWs/slave labourers. However, Nagasaki and Hiroshima were only in a limited sense 'battlefields' in that major ground, naval or air forces of either side were not engaged in what happened in August 1945, so the nature of tourism to these sites is more one of seeking education in the folly of war and remembrance on the part of a falling proportion of domestic 'veterans', with a small addition of those perhaps seeking the macabre so readily available in the museums themselves, rather than one of battlefield tourism *per se*.

Nevertheless, there is a strong tradition of battlefield tourism in Japan in relation to the Pacific War, promoted by many of the same type of organisations that do so for other combatant countries, the returned services leagues and 'families of the war dead'. These organisations are supplemented by battlefield tourism-oriented travel companies whose tours cater for all sides in the conflict, and who attract at least some Japanese veterans and/or their families. But perhaps the most positive aspect is that younger generations of Japanese and some of the remaining veterans themselves are no longer willing to put up with the official silence on past actions, and are prepared to visit battlefields or enter into media debate to try to aid understanding of how the dehumanising processes of war come about.

Conclusions

While this survey of Japanese battlefield tourism cannot be considered definitive (not the least because there are no reliable statistics available at the time of writing), the results tend to support Yoneyama's thesis that representations of Japanese sites such as Hiroshima and Nagasaki have helped to produce (or at the very least, reinforce) the image of post-war Japan as a peace-loving, harmless nation faced with overwhelming victimisation (Yoneyama, 1999, pp. 213–214). Visitors to the Nagasaki Peace Park do appear to identify with this portrayal (Cooper, 2006), although how far this success in getting them to do so can be used to support the idea of a deliberately induced national amnesia in relation to the other events that the Japanese military and Colonial Service was engaged in during the early to middle 20th century is problematic to say the least.

The rewriting of the history of the *Diatowa Senso* to deny wartime atrocities (Restall, 2005) is a significant problem for the study of Japanese battlefield tourism in the Pacific and in Asia. As a result, it is extremely difficult to obtain any reliable statistics on the flows of Japanese tourists specifically interested in battlefield tourism outside of Japan. Anecdotal evidence suggests that a small number of veterans do make some pilgrimages annually to some of the battlefields, but these sites tend to be those of conquest in the Pacific or those on Sakhalin, not of mainland Asia. And as of course such veterans are now octogenarians, it can be expected that this source of battlefield tourists, along with those of Japan's then enemies will cease to be important quite soon. The big question is whether a tradition of visiting parents' and grandparents' former battlefields like that which appears to be happening with Australian young people to the battlefields of France, Gallipoli and Asia has or will develop in the years to come. Again, anecdotal evidence suggests that it will be based strongly on a desire by young people in Japan to negate the censorship imposed on their traditional sources of information as they visit Saipan, Guam, Hellfire Pass in Thailand and Honolulu as tourists. In short, as in other forms of tourism, Japanese young appear to reflect travel patterns similar in style to the young of their western counterparts, including a questioning of past traditions.

Chapter 7

The Battles of Rangiriri and Batoche: Amnesia and Memory

Chris Ryan

Introduction

On leaving Auckland, New Zealand, to drive south along State Highway One, after approximately an hour the driver will pass between Lakes Kopuwera and Waikareto to his or her left, and the Waikato River to the right, just by Te Kauwhata. Te Kauwhata is a small rural town of 1,050 inhabitants servicing dairying and a growing viticulture industry. A sign points the way, and usually there is parked by the junction a large white van bearing the legend that fresh oysters can be purchased there. But 5 minutes later the driver will have left the community behind, with little having marked the fact that the road has gone through a Pa (a Maori fortification) that was the site of what has been described as one of the more important battles of the New Zealand land or Maori Wars in the 1860s. A brown tourism sign beckons, almost feebly it might be said, the curious to the remnants of the Pa, but no interpretation is provided on the site.

On the other hand, the visitor to Batoche in Saskatchewan, Canada is left in little doubt that this, the site of the last battle of note on Canadian soil, possesses an importance that reverberates down the years. Today a multi-million dollar interpretation centre stands ready to host the visitor curious about the Riel Rebellion and the role of the Métis peoples. A number of displays exist to complement the story of the battle told in an audio-visual presentation that involves high levels of technology. The social significance of the events is examined and a bookstore is present where various history books and socio-political texts can be purchased, while the visitor can also purchase refreshments. From the visitor centre, the visitor can then visit the battlefield site and see the memorials to the participants and the grave of Gabriel Dumont. The Province each year re-enacts the trial of Louis Riel in Regina, the Province's capital, an event that continues to attract many visitors, local, regional, national and international. It has become part of many a school child's education in that part of Canada.

The parallels between the events that are recorded are many; the difference in interpretation and recognition of those events is eloquent. Both battles relate to indigenous
peoples that early in the twenty-first century still seek recompense and recognition for
their position and histories. Personal histories are intertwined with the more formal histories of text, treaties, monuments and artefacts. Thus, for example, in 2003, Jean Teillet, an
Aboriginal rights lawyer with the law firm of Pape & Salter, represented two Métis brothers, Steve and Roddy Powley, in a case finally determined in their favour by the Supreme
Court of Canada. The case sustained the hunting rights of Métis Indian peoples as protected by Section 35 of the Constitution Act, 1982, which stated that "35 (1) The existing
aboriginal and treaty rights of the aboriginal peoples of Canada are hereby recognized
and affirmed. [And] (2) In this Act, 'aboriginal peoples of Canada' includes the Indian,
Inuit and Métis peoples of Canada". The personal history is that Jean Teillet is the great
grand niece of Louis Riel (http://p087.ezboard.com/ — accessed on July 2006). Similarly,
personal histories are alive in the North Waikato where today the Maori King,
Tuheitia, is a direct descendent of Potatau, the first King. It was Potatau's son, Tawhiao,
who was present at the Battle of Rangiriri, but who escaped to take up residence in the
King Country south of the Waikato region. Additionally many Tanui who live in the region
today have direct descent with those who fought in November 1863.

This chapter will extend the parallels between the two battles by briefly describing
the events that led to the conflict and the subsequent major battles recorded at these sites.
It will then comment upon the patterns of interpretation of the two sites to question
whether the differences reflect current uncertainties within the dominant cultures of both
New Zealand and Canada.

The Battle of Rangiriri: 20–21 November 1863

In 1840, the British, fearing possible French and even Russian incursions into the Southern
Ocean, and New Zealand in particular, concluded a treaty with Maori chiefs at Waitangi in
Northland. At this time, in New Zealand, Maori were the more dominant in numbers and
the British concluded that an alliance was necessary to sustain their own presence. Maori
themselves had previously reacted to the presence of Europeans and, in July 1835, 52
Maori chiefs (including Te Wherowhero of the Waikato Tanui) had signed a Declaration of
Independence. In 1836, this document was sent to the British Crown by James Bushby,
'resident' and effectively Acting Consul in New Zealand. The Declaration retained all sovereign power and authority in the land (*Ko te Kingitanga ko te mana I te w(h)enua*) in the
hands of the Maori chiefs. However, the intent to meet annually to exercise such power was
never put into action and, by 1840, more pressing concerns were not only the possible presence of 'foreign' powers but also a means of legalising land purchases by trading companies. On 6 February 1840, the Treaty of Waitangi was signed by the new Consul, William
Hobson, and 40 chiefs. Copies of the Treaty were hurried to other tribes and by September
1840 over 500 Maori chiefs had signed the Treaty — for the most part that version in the
Maori language, although 39 Waikato chiefs signed an English language version at
Manakau Harbour and Waikato Heads. The issue of language has subsequently proven
important as some discrepancies in interpretation arise from the two versions of the Treaty.

The Treaty itself was a relatively brief document, comprising three articles. In English these are, first, the giving over of sovereignty to the British Crown, second, the right of the chiefs to possess ownership of the land and a right to sell land to the British Crown is recognised, and by the third article Maori possess full rights of British citizenship. The second article, in the Maori version, provided for 'tino rangatiratanga', which can be translated as entire and full chieftain rights over the lands, property and 'treasures' (*taonga katoa*), a difference of translation, which remains a source of tension within contemporary New Zealand.

Subsequent actions on the part of the colonial power began to undermine the intent of the Treaty. For example, the 1852 New Zealand Constitution Act established a Parliament that excluded Maori participation, thereby denying some rights of British citizenship. The establishment of a Native Land Court in 1862 also undermined chieftain authority by recognising, contrary to Maori tradition, private Maori ownership of land that effectively gave rise to many dubious 'purchases' of land by colonial business and private interests. Disputes over land had commenced as early as 1843 when in Nelson on June 17, 1843, the Maori warrior chief, Te Rauparaha, violently resisted constables sent to detain him after disputes over land surveying and alleged purchase in skirmishes between armed groups. By 1845 the British army was involved in three actions against the chief, Hone Heke, in what came to be known as the Northern War of 1845–1846. In 1846 military conflicts occurred in the Wellington-Hutt area and in Whanganui — the latter to break again in yet more fierce fighting in 1860–1861.

By the early 1860s, business interests in Auckland were seeking an expansion of land ownership to the south; an expansion blocked by Maori fortifications at Meremere. By 1863 the Waikato Maori, alarmed by the events described above, had come together and created a more centralised command structure under the first appointed Maori King, Te Wherowhero, who took the name Potatau, and whose support spread as far south as Horowhenua. In 1860, he was succeeded upon his death by his son Tawhiao. In 1863, the passing of The Suppression of Rebellion Act, which authorised the taking of land from 'rebellious Maori', did little to settle Maori fears. A combination of factors thus led to Maori constructing a significant defensive line south of Auckland at Meremere completed with cannon of varying age and quality to control access via the Waikato River. At one period it is estimated over 1,000 warriors barred the way south to the colonial forces.

In August 1863, the colonial government ordered the steamboat 'Avon' to sail south down the Waikato River to reconnoitre the defensives. An exchange of artillery took place. Later, in October, the gunboat 'Pioneer' repeated the process, and again, albeit on a larger scale, and over several days, an artillery dual ensued. Then, on 31 October, 600 men were dis-embarked from the 'Pioneer' to attack the fortifications. Artillery support was provided by the guns of the 'Pioneer', the 'Avon' and smaller towed gunboats. After attempting to dislodge the 14th Regiment from their positions, Maori then retreated to prepared positions further south at Rangiriri. On 16 November 1863, the colonial government then despatched a further 900 men for the Thames Gulf to engage with Kingite forces who were in a position to harry the rear of the Colonial forces under the command of General Cameron. For his part Cameron had decided the best way to reduce the risk was to move further south, thereby forcing Maori to retreat or be isolated. By the 20 November 1863, the gun boats 'Pioneer', 'Avon', and four others were at Rangiriri with a total force of 850 and significant gunneries. The attack on the pa (fort) began with a 2 hours bombardment from 3 Armstrong guns to be followed by a sally on the fortifications by men of the 65th Regiment supported by others from the 14th Regiment. The outer defences were overrun, but Maori resistance was sustained at the central redoubt, as the scaling ladders were too short to reach the top. As the action raged, men from the 40th Regiment were landed south of the Pa and began to attack from the rear. Cameron then ordered further attacks on the central redoubt, but these were repulsed with significant loss of life on both sides. During the night of 20–21 November, many Maori made good their escape, including Tawhiao. The next morning the British made an attempt to mine the main Pa and blow it up — only to find that a shortage of fuses hampered their efforts. By noon the Maori broke out a white flag. The defenders now numbered 183, but today controversy still surrounds the details of the actual surrender, with Maori maintaining that they sought only negotiation and not surrender — but whatever the truth of the confusing events of the early afternoon of November 21, the outcome was a cessation of the battle. Many Maori of high rank were taken prisoner, including Ta Kerei ('Sir Grey'), te Rau-angaanga, a close relative of the Maori King.

The Battle of Rangiriri did not bring to a close the conflict, which was to drag on for several months. Maori were to establish many strong sets of fortifications, as at Paterangi, but perhaps one of the worse episodes of the war was at Rangiaowhia where many old people, women and children were killed in fighting in February 1864. Finally, an uneasy peace was established and the area from Te Awamutu to Cambridge became marked with garrisons and fortifications as the frontier between the Colonial north and the Kingite south for much of the 1860s.

The Battle of Batoche

The Battle of Batoche possesses many themes common with those of Rangiriri. The 1870–1880s were times of westward expansion in Canada. There existed many tensions, not only between indigenous peoples and colonial government, but also between a growing commercial class that wished to be freed from the constraints imposed by a colonial government — a government that itself was aware of the relative lack of resource in facing the challenges of new lands yet wanting to reduce its own dependence upon Westminster and the United Kingdom. These commercial and political aspirations led to a close relationship between entrepreneurs and government in Canada in the early 1880s. Motivated by an urge to develop a country and unify it through railway building, land was sold in lots to help develop the Canadian Pacific Railway, and fortunes were won or lost via the routes selected. Towns prospered or declined based on their proximity to the railway. Of course, in the events described below, the parallels between the situation of Métis Indians and New Zealand Maori are evident, but important differences also existed. Canada had a European history that predated that of New Zealand by over a century. There was less cultural homogeneity among native peoples. Canada had a neighbour to its south with which it shared less easy relationships than those that existed between the colonial governments of Australia and New Zealand. It was also mindful that its neighbour had endured a horrific Civil War followed by the Indian Wars. There was also the fact that in the mid-nineteenth century Canada had not yet established the federal state of government that came to exist by 1905. Hence, commercial and entrepreneurial expansion westwards was mutually symbiotically tied to the development of the constitution.

Caught in the forces of emergent industrialisation, westward expansion and governmental sensitivities were the Métis Indians. The Métis considered themselves separate from the descendants of the French settlers and Amerindians. Dickason (1986) states they had not been a separate ethnic group at the time of the MicMac wars of the eighteenth century. Nonetheless, French speaking and influenced by French Catholicism they emerged from liaisons between French settlers and the Indian nations of Acadia, to become both more numerous and slowly more distinct. By the nineteenth century they had migrated westwards in attempts to retain their own identity and patterns of life based on traditional Indian patterns of hunting, and by the early 1870s had sought to establish land rights in Manitoba and the North-West Territories. These latter had been transferred to the Dominion of Canada in 1870. Alberta and Saskatchewan were to become Provinces in 1905. In 1870 the Dominion Government completed negotiations with the Hudson's Bay Company and the Manitoba Act was passed which sought to extinguish the land claims of Métis through the setting aside of 1.4 million acres of land for Métis usage and ownership. At that time land issues further to the west and north-west were left unsettled.

Métis claims and opposition to these policies had been gathering pace long before this period. There had been armed resistance in 1869–1870, and in 1881 the Catholic clergy had aided in a campaign of petitioning the Canadian government to recognise land claims. McLean (1986) notes that as a result of this campaign limited gains had been made but Métis resident on lands previously owned by the Prince Albert Colonization Company (which had owned extensive lands in the west and north-west) had neither been surveyed or received title.

Into this cauldron of unease, distrust and conflict there needs to be made mention of the personality of Louis Riel. As a Métis leader, Riel had refused to recognise the appointment of the Manitoba Lieutenant-Governor in 1870, and for a brief period had established a Métis Provisional government following an election. During this period he had commenced negotiations with Ottawa, had suppressed an uprising by Canadian residents in the region, had executed one of their leaders, the Ontario Orangeman, Thomas Scott and had issued a proclamation endorsing full democratic rights and the appointment by election of many local governmental positions. He also accorded equal status to the English and French languages and respect for all traditional rights existent at the time of the hand over to the Dominion Government. The Federal authorities, in a precursor of what was to happen in 1885, responded by sending military force, and Riel, lacking confidence in the Métis ability to resist fled westwards and then eventually to the United States.

In June 1884 he returned to Canada at the invitation of the Council of the Métis that had been established at Batoche in Saskatchewan. He again established a provisional government and sought to open negotiations with Ottawa, while in addition tried to obtain alliances with native American groups in the region. Some of these, including Cree, had taken refuge in the region after the American Indian wars, and had little inclination for further military involvement. However, on this occasion the Government was not prepared to negotiate. Indeed, McLean (1986, p. 84) goes so far as to suggest that the government specifically sought through not meeting Métis land claims to "goad them (the Métis) into armed rebellion" in a complicated plot that involved "top ranking officials of the Canadian government working on behalf of the executive of the Canadian Pacific Railway" (McLean, 1986, p. 85). Whatever the truth of this claim, and it is not without substantiation, it is evident that the government commenced mobilisation of its troops early in March 1885. The spring that year was one of varied weathers that veered from heat wave to blizzard and many soldiers experienced harsh conditions. Although many troops were shipped westwards by train, most of the carriages were open and men froze in the conditions. The displays at Batoche include copies of contemporary drawings of men marching westwards in blizzards. Many died before they reached the eventual battlefield. The 9th Battalion found itself guarding supply routes in Alberta along the Canadian Pacific Railroad, where perhaps mindful of their extreme circumstances they became noted for the care and generosity they demonstrated towards the Indian bands with which they came into contact.

The Riel–Dumont government now claimed the surrender of police barracks at Fort Carlton and Fort Battleford. The police assistant commissioner ('Paddy' Crozier) refused to surrender, and in March set out to Duck Lake with 55 men to secure ammunition stores held there. He was ambushed by Dumont and 12 were killed and 11 wounded. This skirmish initiated a number of Indian reprisals against settlers. The government, as noted, had begun mobilisation, and by the end of April Major-General Frederick Middleton had over 8,000 troops at his disposal across southern Saskatchewan toward Calgary. By the third week of April government troops secured Fort Battleford, and on 2nd May had fallen back on Battleford after various skirmishes and minor actions with the 'rebels'. However, by that date the main action had been joined at Batoche. Middleton had advanced with caution. Dividing his troops on either side of the South Saskatchewan River, Middleton then engaged Riel and Dumont on 24th April on the east of the river. However, being well dug in, the Métis repelled the government forces and two weeks were to pass before Middleton recommenced action. On May 2nd, after a period of exercising his troops, the siege began in more earnest with a newly arrived gunboat supporting Middleton's forces with gunfire on the Métis positions. With a significant superiority in artillery, Middleton commenced a bombardment, but his caution induced increasing degrees of frustration from his more junior officers. Finally, on May 12th, two colonels led their regiments in a direct attack, and easily captured Métis positions and the village of Batoche. The Métis lost 12 dead and three wounded, the government forces lost 8 dead and 46 wounded. On 15 May, Riel surrendered, was tried and then subsequently hanged on 16 November 1885.

Parallels and Differences

The parallels between the two battles and the circumstances surrounding them are obvious. Both involved indigenous peoples facing a British colonial government that, in its expansion, was acquiring a new confidence. Both governments sought land to both help further and finance expansion, and both New Zealand and Canadian governments wished to encourage land settlement and entrepreneurial interests who required land and the new markets they represented. Both colonial governments had a history of land misappropriation. Both battles arose from issues pertaining to non-recognition of indigenous rights.

Both battles involved superior colonial forces. Both battles had a river-based action and both involved gun boats that provided artillery support and troop movement support in the stages immediate to the main conflict. Both battles might be cast in the light of the modern and pre-modern societies coming into conflict. Yet both battles saw the respective indigenous peoples acquiring 'western' arms and proving to be bold enemies. Yet again, neither group of indigenous peoples were able to call upon wholesome support from other indigenous groups — indeed in New Zealand long standing tribal differences saw some Maori tribes fight almost consistently on the side of the British.

There are also significant differences. Maori proved to be adept builders of military fortifications and time and time again (as Belich, 1988, 1996, demonstrated in his histories of the Maori land wars) were able to successfully resist the colonial forces. What they were unable to sustain was the economic costs of maintaining forces in the field throughout the year and at key times the needs for harvesting and other tasks denuded their forces. Nonetheless, Maori after the military events of 1863 were able to sustain for almost a decade a frontier that barred colonial settlement from both north and south in the King Country, while other areas such as the Te Urewas saw very little European settlement apart from logging interests. Maori retained a strong sense of identity that was always recognised by successive New Zealand governments. For Métis the opposite was the case whereby for much of the intervening period between the time of the events described above until the latter part of the twentieth century they held a non-status Indian position and thus could not claim rights that were otherwise slowly being conceded to the 'First Nations' of Canada.

Differences in Remembrance at Battlefield Sites

Given the parallels between the two events, it therefore seems almost unbelievable that such a tremendous gulf lies between the commemorations of the two battlefields with reference to the status of the two visitor centres. At Batoche there remains the church of St. Antoine de Padouche and its rectory, shallow rifle depressions, the Métis Mass Grave and the tomb of remembrance of Gabriel Dumont. The visitor can stand on the banks of the South Saskatchewan River, now peaceful for the most part as it slowly wends its course north and south of the site. But the visitor is informed by the regional park and the visitor information centre. Indeed, on parking the car the Centre stands immediately both visible and welcoming. In many ways it represents 'good practice' for it provides refreshments, toilets, and in its audio visual and professionally mounted displays it relates the details of the engagements and provides information on the social and political context that gave rise to the events. Given, as demonstrated by the Powley case, that the issues of land, ownership and traditional practices are living questions it is perhaps too easy to be critical of some of interpretation being offered. It is arguably contextualised within a given and too specific a period of time relating to the events surrounding 1885, but that too is very understandable given the location of the centre. The rationale for the Centre's existence is the Battle itself. As noted above, the bookshop provides many texts for the more curious who wish to study the aftermath of the battle.

But what of Rangiriri in New Zealand? There stands no government-financed visitor centre. Rather next to the rather more imposing Rangiriri pub is the Rangiriri Battle Site

Heritage Centre — grandiose in title but in reality it might be described as a tea shop with a difference. The visitor buys his or her tea and sits in surroundings of tables and chairs as in any small tea shop, but around the walls lay the trophies gained by its past owner. Painstakingly, over the years, a retired British army officer, Mr Pat Gaitely, has sought to bring to the attention of the visitor the history described above. His walls display weapons, military uniforms and a model of the action. In an adjoining room, visitors and school parties can view an audio-visual presentation of slides and commentary describing the battle. Not the flashing lights and anatomic models of Batoche, but simply a black and white slide show: simply stated, but stated with conviction that now both parties must remember the past as they face a future together. In 2005, because of failing health and not being able to attract either national or local government support, Mr Gaitely finally sold his tea shop and all its contents to a local Hamilton-based Maori business family. It is they who also sell the oysters, and thus today the heritage centre is also marked by a balloon that floats above the premises promising fresh oysters.

The difference in interpretation resource is stark. Cardow and Wiltshier (2003), in a paper given at the New Zealand National Tourism and Hospitality Research Conference, trace the remnants of the history of the Maori Land Wars along the old Great South Road. They note the abandonment of remains of the troop movements and the near dereliction of what still stands. Thus they write:

> Maori who were part of the rebellion against the British rule often had some or all of their land confiscated by the British Crown, in turn those that fought with the British were similarly rewarded. Such land alienation at the time went against the spirit of the recently agreed treaty between Maori and the British crown. In some respects a line may be drawn that connects such land alienation with modern day political disagreements between Maori and the present representatives of the British Crown, the New Zealand government.

It is therefore not surprising that in the nation's consciousness, the battle sites and physical evidence of the civil wars have been, for the most part, removed from society's gaze. In doing so an important formative stage of the New Zealand social history is being eroded. War monuments and the associated heritage sites that may accompany them are significant not only for the events which are remembered but by omission those events that the citizen or society would rather collectively forget (Walsh, 2001). It is as if by simply refusing to acknowledge the events surrounding the civil wars the difficult concepts of trust, betrayal and consequence need not be remembered. They have in some respects ceased to have a place in the modern world. Unlike, for example, monuments to the fallen of the Great War or World War II, and in some towns of New Zealand there can be found monuments to the fallen of the Boer War, but seldom are there visible monuments to the fallen of the Civil War.

A sense of collective amnesia is apparent when looking for the sites of action during the civil wars (Cardow & Wiltshier, 2003).

Chapple (2006), in his account of walking through North Island, New Zealand, offers two views: (a) New Zealanders do not care, but (b) would care if there was something to see.

Belich (1988) in his history of the wars also implies that the remnants of Victorian interpretations still colour contemporary perspectives of those wars and these include a reluctance to admit that the supposedly pre-modern Maori proved time and time again to be a military match for the forces placed in the field by the British Empire. This author would offer as evidence of the reluctance to provide a fuller interpretation the photograph shown in Figure 7.1. This weather-beaten notice board, almost at times lost in the hedgerow at the perimeter of a field in which maize is usually planted, bears the text in English (with a Maori translation):

> In this locality on the 27th May, 1865, Wiremu Tamahana Tarapipipi Te Waharoa of Ngati Haua, the Maori Kingmaker, met Brigadier General Carey to sign a covenant of peace with the government. Later Tamahana wrote to Governor Grey 'These are my thoughts'. Peace is made, an end to the fatigue and weariness of war. The weapons of war have been cast aside and thrown away. We and our weapons are at rest. The cutting edge of the patu has been turned aside in peace.

The notice was constructed by the New Zealand Historic Places Trust. However, while the lack of any other monument much less a visitor centre at a place of significance is eloquent of a silence, an alternative explanation can also be offered. Namely, the notice board symbolises a lack of resources for the Trust. The Trust is under-funded for its work and of

Figure 7.1: Author by the only signage of the peace making between Maori and Colonial Government to mark the end of the Waikato Maori Land War (Photograph by Gu Huimin).

course many sites remain in private and not public ownership. In the 2003 budget, the New Zealand government established the national heritage preservation incentive fund to develop historic sites on private land, but this has only NZ$563,000 (approximately US$343,906) per annum. Do such levels of funding reveal a lack of public interest in New Zealand's past generally and the Land Wars specifically? The viewing figures associated with the televising by Television New Zealand (TVNZ) of a dramatisation of James Belich's work indicate that an interest does exist, but the enthusiasm engendered by that television series has not really been capitalised upon apart from a small stream of bookings for specialist tours of battlefield sites that are offered by various tour companies — which, for the most part, are small in size with the product being offered by history enthusiasts who often find their markets are those of school parties and overseas visitors.

The contrast with Batoche is evident. Possibly, one factor that helps explain this difference is that, within Canadian history, past explanations of the events at Batoche have centred upon the strong personality of one contentious and much re-interpreted individual — that being Louis Riel. Riel has long been a controversial personality. He has been interpreted as being a visionary, prophet, insane, unstable, a revolutionary, a fighter for freedom, a murderer and much else (Stanley, 1986). In the interpretations offered at Batoche it has been stated that one reason for the bravery of the Métis was that Riel had convinced them that God was on their side and they would be invulnerable to the bullets of the enemy. Many contemporaries thought him mad. His very outspokenness may well have been one reason as to why many among the Cree and other Indian groups failed to support him. Indeed, in an interesting side note to history, in 1886 a group of Cree and Blackfoot chiefs who had not supported Riel were invited to the unveiling of the Joseph Brant Monument in Brantford, Ontario — Brant being a Loyalist Mohawk leader who had fought on the side of the British in the Revolutionary War. Riel also did not always enjoy an easy relationship with Dumont, who in the events leading to the Battle of Batoche was critical of Riel's 'humanitarian counsels' and reluctance to engage with Middleton's forces, perhaps because he still hoped for a response from his political overtures to the Ottawa government (Fieguth & Christensen, 1986).

Given the nature of Riel, one consequence is that the audio-visual show at Batoche centres on his personality. As noted previously, this interpretation, based upon an individual rather than broader social forces, is reinforced by the above-mentioned annual re-enactment of his trial in Regina. While it negates more complex interpretations now being offered by social historians, it also offers advantages in creating a 'sellable' story. In this respect, a parallel may be offered with Bosworth Field in the United Kingdom, where popular conception of an 'evil' usurper of the throne who killed innocent princes in the Tower is fixed in popular imagination and thus helps sell the site to tourists (Piekarz, 2007).

In noting the imbalance between New Zealand's apparent forgetfulness and Canada's act of remembrance it should be noted that the latter's act is primarily performed at Batoche. Other incidents marked the events of 1885, and elsewhere these are marked by signposts or monuments just as simple as that noted at Tamahere in New Zealand. At Fish Creek, where with but a few men, Dumont had ambushed 400 troops under Middleton there now exists a national historic site. However, interpretation is limited and only a few cairns mark the spot, albeit not too accurately according to some. At Frenchman's Butte, another site of skirmishing, is also another historic national site, and the rifle pits dug by the Plains Cree Indians are still visible. Yet again, however, interpretation is primarily restricted to a monument with some wooden stakes indicating sites of the action. To this author's mind, the very simplicity and silence associated with such sites possess an eloquence wherein the imagination can roam and thus it is the 'gazers' on the spot who provide their own interpretation of events. Rises and falls in the ground become a site where men (and women) hid, frightened or vicious as the case may be — but as ever in such imaginations there are dangers that the mind creates pictures divorced from reality — and thus the professional interpretation offered at a site like Batoche is important in providing a factual catalyst for the emotional and affective to take wing. The overall management of the sites thus, in Canada, permit an appeal to both the cognitive and affective parts of the mind, while also having the virtue of retaining costs to the minimum at sites other than Batoche.

The difference in interpretation may also be reflective of different mind-sets between the nations of Canada and New Zealand as migrant societies. The former speaks of a mosaic of cultures and ethnic identities where difference is to be celebrated. New Zealand tends more to an ethos of assimilation; while it has created a culture of modesty wherein the 'tall poppy syndrome' as it is called also seeks to reduce difference based on talent or achievement. Whether this latter observation is true or not, the fact that it is discussed within New Zealand is indicative of sensitivities towards difference based on race, achievement and income, a sensitivity that arises from the initial essential egalitarianism of an early twentieth century agriculturally based community. To this must be added an awareness that in its treatment of Maori past government retreated from those principles and thus again a challenge to those principles arises as claims for compensatory recognition are now made. Canada has also had to face similar issues, but perhaps even factors such as physical size has aided Canada wherein it has been possible to demarcate specific lands for Indian peoples in a way practically denied to New Zealand because of its smaller size. In short, interpretation of past conflicts are not solely issues of assessing a factual record of what happened when, but a matter of interpreting why things happened, and what are the consequences of those events. The military historian is thus drawn into differing perceptions of what constitutes social realities, and thus interpretations themselves become matters of contention.

Chapter 8

Seventy Years of Waiting: A Turning Point for Interpreting the Spanish Civil War?

Hugh Smith

Introduction

The Spanish Civil War took place over a period of 33 months, from July 1936 to April 1939, causing the deaths of at least half a million people (de Meneses, 2001). It was a war that could be categorised into three distinct conflicts: a civil conflict including Republicans against Nationalists; an international conflict with nations such as Italy and Germany providing support for the Nationalists and Russia supporting the Republicans, and an ideological conflict with the involvement of the International Brigades including anti-fascists (Thomas, 2003; de Meneses, 2001; Preston, 2006; Beevor, 2006). Ultimate victory for the Nationalists led to the dictatorship of Francisco Franco who ruled Spain until his death in 1975. However, the Spanish Civil War "remains a huge touchstone of political importance..." (Graham, 2005, p. 138).

The many remnants and reminders from the civil war such as battlefields and monuments together with memorials erected following April 1939 are increasingly recognised as important types of heritage. It is the victors of the war that usually have the political power and opportunity to tell the story, resulting in conflict or dissonance (Tunbridge & Ashworth, 1996; Ashworth & Hartmann, 2005) related to the interpretation at the sites as time passes. This is particularly relevant following a civil war where a nation shares the same heritage (Graham, 1996; Timothy & Boyd, 2003). Prior to considering selected sites from the Spanish Civil War to highlight the challenges for those responsible for the management and interpretation of the sites, some 70 years after the start of the civil war, a short history of the war is offered to provide context.

Battlefield Tourism: History, Place and Interpretation
Copyright © 2007 by Elsevier Ltd.
All rights of reproduction in any form reserved.
ISBN: 0-08-045362-7

The Spanish Civil War

The research that continues to be produced on the Spanish Civil War is extremely complex, and this short chapter cannot therefore consider all of the conflicting circumstances and political implications that are essential to gain a full understanding of Spain prior to, during and after the war.

The Spanish Civil War officially began on 17–18 July 1936, when General Francisco Franco ultimately led a military uprising against the Second Republic, starting in Spanish occupied Morocco (Graham, 2005). The following day a rebellion took place on mainland Spain, thus beginning 33 months of civil war between the Nationalists led by Franco (and two other Generals) and the Republican Government, with casualties estimated between 500,000 and 1,000,000 (Preston, 1996, 2006; de Meneses, 2001). The Nationalist victory, formally declared on 1 April 1939, led to 36 years of rule by Franco.

Political scene prior to the war

It has been argued that the origins of the war go back further than the unstable times of the Second Republic, which was established on 14 April 1931 (Carr, 1986; Graham, 2005). At the end of the nineteenth century, Spain lost its last remaining colonies in Cuba, Puerto Rico and the Philippines. However, new conflict arose when Morocco was taken as a protectorate. This action led to serious internal tension that culminated in protests all over the country. A *coup d'etat* subsequently took place on 13 September 1923, led by General Jose Antonio Primo de Rivera. While some successful policies were adopted by the dictatorship such as ending the war in Morocco and developing local government, the aim of returning Spain to a monarchy failed and following elections, the Second Republic was formed (Beevor, 2006; Thomas, 2003).

Spain under the Second Republic was not stable. The government's proposed reforms included redistributing estate lands, separating State and Church and attempting to dilute the power of the military (Thomas, 2003). By 1934 the coalition government that was in place suffered from internal disagreements with increasing strikes, violence and persecution. Instability continued despite the formation of a new Popular Front government in 1936 that had support from parties on the left and centre, but not from those on the right. Assassinations, political violence, destruction of religious buildings and general strikes in major cities such as Zaragoza and Valencia together with street battles in Madrid and Barcelona added to the feelings of insecurity (Beevor, 1982; Preston, 1996). The increasing tensions led to a significant event — the killing on 12 July 1936 of a lieutenant in the Assault Guards and socialist party member, Jose Castillo, by an extremist 'far right' group. In retaliation, a Member of Parliament, Jose Calvo Sotello was killed on 13 July 1936 by a group of Assault Guards (Carr, 1986). Within four days the civil war had begun.

In addition to the factors described above, other important considerations were the uneven levels of development in Spain that had been evident for some time, the strong role of the Spanish church and the past roles of the army. The war could in fact be categorised on many levels, for example, urban against rural, religious against secular, centre against periphery plus generational conflicts (Graham, 2005; Beevor, 2006; Preston, 2006). A final extremely significant factor was the comparison made between the military uprising in

Spain and the fascist takeovers that had already occurred elsewhere in Europe — Mussolini in 1922 and Hitler in 1933 (Thomas, 2003).

Main events of the war

The division of support for each side is complex but can be loosely summarised in Table 8.1.

This information provides a general view of the type of support for each side in the war — the reality was far more complex. For example, the Nationalists stated their support for the Catholic Church (and the church's reciprocation) to defend the church against censorship by the Republicans, in effect termed by the Nationalists as a 'crusade'. Many churches and other religious buildings were subsequently burnt and destroyed by Republican supporters. Throughout the war and aftermath, Franco's strong religious beliefs ensured an important role for the church in Spain, not least in the role of educators (Beevor, 1982, 2006; Preston, 1996, 2006; Thomas, 2003).

This chapter does not seek to provide a chronology of all major battle events but some important events should be considered. Foreign interventionist and non-interventionist policies were important for the outcome of battles for both sides of the conflict (Alpert, 2004). As early as 26 July 1936, Germany and Italy confirmed support for the Nationalists with the provision of troops, tanks, aircraft and weapons. Spain in effect became a testing ground for new weapons and warfare by both Germany and Russia (supporting the Republican side) (Alpert, 2004). This was at its most evident in the total destruction of the town of Guernica by the German Legion Condor on 26 April 1937. Civilians were regarded as almost legitimate targets for bombing raids. This was the first conflict in Europe for such atrocities, with Guernica being forever remembered in Pablo Picasso's famous interpretation of the atrocity (Thomas, 2003).

The United Kingdom maintained a policy of non-intervention and proposed an arms embargo on Spain. However, international concern grew as the conflict progressed, and in view of the conflicting or ambivalent policies pursued by other nations, volunteers came from many countries to fight in Spain for their 'cause'. These were known as the

Table 8.1: Support for Nationalists and Republicans.

Nationalists	Republicans
Fascists	Urban workers
Carlists	Peasants
Monarchists	Educated middle class
Spanish Nationalists	Liberals
Conservatives	Basque and Catalan Nationalists
Catholic Church	Socialists
Businessmen	Communists
Army	Anarchists
Landowners	

'International Brigades'. In the increasingly fractious Republican side infighting and dissention became more common and whole parties such as the POUM (Worker's Party of Marxist Unification) were ultimately labelled as 'fascist' and disbanded (Beevor, 1982, 2006).

The fall of Catalonia was completed by mid-February 1939, and by the end of that month the United Kingdom recognised the Franco regime, signalling that other nations felt that the war was over. However, it was another month before Madrid was taken by the Nationalists on 28 March 1939, with Valencia surrendering the following day. Franco declared victory on 1 April 1939 (Thomas, 2003; Alpert, 2004).

The Battle of Belchite

As a focus for this chapter, the Battle of Belchite was part of the Republican's major offensive in Aragón in August 1937. The Republicans experienced many difficulties in occupying towns such as Belchite, situated some 40 km from their eventual target, the regional centre of Zaragoza (Preston, 2006). Poor communications, extreme heat, lack of water and the military superiority of the Nationalist forces all contributed to the failed offensive with the battles of Brunete, Belchite, Teruel and the Ebro, all being classed with hindsight as 'disastrous repetitions' (Beevor, 2006, p. 428).

Although the offensive in Aragon commenced on 24 August, the focus turned to Belchite on 1 September 1937 (Beevor, 2006). Using Russian-trained Spanish pilots in addition to artillery, the battle left Belchite as "a smoking ruin of death, smashed masonry, dust and corpses, both human and animal" (Beevor, 2006, p. 298). Belchite surrendered on 6 September 1937 (Thomas, 2003). The number of dead totalled some 6,000 people. The delays caused by this battle did, however, allow the Nationalist forces to engage reinforcements and the Republicans' offensive towards Zaragoza failed accordingly.

Aftermath and Legacy

Following the social, economic and political devastation caused by the war, it took decades for the country and its economy to recover. The Franco regime adopted a no tolerance policy towards trade unions, opposition political parties and supporters of the Second Republic. Many supporters of the defeated were jailed, forced into exile or killed. There were also atrocities instigated by the Republican side resulting in the deaths of priests and religious supporters (Graham, 2005). It is estimated that some 400,000 Spaniards sought exile following the war. Other unfortunates included around 10,000 Republicans that were sent to Nazi concentration camps — mostly Mauthausen. A large network of concentration camps was established around Spain where many 'political' prisoners were held (Molinero, Sala & Sobreques, 2003; Museu d'Historia de Catalunya, 2003). For example, Republican prisoners were posted to Belchite on the basis that as they destroyed the town they should rebuild it (Beevor, 2006). In addition, prisoners were used in the creation of the Valley of the Fallen, Franco's monument to the war dead and victory (Molinero, Sala & Sobreques, 2003). Following the death of Franco many publications appeared, analysing the civil war from differing perspectives, published by both Spaniards and non-Spaniards. It has been estimated that in excess of 15,000 books have been published which is almost equal to the number of publications on World War II (Graham, 2005), for which the Spanish Civil War in many respects was a testing ground for many of the weapons and tactics of war.

What Happens to the Battle Sites after the War?

Over time many of the sites of battles, graves, prisons and other remnants of war will be preserved, restored, re-developed or in some cases neglected and allowed to fall into disrepair. Carman (2002, p. 18) argues that the remains of twentieth-century war are 'supremely culturally significant' as war exemplified the century. Equally, sites that have been interpreted can add value to any visitor's experiences by enhancing appreciation in a manner they may not have considered had the interpretation not been extant (Ames et al., 1997). Beck and Cable (2002, p. 2) state that interpretation is "a process, a rendering by which visitors see, learn, experience, and are inspired firsthand". With a focus on war sites they add there is an overriding need for sensitivity without omitting or obscuring the 'truth' (Beck & Cable, 2002, p. 75). Such interpretation should "go beyond statistics" but it is not necessary to interpret in a "gruesome, sensationalistic manner" (Beck & Cable, 2002, p. 75). Tilden (1977, p. 9) argues that "The chief aim of interpretation is not instruction, but provocation … [and that] interpretation should aim to present a whole rather than a part". Although specifically referring to nature-based heritage, Tilden's additional argument that interpretation is the revelation of a larger 'truth' that lies behind the statement of fact has resonance for this chapter. Consideration has to be given to who is doing the interpretation and how the visitor reacts to it. The use of the word 'truth' also raises the question — whose truth? Interpreting history is based upon "interpreting other people's interpretation of events … interpreters find themselves interpreting interpretation" (Beck & Cable, 2002, p. 73). This is further complicated by the ever-changing evaluation of the history that is being interpreted. The challenge for the manager and interpreter is to present the 'truth' about the historical period and events under review without the influence of any 'political correctness' then current at the time of creation of the interpretation. However inevitably, controversy surrounds sites of atrocity being interpreted in any manner, especially as any culture formally dominant becomes increasingly questioned.

Spanish Civil War Sites as Heritage and Tourism

During the war, in 1938, the Nationalists felt sufficiently confident about victory to produce a 'tourist map' of battle sites (see Figure 8.1), which indicated routes in Andalucia in the south, the Basque Country and Asturias in the north and the region around Madrid and Zaragoza (de Meneses, 2001).

Such tours were aimed at the travellers of Europe in a brochure entitled 'Visit the war routes of Spain' (Virr et al., 2001; Imperial War Museum, 2005). The 'War Route of the

Figure 8.1: Tourist map of battlefield sites (from de Meneses, 2001).

North', in particular, has been considered in depth by Holguín (2005, p. 1399), who states that the tours attracted "thousands of people from throughout Western Europe". The Nationalists were also keen to attract journalists, and an article by Ruiz (2001) provides an account of the experiences of Portuguese journalists who travelled the war route of the north. Present-day versions of such tours attract interest. Battlefield tour operators Midas Tours state that "Our eight-day tour to Spain takes you to the scenes of some of the most important aspects of the conflict" (Midas Tours, 2005, p. 25).

Despite well-known representations of the war through artists such as Dali, Miro and of course Picasso's Guernica, and through literature such as Hemingway's novel *For Whom the Bell Tolls* and Orwell's *Homage to Catalonia*, it is unlikely that such tours would be the main focus of a holiday for the majority of tourists and they exist more as a niche area of interest. In addition to the primary battlefield sites and other buildings and sites that witnessed the conflict, Spain's cities and towns contain additional representations of the war in the form of memorials and monuments, albeit from a mostly victorious view-point as argued by Graham (2005, p. 137): "While the Francoist dead had war memorials and their names carved on Churches — *'caidos por Dios y por Espana'* ('those who fell for God and Spain') — the Republican dead could never be publicly mourned".

The general lack of museum coverage of the war is also noted by Graham (2005, p. 145) who states that "Such representations are much more likely to be found at the periphery — most notably in Guernica in the Basque Country, which has the nearest thing to a modern Civil War exhibition". However, a recent exhibition in Barcelona (Museu d'Historia de Catalunya, 2003) interpreted the controversial and disturbing 'Franco's Prisons'. The exhibition ran from November 2003 to April 2004 and was the first publicly funded exhibition to deal with this topic.

Belchite

With the passing of time many of the battle sites have become places of heritage such as the town of Belchite. Franco decreed, following the war, that this town should be left in a state of destruction as a 'reminder' of the damage caused by the Republican forces. The new town of Belchite has been built next to the ruined former town, and visiting the latter site today gives a sanitised version of what the town must have been like at the end of battle almost 70 years ago.

The town of Belchite is situated some 40 km to the south of Zaragoza, next to a main route between Zaragoza and Teruel. From Zaragoza the new town of Belchite appears first but the ruins of the old town are clearly visible. Franco's decree that the old town be left in a state of ruin has been diligently observed over the years. The remains of the town continue to crumble and despite evidence of some attempts to shore up some buildings and brick up some entrances/exits, the overall feeling is one of neglect. The remains of some of the buildings are striking, particularly the churches and clock tower and there is evidence of detailed sculptures that adorn the remains of some of the domestic buildings.

For the visitor, of whom there are estimated to be between 10,000 and 12,000 per annum (Malvar, 2005), there is little restriction on where to wander within the ruined townscape. The area around the crumbling buildings is filled with piles of rubble, broken security fences and overgrown weeds. Yet within this area it is possible to gather some idea of the original townscape from the position of the churches, the pattern of the streets and the placement of a fountain and irrigation implements.

In view of the neglected state of the site it is not surprising that interpretation boards are largely non-existent. However, they do appear at the entrance to inform the visitor that they have arrived at the old town of Belchite and that the town has been declared a historic ruin. In addition a single sign warns of danger due to loose masonry. As the visitor wanders around the site climbing over torn down security fences and through crumbling buildings, the question of safety and liability for any injuries sustained is raised. Additional signs inform the visitor of the names of the churches together with the arch at the entrance to the town. It is at the arch that it is most apparent that steps are taken to control visitor flow and maintain some level of safety. A simple brick wall has been built preventing visitors from walking through the archway. The lack of sympathetic treatment of the old building has, however, attracted graffiti questioning why bricks that would be used to build farm buildings are being used on a historic site such as Belchite. See Figure 8.2 for an impression of the site.

This feeling of overall neglect is apparent throughout the site not withstanding evidence of some restoration work around the old clock tower built in the mudejar style. A tender was issued for work in 2002 (Department of Culture and Tourism, 2006). A notice confirms that the project also attracted European funding. Whether any additional work is to be carried out remains to be seen. Some consideration has been given in the past to the development of the site as a type of archaeological theme park (Malvar, 2005). However, the cost implications of such a project have meant that no real progress has been made.

Figure 8.2: The ruins of Belchite (Photo courtesy of Hugh Smith).

The town has been utilised as a film set in projects as diverse as Terry Gilliam's *Adventures of Baron Munchausen* from 1989 and exhibitions such as Francesc Torres' exploration of "the parallels between military and civilian life in cultures under siege" (Torres, 1988, p. 69), where images and models of the ruined town of Belchite were fused with images from South Bronx, New York.

Visitation to the site at Belchite in its current dilapidated state does provide an exhilarating experience. However, there is little possibility of the site attracting large numbers of tourists due to logistic and safety reasons. It is perhaps accepted that the site will solely continue to attract casual tourists in small numbers. Niche tourists with battlefield tour operators such as Midas Tours (2006, p. 5) can "walk along the silent and abandoned streets of Belchite, a stark reminder of the horrors of this war". This may, however, change in the future bearing in mind the town's close proximity to Zaragoza, the venue for Expo 2008.

Although there is evidence of some restoration, it will take considerably enhanced investment to make this a site suitable for substantial visitation. The site would benefit greatly from at least some additional interpretation boards to tell the 'story' of the battle, the casualties, life before, during and after the battle and the role of the political prisoners after the war when they contributed to the building of the new town of Belchite. The challenge would be to represent the views of the many interested parties. Perhaps the ongoing development of another nearby site connected with the civil war will encourage further development at Belchite.

Orwell's Aragon

Thus it is of interest that another small site to the east of Zaragoza in the area of Los Monegros has been developed with the assistance of European Union funding to recognise the area's civil war heritage. Towards the end of 2006, the 'Ruta Orwell' was officially opened to include interpretation of trenches on both the Republican and Nationalist sides. The route has been developed in recognition of the seventieth anniversary of the start of the civil war with the interpretation being linked to George Orwell's work *A Homage to Catalonia*. Well-designed maps, booklets and a DVD accompany the interpretation boards installed at the site, which is based in the Sierra de Alcubierre. The trenches that have been created follow the design and position of the original trenches as far as possible. The visitor can walk along the trench areas, enter areas such as the stores and view the surrounding countryside through the sandbags. Detailed interpretation boards are well situated throughout the site. The culmination of the project will also see the creation of an institute for study and documentation related to the civil war that will be based at nearby Robres (Centro de Desarrollo de Monearos, 2006). The president of the Comarca de Los Monegros, Manuel Conte Laborda, one of the main initiators of the project, reports that many local businesses are already noting increased custom as a result of the new signage along the road from Zaragoza to Alcubierre.

The Valley of the Fallen

One site connected with the civil war that does attract substantial annual visitation is the site at the Valley of the Fallen, as described in the Midas Tours (2005, p. 25) guide, "a vulgar reminder of the country's dictatorial past and the final resting place of Franco".

By Decree issued on 1 April 1940, Franco decided that a 'Monument to the Dead in the Spanish Civil War' should be erected at the site. It was to be given the title of *Santa Cruz del Valle de los Caidos* (Holy Cross of the Valley of the Fallen). Franco was able to "impose a view of the world, especially of the past, on others" (Harrison, 2005, p. 5). It is recognised by Patrimonio Nacional (2004) that this work was undertaken in extremely difficult years for Spain with particular regard for the country's isolation during World War II. Although experienced stonemasons were used in the building and parts of the project were awarded to trading companies, much of the labour involved prisoners of war, it is argued, who chose to do so under a 'remission through work' scheme. This meant that the prisoners "could work off up to six days of their sentence with one of toil, although in general the ratio was three for two" (Patrimonio Nacional, 2004, p. 18). The site is managed by Patrimonio Nacional and is included in a list of properties together with El Escorial and the Royal Palaces of Madrid that are considered of historical, artistic, cultural and, most significantly, of outstanding symbolic importance (Patrimonio Nacional, 2005).

There is, however, very little interpretation concerning the Spanish Civil War either in terms of chronology or about the victims at the site. The site is a 'monument to the fallen' in the war — officially to both sides — located in a beautiful and peaceful location. It contains the tombs of Franco and Primo de Rivera and the remains of some 40,000 civil war victims (33,872 according to Pinto & Fleta, 2005) — officially from both sides. The site is also a church, which has a daily Mass, holds wedding ceremonies and contains several small chapels, a choir and all other aspects visitors would expect at a place of worship. The site attracts over 400,000 visitors per annum, although it is argued that most of these are tourists from outside Spain as part of an excursion to nearby El Escorial (Pinto & Fleta, 2005). Additional visitors include those who attend the annual commemoration of the death of Franco. Some 8,000 attended in 2004 (El País, 2004).

It is a combination of all of these factors that encourage descriptions of the site such as "an exquisite obsenity" (Roberts, 2003) and "only a Dictator could have conceived of this monstrosity" (Lonely Planet, 2004, p. 214). Crow (1985, p. 347) adds that there are those who regard the whole project as "Franco's Folly. But there are others who regard the whole thing as an imperishable creation of the nationalist regime, in which church and state were always united".

The mass graves located all over Spain that contain many of the victims from the civil war are a focus of attention for the Association for the Recovery of Historical Memory who had petitioned for the exhumation from common graves of up to 30,000 people. The PSOE (Socialist Party of Spain) lodged an amendment to a recent budget earmarking one million euros to finance the opening of mass graves (Short, 2002). As at August 2006, some 905 bodies had been exhumed although there could be a minimum of 90,000 in mass graves (El Pais, 2006). From these examples, it is apparent that politics plays an important role in the creation and development (or non-development) of the sites remaining from the civil war and this aspect is now considered in more detail.

The Role of Politics in Developing War Sites as Heritage Tourism

The interpretation of many atrocity sites from the Second World War was often propagandist from the viewpoint of the ruling power (Beech, 2000), and this is very relevant to Franco, the Valley of the Fallen and his decree that the town of Belchite be left in its destroyed state. Politics plays a strong influential role in defining the type and theme of interpretation that is presented at a heritage site. It can also determine whether any interpretation takes place at all. As argued by Harrison (2005, p. 7): "Perceptions of the past are closely linked to present hierarchies, and the voices of those at the top are often the most likely to prevail". Political influences can lead to interpretation that is inaccurate or biased, thereby rendering the visitor experience inauthentic and trivial (MacCannell, 1999; Lennon & Foley, 2000; Henderson, 2000). Tunbridge and Ashworth (1996, p. 13) also argued that sites can be susceptible to "locational manipulation for social, political or economic ends" and Crooke (2001, p. 120) adds that "history has more potential to antagonise than to gratify".

Political domination is also highlighted by Duffy (2001) in a descriptive article where he refers to the lack of any interpretation or even recognition at the site of a massacre of 100 Palestinian villagers from the village of Deir Yassin, which was destroyed. As argued by Graham, Ashworth and Tunbridge (2000, p. 69): "The relationship between heritage and atrocity is more complex than might at first appear ... accusation, counter-charge, excuse and denial". This is certainly true for the sites at the Valley of the Fallen (where political domination played a part in the creation of the site) and at Belchite (where political domination played a part in the treatment of the site) and may also play a significant role in their future. As argued by Timothy and Boyd (2003, p. 4): "heritage is not simply the past, but the modern day use of elements of the past. Whether tangible or intangible, cultural or natural, it is a part of heritage".

Certainly, the civil war sites and exhibits potentially fall within the 'dark' tourism (Lennon & Foley, 2000) category, analysed by Miles (2002) to include 'darker' and 'darkest' elements. With reference to the Spanish Civil War, the site of the Battle of the Ebro would justify a 'darker' categorisation than the exhibition 'Franco's Prisons' shown in Barcelona during 2003–2004 (Museu d'Historia de Catalunya, 2003) due to the fact that it is a 'primary' (authentic) battlefield site. However, the interpretation techniques used in the exhibition (film reel, audio and photographs) could provide an overall 'darker' experience for the visitor than a largely non-interpreted battlefield. This reaction may further depend on the nature of the visit and identity of the visitor or indeed the notoriety of the site (as evidenced by the largely non-interpreted site at Auschwitz-Birkenau, Poland).

Attempting to connect with the visitor at a site of atrocity can also be a major challenge. In addition to casual visitors, the visitor audience can comprise the victims of the atrocities that took place or relatives of the victims, the perpetrators of the atrocities or descendants of such perpetrators, members of a minority group that suffered at the site or indeed members of the dominant group. Accordingly, the interpretation adopted at the site with respect to the victims or the perpetrators can lead to the creation of a "heritage dissonance problem without parallel and any attempt to resolve it can have profoundly unsettling, if not dangerous, political consequences" (Tunbridge & Ashworth, 1996, p. 95).

Management and Interpretation of the Spanish Civil War in the Future

The Spanish government of Jose Luis Rodriguez Zapatero have confirmed that they are willing to consider the re-interpretation and orientation of the Valley of the Fallen site, a proposal that was to be placed before the Spanish parliament by June 2005 (Nash, 2005). In 2005 there was much press activity and discussion concerning the idea that a monument or interpretation centre to the victims of the civil war and Franco's reign could be created together with a study centre, an idea that had the strong support of Catalunya's Left Green Initiative (ICV). The aim would be to explain the meaning of dictatorship and the horrors committed. Around the same time the Association for the Recovery of Historical Memory lodged an appeal for the withdrawal of Francoist symbols including the Valley site. Whilst not all agree with these particular proposals, it did appear that all political parties agreed that something had to be done with the site (Pinto & Fleta, 2005). An Inter-ministerial Committee had announced that some 30 associations had submitted ideas for consideration (El País, 2005). However, the Culture Minister had indicated in March 2005, that no plan had been made and, at the time of writing in September 2006, no proposals have been forthcoming.

There are also many calls for the interpretation to remain as it stands with arguments that such a museum or monument to the horrors of war as proposed would be incompatible with the location at the Valley (Mayor de la Torre, 2005). The National Foundation for

Francisco Franco is certainly against any change in the interpretation and there is even disagreement over whether political prisoners were forced to work on the project (Richards, 2002; Fundacion Nacional Francisco Franco, 2005) as in the building of the new town of Belchite. Such ongoing disputes reflect the dissonance referred to by Tunbridge and Ashworth (1996) that can be created with heritage sites, albeit a heritage shared by the same nation with perhaps differing ideologies. The absence of any detail in the current interpretation at the Belchite and Valley of the Fallen sites certainly reduces the potential arguments against what is written. But, even though there is minimal interpretation, what is there still causes disagreement and the fact that some information is not presented causes further issues.

The potential creation of a monument or museum at the Valley of the Fallen, which attempts to interpret fascism and documents the 'truth' about the war and reasons behind the creation of the various sites from civil war is perhaps too extreme. Graham (2005) recognised the lack of a dedicated site to the civil war and indeed the (only) war museum in the capital, Museo de Ejercito, was closed in 2005 and will not re-open until around 2007, when it will be located in Toledo.

The attitude in Spain towards the civil war may however be changing, evidenced by the greater debate and publications about the war (*The Economist*, 2006) and events such as the removal (over night) of the final equine statue of Franco by the authorities from the streets of Madrid in 2005 (BBC Mundo, 2005). Progress on official acknowledgement of the impacts of the war on Spain and its people has been slow. Spain has in fact been criticised by organisations such as Amnesty International (Risi, 2005) for failing to offer truth, justice and reparation to the victims from the civil war.

The events of the Spanish Civil War are still within living memory and still play an important role in Spanish society and politics today. It is perhaps still too early to make significant changes. The 'chronological distance' (Lennon & Foley, 2000) between the occurrence of the events in the 1930s and the present time signifies that sites may and therefore continue to have resonance, albeit the seventieth anniversary of the start of the war has recently taken place. Although small interpretation sites such as the 'Ruta Orwell' have begun to appear, it may take longer for the development of Belchite as a heritage tourism attraction or the reinterpretation of the Valley of the Fallen.

Chapter 9

The Legerdemain in the Rhetoric of Battlefield Museums: Historical Pluralism and Cryptic *Parti Pris*

Craig Wight

... if heritage is the contemporary use of the past, and if its meanings are defined in the present, then we create the heritage that we require and manage it for a range of purposes defined by the needs and demands of our present societies (Graham, 2002).

Introduction

This chapter considers the causal relationship between dominant Western societal discourses and western 'war museums' by juxtaposing Lithuanian 'Genocide' museum rhetoric with United Kingdom 'Imperial War' rhetoric as speculative ontological concepts. It is suggested that although similar motivations and interpretations direct visitation (and non-visitation) to these war-themed museums (and although tragedy is showcased in each instance) visitor perceptions of the past are most strongly influenced by dominant societal discourses of the present about each nation's tragic past. The legerdemain in the battlefield tourism museum experience begins to manifest with the cultural rhetoric of war-museums (e.g., the Museum of *Genocide* Victims in Vilnius juxtaposed with the *Imperial War* Museum, London and Manchester). It is perpetuated in more complex political and societal discursive formations of the past and present that shape visitors' understandings of war-related national tragedy. Each place and period creates its own 'myth' of tragedy using the memory of historical events as the means, rather than the end. The end result of this dialectic between production and consumption of the battlefield tourism 'experience' is often the safest, most select and sanitised history being sold to visitors. Such historical and cultural pluralism is accelerated in Western war museum environments through various interpretation techniques that recreate a perceived 'authenticity' and thereby constantly reinterpret the past.

Battlefield Tourism: History, Place and Interpretation
Copyright © 2007 by Elsevier Ltd.
All rights of reproduction in any form reserved.
ISBN: 0-08-045362-7

Post Modernity and Battlefield Tourism

The emergence of 'alternative tourism' (the pursuit of unusual destinations and activities) has been noted by a growing number of theorists (e.g., Salazar, 2004). This term has come to describe the catharsis amongst the Western petit-bourgeoisie who wish to feel more worldly and better about themselves. The alternative tourists will commonly contrast the morality of their travel activity with that of the elusive 'mass tourist' who do not 'experience' travel in the way the alternative tourists can (Salazar, 2004). 'Alternative tourism' is not, however, isolated to pleasant diversion to ever more pleasant places. It increasingly refers to an interest in a 'new', multi-faceted aspect of tourism that covers a wide range of esoteric experiences and activities (Singh, 2004). One such activity receiving much attention in the media and in the academia is visitation to sites of human tragedy. Indeed, at the time of writing, there is a strong possibility that Josef Stalin's Gulag in Russia will be developed into an expensive tourism destination 'experience'. An article in the United Kingdom's *The Independent* newspaper reports (Osborn, 2006):

> Igor Shpektor; the Mayor of Vorkuta … says he is looking for an investor to turn an abandoned prison complex into a 'reality' holiday camp for novelty-seeking tourists keen to understand what life was like for Soviet political prisoners.

Objections have already arisen about the unethical subverting of such a sacred site through what is described by the developers as 'stylised suffering' (an esoteric form of *nouvelle-vague* tourism).

Researchers in tourism are increasingly trying to better understand the behaviour of tourists and tourism enterprises by recognising that histories, cultures, power relations, and aesthetics combine at a given place to create a context to influence behaviour (Davis, 2001). Hollinshead (1999) suggests that when people, nations and cultures are made 'real' through tourism they represent ideologically constructed places. Stories of peoples and cultures promoted through tourism are often staged authenticities, and visitors are essentially told what (and how) to appreciate (through compelling marketing language and imagery). Because of the immense power of tourism to create meaning, " … travel can be enlightening, silly, deadening or deprived" (Hollinshead, 1999, p. 272). Studies of meaning in the battlefield tourism context have been undertaken using various qualitative methodologies including discourse analysis in guide-books (e.g. Siegenthaler, 2002; Espelt & Benito, 2004) and overt or covert observation and interviewing (e.g., Beech, 2000).

Existing research into aspects of so-called 'battlefield tourism' have commented notably on aspects such as visitor motivation and interpretation of sites (Lennon & Foley, 2000; Beech, 2000; Siegenthaler, 2002). Of importance are the methods employed by 'battlefield' tourism attraction managers in the commoditisation of such sites, and the employed methods of interpretation, such as media, signage and simulation. Lennon and Foley (2000) comment on the evolution of Auschwitz concentration camp in Poland, from its original function into its present capacity as a purpose-constructed tourism 'experience', in which very little of the original structures and artefacts are displayed. Time and space are brought closer to the visitor through the interactive, meaning-laden use of signage, tour guide and guide book narratives, and the positioning of imported structures that together form a logical tour with strategically positioned 'high' (or low) points.

Prejudices and expectations are thereby formed within the context of battlefield tourism sites (viewed as indicative units of culture within wider populations or 'destinations'). The myth of warfare is projected in and by films, novels, games, the media and folklore *inter alia* which are laden with meaning and which often lead to histories being contested. Nonetheless, the visitor experience provided is an easily realised marketing concept that is a 'constructed' cultural tourism interface.

Tracking the Discourses of Tragedy through Tourism: Lithuanian and United Kingdom Examples

There is a growing awareness among museum circles that museums are institutions in which power and societal identities are contested (Whitmarsh, 2001). The nation's collective memory of war often forms part of its self-image (Whitmarsh, 2001), and it is the ever-altering societal attitudes to war (re-evaluating and contesting the past) that are reflected in commemorative environments. Whitmarsh (2001) exemplifies this cross-culturally using the example of Germany, which:

> … has been said to have undergone successive phases of either repressing or attempting to come to terms with its Nazi and Cold War history.

Some useful overarching work has been undertaken in the context of tracking discourse in battlefield commemorative environments by Siegenthaler (2002). Using textual analysis, Siegenthaler makes crucial observations, such as the absence of photographs and images (which he expected to see) depicting human suffering prior to and immediately after the bombings. His observations of the images holistically combine with hypotheses on the written text to later form the conclusion that 'sight sacralisation' underlies Japanese commemoration (the sights, he posits, are advertised to tourists as emblematic of the dedicated rebuilding of post-war Japan, not as shrines to victim-hood).

Such research confirms the relevance of critical discourse analysis in the domain of battlefield tourism, particularly in the battlefield museum context and in academic debates over authenticity and reconstructed histories (as in e.g., Salamone, 1997 & Chronis, 2005). Many 'battlefield' attractions can be described as recreations of history that function through interpretation and commentary, including 'living heritage' and 'live heritage' *inter alia.* 'Living' or 'live' heritage involves the bringing to life of history through acting, re-enactments and narrative amongst others (Schouten, 1995) and can be described as the 'signified' in semiotic terms. Artefacts, and often entire 'dark' attractions and sites are contextualised through the use of interpretation (thus, the 'signified'). Critical discourse analysis helps conceptualise 'meaning' in instances of commemoration of death and disaster. As a methodological praxis, it enables the researcher to make telling observations about the image-rich polyglot of battlefield tourism sites (certainly in the West). Horne (1992, cited in Hollinshead, 1999) views contemporary tourism as a 'festival' and a 'celebrated event' and considers that it conquers territories, storylines and populations through the power of the Eurocentric imagination. Museums (and in this context, 'battle-field' museums) as memorial sites are the primary vehicles of public culture tourism (Hollinshead, 1998). They are the institutional apparatuses of societal beliefs and values. Memory, and in particular the memorialisation process, provides societies with security, authority, legitimacy and identity in the present (Whitmarsh, 2001). Such memory is projected through the (often emotive) language used in and by museums, a language frequently peppered with undertones of coercion and patriotic (sometimes jingoistic) traditional beliefs.

War museums typically showcase architectural features, which possess meaning and present themes to the visitors individually (as exhibits) and collectively (as institutions using exhibits as collective units of interpretation). The meta-narrative of the battlefield museum is therefore rife with artificial signs throughout the temporal and spatial arrangement of the wider texts. Interpretation, in the form of written signage, imagery and narrative frequently acts as the 'signified' when it comes to perceiving artefacts. The proximity of these artefacts, and the way in which they are laid out ('proxemics'), convey singular meaning as artefacts of the time (Jones, 1996), but they also accentuate the inter-relatedness of the wider exhibition through the use of interpretation and spatial arrangement.

Deutschlander and Miller (2004) endorse that language constitutes, rather than reflects reality and that language is used by actors (within the tourism industry) strategically to accomplish an objective or set of objectives in particular settings. The concept is applicable to analyses of the language of war museums and visitor experiences within these. Consider, for example, the semantic reaches of 'imperial' as terminology in the sanitised UK war museum environment. The chronological distance discussed in Lennon and Foley (2000) is relevant here in hypothesising that the type of language used depends on how recent or how long ago the event took place, and depends as much on the chronological passage of large-scale cultural rhetoric. The initial purpose of the Imperial War Museum was to function as 'a memorial to those who died and suffered in the First World War' (Imperial War Museum, 2006), whereas now the museum asserts it: "concentrates on all conflicts concentrating on British and Commonwealth involvement from 1914 to the present" (Imperial War Museum, 2006). The latter signifies more strongly the implications of 'imperialism' in the rhetoric of the museum and this reflects, to some degree, the passage that the discourse of war commemoration has taken in the UK since the museum opened. As Dann (1996, p. 4) concludes, "discourse reinforces 'praxis' and vice versa" suggesting a dialectic, or continuum of discourse between producer and consumer that is directly influential to the visitor experience at a given time. Moral anxieties over the 'human cost of war' have, perhaps in this way, been transferred from consumer to institution and vice versa, in the shape of the Imperial War Museum of the North, Manchester, discussed below.

In 2002 the Imperial War Museum opened their Manchester branch, The Imperial War Museum of the North. This was intended to differentiate the imperial war museum experience by introducing human suffering as a concept through interpretation of events, as recent as the September 11th, 2001 attacks on the World Trade Centre, in New York. A sample of visitors (Wight & Lennon, 2005) provided mixed responses when articulating how the museum experience made them feel and what it made them think about. Responses recorded on the latter question included thoughts on terrorism and on the Iraq war as well as thoughts about World Wars I and II (these were invariably across age groups).

It is the interpretation within the war museum and the language of the war museum experience that brings these emotions to the surface (Wight & Lennon, 2005). These in turn (although not alone) temper the societal discourses of war that go on to inform museum management of approaches that must react to popular demand and that must re-tell events in a way that is acceptable to the public.

The Imperial War Museum, institutionally, showcases 20th century conflict involving Britain and the Commonwealth. War is commonly associated with imperialism, racism, nationalism, patriotism and the unquestioning sacrifice of life (Whitmarsh, 2001). War museums would therefore seem (hypothetically at least) to signify such concepts, yet the interpretation within the Imperial War Museum (in London and Manchester) defies these emotional contagions preferring to confer a sanitised sense of national pride through a celebration of the technology of warfare and through exhibiting such tendentious displays as pristine uniforms (as clean as the day they were issued (Whitmarsh, 2001)), gleaming tanks and other technological 'marvels'. Indeed, as noted in Whitmarsh (2001) the Imperial War Museum, collectively, has projected an ambiguous and controversial message from the start. The war dead are frequently portrayed in the Imperial War Museum as:

> ... the courageous, the heroes who made the supreme sacrifice. There is nothing to raise questions about the appropriateness of this sacrifice, of its necessity or the conditions under which it occurred (Hamilton, 1994, cited in Whitmarsh, 2001).

The Museum of Genocide Victims in Vilnius is the antithesis of 'Imperial' rhetoric and the visitor experience is shaped by a very different configuration of political and cultural influencers. The interpretive setting is one of stark imagery of and about Lithuanian national heroes of war and the political circumstances and human hardships suffered at the time of the events presented.

Lithuania has only recently (about 15 years ago at the time of writing) become independent from its Russian occupiers. Russian occupiers retreated from the capital, Vilnius in 1991. The first museum dedicated to memorialising the persecutions suffered at the hands of Soviets was opened in 1992: the Museum of Genocide Victims. The exhibitions are located in a building that has previously served as, variously, a courthouse, a Nazi Gestapo headquarters and most recently, prior to becoming a museum, a KGB prison for political dissidents.

The visitor experience provided by the KGB museum is realised strongly around a blunt, dauntless language of victim-hood and nationalistic pride of a highly patriotic flavour about a brave partisan movement, who fought the Soviet occupiers persistently right up until independence was restored. Interestingly, what is at best overlooked (and at worst massively perverted) is the section of history that deals with local Lithuanian Nazi collaboration (and Lithuanian Russian collaboration) and the organised execution of tens of thousands of Lithuanian Jews during World War II. Instead what is 'experienced' is cultural *parti pris* of an essentially nationalistic nature, focussing on the violent death of Lithuanian national heroes at the hands of cruel Soviet oppressors. Collaboration between Lithuanian nationals and Nazis is withdrawn from the institution's language almost completely.

Staiff (no date, p. 1) lays the foundations to this argument in a study of the conjuring of images associated with Venice in Italy, "Tourism didn't of course invent the 'myth of Venice' but it continues to stage it, because at the heart of the myth is desire and anticipation". The 'myth' referred to is staged through a 'commodity culture', which is made up of 'rich visuality, dreams, mystery and magic' Staiff (no date, p. 1). The author goes on to argue that 'place', in the sense of the destination, is not a material entity that exists autonomously, but is a habit whereby the material place is defined by a series of discourses that then become inseparable from the material place. Thus, it is possible to observe manifestations of the post modern 'polyglot' in cases of battlefield tourism sites. Attitudes, interpretation, micro- and macro-management (of attractions and destinations) and performative broadcasting combine to form the post-modern language of and about battlefield tourism. Images, symbols, escapism, commentary and narrative influence and perpetuate interpretation. Battlefield tourism can therefore be considered pre-figuratively post-modern (Salazar, 2004), since it is a combination of the visual, the aesthetic, the commercial and the popular.

In Lithuanian 'battlefield' museums, it is the 'Genocide rhetoric' that is emerging as the preferred commemorative language. The dominant institutional apparatus of 'tragedy discourse' in Vilnius is the Museum of 'Genocide' Victims in the centre of this Baltic capital (Wight & Lennon, 2006). In this commemorative environment, the historical circumstances (suffering and state sponsored murder) are chronologically nearby. Indeed, the historical and societal markers of conflict are only now (after a long period of turbulent political history) beginning to be reinterpreted to the public in museums. Tracking the discourses of tragedy in this country's museums is an important exercise in understanding the burgeoning discursive 'myths' of Lithuanian 'battlefield heritage'.

Already, there is contention over the use of the term 'genocide' in the context of the Lithuanian Museum of Genocide Victims. Indeed, the use of the 'genocide rhetoric' is concerning when only (approximately) one mile from the museum gates is the Lithuanian State Jewish Museum, which uses markedly less emotive rhetoric in its title and in its showcasing of Jewish history through exhibits and narrative. This museum prefers, instead, to provide a visitor experience focussed on celebrating Jewish history, whilst interpretation concerned with the Holocaust that was visited on over 90% of the wartime population makes up only a small proportion of the exhibitions (Wight & Lennon, 2006). 'Genocide' is becoming a common term used to signify human tragedy on various scales, according to various definitions. The former Secretary-General of Médicins Sans Frontières complains in a recent BBC article on genocide in Darfur that:

> The term (genocide) has progressively lost its initial meaning and is becoming dangerously commonplace. Those who should use the word never let it slip their mouths. Those who unfortunately do use it banalise it into a validation of every kind of victim-hood (BBC, 2005).

The academic secretary of the Lithuanian Jewish State Museum insists that the Museum of Genocide Victims should commemorate 'victimisation', 'exploitation' and 'Soviet illtreatment' rather than using the term 'genocide' and all that it implies (Wight & Lennon, 2006). The unassuming English speaking visitor to Vilnius could be forgiven for believing in the 'pastoral myth' of the brave persecuted wartime Lithuanian partisan, and it may not be long before Hollywood embeds this image firmly in Western discourse through films.

Conclusion

The legerdemain in the language of battlefield tourism museums exists in a unique system of signs (texts, imagery and narrative) that holistically showcase historical 'myth' for mass consumption. Battlefield heritage is part of the knowledge economy of a nation (Graham, 2002) and such heritage is a social construction with ideologies firmly locked into the language of the tourism experience. Dominant cultural and political ideologies create specific place identities (Graham, 2002), and heritage can take a variety of official and non-official forms. The institution of the Imperial War Museum remains focussed on the technology of warfare through sanitised interpretation. The discourses that are nurtured via such a static institution are sanitised and shaped by inoffensive, 'authentic' interpretation such as technology (for example tanks and weapons), clothing and 'imperial' meta-narrative.

The museums that institutionally commemorate war in Lithuania, however, remain conspicuously unconsolidated in their approach to history and sensational (often shocking) sign systems dominate the memorialisation process. It is these 'non-official' accounts of warfare (demonstrated in this chapter using the example of 'genocide' rhetoric in a Lithuanian museum) that merit closer examination when tracking the evolution of battlefield discourse. The rhetoric of 'genocide' in Vilnius sits awkwardly with the story of Lithuanian Holocaust, and the tragic past of this nation remains partially interpreted and holistically contested. The 'myths' of battlefield history are perpetuated in this way; in ideologically constructed commemorative environments that showcase trendy-tragedy to an increasingly attentive audience.

ACTS OF DISCOVERY AND REDISCOVERY

Introduction

Chris Ryan

Battlefields are places of historic action, locations of conflict that over time, as discussed previously, are subject to 'cooling'. It has also been noted that the passing of time is no neutral process and 'cooling' is itself interpreted and re-interpreted. Subsequent generations come to seek clarification of chronologies and sequencing of battles, of who was where at what time, and military historians come to debate the wisdom of tactics and strategies. Political historians contextualize the battles with processes of aspirations and ideologies, while social historians may seek to give voice to the individuals caught up in events, indicating how they exemplified social conditions so that they speak directly to us over the years through their diaries and observations. Within this process selection and filtering of what is thought important occurs and the events are interpreted and re-interpreted for successive contemporary audiences so that the historic becomes an interpreted and evaluated heritage drawn from a resource of discovered papers, existent relics, literary association and popular culture as well as the writings of scholars.

What motivates this process? First, it is often argued that such events become part of our culture. Indeed the myths and events of past battles have been shown to be powerful sources of identity and yet even further conflict as is illustrated by the Battle of Kosovo in 1389, that was to resonate again in the final part of the twentieth century. The sites and relics found at them are perceived as valuable in themselves and thus need to be preserved. Hence, the processes of categorisation, previously described by Piekarz, and the need for visitor centres and museums. Second, the identification of sites and the stories associated with them as possessing importance is an act of legitimization — it provides a justification for given sets of action and thus potentially acquires political importance. The type of political importance can vary. Claims upon the state for funding support are themselves a political action; endorsement by the state is also a political action as it is a recognition of acts of patronage and legitimization of 'approved' stories. Finally, as has been noted, historic battlefield sites can be used for economic regeneration as in the case of 'Red Tourism' and the Eureka Stockade as discussed by Gu, Ryan, and Zhang (2007) and Frost (2007), respectively in this book.

Implicit in these ideas is that the visitor to battlefield sites can engage upon acts of discovery or rediscovery. It has been noted, for example, by Tunbridge and Ashworth (1996), that such acts can be ones of dissonance whereby dominant ideologies are either legimitized or questioned. Equally, the acts of discovery can be sanitized as different generations are motivated by curiosity about the past, but such curiosity becomes but a part of a wider, more contemporary concern related to the prosaic such as, for example, shopping. It has long been noted in the academic literature of tourism that tourists can be segmented, clustered and often differentiated by the patterns and level of their interests. Equally, it is a cliché to argue that such categorization is a categorization of role, where roles may be temporary and not permanent. Again, the literature is replete with distinctions between sustained, continuing commitment that might be associated with 'serious leisure' and that commitment which is situational and contextual to a specific place, moment or indeed social grouping.

This section contains three chapters that possess obvious overlaps with the other 'acts' of the book, but which have been separately categorized under the heading of 'acts of discovery and rediscovery' because they illustrate the complexity of such acts. The first, by Charlie Panakera describes places very familiar to the author. He spent his youth in the Solomon Islands, became a Member of Parliament and resort complex owner, and took visitors to sites such as the location of the sinking of the patrol boat PT-109 commanded by John Fitzgerald Kennedy, the then future President of the United States who was to be assassinated in 1963. In a sense then, Panakera was one of the makers of myths. However, he uses his chapter to describe several 'acts of rediscovery', thereby aptly describing the complexity of these actions. First, there is an act of rediscovery on the part of the servicemen who were involved in the actions of the Second World War in the Solomon's. Essentially, these members of the forces were of a generation whose sole knowledge of the South Pacific prior to the 1940s would have been derived from, in the most part, a popular culture that contained Hollywood films such as the 1935 Charles Laughton film of the *Mutiny on the Bounty* and the earlier, 1932 film, *Birds of Paradise*, starring Dolores Del Rio and Joel McCrea in a story of a sailor falling in love with a Polynesian girl. The 'hot' war tourism of the Second World War for such servicemen was an opportunity to 're'-discover a different South Pacific and as such Panakera's contribution links with that of Piekarz's chapter in this same section in illustrating how war time participants can engage in acts of tourism. Second, Panakera illustrates how war created a tourism industry for the Solomon's, and how the infrastructure of war came to be used by the tourism industries of accommodation and transportation. Next, Panakera illustrates how the impact of war came to be, itself, a catalyst for social change, which too had implications for the future development of tourism in the islands. Finally, in further evidence of the cooling of hot destinations, Panakera traces the emergence of a nostalgia market (as postulated by Weaver, 2000) in the Solomons and thence the role of Japanese visitors — thereby linking with the chapter by Malcolm Cooper.

Li-Hui Chang and Chris Ryan also describe a 'cooled down' or 'tepid' destination wherein the infrastructure of past conflict, namely the tunnels and barracks on what was the very heavily fortified island of Kinmen (Quemoy), have become a touristic backdrop to growing tourism flows. Within these flows, the citizens of Taiwan and in particular Fujian Province of the People's Republic increasingly intermingle to engage in sightseeing, business and recreational tourism. For many on both sides of the straits, not only are the honeycomb of tunnels part of the tourist product, so too is the opportunity to have a direct line of vision of former enemy positions. This chapter is interesting in many respects. First, it might be said that the commodification of experiences through the packaging of tours offers a sanitized way acceptable to both sides of a political divide whereby the serious business of making money can be permitted in spite of continuing outbursts of political tensions between the various involved stakeholders. Packaged tours have long been an accepted part of the holiday business, and thus while often derided as being controlled experiences, their very structure ensures their acceptance within the current political regimes. Second, however, the text also hints at the fuzziness of boundaries of these packages, wherein the economically advantaged are able to use the political status of the island — a status that owes much to its past as well as its geographical position (indeed the two are mutually and symbiotically associated) — for individual pleasure through shopping and nightlife experiencing. In a sense, the battlefield site were the Straits and the Island of Kinmen itself, and so today visitors flow through the site of past hostility, which embraces them and reminds them as they rediscover past, living commonalities of family linkages that have been sustained and are being reborn as past hostilities become more distant even while the echoes remain strongly audible.

The third chapter in this part of the book is a further contribution by Mark Piekarz and, in many ways, brings to the fore that which is implicit in the previous two chapters, and links with the earlier chapter by Prideaux. Piekarz's thesis is that tourism is not just a matter retained solely for a cooled down site — that even in the midst of extended periods of tension, many of those associated with battle will engage in tourism-related activities. Equally, with the cessation of hostilities, there emerge a group concerned with physical, social, economic and political reconstruction — and these too visit places with the eyes of the newly arrived, buying souvenirs, interacting with locals and taking photographs. The very context of war thus becomes the catalyst and embryo of tourism. Piekarz also notes, as Wight has done already in this book, that these are not new phenomenon. Past conflict indeed attracted spectators to the very site of battle, as was evident in the initial battles of the American Civil War.

It is evident that battlefield sites are subject to different articulations almost from the outset. While it is natural to believe that the dominant story is one of fighting, troop movements, tactics and the technologies of weapons, almost from the outset there are potentially other stories springing up almost simultaneously. There might be spectators with their stories, there are, as Panakera notes, the inhabitants of those lands where conflict occurs, there is the interaction between combatants and those peoples, there are the peacekeepers who follow — all have stories as well as the differing perspectives of the two or more opposing forces. Attempts to contextualize battles and to assess the nature of their impacts upon societies require decisions as to whether these voices are to be silenced or permitted to speak — and these decisions are never made in perpetuity but are revisited time and time again as social conditions change and representatives of past stakeholders make claims and counter-claims. Implicit in this argument is a view that evidence continues to exist of hitherto silenced voices, waiting to be rediscovered. Arguably, in the instance of battles several hundreds of years ago, such evidence becomes lost, while in a contemporary age, the issue potentially becomes one of sifting through an excess of data if one is to examine the blogs and e-mails as well as the official manuscripts of contemporary warfare. Certainly, the Second Gulf War has already proven that what is recorded by participants on the internet is important. For example, it has significantly shaped interpretations of legitimacy of American presence in Iraq when one considers the photographs of Abu Graib. Thus the internet has proven to be a means by which silenced voices become a dominant discourse even as the Bush presidency has sought to control media coverage of the war — for example, by banning news images of returning coffins from Iraq and embedding reporters with American forces. Today the processes of discovery and rediscovery are complex, but what is disturbing in the interpretation of battlefield sites is how the photographs of Abu Graib might be likened to the photographs taken by 'normal' tourists — for these too were souvenirs that recorded presence and acts of 'being there'.

Chapter 10

World War II and Tourism Development in Solomon Islands

Charlie Panakera

The demand by American Marine and Army personnel for such things as sea shell carvings, walking sticks, grass skirts, combs and so on resulted in even people my age focusing on making or finding something to sell. I was fourteen years old in 1942/1943 and actively involved in making walking-sticks, combs and grass skirts.

Sir Frederick Osifelo of Malaita,
Solomon Islands

Introduction

World War II was a watershed event in the history of the Pacific region (Oliver, 1961; Grattan, 1963). These islands witnessed some of the most prolonged and ferocious fighting of the war. To wage their military campaigns, the Allies and Japanese poured hundreds of thousands of troops and millions of tons of material into islands once isolated on the colonial fringe. A sudden confrontation with the military power and economic resources of Japan, America and Allied forces left deep and enduring marks on post-war history and culture in the area, especially in the Solomon Islands. In many areas, intense wartime experiences and cross-cultural interactions have been linked to subsequent struggles for increased autonomy, power, and wealth-struggles to redefine economic and political relations with ruling colonial authorities (Worsley, 1968). World War II was the largest and most violent armed conflict in the history of mankind (Frank, 1990). However, the six decades since that conflict has exacted its toll on collective knowledge of that period. While World War II continues to absorb the interest of military scholars and historians, as well as its veterans, a generation has grown to maturity largely unaware of the political, social, and military implications of a war that, more than any other, united the Solomons as a people with a common purpose (Inglis, 1998).

Therefore this chapter has two main themes and a related subsidiary. The fighting in the Solomon Islands in the Second World War was savage and by land, air, and sea. Yet, in the midst of the carnage servicemen from the United States and elsewhere had contact with peoples of the Solomons; and both groups underwent change. Part of that interaction was that servicemen acted at times like tourists in wanting souvenirs of the strange places and times in which they found themselves. For their part Solomon Islanders began to learn that even in wartime their traditional culture and crafts possessed a monetary value. Therefore this chapter first describes this wartime tourism. Additionally the infrastructure left by the war also helped develop tourism resources, and these too will be described. Second, the war left its scars upon land and sea; and these places of conflict have served as tourist sites for the decades since the war. Consequently the chapter will describe some of the ways in which these have been capitalised upon, and the ways in which overseas powers have structured their own interpretations upon a Solomon Island landscape. Finally, civil unrest has itself impacted upon tourism in more recent times in the Solomon Islands, and therefore some brief mention is made of the ways in which these conflicts have impacted upon Solomon Island tourism.

The Guadalcanal War Zone, the Solomon Islands, and Wartime Tourism

The Past

In 2005 the Allied Forces, USA and the Japanese participated in the 60th anniversary to commemorate the end of World War II, and in particular the Guadalcanal War in the Solomon Islands. The commemoration included the publication of various materials to help educate Americans, Australian, New Zealanders, Pacific Islanders, and Japanese people about that war which was waged on land, on sea, and in the air over several diverse theatres of operation for approximately six years (Innes, 2005).

On 7 December 1941, Imperial Japanese forces turned their war on the Asian mainland eastward and southward into the Pacific with simultaneous attacks on Pearl Harbour, the Philippines, Wake, Guam, Hong Kong, and the Malay Peninsula. The rapid southward advance of Japanese armies and naval task forces in the following months found Western leaders poorly prepared for war in the Pacific (Dunningan & Nofi, 1998). Nevertheless, they conferred quickly and agreed that, while maintaining the 'German first' course they had set against the Axis, they also had to blunt Japanese momentum and keep open lines of communication to Australia and New Zealand. As the Japanese closed on those two island democracies, the Allies scrambled to shore up defences, first by fortifying the Malay Barrier, and then, after the Japanese smashed through that line, by reinforcing an Australian drive north across New Guinea. To make this first Allied offensive in the Pacific more effective, the Americans mounted a separate attack from a different direction to form a giant pincers in the Southwest Pacific. This decision brought American and Allied forces into the Solomon Islands and US Army troops onto the island of Guadalcanal.

Between March 1942 and December 1944, the Southwest Pacific was the scene of major troop movements, battles, and the construction of large military bases. The Solomon Islands became the focal point of an intense struggle between Allied and Japanese forces from August 1942 to August 1943. Approximately "half a million allied and Japanese servicemen served in the Solomons" during that time (Boutilier, 1979, p. 8).

Infrastructure and War

The war was, of course, destructive of the islands as well as the lives of Islanders. It also brought positive changes in the form of facilities and economic infrastructure and new work opportunities for Islanders. The wartime creation of an economic infrastructure and attendant new social relations between Islanders and servicemen led the way for subsequent social and economic changes, including tourism, in the region. Building airfields, roads, wharf facilities, communication systems, hospitals, and housing were major activities undertaken to support combat and military administration in the Southwest Pacific (Bedford, 1973; Bellam, 1970; Philibert, 1976). At the same time, the events of the war and its immediate aftermath created significant places and visible reminders of the conflict that have become tourist sites (de Burlo, 1984).

Developed infrastructures did not exist before the war on many Islands (Garrison, 1983). The present capital of Solomon Islands, Honiara, came into being after World War II, when the British administration moved from Tulagi on Nggela Island, to Guadalcanal. Before the war, the town was only sparsely settled. The establishment of military bases created such basic infrastructure as all-weather roads, wharves, water systems, and airfields important for future economic development in the islands. Honiara was born of war's necessities. Honiara takes its name from the 'local' description of its site: 'naho ni ara', meaning 'facing the east and southeast wind'. Henderson Airport was begun during the war by Japanese forces (including Korean labourers) and completed by American forces after their landing on Guadalcanal. Its capacity made it the country's international airport. On outlaying islands there are also airstrips built during the war; these airfields, key goals of military construction efforts during World War II, are critical for the growth of commercial aviation in the islands as well as tourism development in provincial areas.

The place names of land battles — Tenaru River, Matanikau, 'Edson's Ridge' (Bloody Ridge) on Guadalcanal, and Tulagi on Nggela — and of naval battles — Santa Cruz, Vella Gulf, Kula Gulf, Cape Esperance, and Tassafarango — live on in the memories of veterans of the Japanese, American and Allied forces, as well as in those Solomon Islanders who witnessed these encounters. Today wartime history, relics, and memorials are themselves among the main tourist attractions of Solomon Islands and other Pacific Island areas. War scars and memory are inscribed in the hills, valleys, and rivers surrounding the airport, reflecting the savage fighting that took place there as the Japanese attempted to retake the airfield over the course of six months in 1942 and 1943. On top of this geography of war, one now finds another layer of memory in the form of plaques, monuments, and memorials placed as significant points and as public reminders of the events that once made the Solomon Islands the centre of world attention. The international visitor arriving by air in the Solomon Islands is not long in the country before encountering reminders of World War II. Immediately upon exiting the small air terminal, the visitor faces three memorial obelisks dedicated by US Marine veterans in 1982. Just down the road, at the base of the original control tower, another monument and bronze plaque were installed by American veterans in 1992 during the 50th anniversary of the Guadalcanal landings. Just as the war and its relics were the products of foreign powers, so too are these reminders of war the products of foreign ways of remembering.

The Guadalcanal War was, after all, a war between the Allies and Japan, fought over the terrain of colonised societies. The monuments and plaques that memorialise it have been installed by veterans and government wishing to commemorate the sacrifices of their citizen-combatants, often with references to the roles of Solomon Islanders in supporting the war effort. But what are the meanings of the war for indigenous Solomon Islanders? And what, for them, would be the purpose(s) of preserving them? Answers to these questions are complex, entangled in the political realities of new nations attempting to articulate their own identities and histories, while at the same time attracting investment and tourism from former colonising powers.

Location

The Solomons Island archipelagos are practically innumerable. A thousand and one, it is said, make up the cluster called the Russell group, and at least as many more festoon the southeast shores of New Georgia, centring the whole complex of archipelagos. The more practical estimate lists 13 large islands nearly enclosing a central passage which, ever since the war, has been called The Slot, and which runs southeast and northwest between 5 and 12 degrees south latitude and 155 and 170 east longitude. At the top end are Bougainville and Buka, now part of Papua New Guinea (PNG); all the rest being grouped as the Solomon Islands. On the eastern and northern side of The Slot are Choiseul, Santa Isabel, Malaita, and San Cristobal; on the western, New Georgia, Rendova, Kolombangara, Vella Lavella, the Treasuries, and the Shortlands. In a central position lies Florida, Guadalcanal, the Russells, and to the south, well away from the crowd, is Rennel and Bellonal. Most of the indigenous inhabitants are Melanesian, some extremely dark with fair, tawny hair; but ocean-wandering Polynesians have settled in many of the distant outliers: Rennell, Bellona, Tikopia, Sikaiana, Ongtong Java, Taumako, and Anuta.

Total land area is 29,800 km^2. The terrain is rugged and scatted with dormant volcanoes. High rainfall and tropical temperatures make for dense rainforest vegetation. Birds, butterflies, and reptiles exist in abundance and the seas are rich in marine life.

The Solomon Islands is a parliamentary democracy within the Commonwealth, with a unicameral Parliament and a ministerial system of government. It has a population estimated to be 538,000 in 2005. The British monarch is represented by a governor general, chosen by the Parliament for a 5-year term. The national Parliament has 50 members, elected for 4-year terms. For local government, the country is divided into 10 administrative areas, of which nine are provinces administered by elected provincial assemblies, and the 10th is the town of Honiara, the capital and administered by the Honiara Town Council.

Aviation and Accommodation

The British colonial government of the Solomon Islands paid little attention to developing tourism (Boutilier, 1979; PATA, 1985a); nor has the national government since independence in 1978. Tourism has therefore evolved slowly, based on emerging patterns of niche tourism demand seeking a different location outside the main tourist flows, or alternatively a demand associated with a specific wartime relationship with the islands. World War II radically changed the South Pacific by leaving a legacy of advanced aircraft design and manufacture, a surplus of aircraft, an increase awareness of other cultures and geographical locations. A significant growth of tourism in the South Pacific began in the mid-1960s when large-capacity jet aircraft operating on trunk routes and packaged tours made the area more accessible to wider markets. Fiji became a regional hub and tourist destination. On the other hand countries such as Vanuatu, the Solomon Islands, and PNG had only nascent or no tourism, being off the main air service routes. The emergence of long haul routes served by aircraft not requiring mid-Pacific refuelling stops also impacted on island tourism in the 1980s.

Nonetheless by 1960, ex-service men from Australia, New Zealand, USA, and Japan were making regular tours to PNG and Solomon Islands. To capitalise on movement of veterans between the two countries, a regular charter service between Solomon Islands and PNG was established in 1962. A domestic airline, *Solomon Islands Megapode Airline*, was established in 1963 by Captain Crowley to operate out of Henderson field, a wartime strip, at Honiara on Guadalcanal.

A de Havilland Dove was acquired and offered a regular service to major ports in the region. In June 1986 a PNG operator, *Macair*, purchased Megapode and dry leased another Dove. The new airline was renamed *Solomon Airways* (*SolAir*). In 1975 there was a take over by another PNG operator, *Talair*. At this stage *SolAir* was recognised as the smallest international operator in the world, its international route being between Honiara (Solomon Islands) and Kieta, in Bougainville (PNG), while operating two Doves and two Beech Barons (Pacific Regional Transport Study, 2004). In addition to the veteran market, there was a large expatriate population of over 10,000 people, primarily employed by the Bougainville Copper Mine (BCL).

This market and route provided *SolAir* with its highest yield for many years and further prompted the development of inter-regional tourism between PNG and Solomon Islands. Expatriate visitors from Bougainville and their families regularly visited and still visit the Solomon Islands for wreck diving, snorkelling, and fishing.

In 1976 the Solomon Islands government became directly involved in *SolAir* by purchasing 49% of the shares with an option to purchase the remaining 51% within five years. Eventually, in 1984 the government did purchase the remaining 51% of shares making *SolAir* a fully government-owned airline. Political involvement in the airline affected the company almost immediately. For example, there were at one stage, three general managers within a 12-month period. The government also found that accumulated losses were higher than they had believed when taking over the airline.

In 1989 the airline decided to expand its international services independently. It leased a 737-200 from International Lease Finance Corporation (ILFC) and began services from Honiara, Auckland, Nadi (Fiji), Port Vila (Vanuatu), Port Moresby (PNG), Cairns, and

Brisbane. On all routes, except those to Australia, the seating capacity was shared between the Solomon Islands and a designated carrier of the destination country (Pacific Region Transport Study, 2004). A new service to Tonga was introduced with code sharing arrangements with Royal Tongan Airlines. Internationally, *SolAir* operates a virtual airline strategy. It does not own any aircraft for its international routes but has series of arrangements with Air Vanuatu and Air Nauru, under which it charters and/or code shares aircraft owned by those airlines (World Bank, 1993).

Formal accommodation for travellers in the Solomon Islands prior to the World War II was non-existent. When the Allied soldiers went home after World War II they left behind the foundation for a Solomon Islands tourist industry. Networks of roads, bridges, port facilities, and airfield as well as telecommunication systems, refrigeration plants, water pumping stations, and building were scattered about (PIM, 1942). In Honiara, enterprising expatriate Kenneth Dalrymple Hay took over some officers' facilities in 1948 and opened it the following year as the nine-room Woodford Hotel. The opening was performed with a hatchet, the licensee having lost the key (PIM, 1949). The Mendana Hotel, which replaced Woodford, was opened in 1958. Mendana Hotel remained the only significant hotel until Arthur Blum, a US marine who had visited Solomon Islands as part of a medical corporation and who returned in 1954 with a mission to promote the Bahai'i faith, built Blums Hometel in 1966. Blum was encouraged to build the Hometel when one evening he found a senior Ni-Vanuatu government representative outside Mendana Hotel saying he had been refused accommodation by Dalrymple Hay who was well known for his racist policies. As a Bahai'i Blum believed in 'oneness of mankind' and this incident enraged him. Between them, Dalrymple Hay and Blum generally took care of most needs of the Honiara community. The former had ice plant, the butcher shop, a general store, and the hotel; the latter had the bakery, a general store, and the Hometel. The former also kept the last hotel in the South Pacific to have 'closed door' against non-white people:

> You run a hotel as a business, not to please people who might have ideas. I keep out the Solomon Islanders because I don't want to lower my standards. They accuse me of discrimination but that's rubbish. Solomon Islanders can't stay at my hotel because they are not at all at the stage where they are fit to stay here. Certainly some of them are, but if I let some in but keep most of them out then that would be discrimination (cited Inder, 1966).

A sign that the *status quo* was changing came when Peter Kenilorea, later to be Prime Minister, wrote to *Pacific Islands Monthly* suggesting that while he was encouraged to note that the opinions and attitudes of Mr. Dalrymple Hay were in the minority, "he will have to change his ideas and measure up to the demands of the majority or else learn that there is such a word as 'commandeer' in the English language" (PIM, 1966). Sir Mariano Kelesi, past Chairman of the Solomon Tourist Authority and Member of the Legislative Assembly, recalled being "thrown out" of the Mendana Bar by Dalrymple Hay when a group of young local Members of the Legislative Council tried to drink beer but had yet to still get a permit to purchase spirit (BSIP, 1962). "He ordered us out practically at gunpoint so we went and changed the legislation which he couldn't cope with. It was not whiskey Solomon Islanders wanted but freedom" (BSI, 1964).

In 1984 Mendana Hotel was purchased by Kitano Holding, a Japanese hotel franchise, and renamed Kitano Hotel to cater for the growing Japanese market.

Blums Hometel was named Hibiscus Hotel when a new owner took over in 1979. In 2003 Islands Hotels Limited, an Australian public company, together with other investment properties and hotels in Solomon Islands, PNG, and Australia, purchased Hibiscus hotel and renamed it King Solomons Hotel.

Accommodation during the 1960s and 1970s was mainly centred in Honiara. There were small guesthouses on Malaita, Munda and Gizo, and Kirakira. In Guadalcanal, three resorts were built, the beachside Tambea resort, and two very small 'hideaway' facilities, Tavanipupu and Ngarando to which visitors had to take their all food supplies and which were used primarily by resident expatriates seeking to escape Honiara for a weekend. The Travelodge group had been promising for many years to develop a two acre beachfront site in Honiara with a hotel worth over AUD$1million (PIM, 1971) but by 1980 those responsible for tourism were still stoically announcing no further development projects had been proposed let alone completed (STA, 1980).

One of the more controversial tourism developments occurred during the 1980s. Accompanying a small surge of international tourism investment during this period by French and South Korean interests, Hong Kong Chinese proposed a 'sub-sea village' (Islands Business, 1984). In the end the proposal of an Australian company, Pacific Resorts Ltd was the only one to be completed. The luxury Anuha Resort, costing some AUD$480,000, was opened in 1984 in the Nggella Islands. Controversial Australian resort developer, Mike Gore, who had a track record of ambitious projects in Australia, took over Anuha in late 1987, just as difficulties between the island's custom owners and resort management were coming to climax (Sofield, 1993). The Australian government had to step in to evacuate a building team refurbishing the resort when fighting broke out between workers and the owners. There followed several months of allegations in the media of both countries concerning the 'bottom of the harbour scheme' (tax evasion by Australian investors), gold smuggling, drug running, and other nefarious activities with covert suggestions that the resort was somehow involved (*Island Business*, 1988). In November 1987 Anuha was badly damaged by fire with each side accusing the other of causing it. The ruins remain a monument to the difficulties of negotiating land leases satisfactory to both locals and investors in Solomon Islands.

The first financial participation in tourism by Solomon Islanders with foreign investment was at Tambea Village, 40 km west of Honiara, where local villagers as landowners entered into a cooperative arrangement with Olli Tolling, an expatriate and ex-government officer. Solomon Islanders had 8% share of the venture. The bungalows were Melanesian in architecture, the focus of much of the entertainment was the nearby village and the main sources of tourists were from neighbouring PNG and Bougainville. In the earliest days of opening there was an expectation that tourism from Japan would increase significantly following the ceremonial interring nearby of the ashes of some 24,000 Japanese soldiers killed in action during World War II. By the 1990s the resort was in serious decline having never recovered from Cyclone Namu in 1986.

War Influence on Craft and Art

The presence and concentration of military personnel at Allied bases created new market opportunities. Allied soldiers were eager to exchange food, clothes, tools, guns and such goods for local handicrafts produced in the villages, as well as old pre-Christian artefacts that the villagers brought out for sale. Many Solomon Islanders living near large bases became petty traders and craftsmen using their skills in producing cultural artefacts to use in gift exchange and trade with servicemen. These skills would later be significant in the tourist trade (Boutilier, 1979; Philibert, 1976; Weiner, 1982). The result in many areas was a thriving industry of 'tourist arts' where carvers began to revive woodcarvings and carved copies of traditional artefacts as well as new items meeting a booming market of a scale not surpassed since. The war years introduced commercial cash-based woodcarving in a systematic way. For the first time there were large numbers willing to give money to villagers for woodcarvings and other artefacts. The war acted as an 'eye-opener' for villagers in many ways and the wartime introduction of a cash economy greatly enhanced the production of wood carvings and other handicrafts. The colonial practice of collecting local artefacts for free came to halt when the locals realised the monetary value of their material culture, which realisation continues to the present time.

The Allied soldiers' quest for local artefacts as souvenirs led the British Solomon Islands Protected (BSIP) district officers to organise 'curio shops' in 1944 in the Western District. Similar shops had already been operating on Guadalcanal since the previous year, with an attempt being made to control the trade and to standardise prices because BSIP officials were worried that the American dollar was spoiling the locals (Akin, 1989). In the Western Districts, shops were opened in Hombuhombu (Roviana) and Vella La Vella to "regulate the sale of native objects of art and craft to the Allied Forces, both from the native and soldier's point of view, and to stop Allied soldiers roaming native villages" (Clement, 1945; BSIP 1/III, F 14/19: 63). However, the soldiers remained reluctant to purchase from shops and still went to the villages. They sought to establish personal contacts with locals and thereby add 'authenticity' to their purchases.

The most popular artefacts bought by soldiers were grass skirts, carved sticks and clubs, and woven baskets. The carved sticks were mostly ebony walking sticks often with shell inlay applied, and carved motifs of various animals, such as dolphins and sharks. The carved clubs of New Georgia style have not been produced since World War II, except very occasionally, and they are rarely seen on contemporary handcraft markets (Kupiananen, 2000). The allied soldiers not only introduced the system of cash-based trade of artefacts in the Solomon Islands, they also influenced local material culture and artefacts production in various ways that have continued to the present time. There was a definite emphasis on small, portable items since soldiers could transport them more easily. The soldiers also encouraged the production of marine carvings (e.g. fish, sharks, dolphins); these were small in size, matched conventional ideas about souvenirs, and their motifs were undoubtedly familiar to both European and Americans. Akin (1989) also mentioned that the soldiers encouraged and even taught locals to weave grass skirts and hats in the islands where they had never been produced before the war, such as Mono Island.

It is evident throughout the Solomons campaign that the Allied soldiers were collecting whatever local artefacts they could find in villages on different islands where fighting took place, and corresponding narratives have been noted from across the archipelago (e.g. Akin, 1989; Laracy, 1988). For example, veteran politician Gedion Zoleveke noted of Vella laVella that "villagers were able to make a living by selling carvings and other arte-facts to the troops" (Zoleveke, 1980, p. 26). Another account from John Havea from Mono, Shortland Islands stated: "The Americans and the New Zealanders used to come to the village to play music — they formed bands! So we could hear them. When they wanted souvenir, they went up too. Never did they miss a day looking for souvenirs... Small out-rigger canoes, hats and grass skirts mostly" (Havea, 1988, p. 100). Likewise Sir Frederick Osifelo wrote of Malaita that:

> The demand by American Marine and army personnel for such things as sea-shell, carvings, walking sticks, grass skirts, combs and so on, resulted in every people of my age focusing on making or finding something to sell. I was fourteen years old in 1942/1943 and actively involved in making walking sticks, combs and grass skirts. At night we went out to the reef with torches or lit coconut leaves in search of seashells. Sometimes we sent of our stuff to Lunga (Guadalcanal) with relatives working in Labour Corps so that they could sell them for us, at times we sold them ourselves when warships visited Auki (Malaita) (Osifelo, 1985, p. 23).

The widespread demand for souvenirs, paid for with dollars, evoked a vigorous response from Islanders. Father Emery deKlerk looked out from his mission station on Guadalcanal one day in May 1943 and observed "a whole fleet of native canoes travel-ling towards Lunga in Guadalcanal to trade with American soldiers' (de Burlo, 1984). The increase in demand also produced a sharp inflation in the prices of local artefacts. The result in many areas was a thriving industry of 'tourist arts' which still continues.

In the post-war years, especially in the 1950s, there were some changes in the policies towards handcraft production. Consequently, and due to fluctuating copra prices, men began to do wood carvings and women started to weave from pandanus and coconut leaves for the emerging local markets to be sold in Honiara. In the 1950s and early 1960s a small but growing number of men took up woodcarving as they went to work on colonial plan-tations. Wages were very low so locals began woodcarving in their spare time. The buyers were mainly European expatriates, Chinese business people, and crew of visiting copra-boats (Kupiainea, 2000). Immediately after the war Western Province woodcarvers were producing miniature war canoes and various fighting club replicas for tourists.

Post-War Attitudes

As elsewhere in the Solomon Islands, the contrast between the casual and egalitarian atti-tudes of the Allied and USA soldiers and the paternalistic and hierarchical BSIP officials left people disillusioned with colonial rule. In Malaita, Guadalcanal, Florida Islands, and Isabel, *Maasina Rule* movement meant considerable hardships for the returning BSIP officials in their attempt to resume colonial authority after the war (Bennet, 1987; Fifi'I, 1989; Kessing, 1979; Larcy, 1983; Akin, 1993). In the New Georgia group, the anti-colonial sentiments were not particularly directed at the colonial government but rather at the Methodist Mission and its long time leader Reverend John Goldie when Silas Eto, a lay missionary from Kusaghe on North New Georgia, established his own following, known as the Christian Fellowship Church (CFC) (Harwood, 1987; Tuza, 1986). Judith Bennet has noted that:

> Eto protest focused on the real political force in the Western Solomons — the monolithic authority vested in the chairmen of the Methodist Mission — rather than on the apparent authority, the government... Yet, by the mid forties and fifties groups of Solomon Islanders, many who were deadly enemies, were able to organise themselves into movements sufficiently large and cohesive to force both civil and religious authorities to take their wishes seriously for the first time (Bennet, 1987, p. 301).

A central underlying factor in these endeavours was the increased local awareness of global affairs and the position of Solomon Islanders within them, directly induced by the effects of World War II.

Tourism and Motivation

One conceptual framework about tourist motivation is Dann's (1977) push and pull theory where tourists are motivated by push and or pull of destination. Push factors "refer to the tourist as subject and deals with those factors that predispose him to travel" (Dann, 1977, p. 186). Pull factors are motivations "which attract the tourist to a given resort...and whose value is seen to reside in the object of travel" (Dann, 1977, p. 186). Crompton (1979) and Taylor (1974) note the travel industry has also been conditioned to focus on pull factors. MacCannell (1989) supports this in his discussion on the language of tourism. For him a tourist attraction is a sign; it represents (marks) something (a sight) to some one (the tourist). Hence war tourism sites use markers with language to pull tourists to the site. The "rhetoric of tourism is full of manifestations of the importance of authenticity of the relationship between tourist and what they see: this is a *typical* native house; this is the *very* place the leader fell; this is the *actual* pen used to sign the law; this is the *original* manuscript" (MacCannel, 1989, p. 14).

With reference to war-based tourism in the Solomons an individual might be 'pushed' to visit war sites in Guadalcanal because a close relative was killed there during World War II. However, the sight/site itself may be commemorating a special anniversary and be offering a conducted tour, which further pulls the individual to the place. This individual might experience both push and pull facts simultaneously. Furthermore, an individual is not limited to experiencing just one push factor, nor is a site limited to offering one pull factor. Many World War II sites, war relics, and memorabilia affirm both education and remembrance in their mandate.

With specific interest in War Tourism, the literature indicates that a number of individuals visit war sites for personal reasons. Some visit such sites as a socially feasible way of expressing interest in death and disaster. Some come to learn about history behind an event, like those who visit 'Iron Bottom Sound' because of interest in military naval tactics. Some visit to commemorate family, friends, or their own experience, such as war veterans and their families. Similarly, those affiliated with sites may also come to affirm their cultural identity. Some come because of guilt and finally some may come to simply out of morbid curiosity. These are construed as push factors.

Conversely, war tourism can pull visitors to destinations, with the most common explanation being education and remembrance. However, a number of people who have neither direct nor indirect connection with war tourism events visit sites because of heritage motivation. It must be noted that those motivated by heritage do not solely visit specific sites of death and disaster: they might visit representative sites such as museums and reconstructions. Paying homage to someone they identify with can help formulate their heritage.

An interesting aspect of war tourism is the "historical motivation." Thus "Battlefields are of particular interest to two diverse groups: history buffs and military strategists, both real and armchair, who tramp over the area with books in hand, studying such details of the battle as it relates to terrain, to ground cover and troop movements" (Smith, 1996, p. 257). Consequently, visitors do not need to be directly affiliated with a death or disaster site or event to be attracted to it: some are simply interested in history.

By looking at the wide range of products, and tours available to visitors, it may be understood that history does incite visitation to sites in Guadalcanal, Tulagi, Munda, Rendova, Vella la Vella, Kolobangara, Gizo and Mono in the Shortland Islands. One reason for the popularity of various tours (products) is that they provide experiential learning. Through first-hand experience either with land tours or wreck diving, World War II events can be brought to life. To trace the actual path of a sunken submarine, warship, or a corsair fighter located in a lagoon has much bigger impact than to simply read of it in a book.

Literature also reveals that places of war tourism can act as research sites. They act as archives for social conditions, political climates, and environmental hardships. One of the difficulties with this, however, is the manipulation of history by prevailing cultural values and the power that dictates them. Hence war tourism sites provide learning experiences but visitors must question whether the whole story is being communicated.

World War Tours, Scuba Diving, Collectors, and Heritage

Tourist destinations require a supply of attractions as well as a super- and infrastructure to meet travel market demands. As with infrastructure, the islands rely not only on natural resources such as climate, coral reefs, beaches, and indigenous cultures, but also on what World War II left behind. In addition to natural and cultural attractions, war relics and battle sites have for many years been basic attractions for tourism in the Southwest Pacific. These places and relics of the war are now so much part of the tourist itinerary in these islands that they constitute tourist "sights" (MacCannell, 1976, p. 135). For veterans, a growing number and variety of tour packages is offered by specialised operators (Solomon Tours, 2006). In 1972, a former member of the First Marine Division and Guadalcanal campaign veteran, Al Bonney, created a 'Sentimental Journey' tour to the South Pacific for a group of veterans, including a visit to Guadalcanal. Bonney tied this effort to the Guadalcanal Veterans Association, whose newsletter he edited, and in 1984 he formed a larger group, the South Pacific Veterans Association. He organised more than 10 veterans' tours from 1975 until his death in 1984. The tours included visits to sights in Australia, such as the Shrine of Remembrance in Melbourne and the Marine Memorial at Ballarat, and in Guadalcanal (Bloody Ridge, Red Beach, Tenaru River, and air 'flight-seeing' of Tulagi) (de Burno, 1984).

Valor Tours is devoted solely to veterans' tours of the Pacific and caters to a wide range of veterans' groups including the First, Second, and Fourth Marine divisions, Seabee battalions, the Fifth, Thirteenth, and Twentieth Air forces, and others, and package tours to PNG, the Solomon Islands, Vanuatu, the Philippines, Saipan, and elsewhere (Reynolds, 1985, http://www.valortours.com/tours.html, accessed June 2006).

In August 1982, 100 American and Japanese veterans of Guadalcanal met there with former Solomon Islands coastwatchers, scouts, various ambassadors, to dedicate a memorial at Henderson Field (Bonney, 1982; Mohs & Dunn, 1982). These international meetings will continue, given the importance of the events they commemorate and the appeal they make to the sense of history shared by the combatants. In 2005 the cruise ship Pacific Princess, carrying more than 600 veteran and tourists visited Honiara as part of its 'Islands of the Pacific Theatre Cruise' and visited World War II sites including the US War Memorial at Skyline Ridge, Henderson Battle sites, and the Bloody Ridge east of Honiara (*Solomon Star*, June 8).

Veterans are not exactly standard holiday tourists. Veterans who return to Solomon Islands battlegrounds are making both group and personal pilgrimages. Not only do they leave everyday lives at home for a valued journey that takes them into 'a non-ordinary sphere of existence', they return to a time and place (in mind and fact) that was in their earlier life quite extraordinary. They return to exotic places they last saw as members of a special kind of 'tour' group (the military), during a time of fighting, fear, and destruction. These are 'memory tours' of unique times and places, not just a departure from the workaday world for leisure and recreation. Most tourists require modern facilities and transportation. Veterans on tour are like other tourists in this regard. They use tour operators' packaged services that include international-class hotels, airlines, cruise ships, and professional guides or tour leaders. Because of their age or retirement, veterans who take remembrance tours may not have the time and money to travel to outer islands. Their special experiences provide them with the interest to make courteous (as well as profitable) tourists for island nations to encourage. The interest veterans have in the islands helps to create an atmosphere of mutual respect in their encounters with Islanders.

Heritage

World War II wreck and historical shipwrecks represent an important source of archaeological and historical information. They have often been likened to time capsules because, when wrecked, everything on board these floating communities was often preserved together in one place, and can be accurately dated to no later than the date of the wreck. Details about how vessels were built, the daily lives of the crew and passengers, cargo composition and stowage, navigation instruments, crockery, tools, clothing and even foods and medicines used aboard the ships can provide new historical insights. The anaerobic or low oxygen underwater environment means that material — particularly organic remains — not preserved on other archaeological sites can be found on shipwrecks.

There are many different reasons why someone may choose to dive on wrecks. For some, it is a hobby, an opportunity that wrecks provide for underwater photography. A wreck will provide a perfect habitat for many fish and other marine creatures concentrated in a small area. Another reason people may dive a wreck is historical significance that might include its designation as a war grave. Many of the ships that sank in World War II went down with everyone on board, and as such, they are essentially someone's final resting place. And for others, as Crompton (1979, p. 412) pointed out, the motive for pleasure is present, "to dive wrecks just out of sheer curiosity, novelty, the tingling excitement of exploring somewhere that used to be an everyday part of life."

The sunken American and Japanese World War II wrecks have become an important mainstay of the Solomon Islands tourism industry and still conjure up memories of pain, bravery, and brushes with death. 'Iron Bottom Sound' is best known as a mecca for scuba divers, who can explore the dozens of war wrecks that litter its bottom. From fighter planes and tanks, to cargo ships and destroyers, 'Iron Bottom Sound' has become a kind of underwater museum. Major wrecks include the American cruiser *Quincy*, the Australian heavy cruiser *Canberra*, the Japanese aircraft carrier *Kinugasa*, and the battleship *Kirishima*. While most are in water too deep to be visited by recreational divers, more accessible wrecks have helped make the Solomon Islands a world-famous destination for divers.

Along the coast of Guadalcanal are the Japanese transports *Hirokawa Maru* and *Kinugawa Maru* close to the beach near Bonegi Creek, about 8 miles (13 km) west of Honiara. Another transport, *Azumasan Maru*, lies a little further west near Tasivarongo Point. The big Japanese cruiser submarine *I-1* lies on the outside of the reef off Tambea, which is a small village about 25 miles (40 km) west of Honiara. The American troopship *USS John Penn* lies on its starboard side off Lungga Point, east of Honiara, at 180 feet (56 m). The cruiser *USS Atlanta* lies off Honiara at 430 feet (130 m) well beyond the range of recreational divers.

In Gizo Island, Western Province the 450-foot-long Japanese transport *Toa Maru* lies on her starboard side in 40 feet of water. Artefacts are scattered across the seafloor around her, ranging from Saki bottles and small jars to gas masks and cooking gear, medical supplies, and office equipment. Ammunition still lies stacked in her holds, waiting for guns long silenced. One can almost see the chaos that accompanied her sinking. In waters close by sit the wrecks of two American aircraft that wrought havoc in Vella La Vella air combat. The Hellcat was a nimble dogfighter that held deadly aerial duels with Japanese fighters. The Corsair, with its distinctive bent, gull-shaped wings, was another air combat workhorse. Both planes sit quietly on the bottom, their powerful engines mute, their wings covered with sponges and coral (SIVB, 2006).

Dive sites in the Solomon Islands are so widely scattered, live-aboard diving is mandatory if one wishes to see a representative selection of the best diving in the country, thereby giving rise to specialist small cruise businesses catering to the market.

Threats to Historical Sites

Solomon Islands shipwrecks represent a fragile, non-renewable resource that is of immense national and international archaeological and cultural significance. However, this historical heritage has been exposed to some destruction and impairment by a number of factors, which leaves the country with little compared with what existed after the Japanese surrender in September 1945, but with a great deal when compared with other historic battlefields and sites. The World War II remains have become national assets and as such they are in need of proper management, now more than ever. Spennemann (1992) noted:

> There are four horsemen of the apocalypse for historic sites: the first is war and the impact wreaked on sites and collections; the second is neglect and destruction labelled modernization or development; the third is the army of avid collectors, raping and pillaging sites, as well intentioned as some of them may be. The fourth of the horsemen of the apocalypse is about to visit upon these sites: *the tourist.*

From the late 1950s until the mid-1970s, foreign entrepreneurs pillaged these sites in search of scrap iron and especially non-ferrous metals. These scrap metal drives continued the destruction of the historical resources at an unprecedented rate. While a bombed and burned-out generator station was still easily recognisable as such, these generators were cannibalised for the copper wiring of the anchors, the fly-wheels, and the like. What remains is often a sorry sight. In retrospect, the scrap metal collectors, as well as the well-intentioned cleanups and the removal of unexploded World War II ammunition during the same period caused more structural damage to the World War II heritage than the war itself.

Now a new threat has developed from people collecting war remains, labelled 'relics', to increase their spiritual value and thus the collector's justification for taking them in the first place. These artefacts end up in their private collections or for sale to major US and Japanese museums specialising in this line of business. These collectors range from one-time individuals — who encounter a number of artefacts and take one 'for the fun of it' — to 'fanatics' driven by the desire to possess a complete collection of all Japanese infantry gear or the like. Apart from these individuals, there are also a few who come to the islands to obtain war planes and other remains for eventual restoration and resale to museums. Their argument is commonly that they will take a number of plane wrecks in order to return one restored plane to the community. In the end, this most likely does not happen, but the island is stripped of all plane remains since it takes parts of more than one wreck to restore a plane.

In 2005 a local newspaper, *Solomon Star*, highlighted a dispute involving a local community in Shortland Islands not wanting to move plane wrecks overseas for restoration. Locals were suspicious of a foreign investor who claimed he had the support of Solomon Islands government to take aircrafts overseas to be restored. The Solomon Islands Museum subsequently intervened and denied permission for the investor to move historical and archaeological items.

In addition, shipwrecks pose threats to the environment. Sixty years after their destruction, some wrecks are beginning to leak oil, imperiling coral reefs, and beaches. Some biologists say reefs around Western Guadalcanal are dying from oil pollution. To address the problem, officials have been working on plans to remove oil from some wrecks — without destroying their value as historical sites or memorials to those who once fought fiercely over the South Pacific. On many islands, where sites have been left untouched, vegetation has reclaimed the ground, hiding material, and human remains.

Scuba diver operators in the Solomons have also reported a new kind of threat — the 'underwater graffiti artist'. Operators have identified and are looking at ways to discourage Australian divers from inscripting their names and dive clubs on heritage wrecks (Solomon Star, 2005). Recognising these interests and threats of foreign collectors, the Solomon Islands government passed a War Relics Act in the 1980s with the intention of prohibiting the export of war material and limiting profiteering by outside interests. The major difficulty with the Act has been enforcement. Except for the installation of an x-ray machine in the national airport to detect foolish attempts to transport World War II munitions on board jet aircraft, the Act is largely ignored. In a few cases, local provincial governments have taken responsibility by setting up cultural offices that monitor the trade in artefacts. The Western Province, which passed its own cultural policy and created a Cultural Affairs Office to administer it (Lindstrom & White, 1994), was so successful in confiscating war relics (usually from recreational divers) that it faced a storage problem. For the most part, however, the vast array of war artefacts remains outside any organised efforts at public interpretation or conservation.

A Political Economy

Despite the lack of sustained national projects aimed at developing the war's cultural resources, the Solomon Islands government has responded to foreigners' interests in war memory, especially for purposes of promoting tourism. For the 50th anniversary of the battle for Guadalcanal, the Solomon Islands government designated 1992 as the Year of Tourism in Solomon Islands and allocated a budget of US$100,000 to support local planning for commemorative events. However, despite the creation of a Solomon Islands planning committee, the agenda for the 50th anniversary events was largely set by the former Allies, even resulting in the exclusion of the Japanese, who contribute more international aid and investment in the Solomon Islands than the United States. The US World War II 50th Anniversary Committee (a Department of Defense program based in the Pentagon) organised an entire Task Force, called 'Operation Remembrance', to undertake an island-hopping campaign for the purpose of supporting American veterans groups and military units participating in official ceremonies throughout the region (White, 1995). On Guadalcanal, the centrepiece of the 50th anniversary commemoration was the dedication of an impressive monument consisting of a walled compound with large marble panels telling the story of the Guadalcanal campaign. Perched on top of Skyline Ridge overlooking the major battlegrounds, the monument was conceived as a counter-measure to the imposing Japanese 'Peace Memorial' that had been installed in 1983 on a neighbouring ridge overlooking the capital. Funded by the US Battle Monument Commission and by donations from American veterans, the monument cost about US$500,000. The scale of plans for the monument and dedication ceremonies did raise some local eyebrows. The cost of the Skyline Ridge Memorial in Guadalcanal would have paid the entire budget of the Solomon Islands National Museum for several decades.

The potential for the Guadalcanal anniversary to attract worldwide attention was anticipated by many entrepreneurs in the business of producing historical materials for popular audiences. Thus, the same team that mounted an expedition to find and photograph the *Titanic* organised a similar project, using advanced underwater technology, to locate and film many of the sunken warships that gave the waters off Guadalcanal the name 'Iron Bottom Sound'. Sponsored by *National Geographic* and other investors, this project produced a made-for-television documentary film introduced by former US President George Bush and a glossy coffee-table photograph book (Ballard, 1993).

The dilemma for national planners is that sites of war memory developed for the purposes of tourism inevitably speak to foreign audiences interested in objects, people, and places that fit within their own conceptions of history. But the disparity in efforts to preserve and commemorate war memories is more than economic. The economies of memories are here undergirded by more basic questions about the meaning and relevance of 'preservation', particularly preservation of World War II memories. To date, most of the initiatives and financing for preserving and/or commemorating island war memories have come from the metropolitan powers.

Today tourism in Solomon Islands is increasingly oriented towards the pleasure-seeking and adventure tourist market. Its scale will mean challenges to the physical and social capacities of the islands. In 1990 about 10% of visitors to the Solomon Islands were returning veterans; at least 50% were Australians and New Zealanders on business or holiday trips (Solomon Islands Ministry of Tourism, 1991–2000). Tourism is already contributing to changing relations with outsiders, and a younger generation of islanders has grown up that does not recall the war and will establish different relationships with foreign visitors. As tourism expands and time passes, special tourist types such as veterans become lost in masses of tourists. As the generation of veteran servicemen and Solomon Islanders directly involved in the events of 60 and more years ago pass the present relationship between the wartime heritage of the islands and the attraction of veterans becomes increasingly distant. It also needs to be recognised that in the period 1999–2004 overseas arrivals to the Solomon Islands declined from over 17,000 to about 6,000 because of social unrest and the accompanying violence surrounding the issue of Bourgainville. One further consequence is that tourist resources have become under-utilised, suffered degradation and now need capital investment to meet the needs of an experienced tourist class.

In recognition of the mismatch between supply and demand, and the need to reestablish coordination functions associated with management of tourism, the Australian government, through its AusAID/RAMSI program is providing assistance under the 'Tourism Strengthening Program for the Solomon Islands'. The intension of this AID is to provide assistance to enhance understanding of tourism demand, stimulate additional tourist activities and support the efforts of the Solomon Islands Visitors Bureau, National Tourism Industry Associations, and the Ministry of Tourism and Aviation (GRM, 2006; http://www.ramsigsf.org.sb/index.htm, accessed June 2006). Under the auspices of the programme a tourism marketing plan has identified the World War II heritage as a component in the total tourism portfolio.

Conclusion

World War II swept into Solomon Islands with incredible speed and force — a force made even greater by the relative isolation of pre-war island communities. The sheer magnitude of the war would be enough to ensure its place in island memories. On the island of Guadalcanal, for example, the number of Allied and Japanese who died on the island in just nine months of fighting was nearly double the total indigenous population of 15,000. But, for most Solomon Islanders, the events which unfolded between 1942 and 1945 amounted to much more than a massive military confrontation; they marked a turning-point in the history of race relations and the development of island nations. It is this story, and the story of massive cross-cultural encounters and social disruption that to a large extent still remains silenced in the histories of the conflict.

The war came at a critical moment in the history of many island communities struggling to define their relations with colonial authorities and the wider world. For some people, the war presented opportunities for improved status and government involvement; for others it offered new ideas and skills which could be used to challenge entrenched colonial regimes. In areas where Islanders had become increasingly restless with domineering colonial officers, the encounter with powerful, exotic, and often friendly military personnel was a catalyst for change.

Like any major event in the history of island societies, wartime experiences have been incorporated in local oral traditions — historical 'archives' that depend for their existence on the memories of a disappearing generation of Solomon Islanders. The historical significance of the war in peoples' lives is primarily expressed in songs, stories, and ceremonial practices enacted in village settings. In the rural Solomon Islands, where literacy is only slowly making inroads, history is largely oral. Translating these histories into relevant forms in books, films, museum displays, and so forth, requires sensitivity to the different ways in which history itself acquires relevance for peoples' lives. For future generations, the cultural and social impact of warfare will be as important a matter for interpretation as the simple retelling of military action and acts of heroism that tend to be the current subject matter of story telling oriented towards the international tourist. While the past events of conflict are currently encapsulated in the wrecks, the consequences of the social impacts continue to echo, and interpretation and reinterpretation are required for contemporary and future generations so that they may understand the forces that shape their daily lives. Thus the stories are never complete, but evolve with emerging and decaying themes as they seek their own authentifications and authorisations to provide meaning for their own perceived realities.

Chapter 11

Xiamen and Kinmen: From Cross-Border Strife to Shopping Trips

Li-Hui Chang and Chris Ryan

Introduction

Today, in the Taiwan Straits, the island Kinmen, formerly known as Quemoy, hosts several thousands of tourists. Four categories can be devised: 450,000 Taiwanese primarily tour the island from which they view the Chinese mainland. Second, there are business people in transit travelling to and from China and the rest of Taiwan. These number about 150,000. Third, there are 100,000 residents in Kinmen who travel to China for purposes of seeing relatives, going shopping and enjoying the nightlife of Xiamen. Finally, there are those numbering, in 2005, about 15,000 from Fujian who usually take two-day tours, staying overnight and satisfying their curiosity about life in Taiwan. Yet, just over 20 years previously, the skies between Kinmen and China would be lit by shells fired from the Chinese Mainland. How did this transition occur, and what does it signify?

Following the end of the Cold War, significant changes occurred around the world. The Soviet Union split into the Russian Federation and separate states. Russian communism retreated in the face of the Mafia and capitalism only to re-emerge in some form of reformed central planning under Putin but with a private industrial sector. Other states like Yugoslavia collapsed into war. Slowly, however, a post-Cold War world has emerged and many formerly sensitive regions have been opened one after another, allowing tourists freely to travel. With a growth of tourism in these states have emerged new tourist zones with an attendant growth in incomes, employment, capital structures, trade and transport; and equally new sites of social, community and environmental discourse.

The past history of these formerly difficult to access zones of the Cold War appeal to some due to the frontier images of past politically disputed zones and the often intact natural scenery of less developed countries (Boyd, 1999; Butler, 1996; Essex & Gibb, 1989; Gibbons & Fish, 1987; Herzog, 1990; Lintner, 1991; Slowe, 1991; Timothy, 1995, 2000). In particular, border zones have specific appeal as sites of formerly restricted movement, sites of conflict and tense relations between states characterized by the hardware of conflict.

Similarly, discrepancies may exist between peripheral zones and their hinterlands. Often peripheral zones at the boundary are the poorest within a nation or zone. Tourism thus assumes even more importance as a source of economic development for these frontier regions.

East and West Germany, North and South Korea and China and Taiwan, after World War II, were separated in the period when communist states challenged the democracies of the West. Some sites of division achieved iconic tourism status in this period such as Checkpoint Charlie and the Berlin Wall, or the Demilitarized Zone dividing North and South Korea. During the Cold War itself, a platform was built in West Berlin to enable the public to observe the forts and communities of East Berlin (Koenig, 1981; Maier, 1994). In 1988 trade negotiations opened between Seoul and Pyongyang and, as a result, South Korean businessmen, since 1989, have continued to visit the North within certain restrictions for purposes of trade (Kim & Crompton, 1990). As indicated below, previously a hostile separation had existed between Taiwan and Mainland China since 1949 but, in 1979, a slow rapprochement commenced when both sides began contacts and cooperation (Yu, 1997). In 1987 Taiwan ended many restrictions on trips to the Mainland and cross-strait tourism hereafter began to flourish. Under the premises of the three 'non-links policies' of no direct trade, post or travel, tourists residing in Taiwan are approved to legally enter China but via a third party area, usually Hong Kong.

Of interest under the easing of travel is the position of the frontier island of Taiwan, Kinmen, which has become an experimental region for policies between Taiwan and China. Kinmen, formerly known as Quemoy, was a disputed island and the site of the 1958 823 Artillery War (also known as the Kinmen Artillery War). Because of its military importance as a heavily fortified area, Kinmen was closed for a period of nearly 40 years when neither residents nor trade could freely circulate to or from other zones. Following the commencement of cross-strait relations in 2001 under the 'mini three links policy', Kinmen has become an experimental region for Taiwan's policies towards China. Consequently, Kinmen has become a point of access to China for Taiwanese travelling to the mainland for trade and/or tourism. As seen in the accompanying maps, for many this is a more direct route than via Hong Kong or possibly Macau, thereby potentially saving time and expense. The process was not immediate. First, there was permission for Taiwan residents to tour Kinmen, second, those resident in Kinmen were allowed to trade or tour in China, and third, Taiwanese businessmen trading with China could then do so by way of Kinmen if possessing suitable documentation and last, residents in Fujian received permission to visit Kinmen. Thus a tourism circuit of Taiwan, Kinmen and Xiamen has taken shape. From the battlefield to attraction site, Kinmen has gone through a major transformation, not merely socially or economically but in terms of thought, perceptions and attitudes. This chapter examines the relationship of conflict, global movements and symbolic meaning in the establishment of Kinmen as a tourist destination.

Theoretical Foundations of the Study

The chapter is premised on the two concepts, those of first (a) the border as a point of crossing and travel and (b) the shaping of a tourist gaze and the dialogue to which it gives expression as a means of shaping a tourist experience. These concepts are illustrated in Figure 11.1, which also serves to show the means by which data were generated to inform

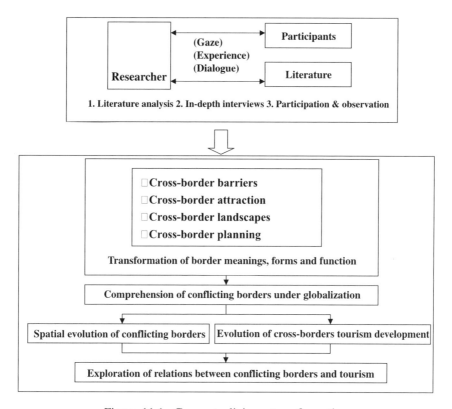

Figure 11.1: Conceptualizing a transformation.

this text. First, a process of literature review and interviews were collected to subsequently create a discourse of cross-border attractions and how the process of travel within a past history of conflict and tension shapes and reshapes the relationship of borders and tourism.

The terminology of the tourist gaze is derived from Urry's work, which in turn was derived from Foucault's analysis of how perceptions of a post-modern world changed at some point in the mid-twentieth century due to social, political and technological change. All foreign travel requires the crossing of a border, but borders possess additional political meaning as evidenced by the examination of passports and other travel documentation. In zones of past conflict, the transformation of a border not only influences local tourism but reshapes a gaze of what lies on the other side of a boundary.

Any tour is framed by social groups, historical periods and personal experiences. A border of past battles that undergoes a transformation is thus an interesting place of changing cognition and perception. The tourist gaze is shaped through the contrast of attraction sites with the existence of a certain difference itself shaped between imagination and reality. During the process of 'looking' and 'being looked at', the gaze becomes a function and relationship between knowledge and power. The interpretations of sites and their history through both authorized and non-authorized storytelling becomes a powerful shaper of thought, and symbols come to possess meanings that themselves can be used to legitimize the symbol itself and the artefacts that shape those symbols in a continuous process of mutual reinforcement.

This process itself does not occur within a vacuum. The decade of the 1990s saw the rise of new technologies and significant improvements to older ones that have reinforced a process of time-space compression. This time-space compression has permitted a swifter mobility of tourists from one place to another (Bauman, 2000). This mobility is characterized by new social connections and associations that are worldwide in nature, while places are transformed to fit the attribute of mobility. Consequently, the production of all absorption and "viewpoints of local consumption" appear almost everywhere worldwide (Urry, 2002). A possible consequence is a growing 'travel reflectance' that is the creation of an ordered, programmed and standardized reflexivity that makes it possible to monitor and assess any location and to develop its tourism potential in the globalized tourism model. While the majority of people are not global travellers, the places where they live and the associated environments, natural, ethical, social, culture, political and traditional all become part of a global tourism. As a result, the border zone is not solely the core of a recognition of national differences but also a specific area of scenery, food, beverages, art — all the subject of tourist consumption and thus interpreted by the standard reflevities of international tourism (Light, 2000).

Borders exist, almost by definition as peripheral regions, and many such regions possess characteristics of being distant, away from the mainstream of activity and are often the least developed part of a country (Page, 1994; Wanhill, 1997; Timothy, 2000, 2001; Weaver, 1998). As noted above, tourism is then labelled as a way of economic development for such boundary regions (Friedmann, 1966; Husbands, 1981). In one sense, they possess the attraction of being zones of communication between differences and this coupled with the need for people to pass through key points represents an opportunity for development, sometimes without effortful planning (Page, 1994).

Functional Transformation of The Border Island: From Offshore Frontier to Cross-Strait Interactions

Kinmen consists of 12 islands, facing the Taiwan Strait in the east, being 277 km away from Taiwan and is surrounded by China in three other directions. It is located near the shore of China's Fujian Province, roughly 10 km distant from Xiamen in Fujian. It thus has close cultural connections with Xiamen on the mainland. It has also, since 1949, been claimed by Mainland China. It is thus a disputed territory, and one where the dispute has boiled over into military action. See Figures 11.2–11.4 to assess the geographical location of Kinmen and its proximity to Mainland China.

On 25 October 1949, 20,000 troops from the People's Liberation Army succeeded in landing in an attempt to occupy Kinmen. Although initially successful in breaking the defence line of garrison troops, it was then subsequently defeated by the Kuomintang Army at the Battle of Guningtou. Since then, battles or conflicts have occasionally occurred. On 23 August 1958, China bombarded Kinmen for 44 days. In total, over this period, it is estimated that 47,000 shells landed on the island. To guard Kinmen, Chiang Kai-shek stationed a permanent garrison of 10,000 soldiers on the island and Kinmen became an island honeycombed with underground bunkers and shelters. These underground galleries became almost home for both military personnel and civilians and thus protected Kinmen. Nor was Kinmen purely defensive. Its position meant that it was continually able to monitor ship movements in the Taiwan Straits and air movements.

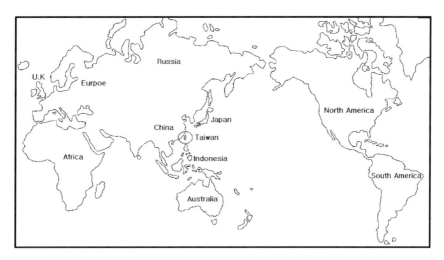

Figure 11.2: Location of Taiwan.

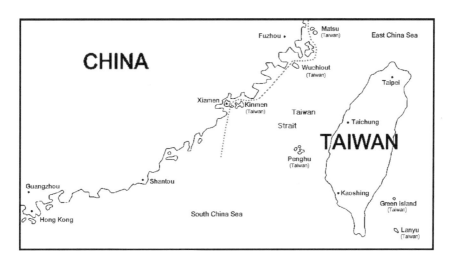

Figure 11.3: Locations of Taiwan, Kinmen and China.

These battles caught the world's attention, especially if taken to a point where United States involvement became an issue. This was particularly so during the period of the Korean War. A constant question was whether Kinmen would be the fuse triggering military actions between the United States and China. At that time, Kinmen and Matsu were regarded as the outposts of the free world struggling against the shellfire from the Mainland. In 1960, as Eisenhower, President of the United States of America, visited Taiwan, Kinmen again suffered from an onslaught from China for three days, with the People's Republic of China (PRC) firing an estimated 175,000 shells. Indeed, this signalled the start of a regular firing of shells at Kinmen on each odd numbered days for 19 years; the firing only ceasing on the

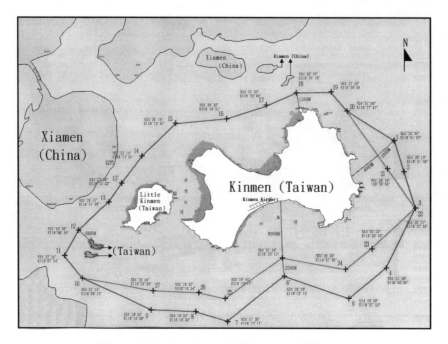

Figure 11.4: Locations of Kinmen and Xiamen.

establishment of diplomatic relations between the USA and PRC in 1979 under the 'ping pong' diplomacy initiated by President Nixon.

The period from 1949 to 2006 can be categorized as falling into four periods. The first one is that of tense military actions (1949–1958), the second, the period of defence (1959–1979), the third, developing rapprochement and beginning of an underground economy (1980–2000), and finally, commencing in 2001, the growing transparency and legitimization of trade and tourist movements.

Establishing the Entry Model of Tourists Transferring via the Third Region to Enter China

The period of 1979–1987 was when tourist movements started between Taiwan and China via third regions such as Singpaore, Hong Kong or Macau. In 1987 the Taiwanese government removed restrictions on travel, thereby making it easier for Taiwanese subjects to visit China. Initially, movements were restricted to those with family relationships on the mainland and Taiwan, but tourist and trade movements had become freer and, in 2001, it became possible to visit China directly from Kinmen and Matsu. Restrictions however, still exist, and these are based upon quotas, residential rights and similar considerations. As ever, where restrictions exist, people find ways of bypassing those restrictions. For example, some Chinese travel to Taiwan via Thailand and obtain a 7 or 15-day effective entry permission to Taiwan from the Taipei Economic & Cultural Office in Thailand through the use of separate travel documents.

Breakdown of the Virtual 'Offshore Berlin Wall': Kinmen as the Demonstration County of Cross-Strait Interactions

The abolition of martial law in 1987 by the Taiwanese authorities has been a mixed blessing for Kinmen. Each year fewer troops are stationed on the island and this in turn means that the businesses and producers that depended upon the military presence have had their livelihoods threatened. Tourism thus represents a means of correcting that economic loss. See Figure 11.5 for a diagrammatic representation of this process.

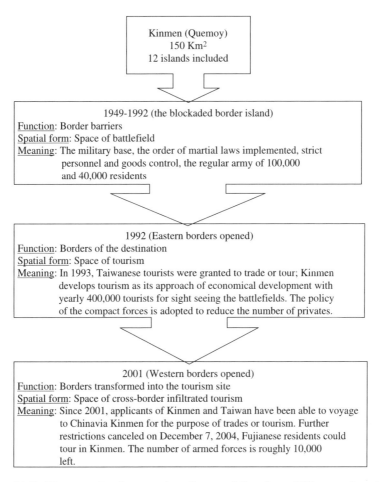

Figure 11.5: The cross-border meaning, form and function of Kinmen since 1949.

The island possesses significant tourism resources. As an island close to the mainland, Kinmen developed a culture and civilization prior to Taiwan and thus it maintains a number of heritage sites and museums. It also possesses an infrastructure of hotels (numbering 22 supplemented by 29 home stay accommodation), and in total 1,256 rooms were available in 2005. The number of tourists arriving, primarily from Taiwan, in 2005, was about 450,000. One result has been a construction boom on the island and rental property, in particular, has attracted investment because of yield of 5–6 percent compared to 3–4 percent on Taiwan. Indeed, there has been a spillover effect into Xiamen on the mainland, where Taiwanese business people have purchased houses and converted them into hotels. By 2006 at least 4,000 properties had been purchased in Xiamen by owners registered in Kinmen to a value of NT$0.34 billion. In part, this flow of funds has been aided by the rapid development of the Mainland economy, poor returns on the Taiwanese stock exchange and low interest rates in Taiwan, and it has been estimated that in total Taiwanese investment in Xiamen has been worth nearly NT$2 billion. Additionally, people have begun to migrate from Taiwan and Kinmen to Xiamen.

Tourist and business flows are not wholly one way. In the period 2001 to the end of 2005, a total of 15,984 tourists from Fujian had visited Kinmen. Most were on organized tours of two days with a one-night stop over; most saw the historical sites and purchase local crafts, but few went to the August 23rd Artillery Battle Museum and Guningtou War Museum, which commemorate Nationalist victories.

Among the tourist sites are undoubtedly those of the fortifications developed between 1949 and 1979. As noted previously, the island is honeycombed with fortifications. Additionally, as is the case of Demilitarized Zone between North and South Korea, the prohibitions on construction in some zones and inhibitions on marine developments have created a heritage of a near pristine environment near the remnants of warfare. Spaces have also been left unspoiled for other reasons. There remain areas that are still mined. Former and continuing artillery training areas, ammunition depots and similar areas remain marked off. Signs warning of 'dangerous minefields' restrict movement — but also serve to provide a minor thrill of potential danger for visitors on guided tours. From a religious perspective, some areas are avoided by residents for fear of awakening the spirits of the dead. Deserted villages also exist — it is estimated that 157 abandoned villages exist — protected still by rings of pillboxes or barracks — but not protected against the growth of vegetation that reclaim the land. In addition, as noted, there are also the museums that recall triumphs and warfare, but with notices still heavy with the messages of resistance to communism.

The island thus possesses a landscape both natural and constructed. The shores facing the Mainland possess fortifications, artillery outposts and the traditional older architecture of Southern Min — all increasingly intruded upon by hotels, reused pillboxes for recreational use, scenic look out and photographic spots and the like. The island becomes a paradoxical mix of entertainment, prohibition of entry to some places, memory of past conflict and a wish to forget the past to pursue the commercial interests of the present.

The cross border is reinforced by observation of the mainland through telescopes, through being able to receive cell-phone messages from the Mainland, of taking photographs of signs that ban the taking of photographs and of stepping over into prohibited zones. Mashan is the closest military base to the Mainland, and through telescopes from this base it is easy to observe life on the Mainland — thereby making this a popular location for Taiwanese tourists. At night it is easy to see the lights from skyscrapers and other buildings on the Mainland. The sense of tension is also reinforced by the propaganda messages that themselves are now tourist attractions. On the shore in Xiamen facing Taiwan, the Chinese authorities have erected a huge sign reading 'Two systems in one nation unite one China', while for their part, the Taiwanese, on the island of Dadan, facing Xiamen, have erected a sign stating 'The Three Principles of the People Rule One China'. Indeed, local rumour has it that when the Taiwanese took down some neon signs advocating their vision of China, the Xiamen tourist authorities asked them to restore them as they attracted Chinese mainland tourists to Xiamen!

The past clash of ideologies has become a current meeting of tour boats in the Taiwan Straits as tourists take the boats for a round of the island of Da Er Dan to take photographs of anti-communism messages and tourists wave to each other as boats from both shores cross each other's path. Indeed, the meeting of peoples is officially sanctioned on the date of the Moon Festival when each side set off fireworks after a symbolic meeting of two boats in the middle of the Straits where a large moon cake is cut in a declaration of peace. This ceremony and the following fireworks attract hundreds of tourists on each side of the Straits. The first such celebration was held in 2001, when the Kinmen magistrate, Chu-Feng Lee and Xiamen Vice Magistrate, Chuang-Chou Chan, formally gave presents to each other. This was followed by the rendering of the song 'The Same Moonlight' by the popular singer Hui-Mei Chang.

Another facet to the tourism is that of shopping. With access to the developing urban sprawl of Xiamen with, in 2006, 1.2 million residents and 7 million visitors a year, Kinmen is a popular route for Taiwanese visitors wishing to take advantage of the wide choice, good quality and cheaper prices that Xiamen has to offer. But Xiamen has not only shopping to offer. Sex clubs can also be found, and as gambling and prostitution is illegal in Kinmen, these services are also popular with several Taiwanese. It has been noted that the only late-night stores open in Kinmen are 7-Eleven stores. By comparison, Xiamen offers a cornucopia of temptation.

Conclusion

Kinmen therefore represents a place in transition from a site of war to a place of normalization not yet fully achieved because of past conflict. Yet the past conflict represents a rationale for the new patterns of tourism and trade that are emerging, and as noted many visitors from both sides of the Straits use Kinmen and its location and history from which to gaze on, and visit, a past enemy. A state of 'tepid war' might still be said to exist wherein past ideologies conflict with the necessities of trade and commerce to create a still sensitive situation, but one within which people can increasingly travel and meet their business needs and those of family reunification and simple curiosity. Like many borders, Kinmen and its adjacent Chinese Mainland sustains a sense of difference. It is a place of pragmatism and ideological difference, and a place of transition in many different senses.

Chapter 12

Hot War Tourism: The Live Battlefield and the Ultimate Adventure Holiday?

Mark Piekarz

Introduction

The media enjoy using the juxtaposition of holidays and war. Headlines such as *Backpackers Risk all for the Thrills of Kabul* (Meo, 2001), or *Terror Tourists Queue for Trips to War Zone* (Bryne, 1997), or *Battledress and Bermuda Shorts* (Calder, 2000) illustrate this. Holidays are generally associated with having fun, enjoyment and relaxation, which take place during leisure time. War, and the associated atrocities it can induce, is an event filled with tragedy and horror, which destroys families, can break-up decent, law-abiding societies, shatters economies and ruins environments. It is essentially a destructive force that exemplifies everything that is bad about human nature, revealing the depths of barbarianism to which people can sink. Furthermore, war can be viewed as the key cultural time marker for a society (Smith, 1998), with Churchill describing battles as the "the punctuation marks of history", with battlefields the "fragmentary pages on which those punctuation marks are written in blood" (cited by Stevens, in *Guest and Guest*, 1996, p. 6). No surprise then that it can initially seem incongruous that an industry, which is so intimately linked with delivering human happiness, should be associated with a phenomenon which delivers so much death, destruction and misery.

Yet on closer examination one soon realises that war and the leisure and tourism industries are in fact deeply entwined and on a huge scale. It is evident in the number of battlefield attractions, memorials, museums, re-enactments, films, TV, literature and even children's toys and games. Indeed, Smith (1998) argues that war and the memorabilia of warfare and allied products probably constitute the largest single category of tourist attractions in the world.

There is, however, a difference between these more mainstream types of war tourism services, and the forms of war tourism the headlines are identifying. Generally, tourist attractions that use war as the basis for its service have allowed a passage of time to take place, resulting in the dangers to diminish, landscapes to recover and people to return to some notion of normality. In this sense, the sites and events can be said to have gone 'cold'. The type of war tourism associated with the opening headlines is different, as it often operates within an unstable political environment, where the risks to the individual, or organisation, are much higher, together with the opportunity to see a raw, dark visual aesthetic of battle, along with the possibility of experiencing the vicarious thrill of war first hand (Creveld, 1994, p. 86); factors that would make the locations 'hot'.

War in the 21st century shows little signs of abating. At the same time, tourism and the experiential economy are forecasted to continue growing. The result is that tourism and war seem set to increasingly bisect in the future, with more examples of hot war tourism becoming identified. This chapter examines this phenomenon of hot war tourism. Its primary aim is to give conceptual recognition and distinction to the phenomenon, stressing that it is neither a new activity, nor a fringe activity pursued by a small group of thrill seekers, but one which can be highly segmented and seems set to continue growing in the future.

Establishing the Conceptual Parameters of 'Hot War Tourism'

Arriving at a precise definition of hot war tourism is fraught with difficulties. These arise from the problems of defining each of the concepts of 'hot', 'war' and 'tourism'. Defining one can be challenging enough; defining all three can mean shortcomings and exceptions can always be found with any definition put forward. Yet it is still important to define the concept in order to set the parameters of the discussion, and to distinguish it as a discrete aspect of tourism.

In relation to tourism, the United Nations' World Tourism Organisation's definition (World Tourism Organisation, 2003) takes account of both recreational and business-related travel. The latter aspect is one that is perhaps sometimes underplayed in tourism literature, which is surprising considering its importance, representing approximately 40% of travel (World Tourism Organisation, 2003). This appreciation of travel for both recreation and business is central to this discussion on hot war travel, helping to move the analysis beyond the narrow focus of thrill-seeking backpackers travelling to war zones.

In Swarbrooke and Horner's (2000) typology of business tourism, they illustrate the diversity of business tourism, which can range from paid to voluntary aid work; and includes non-governmental organisations (NGOs), diplomats and military personnel who are away from their normal home bases. The inclusion of the military here is particularly interesting. To call the thousands of soldiers in Iraq tourists would be wrong and trite, as they are engaged in active military operations (although it is of interest how many of the soldiers exhibit touristic like behaviour, particularly with the taking of photographs, even during battle, as Sontag, 2004, noted).[1] If, however, one looks at the impact the numerous peacekeeping forces have had around the world, together with the many aid agencies, volunteers and business travellers who will visit conflict zones looking for new market contracts, it begins to reveal that far more people are likely to travel to war zones (or immediate former ones) than just a small group of thrill seekers.

---

[1] The touristic behaviour of soldiers was even noted during the English Civil War (1642–1649), where soldiers who had rarely ventured beyond their own villages, were exposed to many new sites and experiences, with their diaries displaying the 'enthusiasm of modern tourists' (Carlton, 1992, p. 104)

In relation to defining 'war' there are a number of difficulties. In the past, wars were frequently fought between nation-states that would make official declarations of war, then distinct armies would meet in an open field, with the majority of the casualties being soldiers (Pelton, Aral & Dulles, 1998). Today this is rarely the case. Between 1945 and 1998, according to the United Nations, of the 82 armed conflicts, only 3 were between nation-states (Pelton, Aral & Dulles, 1998). Declarations of war are also rarely made, as the Vietnam War illustrates.[2] Contemporary wars tend to be internal conflicts, where frequently the combatants have a mixed array of uniforms, the combat often taking place in urban environments and "the majority of the casualties are civilians rather than the combatants" (Paris, 2004, p. 2). There is also ambiguity between insurgency, guerrilla campaigns, terrorism and when they become defined as being at war. War, it seems, can be in the eye of the beholder and can escalate or de-escalate from insurgency, terrorism and war (Wilkinson, 2001; Black, 2000). Despite these difficulties, war in essence can be said to relate to the notion of organised groups using violence and aggression to achieve some goal, which can range from promoting a doctrine, securing resources, alleviating security fears or distracting people from domestic problems (Kegley & Wittkopf, 2001; Wight, 1994). Sollenburg, Wallenstein and Jato (1999) develop a more precise definition and measure of war, but use the term 'major armed conflicts', which are described as:

> the prolonged use of force between the military forces of two or more governments, or of one government and at least organized armed group, incurring the battle-related deaths of at least a 1000 people during the entire conflict and in which the incompatibility concerns government and or/territory (Sollenburg, Wallenstein & Jato,1999, p. 15).

This is a useful definition and helps give a more precise location to 'conflict' zones that can be deemed as still 'hot'.

The concept of 'hot' used here may be less familiar to many. Essentially the term has two sources. The first stems from the use of the terms 'hot' and 'cold' wars, where a 'cold war' had all the characteristics of war, "without the actual violence" (Duncan & Opatowski, 2000, p. 3). The second aspect of hot relates to the idea of hot cognition and dissonance. The notion of dissonance is frequently used in marketing and in discussions on dark tourism. Essentially, it refers to a cognitive discordance, or tension (even discrepancy and incongruity) caused between an individual's actions, values or beliefs (Tunbridge & Ashworth, 1996, p. 20). This dissonance in turn creates arousal, which is interpreted as an emotional experience, with people striving for an "optimal level of incongruity" (Tunbridge & Ashworth, 1996, p. 20).

Hot cognition can be provoked in a variety of ways, which in turn will influence the type of emotional arousal experienced. In Uzzell's work (1988), his prime focus was on war sites provoking feelings of sadness, anger, disgust and empathy, in order to help make learning possible. Hot war zones can not only make these feelings even more keenly felt,

---

[2] For all the years of bloody conflict in Vietnam, America was never officially at war; this was a conflict driven by the presidency, as no Congressional declaration was ever given. In the American constitution, only Congress has the powers to declare war.

but can also arouse other emotional states, particularly in relation to fear and excitement prompted from the risks posed to life, limb and property: as Churchill remarked "nothing beats the thrill of being shot at" (Pelton, Aral & Dulles, 1998). These factors can be regarded as some of the key distinguishing features between a cold war and hot war site, which can also begin to give an insight into some of the possible motivations for travelling to hot war zones, as some of the cuttings begin to illustrate in Figure 12.1.

One of the factors that can also influence the degree of hot cognition relates to the rawness of the visual aesthetic in the aftermath of battles. For soldiers from the developed world, conflicts can be waged with almost clinical precision, with casualties generally removed from the conflict zone very quickly. For other parts of the world, wars and battles can still be fought with a ferocity and rawness familiar to past conflicts, where the sites of conflict can remain hot for years, owing to the lack of resources, desire or time to remove the detritus or mess of war, such as the damaged vehicles, buildings and even bodies. Whilst time can gradually help to reduce the heat in the aesthetic

> *The following sample cuttings (some of which are illustrated below) reveal the diversity of evidence for examples of hot war tourism which can be gained from a variety of publications:*
>
> - *"We're all going on a grimmer holiday" (Merret, 2002) from the Daily Mirror*
> - *"When the war is" (Spink, 2004) from the Outdoor Photographer*
> - *"Rubbernecking in Hell: Why do people holiday in war zones?" (Wakling, 2005) in the Adventure Travel magazine.*
> - *"Into harms way" (Chesshyre, 2006) in the Geographical magazine.*
>
> *It must however, be emphasised that these sort of stories can be a little misleading. In the first instance, people visiting hot war zones can be for altruistic purpose, not just for voyeurism; secondly, although the media enjoy using the juxtaposition of war and holidays, when one grounds the phenomenon of hot war tourism in a framework of optimal experience, one should be less surprised by the trends. These people can be classified as the 'counter-tourists'- - the people who go to the non-zoned, designated tourism areas (Carter, 1998).*
>
> *These headlines can also skew the thinking and focus of attention away from perhaps the most significant part of hot war tourism, which relates to business travel, particularly in the context of the growth of the peace keeping industry.*

Figure 12.1: When war attracts tourists!

witnessed, such as helping to soften landscapes with plant growth and human activity, it may not be enough in itself. Lloyd (1998, p. 96), for example, gives a description of how people travelling to the battlefields in Iraq and Palestine in the 1920s still saw the "bones of the dead" lying on the ground or in the trenches: images that would make these battlefields 'hot'.

A critical element affecting the amount of heat left in battlefield is the degree of 'tidying up' that has taken place at the sites, as Figure 12.2 illustrates. These rounds of interventions, or land management actions, range from establishing proper cemeteries, removing or repairing damaged buildings or machinery, erecting memorials, making sure the sites are safe from unexploded ordinance and even setting up interpretive services for visitors. All can be regarded as a process that can lead to the commodification of the battlefield, which can eventually be presented to less adventurous, more mainstream visitors. As a site is increasingly managed, it progresses through successive rounds of filtration, whereby the heat is steadily dissipated, until it becomes a cold war site.

These definitions of 'hot', 'war' and 'tourism' mean a definition of 'hot war tourism' can be established. Hot war tourism can be said to refer to the phenomenon of people travelling

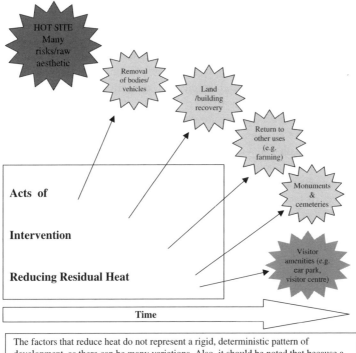

Figure 12.2: Factors determining the residual heat of a battlefield/conflict zone.

and staying in locations, which are currently experiencing conflict and violence, or are still recovering from such events, and can either be directly sought and experienced, or else is an indirect experience, acting as a startling backdrop to the travel event, as the people involved are motivated by other purposes, such as travelling for work, or as part of a pilgrimage. Underpinning this type of tourism are stronger elements of the unknown, risk and rawness to the possible aesthetic of war, all of which can help contribute to provoking hot cognition and powerful emotional experiences, which can include fear, empathy, excitement, sadness and anger.

Is 'Hot War' Just Another Aspect of 'Dark Tourism'?

It is important to acknowledge that the concept of hot war tourism as it has been presented so far is not necessarily a phenomenon which has gone unrecognised in literature. Hot war tourism, for example, can be understood as a form of 'dark tourism', which relates to "visiting places associated with death, disaster, and atrocity, such as battlefields, graves, accident sites, murder sites, places of assassinations and death camps" (Lennon & Foley, 2000, p. 4). Seaton (1999) gives a variation of dark tourism with the use of the term 'thanatourism', a form of travel that is characterised by travel to a location wholly, or partially motivated by the desire for "actual or symbolic encounters with death". Other terms that can be used to describe forms of hot war tourism have been "terror-tourism" (Bryne, 1997), relating to travel to locations at war or where terrorists atrocities have taken place; "testosterone tourism" (Harris, 1998), which relates to the excitement of visiting an active war zone; "danger zone" tourism and "reality tourism" (Roosevelt, 2001), which relates to travelling to the world's political hotspots.

The problems with these concepts are that they cannot fully cover all the aspects of hot war tourism. Terms like thanatourism and dark tourism tend to focus on the motivation of travel to encounter death and violence; the difficulty with this is that it would not adequately cover those who may travel to such locations in a working context, paid or voluntary, such as aid workers, peace keepers, contractors, etc. In relation to the other terms, such as terror tourism, or testosterone tourism, the focus is on the more descriptive, emotional states, which can also reflect the need for a good, provocative news headlines, as Figure 12.1 also illustrates. Furthermore, these terms do not adequately cover the business/working travellers, nor reflect the diversity of hot cognition that could be initiated.

The Historical Context of 'Hot War Tourism' and Current Trends

There is a long history of people travelling to places associated with death and destruction, with Lennon and Foley (2000) making the comment that travelling to such places has always been a significant part of the tourist experience, particularly in the context of pilgrimage travel to battle sites, tombs of saints and locations of infamous deeds. It seems to be part the human psyche to be attracted to this inescapable 'dark' aspect of our world, which is reflected in so many ways, ranging from literature, films, TV, memorials, etc.

(Dyer, 1998; Black, 2000). In relation to tourism, whilst these examples reveal the long historical interest of dark tourism, they are not, necessarily all examples of hot war tourists.

There exist numerous scattered historical references that testify to the existence of hot war travel before the post-modern age. During the 1642–1649 English Civil War, there are descriptions of families travelling to battlefields to try and find the bodies of family members, or others travelling to pillage the corpses, dispatch the wounded and rob other visitors to the site (Carlton, 1992). At the battle of Culloden, in 1746, there are records of the civilians coming out to watch the fighting, but were then subsequently slaughtered by the Hanoverian soldiers. During the 18th century and the age of the Grand Tour, war and battles were constantly affecting travel, with some opportunities to witness first hand the actual battles (Black, 1992). The Crimea War produced the first war correspondents,[3] together with people volunteering to help the wounded soldiers, or travelling out to watch the siege and fall of Sebastopol (Gordon, 1998). Shortly after the American Civil War ended, Thomas Cook reinstated his tours to America, which included travelling to many battlefields which could still be deemed as hot in relation to the raw visual aesthetic that could be witnessed, as so many bodies had still not been interned (Brendon, 1994; Bates, 1994). Indeed, the First Battle of Bull Run of the American Civil War was made even more chaotic by the retreating Union troops becoming mingled with the fleeing spectators who had driven out from Washington in the expectation of a pleasant afternoon's excursion watching the fighting! The Boer War in 1900 also saw many people travelling out to see the sites of conflict, with Cook organising tours long before the fighting had finished, much to the annoyance of the British High Commissioner who felt tourists were impeding the war effort (Lloyd, 1998).

Seaton (1999) puts forward a convincing argument that the Battle of Waterloo, in 1815, was one of the first great battles to be visited by significant numbers. The societal and economic figurations allowed for more people to visit the battle on a previously unknown scale. Accounts are given of people going to the battle not only immediately after the battle was over, but even during the conflict. Those visiting the battle later helped create a demand for battle mementoes, ranging from swords and bits of uniform; and once the original sources were exhausted, a small cottage industry of fakes was created. The battlefield thus became an important economic resource for the local peasantry, with veterans acting as guides; a pattern of battlefield exploitation places today familiar in places such as Vietnam and Cambodia.

The Thomas Cook archive in Peterborough provides a particularly rich source of historical data on travel to many war zones. For example, as soon as the siege of Paris by the Prussians came to an end in 1871, Cook dispatched one of his staff, John Bedall, on a reconnaissance mission to check the feasibility of resuming tours to Paris. Bedall's correspondence provides

---

[3] William Russell (the first real modern war correspondent) of the *Times*, who accompanied the British troops to fight in the Crimea War in 1850s wrote such vivid descriptions of the conflict, that it helped bring home a distant and far-off land and the many tragedies and incompetence, with his call for the 'daughters of England' to help nurse the sick, helping to inspire and motivate Florence Nightingale to lead a team of nurses to the Crimea. There are also many photographs of the tourists who travelled out to witness the siege of Sebastopol.

some moving descriptions of the devastated landscape (Bedall, 1871), with Cook himself later travelling to Paris, but being slightly more sanguine, saying:

> During my visit I drove and walked though all the principal ruined parts of Paris, and after a most careful examination I failed in finding the slightest disagreeable odour, or appearance of filth or refuse of any description; but on the contrary, the streets were being swept and watered as in the old days. The barricades were all removed, and in a few days nothing will be left to be seen in the street except the frightful ruins in the modern Pompeii, and I should advise all those who are anxious to gratify a morbid curiosity to go at once (Cook, 1871).

Perhaps the high point of hot war tourism was the period immediately after the First World War. The scale of the devastation, the nature of the warfare, together with the economic, social and technological changes or figurations, meant that an unprecedented number of people could visit the sites of conflict: something which Lloyd (1998) comments was done out of both a mixture of remembrance and mawkish interest. The battlefields, which stretched from Belgium, France, the Italian Alps, Palestine, Egypt, Iraq and Turkey, provided numerous opportunities for visiting hot war battle sites. There are even accounts of battle souvenir hunters, in 1914, searching for mementoes immediately after battles were over (Lloyd, 1998). Furthermore, it was estimated that as many as 75% of enquiries about travel to France, in 1919, were related to visiting the battlefields. Lloyd gives a vivid description of what these visitors faced:

> The first parties (to the Western Front) of relatives faced, not only the desolations of the battlefields, which were a veritable desert, but also the depredations of gangs of deserters, who attempted to prey on isolated groups whom they caught in the vast wilderness of the Western Front. Enid Bagnold wrote that immediately after the war a 'certain' lawlessness was abroad in the lonelier areas of the battlefields. Odds and ends of all armies, deserters, well hidden during many months lived under the earth in holes and cellars and used strange means to gain a living (Lloyd, 1998 p. 102).

What is also of interest from Lloyd's work is the recognition of how some destinations became less attractive, as time went on and the heat dissipated, which is of interest in relation to the life cycle of a hot war destination.

The Spanish Civil War and the Second World War also provide many more examples. The Spanish Civil War in particular provides a rich source of evidence. In addition to the thousands of volunteers who travelled to support a cause (McCabe, 2000) — finely articulated through the writings of Orwell, Hemingway and Lee — there were examples of people being invited to see 'history in the making' whilst the war was still on. Thomas Cook also tried to resume tours soon after the war was over, but issuing a warning on their brochures saying "members of the tour are particularly warned against touching grenades, shells, loose wire and such like objects". In relation to the Second World War, the evidence for hot war tourism is less obvious, but can be found, such as in Gordon's (1998) interesting work on Germans travelling to Paris during the war and how their travel patterns became gradually modified as the war progressed.

Currently, despite the initial optimism that the collapse of communism would usher in a new peaceful world order, the pattern that has in fact emerged is one where war and violent insurgent activity has escalated (Black, 2000; Creveld, 1994; Duncan & Opatowski, 2002). According to the SIPRI 2005 Data Base, there were 19 major armed conflicts (which is defined as having over 1,000 deaths) in 17 locations, which were primarily intra-state conflicts, many of which have international dimensions and spillover into other countries (Dwan & Homqvist, 2005). If one was to use Pelton's (2005) much looser definition of conflict and a war zone, it can be argued that there were approximately 80 conflicts around the world in 2005 (Pelton, 2005). Whatever the true figure, what is clear is that war, or conflict zones are a fixture of the post-Cold War world, which partly explains the steady increase in governmental travel warnings (Sengupta & Marbeau, 2003).

The forecasted continued growth of tourism and the emergence of the experiential economy (Mintel International Group, 2002; World Tourism Organisation 2003; Franklin, 2003), together with the permanency that war, insurgency and terrorism has developed in the modern world, means that tourism and war seem likely to increasingly bisect with each other. In the context of this discussion, what is particularly of interest is the growing number of people who consciously seek to travel to hot war zones in both a recreational and business context, which leads to the question of who they are and why do they want to travel to these hot war locations?

Demand Analysis: How Significant are 'Hot War Travellers'?

The discussion of the historical context of hot war tourism and travel helps to more clearly identify the phenomenon. What it does not do is give any real indication of the scale, or significance of the occurrence. A great deal of evidence for the existence of hot war tourism tends to be found in news clippings and magazine stories. For example, Bryne (1997) reported that there are hundreds of British travellers who consciously seek to witness war and famine, with embassies serving war-torn countries reporting an increase in the number of tourists wanting visas, such as in Rwanda, Bosnia and the former Soviet Republics. Jennifer Cox of the Lonely Planet guidebooks also reported that 'terror tourism' seems to be becoming more popular, with Casodo (1999) commenting on how such things as a Foreign Office Travel Warning are read not with fear, but with renewed interest by some. He says the appeal is the historical richness, low prices or geographical beauty, but also the thrill of being in a potentially dangerous place.

The problem with these cuttings is that they focus too much attention on hot war tourism in a recreational context and further strengthen the notion of it being a fringe activity; an argument implicitly reinforced by Lennon and Foley (2000) who acknowledge hot war tourism, describing those who travel to the "most dangerous places on earth" as the "vanguard of dark tourism" (Lennon & Foley, 2000, p. 9). They conclude that these vanguard tourists are few and possess limited economic, political and social significance.

Whilst there seems little doubt that these vanguard tourists are in quantitative terms small, this does not mean they have little significance as Lennon and Foley suggest.

Their importance is not in their number, but in the portentous significance these travellers play in pioneering, or opening up destinations, setting the trail for others to follow (Pryer, 1997). The paradox of war (perversity even) is that whilst it is a destructive force, it can also serve to protect a tourist destination from the tourist hordes, allowing for a more intense, personnel travel experience to be gained by certain types of travellers.

It is perhaps not surprising that many former war zones can become the new destinations of tomorrow (O'Connor, 2002; Mintel International Group, 2004), and in a remarkably short period of time. In the Mintel International Group (2004) report on *Emerging Destinations*, they identify the top 10 countries that are noted for their 'extraordinary' market growth, which includes the former war-torn countries of Cambodia, Vietnam and Croatia, with a number of the other destinations having been affected by conflicts in other countries. What should be appreciated is that many countries at war, or in the process of state rebuilding, can be attractive destinations to certain types of travellers, which can relate to Plog's (1973) allocentric traveller; Cohen's (1973) drifter and explorer; Vogt's (1976) wanderer; Carter's (1998) counter tourist or Elsrud's (2001) budget traveller. Together they form a collective group of travellers that has tended to be under-valued in their economic and social impact, together with the complexity of the way they can be segmented (Pryer, 1997; Elsrud 2001). Furthermore, these more adventurous groups should not be understood as just young backpackers seeking out a meagre existence on minimal money; they can also include mature, credit card wielding travellers who can afford many more expensive items of travel, such as internal flights, rather than the more time consuming overland travel (Pryer, 1997).

Business travel to former, or actual, war zones gives another dimension to the phenomenon of hot war tourism. Oil and mineral companies have long sent workers to war zones, representing one of the more obvious examples of hot war business tourism. What is significant today, however, is the growth in the number and diversity of organisations that will send people to war zones, particularly in the immediate aftermath of a conflict when a process of state rebuilding begins to take place. Paris (2004) noted that the significant increase in the number of armed struggles in the 1990s (with 94% of them being civil or internal in nature) has seen a mixed response from the rest of the world, certainly in terms of preventing the conflicts. What has occurred, however, has been a pattern of brokering peace deals between the different factions, followed by assistance in rebuilding economic, social and political institutions, in order to ensure future state viability. The result of all these many civil wars breaking out, followed by a state rebuilding process, is the growth of what has been described as a peacekeeping industry (Paris, 2004; Duncan & Opatowski, 2000). This industry can involve a vast array of workers, ranging from lawyers involved in writing laws and constitutions; people monitoring elections; aid workers and charities; commercial organisations with contracts for infrastructure projects, such as rebuilding bridges, or power plants; diplomats; people involved in educational training programmes of the military, police and government staff; and soldiers involved in peacekeeping operations. In 2004, the United Nations had sixteen current peacekeeping operations, which involved 58,741 military and civilian police, drawn from over a hundred different countries, together with 3,704 international civilian personnel (United Nations, 2004).

   The conflicts in Afghanistan and particularly Iraq have also more explicitly revealed the scale of outsourcing activities for military operations, such as catering[4] and security. Private security in particular has been experiencing a 'bonanza' (*The Economist*, 2004a),[5] with estimates of the number of private security workers in Iraq ranging from 15,000 to 20,000 people (Lister, 2004; Arun, 2004; Traynor, 2003). Not only do all these workers reveal the scale of a particular niche of hot war tourism, they also indicate a demand for the protection of many foreign workers in Iraq, together with the billions of dollars and market opportunities, which rebuilding war-torn countries can represent (*The Economist*, 2004b).

   It is recognised that some of these groups do not fit neatly into a category of business tourism, particularly if they are transported, accommodated and fed by the military. There is also the issue that many of these groups tend to come when, in theory, the war is over. The 'in theory' is worthwhile emphasising here, particularly in the instance of Iraq, where officially the war is over, yet for all intents and purposes it looks and feels like a war zone, even though the descriptors of insurgents or terrorists tend to be used by governments. Whilst wars may have 'officially' finished, there is no doubting that they can carry plenty of residual heat for long periods after the conflicts, in relation to both the dangers which may be present and in terms of the rawness of the battle aesthetic.

   The significance of business-related hot war tourism should not be undervalued. Just as the pioneering backpacker can be portentous of the future development of tourism in a former war-torn country, so too can the peacekeeping and rebuilding operations lay down the foundations for a future, more mainstream recreational tourism industry. This process is illustrated in places like Cambodia, where the many aid workers and peacekeepers in the country helped establish local services such as restaurants, tour guides and, sadly, exploitative activities such as prostitution and supplying drugs.

Demand Analysis: Developing a Typology of 'Hot War Tourists'

What the discussion has so far revealed is that hot war tourism is much older than many would suspect, and more diverse than many would realise. It is therefore worthwhile developing a more sophisticated typology of the different groups who may travel to a hot war zone. Pelton's many books on travel to dangerous places provides a useful initial insight into some of the realities of hot war zones, illustrating many diverse types of people who may be interested in travelling to hot war zones, which can include the mercenary and war correspondent in addition to the 'curious' (Pelton, 2005). Although many have found his work morally dubious and the dark humour difficult to relate to, his work still provides a useful starting point, or prompt for helping to construct a typology of hot war travellers. Using Pelton's work, together with a mixture of literature, ranging from journal articles, archive material and news clippings, underpinned by a number of interviews with

---

[4] In June 2004, Kellog Brown and Root who had the contract to cater for the soldiers in Iraq had to cater for 50,000 soldiers a day, increasing to 130,000 a day in July (*The Economist*, 2004b).
[5] The Halliburton corporation revealed that a third of their $1.7 billion revenue came from contracts related to Iraq (*The Economist*, 2004b).

people who have directly travelled to war zones for various reasons, one can begin to identify a number of different traveller types. These are summarised and presented in Table 12.1.

What should be noted is that the word 'travel' is used self-consciously here, in the sense of its origins, where it referred to the notion of embarking on a journey that could entail

Table 12.1: A typology of hot war travellers.

Type	Description
(i) The innocents	The innocents' category is designed to take account of those tourists who inadvertently get caught up in war or insurgent activity. Whilst these people do not actively seek the danger of war, they are highlighted here to take account of the apparent increase in the number who may find themselves as a target for kidnapping, terrorism or murder. The British tourists on an adventure holiday killed in Uganda in 1999 and the Yemen in 1998, are examples of these innocents who by misfortune became victims of wider conflicts.
(ii) The cocktail traveller	These travellers are not interested in the war directly, but if there is the element of danger, or an opportunity to see the aftermath of a battle, then this only adds to the general experience. The war acts as a startling backdrop to the travel experience, with the possible prospect of danger adding an element of frisson to the travel.
(iii) Remembrance/ pilgrim traveller	A great deal of Northern France and Belgium's tourism industry was established to cater for families and veterans of those who died in battle. This century, the figurations in society have meant that more people than ever can return to locations where loved ones have died. Perhaps, the high point of hot war tourism was after the two world wars in relation to the numbers who could travel and witness the carnage that had just come to an end. In places such as Iraq, the number of people who travel to holy shrines, despite many of the conditions of a war zone existing, also illustrates another dimension of this type of traveller.
(iv) The Duty/ working traveller	The most obvious category of traveller here would be the journalist covering the war zone. One can add to this list the growing number of people who go to war-torn areas in the context of aid programmes, the peacekeeping industry, or seeking commercial opportunities and contracts, particularly in infrastructure rebuilding projects.

(Continued)

Table 12.1 (*Continued*)

Type	Description
	More unusual types can be found with the example of Phil Sands (who kept a diary for the *Independent* in 2003), who left his job to go to Iraq as part of a peace protest and acting as a human shield.
(v) The thrill seeker traveller	This is a category the media like to focus on where the thrill of war is directly sought, whereby it is seen as part of an adventure. It is the people who want to experience the excitement of war and its associated dangers, which can even drift into becoming a fighting volunteer or duty tourists.
(vi) The rubbernecker traveller	This is another popular category for the media to focus on. These are the people who wish to see the consequences of war directly, whilst they are still hot, with the basis of the motivation being more of a curiosity, mawkish interest or are voyeuristic, which has been described as rubbernecking at misery. This group is perhaps the most morally suspect.
(vii) The fighting volunteers	Whether someone volunteering to fight for a foreign side could be classed as duty tourists could be open to debate. There is a long history of people volunteering to fight for a cause, ranging from early crusades in the 11th century, the International Brigade formed during the Spanish Civil War, Bosnia[6] in the 1990s and the more recent conflicts in Afghanistan[7] and Iraq. They highlight the complexity of humans and their motivations, how we are not just satisfied by the search for security, food, love and happiness. There is also the grey area of mercenaries that seems to be a growing area (Kemp, 1998).
(viii) The trophy seekers	For some, going to war zones can be seen as the ultimate travel challenge or culmination of their profession. It was something Hastings (1984) was conscious of with his desire to cover the Falklands war, where he would have a chance to emulate his father's experience of being with the troops during the Normandy landings. A hot war destination could be understood as the ultimate test in their travel or work.

[6] In 1992, an estimated 2,000 'internationally minded mujahideen', some with training in Afghanistan, travelled to fight in Bosnia (Harmon, 2000, p. 144)

[7] The white, middle-class American, John Walker, a Taliban volunteer in Afghanistan is an interesting example of the fighting volunteer, who was discovered after the revolt of Qala-I-jhangi, is a more unusual example (Engel, 2001).

dangers and hardships, yet could also provide experiences that may be valuable and rewarding. It is also a definition that has relevancy in relation to gaining an insight into the motives for travel to hot war zones as will be illustrated in the next section.

It should also be recognised that these types/groups are not presented as rigid, deterministic categories. People travelling to hot war zones, can and do drift between these categories at different times. What the categories help reveal, however, is the complexity of hot war travel patterns in terms of the possible motivations — elements that can be particularly important when exploring the ethics of this form of travel.

Whilst researching and composing this typology, what soon became evident was the strong Eurocentric bias, in the sense that it predominantly focused on people from the developed world travelling to lesser-developed countries. What one soon discovers is diversity in travel patterns from within a country at war (excluding refugees) and from countries that could be categorised as lesser developed. This is particularly true in relation to the 'pilgrimage' traveller and perhaps more controversially the 'fighting volunteer' type. The pilgrimage traveller in particular is worthwhile exploring a little more deeply as it revealed some interesting findings.

A prime example that illustrates the complex pattern of hot war pilgrimage travel, relates to the holy city of Karbala in Iraq, which is 100 km from Baghdad. The city of Karbala grew on the site of the Battle of Karbala, where in 61AH/680CE, the Imam Husayn — a direct descendent of the Prophet Mohammad and the spiritual leader of Shi'a Muslims — along with his followers, was massacred after a protracted period of negotiations trying to avoid bloodshed. The place of his death became a place of pilgrimage, with the date of his death becoming a time of commemoration and remembrance. Under Saddam Hussein's regime the commemoration of this massacre, known as Ashura, was banned. Since the regime's collapse, worshippers are free to mark Ashura, with millions attracted to Karbala not only from within Iraq itself, but also from Iran, Pakistan and many other countries. Although there is little doubt that the violence in Iraq has deterred thousands from travelling to the site, there were still a significant number whose strength of belief compelled them to endure the dangers and visit the site. As many anticipated, the commemoration of Ashura became the focus for a number of bomb and mortar attacks, killing and injuring hundreds of worshippers in 2004, which has only added to the feeling that the country is drifting further towards a sectarian war between the Shi'a and the Sunni Muslim factions. There are too many sad ironies here. The battle which marked the beginning of the split between the branches of Islam over 1,400 years ago, which had long gone cold, is visited by thousands in hot war conditions, with the many subsequent attacks on the people commemorating Ashura and paying homage to the shrine, possibly marking an escalation of sectarian conflict that could become a civil war.

Demand Analysis: Examining the Motivation to Travel

Many media reports tend to place hot war tourism as part of a fringe, adventure type travel. Whilst no doubt this can be part of the motivation to travel, a deeper examination of the subject reveals a more complex process generating human action.

When examining the different possible types of hot war traveller, four underpinning motivational elements can be said to operate. These are:

- Hot cognition (e.g. shock, empathy, thrill seeking, reverence);
- Opportunistic behaviour (e.g. this relates to not only financial gain, but also reputational gain, such as journalists taking risks to cover the story and gain more recognition, or travellers gaining the kudos of a good story);
- An obligated activity (e.g. a peacekeeper, aid worker, with pilgrimage travellers being something of a grey area);
- The search for the new (e.g. a new destination untouched by tourism, or new destination markets).

These are broad categories and again must not be understood as mutually exclusive or exhaustive. For example, when examining the motivation of many war correspondents, such as John Simpson, one can see a complex interaction of motivational forces at play, ranging from the excitement of the war, the deep friendships formed in the face of adversity, the desire to make his mark on history, and the sense of outrage felt which compels him to tell the world of the atrocities taking place (Simpson, 2002). In this sense, all of the underpinning motivational elements are at play. Motivation is thus seen as a cocktail of driving forces, which can vary in their mix and how they influence behaviour.

If one frames these motivational elements in the context of the growth of the experiential, or experienced-based economy, a better understanding can be gained about the phenomenon. Mintel International Group (2002), the World Tourism Organisation (2003) and Franklin (2003), all emphasise how the industrialised world is in transition from a service-based economy, to an experienced-based economy. In the context of tourism, this can involve creating a better, or perhaps it is more accurate to say, a more provocative travel experience, with the opportunity for travellers seeking something different, and a sense of personal discovery (Mintel International Group, 2002).

Theories, such as Csikzentmihalyi's concept of flow, help to give further insights into these trends. Csikzentmihalyi (1992) examined the condition of human happiness and meaningful experiences, noting that happiness is not necessarily the result of good fortune, or something that happens, but is the cognitive interpretation of events, whereby we are all striving for optimal flow experiences. What is of particular interest is how Csikzentmihalyi (1992) is keen to stress that these experiences do not need to give immediate gratification. As he states: "like all good adventures worth having it will not be an easy one" (1992, p. 6). Satisfaction is not always gained immediately with the act itself, but with later reflection — something which is particularly relevant in travel experiences. Furthermore, he also points out that lives disrupted by tragic accidents and other stresses, do not necessarily diminish happiness — the key is how people respond to the stress, "despite the adversity" (Csikzentmihalyi, 1992, p. 70).

The value of these theories is that it encourages one to examine the travel experience beyond the common, narrow focus on relaxation, or the seeking of immediate pleasure gratification. What can give satisfaction and optimal experiences can relate to overcoming challenges, have an element of the unknown, and can involve a wide array of provocative emotional experiences. It can also be used to gain an understanding into the significant growth in voluntary work in remote destinations, where people are seeking a provocative, challenging experience, not one that delivers immediate fun and happiness. If one frames these motivational elements in the wider global political, economic and technological figurations, then one soon realises that there are more opportunities for people to seek optimal experiences, in more diverse ways, which has relevancy for people in both the developed and lesser-developed world.

Conclusion

War in the 21st century is as endemic as ever. The ending of the Cold War was not the end of history after all. Instead of two monolithic power-blocks facing each other, there has been a flourishing of smaller ethnic, religious and political civil wars which, despite the internal state aspect, have had reverberations far beyond their state borders. The pattern that has emerged is that wars seem increasingly to bisect the world's largest industry, whether this is by disrupting and/or diverting tourism flows. People continue to seek new opportunities in competitive global market places, or people desiring more intense, provocative personal, optimal experiences, and these potentially include travel to the conflict 'hot spots'.

Is hot war tourism a new and growing ultimate adventure holiday as so many media headlines, stories and programmes would suggest? The answer is a small 'partly'. Hot war tourism is far from new, is more diverse than many would suppose and should not be understood as just an extension in the growth of adventure tourism. To do this is to bind one's rationality to the phenomenon.

What this study helps reveal is the importance of business related hot war tourism, with the growth in the peacekeeping industry in the 1990s being of particular significance. It is an industry that not only involves military personnel, but also many aid workers, lawyers, trainers and commercial businesses seeking lucrative contracts, as attempts are made to rebuild the failed state. In relation to tourism, these people play a vital role in establishing a tourism infrastructure, for both good and bad, from which more mainstream tourism services may flow from in the future. Furthermore, what also began to be revealed was the complex pattern of domestic travel within war zones and those generated from lesser-developed countries, particularly in the context of pilgrimage travel. This is a discrete area of research in its own right.

What has not been discussed in this chapter is the issue of the ethics and hot war tourism. It is an area that could take up a whole book in itself. For now, only a few comments will be made in relation to making some closing remarks. It is clear that cold war locations can be understood as a tourism resource that have a long history of exploitation. Yet they are not ordinary tourism resources. To treat them as such is to run the danger that the places and the events are trivialised and robbed of their power. In relation to hot war tourism these issues are intensified. For many types of travellers identified, one can raise serious questions about the ethics of such travel. True, for the duty tourists, whilst deep down the motivation may be a desire for excitement, at least there is a moral framework within which they operate; a framework which does not exist for other types, such as the 'thrill seeker', or the 'cocktail traveller' and so one can raise serious questions about the morality of their actions. To treat hot war zones as just another destination or tourism resource is to begin a process of commodification that can distract from the horrors of war and the poor people who have to endure the pains inflicted upon them by the violence unleashed. We should remember those people first, always.

ACTS OF IMAGINATION

Introduction

Chris Ryan

Thus far, among the themes identified by contributors to this book have been those of how does one record the exploits of those who fell far from their own shores and the battles that involved forces fighting far from their home country? Second, it has been continually noted that acts of remembrance can be selective, and that such acts contribute to a culture and its constructed stories. The first of the three chapters involved in this section of the book brings these two themes together to illustrate how the past and its events can be displaced in both time and location in order to create a tourism event that is designed to generate a sense of community, economic yield and quite fundamentally, a 'good day' out for families. Yet, the authors, Chris Ryan and Jenny Cave, maintain that within this construction of a tourism event there exist serious moments of experiential authenticity for key actors within the presentation, and that, for at least some spectators, the acts of falsehood in which this event engages nonetheless generate emotive truths as people face a sense of loss. The event that is described in this chapter is the Armistice Day celebrations at the small township of Cambridge in New Zealand. While Cambridge owes its origins to being a place of settlement by colonial troops in the aftermath of the Maori Wars of the 1860s, it does not directly remember its own military engagements, but takes advantage of being twinned with the French town of Quesnoy. Quesnoy possesses significance in New Zealand military history as, in the dying days of the First World War, it was taken by New Zealand troops, thereby bringing an end to a period of German occupation. On this premise, what is described in this chapter is a replacement of a tradition of a dawn service by a parade of military hardware by re-enactment societies, a presentation of engagements from differing wars that include Vietnam as well as the World Wars, and the enactment of roles of being a representative of foreign nationals by local citizens and guests who, on having to place a wreath at the Cenotaph, then come face to face with their own thoughts of war and personal impacts. In short, a mélange of military traditions are brought to bear on a particular period of the year for both reasons of remembrance and commercial and social gain.

The second chapter in this section is also about the constructions of stories for community well-being, but this time based upon historical events that occurred at the location of remembrance and myth building — but these are stories about which a diversity of opinion exists.

Did the events of the Eureka Stockade in 1854, in what has been described as Australia's only major act of rebellion, represent a strike for personal freedoms, liberty and democracy, or was it little more than simply a case of a bungling colonial government facing irate miners aggrieved about the need for a license and inflamed by a series of mob actions as an alarmed local government sought military support? In his chapter, Warwick Frost identifies the contradictory arguments and notes that in the period of the immediate aftermath there was something of an embarrassed silence that things should have gotten so out of hand. However, he lists the differing interpretations attributed to the events and notes that, drawing on Tunbridge and Ashworth's (1996) concept of a dissonant heritage, that the dissonance is not only one of interpretation of past events, but also of a current nature with reference to the location of the relics and a competing claim to 'authenticity'. Equally, what Frost demonstrates is how, in order to generate economic gain, tourism authorities will seek to generate mindfulness on the part of visitors, but that such attempts are in part determined by the nature of the resource base.

The final chapter is an account of the annual re-enactment of the Battle of Aiken during the American Civil War. Fought in the dying days of that conflict it represented a momentary triumph for the Confederacy as Sherman was beginning to mop up the remnants of the southern armies in 1865. As an event it is attracting larger crowds each year, and thus brings some economic benefit to the small town of Aiken in South Carolina. However, bearing in mind the comments of the opening chapter that the third component of culture is the lived-in experience, this text, having initially described the history of the battle, tends to relate to the motives of the re-enactors and their experience of re-fighting and re-discovering events so that they can light the imagination and knowledge of future generations about events that they feel are being slowly forgotten in a popular culture of sound bites divorced from any sense of history. The motives described range from a concern about accuracy — about the minutiae of costume, weapons and movements that drive a small industry that seeks out diaries and writings from all manners of participants in the original fray — to a wish to personally experience what it must have been like for people at that time. Thus the chapter cites one respondent on his own feelings about charging up a hill where people aim guns at you. This chapter is perhaps one that demonstrates clearly that a living history can be built upon the battles of the past, and in a way it is indicative of a growing interest in re-enactment societies — an interest also touched upon by the chapter on Cambridge's Armistice Day celebrations.

What also emerges from this last chapter is that the passing of time and a growing distance from the past might possibly be said to add an air of romance to the conflicts of history; but it is a tempered romance as many of the political issues that accounted for that specific war continue to reverberate in the south of the United States. The issue of State rights against a Federal government continues, as in any Federal constitution, to be a source of tension. Whether such tensions are constructive or dysfunctional depends to a large degree upon the representations of past conflict, and thus again it can be noted that representations of past battles are not simple matters of record, but living stories with meanings for contemporary generations.

Together it is suggested that a theme of imagination weaves its way between the three chapters. It might be argued that imagination is the embryo of action — and in all three locations local people have imagined a scenario where past events can be brought to life to aid their own senses of community and social well-being. In each case the local initiatives have received comparatively little formal central government support, although local government has provided some monies and local government employees involved in tourism services have provided labour and professional skills to help bring about the presentations and re-enactments. In two of the chapters it needs to be realized that significant planning is involved in the re-enactments. Large numbers of enthusiasts have to be in the right place at the right time. Health and safety legislation need to be considered, logistics of movements are required, roads may be blocked off at given times and police help sought as crowds might need to be marshalled. Commercial interests associated with the sales of memorabilia need to be catered for, and indeed they may represent a source of revenue. Approvals may be sought for camping purposes — in short, a year-long process of planning lies behind these re-enactments. Both the Cambridge and Aiken examples reflect the common themes of wanting to retain memories of past events seen as meaningful and important to an understanding of not only local, but also national identity; but both also have other concerns of entertainment, of being with people of similar interests, and of personal senses of identity. In short, battlefield sites are not simply dead places, devoid of current life; places left to ghosts — in these instances contemporary generations play out for their own needs and those of their societies, the actions of yesterday.

Chapter 13

Cambridge Armistice Day Celebrations: Making a Carnival of War and the Reality of Play

Chris Ryan and Jenny Cave

Context and Background

On the 11th hour of the 11th month in 1918, hostilities ceased on the Western Front to signal the end of the Great War. In subsequent years, throughout the Commonwealth, near to
and far from the battlefields of France, monuments were erected to the fallen to commemorate
their sacrifice for Empire. This was as true of New Zealand as other countries. New Zealand
troops had been involved throughout the Great War, having been quick to respond to appeals
for help from what was still regarded as the 'mother country' or 'home'. In the final days of
the Great War, New Zealand soldiers were engaged in the relief of Quesnoy in France,
successfully expelling German troops on 4 November 1918. That attack is important in
New Zealand military history for many reasons. It was the "New Zealanders' most
successful day of the whole campaign on the Western Front. They advanced ten kilometres
and captured 2000 Germans and sixty field guns" (www.nzhistory.net). In the attack about
90 New Zealand soldiers lost their lives. They were almost the last of the 12,483 who died
between 1916 and 1918 (a total that was greater than in the whole of the Second World War)
earning New Zealand the honour of having lost more men per capita than any of the Allied
nations.

   Between 1918 and the present, the monuments to the fallen collected other names from
other wars, notably from the Second World War, but also from other engagements where
New Zealand troops were engaged such as Korea and Vietnam. Additionally, as in other
Commonwealth countries, the practice took root of commemorating the dead as returning
comrades sought to remember, give thanks for their own survival, share the comradeship
of similar others in the clubs and bars of the Returned Services Association, while also
being motivated to keep alive a memory thought important for succeeding generations.
The 11th November, or the Sunday closest to it, saw various ceremonies being enacted at

Battlefield Tourism: History, Place and Interpretation
Copyright © 2007 by Elsevier Ltd.
All rights of reproduction in any form reserved.
ISBN: 0-08-045362-7

dawn through communities large and small in New Zealand — all with common themes of remembrance, the playing of the 'Last Post' and the laying of wreaths before a cenotaph. The acceptance of this ceremony beyond those who had been involved waxed and waned through the years. In the iconoclastic 1960s, such memories appeared 'old fashioned' — redolent of an age of past values strange to the then contemporary discovery of fashion, teenage years and the rise of popular music as a mass market. However, by the late 1990s, the numbers attending dawn services had increased, and commentators remarked not only on the size of crowds, but also the mixed age groups as young people began to re-assess the contribution of past generations. As the survivors of the First World War dwindled in number and those who returned from not only the Second World War, but also Vietnam, grew grey in hair and increasingly infirm, so it seemed the young wished to know more about the events that had shaped this part of a nation's history. Among both New Zealand and Australian youth, Gallipoli became symbolic of a past age and a birth of nationhood for both these countries (Hall, 2002).

Apart from these acts of remembrance other linkages came to be formed. The small town of Cambridge, in the north of New Zealand established twinning arrangements with Quesnoy in France, partly on the military connections between the two places as noted above. Like many such arrangements, and for many years, the relationships were comparatively low key. Councillors and school children engaged in exchange visits to become aware of each others' history and to share experiences of different places and culture.

In the late 1990s, Cambridge, again like many New Zealand communities, began to benefit from the growth of tourism. A generally well-endowed area, with Class A soils, generous rainfall and temperate climate, the town has one of the highest per capita incomes in New Zealand, being at the centre of a thoroughbred race horse industry and having its share of successful dairy farmers that characterise the rural economy of the Waikato. Additionally, it acts as a rural dormitory town for Hamilton and many professional, higher educated and higher income groups have made Cambridge their home. However, economic success had not been consistent. The dairy industry had survived the loss of farming subsidies in the 1980s to rebound stronger than before, but the industry was still vulnerable to changes in world market prices, adverse movements in foreign exchange and uncertain payments to dairy farmers. Given consistent growth in international tourism, and access to the key market of Auckland, 2 hours drive north for a domestic tourism market, local entrepreneurs began to explore the possibilities of tourism. New accommodation units began to appear, rural- and farm-based stays began to be offered, and the town sought to take advantage of its 'English nature' and its tree lined 'gentility'. Other factors influenced the town. Its nodal location on the arterial State Highway One bisecting the North Island and central access to the pivotal tourism destinations of Rotorua and Lake Taupo means on average that 16,000 cars pass through Cambridge daily. Local government reform meant that the town lost having its own Council, but a larger Waipa District Council invested in Lake Karapiro, local to the town, and a series of events there based upon a new water sports centre began to create more retail and accommodation opportunities. The arrival of one of New Zealand's largest discount retailers, The Warehouse, in 1998, signalled a change in retail mix as small shops trading in records, house ware and second-hand clothes disappeared to be replaced by a mixture of cafes and more upmarket retailers to complement The Warehouse and to serve the greater number of clients it attracted. One by-product of this was an extension of trading hours at weekends. Whereas, in the mid-1990s much of the retail provision in Cambridge closed at mid-day or 1.00 pm on a Saturday, a decade later retailers traded all day Saturday. Additionally, Sundays saw the towns' cafes and restaurants having a successful trade catering to locals, day and longer stay visitors, while the local Lions launched a series of 'trash and treasure sales' and monthly Market Days that gave reason for people to visit, generated business for local cafes and provided a happy bustle to the main street. This new interest in tourism, aided by the District Council's wish to generate yet more visitors, laid the background to what has become one of the town's most successful events.

Cambridge's Armistice Day

The current programme commenced in 2001, and was very much due to the initiative of a dynamic personality appointed to manage the town's Visitor Information Centre. Liz Stolwyz created a position that evolved into a role very different from the purely administrative position that some councillors might have originally envisaged. She quickly saw an opportunity to put Cambridge on the map and identified the development of a portfolio of events as a key component to this. The link with Quesnoy provided the impetus for what is now known as Cambridge Armistice Day. Links with Quesnoy had blossomed further with a local historian and entrepreneur starting tours of Quesnoy and the sites of battle. Quesnoy's councillors had reacted warmly and been courteous hosts, providing special civic occasions for their New Zealand guests. From these seeds Liz's ideas for an Armistice Day celebration beyond the traditional dawn service emerged, and quickly gained the support of key figures in the local community. The Deputy Mayor for Waipa District Council, Peter Lee, a local Cambridge businessman, and a Councillor representing Cambridge, quickly embraced the idea, while the Mayor, Alan Livingston, readily lent support to help offset a perception among some in Cambridge that the 'new' Waipa District Council was too readily predisposed to support initiatives in Te Awamutu, while also liking the very idea itself. The Board of Cambridge Information Centre also comprised local leaders from Cambridge Community Board, and they too fully supported the idea for reasons of local pride, to generate economic benefit and perhaps also to obtain, or retain, a high profile for themselves in local politics.

The idea was basically quite simple, and to a small degree based on an already successful model. The museum at Wanaka in New Zealand's South Island, dedicated to the restoration and flying of old aircraft from past wars had already shown that an event based on nostalgia, pride in New Zealand's participation in past wars and a growing interest in old technologies could prove to a 'crowd puller'. The biennial 'War Birds over Wanaka' started by Tim Wallis was attracting visitors in the tens of thousands, and among these were several enthusiasts drawn from overseas. Thus at Cambridge, the core of the idea was the attraction of military history enactment societies to come, camp overnight in Cambridge prior to the main events on a Sunday, participate in a town parade, and engage in battle enactments while also incorporating the ceremony at the Cenotaph. From the outset, the idea has proven successful from the perspective of different criteria. It has attracted a growing number of visitors. Even in 2004, when the weather was not at its best, it is estimated that 5,000 came to watch the events, while in 2005, blessed by fine weather and more events, possibly twice that number attended. From being primarily covered solely by local media, in 2005 national media including television was present, thereby attracting favourable publicity for the town. The economic impact of the event has grown significantly in as far as can be assessed. Researchers from the University of Waikato's Department of Tourism and Hospitality Management have been connected with the event from the start, being present on the Board of the Visitor Information Centre and the Organising Committee of the Armistice Day Celebrations since its inception. In 2005, as part of the growing number of events, the Department also organised a seminar on the Thursday night prior to the main event. The subject matter was military events and history as tourist attractions, and such was the level of support and attendance that the Department became committed to a similar event in 2006.

The main attraction for both crowds and participants are the presence of the military enactment societies and their 'battles'. Figure 13.1 is taken from the 2005 parade prior to the memorial service. Figure 13.2 is from one of the battle enactments. Another regular feature has been the Boogie Woogie Girls, an Andrews Sisters copy group. This trio has been present at every event and are another important component within event programming.

On the Saturday night before the parade and enactments, a feature of the proceedings is the Armistice Dance. Military uniform and the styles of the 1940s are *de rigueur*, and everyone turns up duly dressed to dance to the Hamilton Big Band playing the music of Glenn Miller and the Boogie Woogie Girls performing the songs of the Andrew Sisters. Additionally, the Boogie Woogie Girls provide a transition from the serious remembrance at the cenotaph to the entertainment of the remainder of the programme.

Figure 13.1: Parade of military equipment by re-enactors (Photograph by Chris Ryan).

Figure 13.2: Skirmish on the cricket pitch at Cambridge Armistice Day (Photograph by Chris Ryan).

Until 2004 there was one main battle enactment, but in 2005 the programme was changed, and three such separate events took place. These were an ambush on one of Cambridge's streets involving a replication of a World War Two action, an enactment of a skirmish from the Vietnam War in the main venue of the Village Square and finally, as the main event, a re-enactment of the relief of Quesnoy. In addition to these events, supporting acts have included flights over the town by War Birds of Wanaka, parachute drops, the presence of New Zealand's armed forces including displays in 2004 of a helicopter, a lolly scramble from jeeps, demonstrations of military vehicles in action such as tanks and armoured vehicles, marching bands and other ancillary events such a military memorabilia tents and trading.

It has been noted that the event has been successful from many points of view. Estimates of the economic impact as measured by net added value by the authors were of about $60,000 in 2002, and $80,000 in 2003. In 2005 the estimates would be significantly higher for a number of reasons. First, there was an increase in attendance. Second, there was evidence of growing use of the serviced accommodation sector and for the first time since the event started local motels reported being full. Third, some of the leakages previously identified were stopped with local Lions mounting stalls selling burgers, fries, soft drinks, etc., whereas initially these services had been provided by out of town sub-contractors. Consequently, it is not unreasonable to say that net added value was double that of 2003.

Next, in terms of reinforcing the links between Cambridge and Quesnoy, the event has been successful. Indeed in 2005, the French Ambassador, Jean-Michel Marlaud visited Cambridge with the Senator for French Nationals abroad, Christian Cointat. At that time Cointat was also Director-General of the European Parliament. Hosted by Alan Livingston, Mayor of Waipa District Council, both were presented with copies of the book *Cambridge WW1 — Something to Remember* by the author Eris Parker — curator of the Cambridge Museum.

With such visits, and the growth of the event, national media coverage has been achieved as has been already noted, but the event also provides significant material for the local press. Figures 13.3 and 13.4 show how the event dominates the front page of the local paper, the *Cambridge Edition*. While this is important in attracting local people to support the event, it

Figure 13.3: Local reporting of the Armistice Day Event – example 1 (Reproduced by kind permission of Wayne Timmo, editor, *Cambridge Edition*, Cambridge, New Zealand).

Figure 13.4: Local Reporting of the Armistice Day Event – example 2 (Reproduced by kind permission of Wayne Timmo, editor, *Cambridge Edition*, Cambridge, New Zealand).

is suggested that such coverage goes beyond just attracting people. In personal communication with one of the paper's reporters it was stated that while initially such coverage was about promotion, it is today as much about confirming senses of local pride and community — something that was perhaps important in 2005 when earlier events at the local high school had divided the community with demonstrations for and against the School Principal.

Deconstructing the Event

It should not, however, be thought that the event has been without its critics in spite of its obvious success in generating favourable publicity for the town, reinforcing a sense of community, generating income and simply adding to the factors that make Cambridge a pleasurable place to live. The juxtaposition between acts of remembrance and entertainment sits uneasily among some members of the Returned Services Association. The traditional time of the Remembrance Service has been changed from dawn to 10.45 am, and for some this represents a break with tradition and reduces a mild level of inconvenience in terms of getting up early — an inconvenience which is a minor sacrifice, but which with the sounding of the Last Post early in the morning has contributed to a sense of stillness and appreciation of the sacrifice made by past generations of primarily young men and women. Yet it can be argued that the dawn itself is a deviation from the actual time of 11.00 am when hostilities ceased. A further issue for the Association is the addition of an indigenous Maori powhiri to challenge and welcome for international dignitaries which, while essential in terms of cultural and Anglican church protocols, does not represent the moves in place in either World War I or World War II. There is the obvious juxtaposition of the seriousness of war, the bloody mess that is war, and the playing at war involved in providing enactments of battles for the purposes of entertainment and economic gain. Is this an example of the sacrifice of past generations becoming commodified?

This issue is one that participants in the re-enactment societies have pondered. In New Zealand, the World War II Historical Re-enactment Society was formed in March 1995, the year of the anniversary of the end of the Second World War. Its web site (http://www.hrs.org.nz/main.htm) notes that "The society formed two units, one allied and one German for a TVNZ display battle and went on to provide extras for several local TV programmes like *The Charles Upham Story*, *The Call Up*, and *Heroes* as well as several short films". It goes on to say that it does not seek to glorify war, but rather "We believe that military history is an important part of our heritage. Re-enactment gives us a little more understanding of our forefathers' sacrifice". Indeed, it deliberately heads its web site with words from the memorial service, namely:

Lest We Forget

They shall not grow old as we that are left grow old
Age shall not weary them, nor the years condemn
At the going down of the sun, and in the morning,
We will remember them

(*ANZAC — Australia New Zealand Army Corps*)

Another major presence is that of The Jeep Owners Club of New Zealand and The Military Re-enactment Society. Their web pages are hosted by Brigadier Colin Jansen of the 16th Field Regiment, and for him the pages and the society's activities were both inspired by, and a monument to, his grand father, Private Neil Yukon Wylie of 24th Field Ambulance Corp who fought in the Second World War.

The main aims of the Military Re-enactment Society are described as being "more complex than the usual re-enactment group. We wish to preserve both the memory of the men and women who served their country in the ground war, as well as the relevant equipment, weapons, vehicles etc., those individuals used in performing their duty, and to educate younger generations through attendance at remembrance ceremonies and live or static displays of the war years and those post World War II conflicts New Zealand and her allied were involved in. We wish to be recognised as a mobile live action museum" (http://www.jeepownersclub.co.nz/mrs/mrsindex.html). Many members of these societies actively contribute to the New Zealand Armed Forces Memorial Project, which seeks to develop a pictorial record of war graves and memorials that mark the sacrifice made by New Zealanders in conflict overseas.

There are parallels with other re-enactment societies whose interest lies in different periods of history. For example, an intense interest exists in the minutiae of design, uniforms, correct presentation and procedures so that historical authenticity is reproduced as carefully as is possible. However, while other historical re-enactment societies present alternatives to contemporary life, these historical re-enactment societies differ in that they see themselves as deliberately seeking to remind contemporary society of past sacrifice that is an important explanatory variable that shaped that society. There are, as for Brigadier Jansen, personal family reasons for their interest and a parallel might be drawn with the current growing interest in genealogy. From a wider societal perspective, as technology and life styles create continuous change, such interests might be said to provide an historical basis for personal as well as societal identity, and are carried into the personal relationships of the Society members, many of whom are close friends, couples or colleagues.

While the motives of those promoting the societies are serious, other facets of presentation possess importance. The members are engaged in serious leisure. It has been suggested that serious leisure has several functions that include definition of self-identity, the gaining of status, and the development of career opportunities.

One of the implications of this for the Cambridge Armistice Day celebrations has been the increasing professionalism of the event. For 2005, the re-enactment was advised and partially designed by Steve Goodman, who had emigrated from the UK to settle in Cambridge. His background included work with the Second Battle Group — a UK military re-enactment group specialising in portraying German troops — which group was involved in the Spielberg film, *Saving Private Ryan*. Goodman was cited as saying "it cost around thousands simply for the blank ammunition for the day. With a machine gun chewing through hundreds of rounds a minute at $1.00 a pop, the cost soon added up. You are looking at $3,000 just for the bangs" (Timmo, 2005, p. 1). The search for authenticity included the use, in the Vietnam re-enactment, of a M60 machine gun valued at $7,000, loaned by the Auckland company, Fire Fight Industries. The main event in 2005, a re-enactment of the taking of Quesnoy, involved 70 enactors and the construction of wooden walls to portray the medieval ramparts of Le Quesnoy.

Against the professionalism of those who handle the explosives, or the parachute jumpers and the 'real' military presence sometimes found, there (in 2004, the New Zealand Navy Air Arm provided a new Kaman SH-2G(NZ) Super Seasprite helicopter to be part of the display — intriguingly enough another display was a Peter Jackson imitation First World War tank that was to have had a role in his 2005 release, *King Kong* — a further example of where the real and the imagined shared a spatial juxtaposition) is the 'amateur enthusiasm' of the organising committee. It should be noted that this is not meant as a pejorative term. The organising committee has more of its fair share of retired people, but these are people active in local affairs, with past business experience, and with time and a 'can do' attitude. But, for an event of the size of the Armistice Day it might be said that they are under-resourced. The main resource is the full-time manager of the Visitor Information Centre, a role with many other functions than simply organising a replica of battle. One implication of this is a budget that is growing, and in 2005 was over-spent. One sign of the growing professionalism is the request for fees for services initially provided free by different participating groups, and thus in 2005, Warbirds over Wanaka did not provide their aerial acrobatics because of cost. A further indicator of professionalism is the emphasis in 2005 on health, safety and security undertaken to ensure the safe operation of heritage equipment, safety of the crowds and security of the vehicles and memorabilia — a difficult task when 'can do' enthusiasts work with professional organisers who are aware of legislative concerns and penalties.

Such a nexus of professionalism and amateurism means that the event, when set in the wider context of meanings and location, begins to appear increasingly nuanced. Tourism is full of examples of temporal and place displacement. It is possible to see Amsterdam in Sasebo, Japan, at Huis Ten Bosch and the African jungle at Disney in Florida complete with wildlife to cite but two examples. At Cambridge there is the remembrance of past events but spatially and temporally re-enacted far from the place of their origins. Indeed, it might be argued that there are many other locations in New Zealand with a closer claim for relationships with Quesnoy than Cambridge. For example, the first New Zealander to scale the walls of the town was Lieutenant Averill from Christchurch.

Whatever the motives, the events in Cambridge are a re-enactment of a past in another place, but it is the nature of such events that they (re)create their own realities, even where they are based upon tenuous attachments to what might be perceived as an objective truth. This became very clear in 2005. As has been noted, one of the solemn occasions is the laying of the wreath in memory of the fallen at the 10.45 am service. A service is conducted by the Vicar of St. Andrews Church in Cambridge. At 11.00 am, as the clock strikes the hour, wreaths were laid by representatives of nations involved in the war. The wording of introductions was ambiguous, but the clear impression was given that these were representatives from the embassies of the countries involved, and thus had official status. However, the Australian representative was a Professor from Australia visiting the Department of Tourism at the University of Waikato. The American representative was a local businessman and a member of the local soccer team board, while the Italian representative was a local retailer and councillor. That the ambiguity succeeded was clearly brought home to the first author as, when talking to the American 'representative' a tourist from the United States made herself known by asking 'Are you from the Embassy, what part of the States are you from'? — for which the answer was 'from California' with no explanation of the position.

Yet, even this lack of authenticity creates an authentic experiential moment for participants. The laying of the wreath possessed meaning for those attending the service; including the 'ambassadorial staff'. In later conversation, the Australian Professor stated that when laying the wreath, he thought of his father, what he had been through, and that for him the moment had a personal meaning through that link. For the Italian representative, when asked what he had felt, had replied, 'I felt a bit funny — after all, I was on the loosing side — I was the enemy — but then I thought — that was the past, today we are all one, and this was my community and it was good that we can come together without enmity, as friends'. The moment too had a reality for him.

Cambridge Armistice Day has several paradoxes within that can be summed as opposing paradigms:

- Serious remembrance of bloody war — spectating and participating at war games
- Inauthentic representation — authentic experiential moments
- Displacement from place and of time — confirmation of community
- Professionalism in presentation — 'enthusiastic amateurism'
- Serious leisure — playful leisure.

Even as a military re-enactment and given the interests of its enthusiastic members of the re-enactments societies, in 2005 there were anomalies that might have offended the purist. Prior to 2005 there had been just one main battle re-enactment. The organising committee, in its need to develop a programme while meeting ambitions to expand the event, in that year as noted above, sought three battle engagements. But it could be seen that Quesnoy was being defended by 'German' troops wearing World War Two helmets, while some of the weapons were from a later period. Equally, in the Vietnam engagement, some troops used pre-1960s weaponry. The smoke, noise and movement created a spectacle — and it was the spectacle that many came to see, especially those who arrived in the afternoon for the main events and therefore were not present during the commemorative service of the morning. Indeed, the service itself attracts a few hundred, while the main street of Cambridge hosts several hundreds more shopping for bargains in the 'trash and treasure' market that has little to do with the main event other than to take advantage of the increased flow of pedestrians. Yet this has its positive side, as the increased number of vendors generates more funds for the local Lions club and enables it to carry out its good works and community services.

Cambridge Armistice Day is indicative of much of contemporary tourism, even while many of its participants might not view themselves as actors in the tourism industry. But actors they are in many senses — parts and roles are being acted, past events are acted out, a sense of community is acted out and acted upon, personal political ambitions are acted upon, local worthies take on roles outside of their normal lives and at least for a time, as in the Armistice Day dance, act out roles, military and non-military, in uniform and 1940s dress. The Day confuses history, remembrance, celebration, fun, fantasy, role play and function in a growing successful kaleidoscope of noise, colour and economic transactions. And, as in many instances in tourism, the main attraction is that of a spectacle, which is an entertainment, an entertainment that possibly threatens to drown out the nuances of meaning that gave birth to it. Nonetheless, each visitor and each participant draws from the poly-vocal event separate meanings; providing yet again examples of the multitudinous nature of tourism as a stage for action, actors and emotions that are perhaps not so much conflicting, but complementary.

Chapter 14

Refighting the Eureka Stockade: Managing a Dissonant Battlefield

Warwick Frost

Introduction

> I think it may be called the finest thing in Australasian history. It was a rev-
> olution — small in size, but great politically; it was a strike for liberty, a
> struggle for a principle, a stand against injustice and oppression. It was the
> Barons and John, over again; it was Hampden and Ship-Money; it was
> Concord and Lexington; small beginnings, all of them, but all of them great
> in political results, all of them epoch-making. It is another instance of a
> victory won by a lost battle (Twain, 1897, p. 195).

Battlefields signify much more than military conflicts. Wars have their origin in ethnic, social
and political contests and these continue well after the fighting of the battle. Accordingly,
much of the interest amongst visitors to battlefields is in the continuing meaning and significance of historic battles to modern societies. These meanings depend on the differing
perspectives of the visitors. The growing literature on battlefield tourism has been mainly
concerned with the difficult issues of managing and interpreting highly contested heritage
sites (Chronis, 2005; Gold & Gold, 2003; Henderson, 2000; Lloyd, 1998; Patterson, 1989;
Seaton, 1999, 2000; Slade, 2003; Smith, 1998; Whitacre & Greene, 2005). As such battlefield
tourism may be seen as primarily characterised by 'heritage dissonance'.

Tunbridge and Ashworth (1996, p. 20) coined the term 'heritage dissonance' to describe
situations where heritage provoked amongst various stakeholders a "discordance or a lack
of agreement and consistency". The term dissonance originally denoted music played in
contrasting and jarring styles. The analogy is most apt for battlefields, suggesting the differing military bands of the opposing armies. Most importantly, dissonance "is intrinsic to
the nature of heritage … It is not an unforseen and unfortunate by-product of the heritage
assembly process" (Tunbridge and Ashworth, 1996, p. 21). However, Tunbridge and
Ashworth paid little attention to battlefields, just noting that they were "usually rather

difficult to ... interpret to visitors" (1996, p. 116) and "it is remarkable that very few are in fact commemorated effectively or at all" (1996, p. 117).

Militarily, Australia's Eureka Stockade was a minor and one-sided affair, hardly deserving much consideration as a battle. Gold miners at Ballarat, protesting at high licence fees and government corruption, took up arms, raised the Eureka Flag (or Southern Cross) and constructed a rudimentary stockade. They were quickly routed by British troops. Their leaders were tried for treason, but were acquitted by juries (Hocking, 2000; Molony, 1984). In contrast to its military insignificance, its broader meaning and importance has been hotly debated for over 150 years. What were the miners trying to achieve? How revolutionary did they intend their protest to be? What was the impact of their stand on Australia's political development? Following Eureka, the British introduced political reforms. Were these the result of Eureka or would they have occurred anyway?

Less openly asked, there are also questions of who are the present-day stakeholders, what are their objectives and how do they influence interpretation and visitor perceptions? For battlefield sites, such stakeholders include (but are not limited to): heritage attraction and site managers, local, state and national governments, destination marketing organisations, local historical and community groups, ethnic and political organisations, historians, filmmakers, artists and descendants' groups. Also of great importance is the media, which may provide a forum for competing perspectives, or indeed promote its own agenda.

The Eureka Stockade provides a valuable case study for examining issues of heritage dissonance. While militarily insignificant, its modern-day battlefield is highly complex. Numerous stakeholder groups hotly contest its meaning. Some claim exclusive ownership of the symbols and values of Eureka. Two main heritage attractions compete for the attention of visitors and for the possession of the key artefacts. The actual site of the battle is still debated. Media representations vary and often reflect modern concerns.

In examining the contested nature of Eureka, this chapter is divided into five parts. The first begins by considering how and why battlefields are typically dissonant tourist sites. The second discusses the utilisation of Eureka for the destination marketing of Ballarat and the contested nature of the resulting branding. The third examines the Ballarat Fine Art Gallery, symbolically sited on the British camp, but holder of the rebel's Eureka Flag. The fourth considers the Eureka Stockade Centre. Sited on the battlefield (though this is disputed), its potential as the focal point for tourists is limited by a lack of artefacts and internal disagreements over interpretative themes. The concluding part speculates on the management implications for such a dissonant site.

Battlefield Dissonance

Much controversy surrounds the management of heritage interpretation. Some are greatly troubled by the subjective choices taken by managers. For Lowenthal, history was factual, 'real' and unchanging. In contrast, he characterised much heritage interpretation as biased and "bad history", at its worst "a partisan perversion" (1998, p. 102–103). For Hewison, heritage was often "a distortion of the past", which promoted "fantasies of a world that never was" (1987, p. 10). Timothy and Boyd described history as "the recording of the past as accurately as possible", whereas heritage was "often the re-creation of the selective past"

(2003, pp. 4, 237). For the USA, Loewen (1999) catalogued a large number of historic sites, including battlefields, where the interpretation was so one-sided that he considered it lies.

However, there is also an increasing recognition of the validity of diverse perspectives, even if this provokes conflict (Frost, 2005; Howard, 2003; Tunbridge & Ashworth, 1996). This dissonance is further amplified by the role of the visitor. Chronis, writing of the Gettysburg battlefield, argued that interpretation was a 'co-construction' between visitors and tour guides:

> Tourists are not passive readers of the text. Rather, they are actively engaged by using their prior background, negotiating, filling gaps, and imagining. Hence, service providers do not simply teach history and tourists do not only learn about the past (2005, p. 400).

Eureka Stockade is a striking example of a dissonant battlefield. There is no single historical interpretation which one can say is objectively true. Instead, in a recent historiographical survey David Goodman identified five distinct schools of thought amongst historians as to what Eureka meant (see Table 14.1). The wide range of conflicting interpretations about the meaning of Eureka is a common theme in academic and popular writing on the battle (Beggs Sunter, 2001; Blainey, 2004; Button, 2004a, 2004b; Molony, 2004; Wright, 2004).

It is this complexity of meaning that makes Eureka important. Battlefield sites such as Gettysburg, Culloden and Little Big Horn represent conflicts between two opposing forces, but these forces are clearly identifiable (North versus South, English against Scottish, US Cavalry fighting Native Americans), and their perspectives are therefore more easily understandable to visitors. However, Eureka stands apart. It was not a battle between different ethnic, social or religious groups. Nor was it a revolution or civil war. The dissonance at Eureka arises not from any tangible differences between the opposing forces, but the ease with which visitors may adopt quite differing views as to what the protagonists were fighting for.

Table 14.1: Schools of historical thought as to the meaning of Eureka.

Liberal	Birthplace of Australian democracy. A fight for freedom against oppressive government
Radical Nationalist	Fight for Australian nationalism and independence from Britain
Sceptical Left	Pessimistic view, little long-term benefit for workers
Conservative Revisionist	Democratic reforms were not caused by Eureka, they would have happened anyway
Capitalist Triumph	The miners were independent small capitalists protesting against bureaucratic government interference

Source: Goodman, 1998.

To understand this dissonance, it may be useful to consider two examples of seeing Eureka through a North American lens. The first concerns Mark Twain. After the nine-teenth-century American humourist and travel writer visited Eureka, he enthusiastically compared it to the American War of Independence. His glowing appraisal represented not only his genuine admiration for the Eureka rebellion, but also stimulated him to reflect on his own country's pioneering history (Shillingsburg, 1988, p. 101). Twain's enthusiasm for Eureka may be contrasted to his visit to a New Zealand memorial to British soldiers in the Land Wars. Reflecting that the British were the aggressors and the Maori were defending their homes, Twain scornfully described it as "the most comical monument in the whole earth" (quoted in Shillingsburg, 1988, p. 170).

A second comparison is with the Alamo in Texas (for a coverage of this battle, see Davis, 1999). The Alamo has three main similarities with Eureka. The defenders saw themselves as upholders of the constitution. Faced by professional troops they were quickly overwhelmed by a night attack. Despite the one-sided nature of the loss, the defenders were ultimately successful in their struggle. However, all similarities are swept aside when we consider that the Alamo was a battle between Spanish-speaking Mexicans and English-speaking Americans. Today, the Alamo may be thought of in terms of ethnic-ity, imperialism and ongoing inequities. The meaning of Eureka is equally contested, but on differing grounds.

The Battlefield as Destination Brand

In the period leading up to the 150th anniversary of Eureka in 2004, the City of Greater Ballarat adopted a destination brand linked to Eureka. Versions of this destination brand-ing combined Ballarat and Eureka followed by slogans such as 'The city that changed a nation', 'A turning point in the growth of democracy in Australia' and 'Discover the birth-place of the Australian spirit'. The extensive publicity for the 150th anniversary was branded 'Eureka spirit' (sic) and 'Eureka 150: diversity, dissent, democracy'. Such desti-nation branding is highly unusual, not only in its utilisation of a battlefield but also in the application of that battlefield's name to an entire destination and its marketing program. Given the dissonance which surrounds Eureka, adopting this brand is contentious and risky.

Choosing Eureka as a destination brand represents a refreshing reversal of current trends in regional destination marketing. Nowadays many Goldfields towns are opting for standardised and sanitised destination brands based on lifestyle and shopping, with cul-tural heritage more as an ambient setting (Frost, 2006b). Where heritage is retained as the destination image, it is often represented in safe and non-threatening terms. An example of this may be seen at Australia's other nineteenth-century battlefield, the site of Ned Kelly's Last Stand (Frost, 2006a). For years the surrounding region was known as Kelly Country. However, in 2006 it has been rebranded as 'Victoria's High Country' and the emphasis shifted to the mountain cattlemen portrayed in the film *The Man from Snowy River*. Ned Kelly — republican, Irish, lawless — has been replaced by the hard-working, respectful *Man from Snowy River*, even though Kelly was a real person and the *Man* only fictional.

Adapting Eureka to a destination brand and slogans raises questions of what is meant and what image is being promoted to visitors and the community. Where the brand, particularly the idea of a Eureka Spirit, has been elaborated upon it is clear there is a broad diversity of meanings.

For the 150th anniversary, the official guide to the event contained a number of quite different interpretations of what these slogans meant. In their introduction, the guide's compilers emphasised nationalism:

> Eureka was a defining moment in Australia's history that left a legacy of freedom, social democracy and cultural diversity. It provided many of the foundations on which contemporary Australian society is built. Next to Gallipolli, Eureka is Australia's most talked about armed struggle (Eureka 150, 2004, p. 2).

A message from Steve Bracks, Labor Premier of Victoria, took a different perspective:

> Eureka has become a potent symbol of the right to democratic protest everywhere .... The principles for which the diggers fought are universal-human rights, justice and tolerance. These principles are as relevant today as 150 years ago (Eureka 150, 2004, p. 4).

The Minister for the Arts focussed on cultural diversity, writing that "Eureka itself was a true cultural melting pot, where ideas, hopes and histories met. It's that energy and innovation that we want to particularly celebrate" (Eureka 150, 2004, p. 5). A fourth interpretation came from the Mayor of Ballarat, who wrote that, "Eureka was the birthplace of the Australian notion of the 'fair go'" (Eureka 150, 2004, p. 6). A fifth perspective came through an omission, the Commonwealth Government not contributing its view.

For the 150th anniversary, the Royal Automobile Club of Victoria, a long established promoter of Victorian tourism, turned to the historian Geoffrey Blainey. The politically conservative Blainey took the opportunity to refute the interpretations of the Labor government and the destination branding strategy for Eureka. He wrote:

> Some politicians even argue that Ballarat in 1854 was the birthplace of democracy in Australia. Such an argument is pretty hard to accept. South Australia, with a quiet and law-abiding population and no goldfield worthy of the name, gained what we call democracy at exactly the same time as Victoria (Blainey, 2004, p. 20).

The Flag in the Enemy's Camp

Throughout the Goldfields, administrative camps were established on non-gold bearing ground. At Ballarat, the government camp symbolically overlooked the diggings. In 1854 it was the base for the British troops and fears that it would be overrun by the diggers led to the pre-emptive strike on the Eureka Stockade. The centre of urban and civic development, it is today graced by probably the finest grand late nineteenth-century streetscape in the world.

The Ballarat Fine Art Gallery sits atop the site of the government camp. Its main attraction is the Eureka Flag or Southern Cross. When the British troops overran the Stockade, the flag was cut down by a Constable John King. He kept the flag as a souvenir, and in 1895 his family donated it to the Ballarat Fine Art Gallery (Button, 2004b, p. 10). It was kept in a closet for many years, before being put on public display in the 1970s.

The ownership of the flag is highly contested. As the Eureka rebels were acquitted, the flag should have been returned after the trial. John King had no legal claim to the flag and accordingly no right to donate it. With the 1998 opening of the Eureka Stockade Centre (see next section), it was argued that it was far more appropriate to display the flag on the site of the battlefield (Molony, 2004, p. 2). The counter argument was that the Gallery has been the custodian for over a hundred years. Commercial considerations also apply. The Eureka Flag is the main reason visitors come to the Gallery, its removal would seriously affect its viability.

There is an intriguing dispute over who designed and made the flag. The commonly held view is that it was sewn by three women and they are increasingly being elevated to a prominent role in discussions of Eureka (Beggs Sunter, 2004; Button, 2004b; Wright, 2004). Less romantically, it is argued that it was sewn by a local tent-maker (Beggs Sunter, 2004; Button, 2004b).

A second issue of contention is the Gallery's organisation of the Dawn Lantern Walk, held annually on the anniversary of Eureka. This commenced in 1993 and follows the circuitous route taken by the soldiers from the camp to the Stockade (Beggs Sunter, 2001). Eureka's Children, a descendants' organisation, labelled the walk as, "offensive in the extreme because it commemorates the march and attack by soldiers on innocent men, women and children" (quoted in Beggs Sunter, 2001, p. 56). In 2001 Eureka's Children created a rival dawn walk, following the movement of the miners from their earlier meeting place on Bakery Hill to the Eureka Stockade (Button, 2004b). Further controversy erupted in 2004 when the walk organisers asked the father of an Australian prisoner in Guantanamo Bay to lead and address it. In response, the Federal and State Governments and the City of Greater Ballarat all distanced themselves from the event (Anon, 2004).

Questions or Answers? A Hollow Centre

The miners held their protest meetings at Bakery Hill, an intimidating location less than a kilometre from the government camp. It was here that they raised their flag and swore an oath to defend their rights and liberties. However, following this defiance of the authorities, the miners retreated a kilometre and a half to a gully known as Eureka and constructed their rudimentary stockade. The stockade's existence was so brief that in later years there was disagreement amongst veterans as to where it was actually located (Harvey, 1994). Such dissonance over the location of sites is common as, for example, in the case of the Sand Creek Massacre in Colorado USA (Whitacre & Greene, 2005, p. 61).

Over time a series of celebrations and monuments were focussed on a reserve that became known as the Eureka Stockade site. These included a formal stone monument flanked by cannons, a diorama and a reconstructed stockade (Beggs Sunter, 2001). In 1998 the Eureka Stockade Centre was opened on what was held to be the authentic site of the battle. Though still located within the reserve, it was slightly away from previous monuments. The centre was built at a cost of $4 million provided by government grants. Since then it has struggled financially and has not attracted visit numbers at the planned level.

Its problems are twofold. First, it lacks sufficient authentic and evocative artefacts. In particular, it does not have the Eureka Flag. This leads to the confusing situation that visitors need to be directed to drive over 2 kilometers away from the battlefield site to see the battle's relics. Without artefacts the displays within the centre lack interest. This incongruity is emphasised by the centre's gift shop selling souvenir copies of the flag and contemporary paintings, even though they are not available for viewing at the centre.

The second issue is that in order to secure government funding, centre management had to promise to provide a 'non-political' interpretation of Eureka. Accordingly, the centre provides a straightforward narrative of the events of Eureka, but without any information on its meaning or effects on Australian history. This combined with the lack of artefacts gives an unsatisfactory hollow feeling to the centre.

Moscardo (1996) argued that cultural heritage attractions needed to encourage 'mindfulness' amongst visitors. Mindful visitors, she argued, were "active, interested, questioning and capable of reassessing the way they viewed the world" (Moscardo, 1996, p. 382). To achieve this, effective interpretation needed to be "multisensory ... personally relevant, vivid or affectively charged ... unexpected or surprising; [and] questions are used to create conflict or ambiguity" (Moscardo, 1996, p. 384). The interpretation at the Eureka Stockade Centre lacks the provocation required to stimulate and satisfy its mindful visitors.

This dissonance is well-illustrated by thoughts on its role expressed by dignitaries at the opening of the Eureka Stockade Centre. The centre manager, Jan Penney, was reported as saying that she:

> Will make no apologies to visitors who leave the new centre with unanswered questions about the battle and its impact on society. She will actually be pleased if they leave more confused than when they arrived. 'I'd like them to go away with a whole lot of questions,' Dr Penney said (Anon, 1998).

In turn, the then Premier of Victoria, Jeff Kennett, proceeded down the exact opposite path. He argued that the most important duty of the new centre was that, "it must leave the visitor with no question unanswered" (Kennett, 1998).

Management Implications

The Eureka Stockade provides a number of management challenges. Significant resources have been invested in developing attractions and adopting Eureka as the destination brand for the city of Ballarat. However, the visitor experience is fragmented. Two attractions claim the visitor's attention. One is on the site of the battlefield but lacks artefacts.

The other, over 2 kilometers away, holds the major relics but is ironically situated on the site of the British camp.

Furthermore, interpretation of Eureka is profoundly affected by dissonance as to its historical and contemporary meaning. In an ideal world, "cultural heritage requires a community-based perspective, where the community that 'owns' the cultural attraction collectively decides" (Timothy & Boyd, 2003, p. 179). However, at Eureka the community stakeholders are fiercely divided, take the concept of ownership quite literally and are unlikely to reach a collective consensus. Nor is the visitor passive. As Chronis (2005) found at Gettysburg, they co-construct interpretation based on their pre-existing values and beliefs.

Three scenarios are possible for the further management and development of this battlefield. The first is that there is a strong possibility of atrophy. The use of the battle in the destination branding of the city is a high-risk strategy. The temptation will always be to abandon this and return to a safer option. The problems associated with the Eureka Stockade Centre may lead to decreased funding from government sources.

The second scenario is for some form of intervention. Advocates of an imposed solution see legal or government action saving the Eureka Stockade Centre by moving the Eureka Flag from the Ballarat Fine Art Gallery (Button, 2004b; Molony, 2004). Such a move, it is argued, would re-unite the battlefield site with its iconic symbol. However, given the gallery's reluctance to part with its most important attraction, such a plan is only likely to be achieved through the heavy hand of government and would exacerbate existing divisions. Furthermore, it is difficult to see the economic or financial value of bolstering one attraction at the expense of another.

The third possibility is for management plans to incorporate and utilise the dissonance, which is such a part of Eureka. Rather than opting for a single, supposedly safe, 'non-political' interpretation, the opportunity exists to embrace the variety of perspectives. Interpretation that highlighted dissonance, which was mindful and provocative, could increase visitor numbers and satisfaction. Such a path was tentatively ventured upon during the 150th anniversary celebrations, though it did upset some stakeholders. Perhaps it is time to move on from ideas of a homogeneous 'community-owning' heritage and recognise that communities are heterogeneous and dissonant.

Chapter 15

Re-enacting the Battle of Aiken: Honour Redeemed

Chris Ryan

Introduction

This chapter refers to the Battle of Aiken, which took place in South Carolina on 11 February 1865. Whereas the penultimate chapter in this book provides an account of the first military engagement of the American Civil War, this chapter describes events surrounding the final stages of that war, and the last Confederate success of any note. The chapter comprises four sections: first, an historical context describing the events that predated the battle; second, a description of the events at Aiken; third, a description of an enactment that has gained growing significance in the Civil War enactment schedule in the southern states to the extent that in both 2005 and 2006, approximately 1,000 enactors were engaged in replicating the events. In 2005, there were over 16,000 spectators. The enactment of the battle has also spawned a mini-industry of recordings with Forbes Film having produced at least two DVDs and a number of books also being published. Finally, drawing on the interviews in the DVDs, plus comments made by those who responded to e-mails that contained questions about the re-enactment, a series of observations about the current status of the battle and its interpretation are provided. It probably needs not be said that such observations are those of the author alone and do not necessarily represent the views of the organising committee or any formal body associated with the battle enactment.

The Historical Context

The summer of 1863 was a key period in the American Civil War. At the start of that year, General Grant was still almost literally stuck in the mud before Vicksburg and the Army of the Potomac, in spite of victories at Antietam, Perryville and Corinth, had failed to deliver a telling blow against Lee in Virginia. Tiredness and some disillusionment with the war had emerged in the north and the Peace Democrats under critics such as

Battlefield Tourism: History, Place and Interpretation
Copyright © 2007 by Elsevier Ltd.
All rights of reproduction in any form reserved.
ISBN: 0-08-045362-7

Clement Vallandigham had made electoral gains. Lincoln had, in November 1862, accordingly removed McClellan from command of the Army of the Potomac, and increasingly McClellan allied himself with Lincoln's political opponents. To add to Lincoln's problems, on 13 December 1862, the Union suffered 10,000 casualties (twice the number lost by the Confederacy) in an attack on Fredericksburg. Sensing a need to sharpen the nature of the debate as to the purpose of the war, on 1 January 1863, Lincoln's Emancipation Proclamation not only sanctioned emancipation as an act of justice but also permitted the enlistment of black soldiers and sailors in the Union army and navy. The southern response was immediate and blunt. McPherson (1988, pp. 565–566) notes Beauregard's call for the "execution of abolition prisoners" and Davis's reaction in his message to Congress on 12 January 1863, where he called the Emancipation Proclamation "the most execrable measure in the history of guilty man". In short, to shore up the war effort in the north, Lincoln had intensified the resistance of the south.

While the Battle of Stones River or Murfreesburg, ending on 2 January 1863, brought some relief to the Union, it was scarce comfort for while Confederate forces had retreated from the field the Union had suffered casualties amounting to 30 percent of its troops and was unable to follow up the 'victory'. Yet if things had not gone well for the Union, affairs were desperate within the Confederacy. By March 1863, Lee's army was on half rations, inflation was rampant in the Confederacy and food was in scarce supply. Indeed, in April riots broke out in Richmond itself, the Confederate 'capital' and only the personal intervention of Jefferson Davis himself avoided bloodshed.

By the summer of 1863, though, the tide began to turn decisively in favour of the Union, thereby bringing to an end the peace feelers that had commenced between north and south. First, Grant got around Vicksburg and eventually after manoeuvrings and a long siege, Vicksburg surrendered in July. In Virginia, Lee opened his campaign with an astounding victory against Union armies twice the size of his own at Chancellorsville, but at the loss of 13,000 casualties, about one-fifth of his army. All was to be undone at Gettysburg, fought over July 1st–3rd. In the first two days of fighting it is estimated that a total of 35,000 became casualties, by the end of the third day about 30 percent of Lee's army, some 28,000 men in number, were killed, wounded or missing. In total, for both sides, some 51,000 were killed, wounded or missing. More bloody battles with high casualty rates followed — at Chickamauga (September, 1863) and Chattanooga (November, 1863) — the last, a major victory for Grant. The implications of these victories and the advances made in 1864 were important for military success and brought political success for Lincoln in the elections of 1864, with a popular vote majority of over 500,000.

By 1864 Sherman had persuaded Grant that the only way to win the war was to adopt a total war philosophy that would undermine southern resistance. To do this he broke off searching for Hood's army and marched through the heartlands of the Confederacy, living off the land, burning and looting all that was not required by his army. Sherman, in his memoirs published in 1886, indicated that it was with some reluctance that he adopted this method, but he had come to the conclusion that given continual southern resistance in spite of economic and manpower problems, the only way to bring the war to a speedy conclusion was to be totally ruthless. Whatever Sherman's doubts, many of the army were more than happy to forage on the best Georgia and South Carolina had to offer, and to burn the homes of those unfortunate enough to lay in their way. His advances were eased by the failure of

Hood's Confederate Army of the Tennessee and it being seriously mauled at Nashville on 15th and 16th December 1864. The scene was now set for the final acts in South Carolina.

By 1865, the only parts of the Confederacy still largely untouched by Union forces were the interior of the Carolinas and Alabama. Sherman was later to assess the march through South Carolina as being more important than that of the previous campaign in Georgia. Symbolically, it was important because South Carolina had been the first state to secede and, under leaders like John Calhoun, it had been the most vociferous in its condemnation of what was perceived as an unjust exertion of Federal power over the states. Starting in winter the engineers cut paths and built roads for Sherman's army of over 60,000, which commenced to advance at 12 miles per day. Dividing his forces into three, Sherman sliced through to Columbia to take the capital.

On Sherman's left flank, to the west, he ordered General Henry Slocum to feint towards Augusta. The cavalry attached to this army numbered about 4,000 and was under the command of Major-General Kilpatrick. Kilpatrick adopted Sherman's policy of torch and burn to the point that it is stated that he specifically purchased 50,000 matches for his troops. This action forms a feature in Christopher Forbes film of the *Battle of Aiken*, but McPherson in his history of the American Civil War notes that such was the state of the Confederate forces at this time that plundering was not restricted to Union forces. He cites a letter appearing in the *Charleston Courier* of 10 January 1865 (McPherson, 1988, p. 810), as saying "I do not think the Yankees are any worse than our own army. (They) steal and plunder indiscriminately regardless of sex". Certainly the march through Georgia and South Carolina added much to the ruin of the southern economy. Adreano (1962) estimated the south lost a quarter of its white male population of military age, 40 percent of its livestock, ruined thousands of miles of railway, ruined many farms and plantations to the effect that the south lost two-thirds of its wealth in the war. Between 1860 and 1870, southern capital declined by 46 percent, while that of the north increased by 50 percent. Table 15.1 provides data on the costs of the War.

By February 5th, Kilpatrick had reached Barnwell, and following Sherman's orders Kilpatrick looted and burnt the town, to consequently refer to it as 'Burnwell'. Two days later he tore up the railway track at Blackville and turned his forces in the direction of Aiken. Facing him was a former West Point colleague, Major-General Joe Wheeler, who commanded the Confederate cavalry in the region which numbered about 4,500. The scene was set for the Battle of Aiken.

The Battle of Aiken

Wheeler's men came from Tennessee, Texas, Arkansas, Alabama and Georgia, and had seen much action in the four previous years. Experienced, hardened, but short of supplies, they had been almost continually in the saddle attempting to throw a shield between Sherman's main forces and the potential targets of the gunpowder works at Augusta and the Graniteville Mill, which was a major source of cotton cloth. Both were vital to the continuation of the Confederate war effort. Rigdon (2001), in his history of the battle, replicates a number of contemporary writings that indicate the destruction and looting being undertaken by Kilpatrick's forces as it closed upon Aiken. The town was naturally fearful of its fate. Wheeler sought to delay Kilpatrick's advance even as defences were being

Table 15.1: Costs of the American Civil War.

The Costs of the Civil War (Millions of 1860 Dollars)			
	South	North	Total
Direct costs			
Government expenditures	1,032	2,302	3,334
Physical destruction	1,487		1,487
Loss of human capital	767	1,064	1,831
Total direct costs of the war	3,286	3,366	6,652
Per capita	376	148	212
Indirect costs			
Total decline in consumption	6,190	1,149	7,339
Less			
Effect of emancipation	1,960		
Effect of cotton prices	1,670		
Total indirect costs of the war	2,560	1,149	3,709
Per capita	293	51	118
Total costs of the war	5,846	4,515	10,361
Per capita	670	199	330
Population in 1860 (million)	8.73	27.71	31.43

Source: Ransom (1998, p. 51, Table 3-1), Goldin and Lewis (1975, 1978).

hurriedly constructed at Aiken and, on 8th February, Wheeler's troops skirmished with advance forces of Kilpatrick's men at White Pond and again at Johnson's Station (Montmorenci). For the most part though Wheeler consolidated his troops in Aiken, being continually advised as to Kilpatrick's movements by the Aiken Home Guards. Wheeler counted on Kilpatrick's confidence and wish to pursue the 'total war' strategy that would require him to advance into Aiken itself, and sought to deploy the classic tactic of creating a V-shaped force with the centre due to retreat leaving then the arms of the V to fall on the extended line of attack from the flanks. On February 11th, Kilpatrick, although aware of the presence of Confederate troops, advanced into Aiken determined to both burn the town and engage the enemy. A contemporary record written by Reed from the 92nd Illinois Mounted Infantry notes that:

> we were within a half mile of the town of Aiken, when we discovered long lines of rebel cavalry. The column halted ... Kilpatrick came dashing up to the head of the column and desired to know the reason of the halt. Just then a locomotive ran out in plain view near Aiken and whistled and whistled. Kilpatrick brought up the artillery and sent a few rifled shells toward the locomotive and into the town. Kilpatrick also called on the 92nd Illinois

Silver Cornet Band to play Yankee Doodle. The next thing in order was for the 92nd Illinois to charge into the town … Now we felt that we were going into a trap, but Kilpatrick took the lead … Gen. Atkins ordered the 9th Ohio into line of battle on the right of the road, flanking the artillery, and the 9th Mich. Cav. into line of battle flanking the artillery on the left of the road, holding the 10th Ohio Cav. in reserve … The ladies of the town waved their handkerchiefs in welcome and smilingly invited the officers and men into their houses. But that kind of a welcome was unusual in South Carolina … It was an additional evidence of danger. In the farther edge of the town the enemy was in line of battle …

However, an Alabama trooper fired too soon and the trap was not fully engaged. Reed went on to write that, after the accidental shot:

(the officers) quickly formed the regiment to charge back again to the brigade, the rebels having formed in line in our rear. Every man in the regiment appeared to be conscious that the only way to get out was to assault the rebel line and cut a hole in it. We road (sic) forward to the charge … the rebels awaited our approach until within close range, when they demanded a halt and surrender, and were answered by every man in the regiment pumping into them the eight Spenser bullets in his trusty repeating rifle … It was a desperate charge, and the men fought face to face and hand to hand … Now the brigade bugle sounded the charge and with a yell the 9th Ohio and the 9th Michigan charged … into the town of Aiken … recapturing a great many of the boys that had been taken prisoners … We were five miles from camp, where the balance of the division lay behind their rail barricades (Montmorenci) … The rebels at Aiken, came thundering down upon our four little regiments, and the five miles back to camp was a battle field all the way … (Rigdon, 2001, p. 77).

Once back at his defensive positions, Kilpatrick held the line against Confederate action and the battle diminished to a series of skirmishes until Kilpatrick on February 12th sought, under a flag of truce, a breaking off of hostilities to recover the dead and wounded. This was duly done and the two forces subsequently rejoined the main armies as Sherman continued his march to Columbia.

As is often the case, confusion exists as to the actual number of casualties. Kilpatrick subsequently wrote in despatches that Wheeler lost 31 killed, 160 wounded with 60 taken prisoners. For his part, Wheeler admitted 50 killed and wounded, and subsequently claimed that the Confederates attack resulted in 53 killed, 270 wounded and 172 captured — a total of 495 Union casualties. Kilpatrick admitted to 25 being killed and wounded.

While, from a military perspective Wheeler had failed to destroy Kilpatrick's forces, the day belonged to the Confederate army in that Aiken was saved from destruction, and certainly if Kilpatrick had entertained any thoughts of marching towards Augusta, such ideas were never put into effect.

In his film *The Battle of Aiken*, Forbes interviews Peters, a local historian, who notes that one ironic outcome of the battle was that many years later the great-great-granddaughter of Kilpatrick, Gloria Vanderbilt came to live in Aiken, partly because of its historical ambience — an ambience that her great-great-grandfather had sought to destroy.

Enactments and Interpretation

Much of the interpretation of the Battle is to be found in the annual re-enactment of the battle that takes place in February each year. Re-enactments of the American Civil War, or, to use its alternative titles, 'The War of the States' or 'The War of Northern Aggression' have become a significant industry and have added impetus to the subject of the War as a well-researched topic. Even a cursory search on the internet will reveal a multitude of historical materials on sale from both private and public organisations. Individual diaries and collections of contemporary letters are readily available, and a multitude of histories can be found. There are also individual regimental histories, various collections and battlefield sites around the country. The appeal of the Civil War as a subject for re-enactment also extends beyond American shores, with enactments taking place elsewhere such as in the United Kingdom.

For those interested in Civil War re-enactments there are many and various specialist magazines and retailers. It would be invidious to mention a few — but the interested reader may wish to look at www.quartermastershop.com, www.TheCavalry.Net, www.heirloomemporium.com, www.mercurysutler.com to just draw a small selection of those who advertise in the *Camp Chase Gazette*, just one of the specialist magazines that exist. Sites specific to this engagement and area include www.BattleofAiken.org and www.27thscvi.org. That interest is high can also be confirmed by the size of the re-enactments. Major engagements that are re-enacted now require strict quotas. For example, the enactment of the First Manassas operates with a quota of 12,000 re-enactors and a limitation of 45 artillery guns to each side. Gettysburg imposes a limit of 15,000 on its re-enactment. Consequently a battle such as that of Aiken is increasing in popularity with both spectators and re-enactors because, as yet, there has been no need to impose limits. Yet, in terms of carrying capacity, the town of Aiken itself has but a population of about 20,000. Of course from the perspective of the enactors, accommodation is camping out on the field of engagement and small tented towns grow on the fields for a few days as the 'troops' and followers congregate. Each enactment is carefully choreographed to ensure that officers and men know the order of battle and to ensure that no accidents occur. While specialist black powder is used for guns and artillery, the author has observed that horses can sometimes be 'spooked' by the sound of battle and care is taken to ensure that spectators are kept behind allocated lines.

Enactments are primarily true to the events themselves as is discussed below, but the movement is producing some offshoots. For example, a combination of searching for something new and a drive for more historical authenticity is leading to shooting competitions with 'live' guns. During the enactments, while there is the marching and firing of guns, and men (and women) drop to the ground, there are careful controls and inspections to ensure that no live ammunition is carried. McBride (2006) writes: "It has always seemed a waste to me that the single most expensive item in our re-enacting kits are our weapons, and we just use them to blow smoke. On top of that, we often don't even blow the smoke right at our enemy. Instead, for the sake of safety, we point our muskets at some point in the sky". Instead, actual shooting competitions not only meet a need for competition, but also provide new information on the effects of rifling, compounds of bullets, the mechanics of matching bullet and powder load.

A second outcome is the development of a fiction about the Civil War. For example, Forbes project in 2006 is the filming of a romantic novel about the Civil War — but of course the use of fiction within a Civil War setting has retained significant popularity even before *Gone with the Wind* was either penned or filmed. The Civil War has even moved into science fiction, as with the novel *Expeditionary Force* by Ken Brittian. The publisher describes the plot on its web site as: "The story of a war between two alien races; one civilized village dwellers, the other savage nomads. With the Sleebok threatening to overwhelm the Kandirians, the village dwellers are willing to grab any chance to save their civilzation from annihilation. An opportunity soon presents itself in the form of a strange portal to another world — a world that turns out to be the State of Georgia in the year 1864" (Port Town Publishing, 2006).

For the serious re-enactor, such outcomes as the latter may be peceived to be frivolous. What motivates the re-enactor? Certainly, re-enactment can be classified as 'serious leisure' and significant sums of money are spent. A cannon can cost US$10,000; cavalrymen may spend in a season as much as US$45,000 on their horses, equipment and travel (personal communication). As is noted in Chapter 13, one strong motive is a wish to connect with ancestors. As one enactor stated at the Battle of Charleston re-enactment, "my great-grandfather fought in this war, and doing this makes me better understand what it was like for him and for his times". Another stated that he had become interested in the Civil War, and then found that four of his ancestors had been engaged on the Confederate side, and this gave him an added reason for involvement, and a wish to perpetuate and disseminate the history of those events.

An additional strong motivation lies in an interest in and a sense of history. The former informant said: "A lot of people still don't want to talk about this war, but it was important. They will tell you it was about the States, about slavery — but what it was about was money and power — as is every war. Today we are in Iraq because of oil, then it was about King Cotton". Such sentiments raise a number of issues about interpretation, of which the following alternatives are but three.

First, are we indeed never able to learn from the past? For the historian of the Civil War, the fact that Vietnam and Gulf War veterans suffer post-traumatic stress is not news. A study of 15,027 Civil War veterans showed that 40 percent later developed mental and physical ailments, with the younger soldiers being most at risk (Pizarro, Silver & Prause, 2006).

Second, are we in danger of forgetting our history? Another enactor provided a long list of speaking engagements at schools that he was engaged in. Yet the National Assessment of Education Progress 2001 survey of 28,000 school students found that 91 percent of 8th grade students could not "list two issues that were important in causing the Civil War" while 13 percent of respondents thought England was a participant in the war (US Department of Education, 2004). Re-enactors thus perceive their educational function as being very important as providing a historical context for the present.

Third, to what extent do we attribute desired interpretations upon events? In short, possibly, there is a romantic notion of a lost cause that possibly appears the more noble for being lost.

While this last motive might be found, in discussions with re-enactors this motive did not emerge very strongly. A strong motive is an interest in history, and a wish to better understand history and the events of a time. That understanding can be at a visceral level. In a phone interview one re-enactor talked about the educational value of re-enactments for children. The events of long ago can seem so distant from today's experience he stated. But in an enactment the visual senses are engaged, "and children can learn things", he said, "that cannot be learnt by reading … They hear the sound of the guns, they smell the gun-powder, they feel the ground shake under the charge of a cavalry brigade, they see bodies scattered on the ground — these things cannot be learnt from books". Additionally, having seen these things, it is natural to ask 'why?' — what lead to these things? However, he then went on to say as an enactor you can immerse yourself in the culture. "You sleep in a tent the night before the battle, and if you listen to your radio or your walkman — well no — you have to do the whole thing … I was engaged at the Battle of Blues Springs in Tennessee, and we ran up a hill a long way and were engaged in hand to hand battle having attacked some cannon, I killed a man, bayoneted another — and then afterwards when it was over my friend asked me — why was I crying? — and I didn't know I was — and I guess it might have been the fear — where else does a man have a rifle directed at him — it's so real in the battle — all that is missing is the lead flying past".

Another re-enactor e-mailed the author and wrote:

> As a member of the Sons of Confederate Veterans we are to 'ensure the true history of the South is told to future generations'. Not slavery, but issues of taxation, state rights, etc., that lead to the 'War of Northern Aggression'. While the battle may be 'entertaining' to the spectator, we encourage them to walk thru the camps, talk with the men, women and children as they portray life in the 1860s of infantry, cavalry, artillery, naval, Provost (military police), cooks, washer-women, embalmers and morticians, doctors and nurse. We want people to realize the hardships on both sides of the battle, view weapons, clothing, food, lifestyles, children's games, period dances, period church services, etc.

The educational motives are important to re-enactors, and the numbers engaged are impressive. For example, prior to the enactment of the Battle of Aiken in 2006, some 2000 local school children were involved in educational talks and/or were hosted at the encampment.

The southern states of the USA have a complex history for all that many people have a notion that after the Civil War the states went into a period of economic decline and subsequently, somehow, rights of emancipation were eroded so that by the 1960s, 100 years after the Civil War, there was a need for a Civil Rights movement to address issues of segregation. There is, of course, truth in this broad, sweeping outline, and in the truth there are generally little known aspects of history that become a form of collective amnesia in that the Jim Crow laws did emerge to create the situation that led to a need to assert a civil rights protest. But equally there are eddies and currents in the stream. It has been noted there were black slave owners, and individuals like Joseph Hayne Rainey (1832–1887) did successfully run for Congress, being voted for by both black and white Americans. The Civil Rights movement of the 1960s had many echoes of the 1860s, with again the rights of States to determine their own policies being a key factor in resistance to, and a constraint upon, the powers of the Presidency and Capitol Hill. And, from some viewpoints, the success of the Civil Rights movement was not simply a success for the Federal Government and the National Association for Colored People, but also a success for those white politicians and supporters of the NACP within the southern states like Alabama who sought change. There is then a need for the voices of the Sons of Confederate Veterans and the United Daughters of the Confederacy to point out the complexities of the past and to avoid the War being simplified as being simply a pro- or anti-slavery issue, thereby creating a pastiche of characterisation of the north 'good' and the south 'bad'. Equally, many re-enactors, even though belonging to organisations like the Sons of Confederate Veterans do not simply take on the uniform of one side. Many re-enactment organisations possess members who own the uniforms and regalia of both sides, and who will, as numbers are perhaps required at an enactment, march on either side.

Nonetheless for many enactors of the Battle of Aiken there is a notable pride in re-iterating that this was a successful engagement for the Confederate forces. In Forbes' film, which is made with the support of those involved in the re-enactment movement, there is an emphasis upon Kilpatrick's perceived failings of over-confidence and seemingly strange behaviours. But there are possible alternative explanations — his actions in burning Barnwell were consistent with Sherman's orders, and while seemingly over-confident in his attack on Aiken it has noted that the majority of his force was left at defended lines at Johnson's Turnout (Montmorenci) to which he retreated and there comparatively easily held off Wheeler's attacks (although it should be noted it was no orderly retreat but a desperate affair which almost cost Kilpatrick his life). Equally, his including Afro-American women at a dance might be seen as a confirmation of their status, although the act seemed bizarre to many southern commentators. In short, while indeed the battle was a Confederate success in that it saved Aiken and perhaps averted a more serious feint towards Augusta, the representation of Kilpatrick as "the worse major cavalry officer of the American Civil War" (Rigdon, 2001, p. 105) might be seen as being harsh given the reputation of some of the other officers involved in the war (that included, for example, Custer). Yet it also needs to be noted that Joe Wheeler continued a distinguished career even after the Civil War and, in 1895, at the age of 64 years was in active service against the Spanish in Cuba and was a significant influence on Teddy Roosevelt who served under his command. Thus, while for the most part, the Battle of Aiken is little more than a footnote in the histories of the American Civil War, the attention being bestowed on it almost 150 years later is not unduly undeserved, and for many spectators, almost by reason of it being comparatively unknown, the enactment brings aboutquestions and thus perhaps more understanding of the time than might otherwise be the case.

ACTS OF REMEMBRANCE

Introduction

Chris Ryan

In the previous section, reference was made to the events that surround Armistice Day. In many Commonwealth countries, the Sunday nearest to the 11th November is an occasion of solemn remembrance of the fallen in past wars. At various battlefield sites, as, for example, described by Hall (2002) and Slade (2003) in the case of Gallipoli to commemorate ANZAC day, specific services are held and it is not uncommon for representatives of governments to be present, including the representatives of those who were once foes. Such occasions are an opportunity for families to recall the dead, for people to note acts of heroism and dedication to service, and a catalyst for thoughts upon the meaning of war. Some sites have these functions on an almost daily basis, and this chapter takes three such examples, albeit they differ as to degree and age. As noted by Pierkarz and Prideaux in this book, and by Weaver (2000), battlefield sites possess their own life cycle of meaning and nature of attraction — and with age they 'cool' to become not simply places of memorial to a recent past generation, but a place of heritage to inform future generations. Equally, as places of heritage they become subject to different nuances of interpretation in terms of how they contribute to a wider sense of culture, shared values and national identities. All three sites in this section of the book demonstrate aspects of this process.

The first chapter illustrates Prideaux's point that the site of battle may not be fixed — and this is literally the case of the *USS Yorktown*, one the major aircraft carriers engaged in Pacific action in the latter part of the Second World War. The ship is now moored in Charleston, South Carolina, and possesses interest for many reasons. First, it is in itself a significant monument by reason of its ability to impress itself upon the visitor by its bulk, sheer size and the stories of the air crew and sailors that manned it during its operational life. Second, for the preservation society, there is a marketing need to recognize that the original motives of wanting to commemorate fallen colleagues and remember shared times of conflict were motives of increasingly less significance for generations who had no direct experience of war and were increasingly distant from the events. Thus, a need for repositioning and new marketing and interpretation has become evident. Currently, the stories constructed upon the vessel are tales of the crew in terms of battles in which they engaged, number of kills made and theatres of operation and conflict with which the aircraft carrier

Battlefield Tourism: History, Place and Interpretation
Copyright © 2007 by Elsevier Ltd.
All rights of reproduction in any form reserved.
ISBN: 0-08-045362-7

was involved. Little other interpretation is offered, and there is an assumption made about the patterns and degrees of knowledge held by visitors about the nature of the Second World War and the United State's participation in it. Of the chapters in the book, this is also perhaps the most personal because it contains a personal reaction to the ship — a text thought appropriate inasmuch as the initial chapter in this book makes reference to symbolic interactionism and the importance of the 'lived' experience of place, time and interaction with others. In this instance, the author on one visit was accompanied by a teenage son, and thus differences of view caused by inter-generational difference was, for this visit, a significant factor that aided an understanding of the nature of the exhibit. Equally, there is one significant exhibit on the aircraft carrier that does personalize the stories of the crew, and that is a film that may be viewed by visitors, and which becomes an important part of the total visitor experience. The use of this medium adds an element to the visitor experience not found in many other sites.

The next chapter, on Culloden, by McLean, Garden and Urquhart, also draws attention to individual responses by utilizing the comments made by visitors. Culloden enjoys a high level of recognition within popular imagination, particularly perhaps among those of the Scottish diaspora, because of the association with 'Bonnie' Prince Charlie and his subsequent escape aided by Flora MacDonald. A combination of the attribution of a romantic legend based upon images created by late Victorian writers including Walter Scott and Robert Louis Stevenson, aided and abetted perhaps by cinematic stories that included David Niven's 1948 version entitled *Bonnie Prince Charlie*, the 1953 *Master of Ballantrae* based on Stevenson's novel with the dashing Errol Flynn in a starring role while no less than seven versions of *Kidnapped* have been made that have included, among others, Peter Finch, Michael Caine and most recently Iain Glen as the hero Allan Breck. While not strictly pertinent to the specific site, McLean, Garden and Urquhart also make reference to the Mel Gibson film *Braveheart* as also contributing to a Scottish image of English defiance.

Yet, regardless of the mixture and juxtaposition of history and image in popular imagination, there would appear to be something specific about the site of the battle itself. On a wet, dismal day, web sites relating to the 250th anniversary of the battle make reference to senses of isolation even among the 7,000 crowd that came to witness the remembrance of the White Cockade Society (Vass, 1996). Certainly, the presence of the words 'British genocide' and 'murderers' on the Cumberland stone at those celebrations reveal the power of resistance that still exists since the events of not only 1746, but the immediate aftermath as described by McLean, Garden and Urquhart. Not for the first time can it be said that the significance of battle is the nature of what befalls the losers. And it is these stories that also become part of the articulation of interpretation — and hence as the authors describe, the creation of problems for contemporary interpretation at the new visitor centre constructed in 2007. These acts of symbolic resistance, some 250 years after the battle, are also part of the story to be told, and thus interpreters are faced with decisions as to how much importance to concede to such things. As in many of the battlefield sites, continuous decisions as to past conflict that may have current echoes need to be made.

That is also true of the third chapter in this sequence. This is the story of Forts Sumter and Moultrie — sites of the first action of the American Civil War, or, as Ryan reminds us, of the Northern War of Aggression. He also notes how the storytelling can be shaped to the nature of the audience by the simple technique of asking audiences from where they come.

It can be envisaged that the telling of the story would differ between a Yankee and a Johnny Reb audience! Like Culloden, the interpretation of the site lies in the hand of a professional parks organisation or equivalent. They are charged with the maintenance of a site, the generation of revenue from visitation, and the nature of interpretation. Thus, to the complexities of interpretation can be added the understanding of its role that a Parks Service may bring to its role as custodian of the site. In this chapter, it can be noted that a specific inclusive interpretation is undertaken. The service flies a copy of all flags that have flown above Fort Sumter, and thus in its inclusiveness it avoids the problems associated with selectivity. Yet the flying of all flags implies an equality of importance and legitimacy, and while the identity of the flags is provided upon the notices, there is a notable absence of evaluation. Fort Sumter represents an interesting case of interpretation because it is pointed out that to engage in the story of the events the tourist has to visit more than one site — for there is interpretation offered at each of the points of embarkation to the Fort by boat, and a fourth location at Fort Moultrie. Together the points add up and, in some ways, the most revealing of all points of interpretation actually stands separate from the main points of interpretation in Liberty Square — namely, a plaque to Septima Clark, an Afro-American teacher. Spatial and cultural juxtapositions all account for nature of the site and its interpretation in this instance.

Together, therefore, all three sites are eloquent because of the resonance of the places for contemporary understandings. Culloden is eloquent in a period of new assertions of Scottish identity in a period of a Scottish Assembly. Fort Sumter refers to one of the most cathartic periods of American history; and its presence speaks also about a silence in much of southern states history — which is the period from approximately the 1880s to the 1960s. Why was it that, after the emancipation of slaves in the period after the Civil War, when Afro-American congressmen were elected from southern states, there came about a situation where a civil rights movement was again necessary in the 1960s? In short, the visitor to a site such as Fort Sumter can come away with as many questions as answers. Equally, the *Yorktown* lies moored, articulating in its presence, a simpler age in terms of American participation in War. It was perhaps the last time that the United States was engaged in a war that unified and not divided its peoples: it evokes in its presentation an age when issues appeared to be simpler, but it remains generally silent about how that War came to an end with the dropping of the atom bomb. Articulation and silence, the two partners in interpretation, are evident in these locations; yet for all of that they possess an ability to evoke even on the sunniest of days, a sense of being at a place of history that, at least for a male Anglo-Saxon, a sense of involvement and history — and thus a questioning of why that should be. Of all the purposes of battlefield sites and their interpretation, this perhaps is of no small importance.

Chapter 16

Yorktown and Patriot's Point, Charleston, South Carolina: Interpretation and Personal Perspectives

Chris Ryan

For they were brave, they were gallant.

Introduction

This chapter relates to the Naval and Maritime Museum at Patriots Point, Charleston, South Carolina. It describes the vessels and exhibits found there, and provides a brief history of the engagements in which those ships were involved. It notes the nature of comradeship that emerged from those times that motivated survivors to spend time, energy and considerable monies in their attempt to ensure that the sacrifices made by those who fell in combat will not be forgotten. There is a specific interpretation at work at Patriots Point based upon a history of ordinary individuals engaged in extra-ordinary events. It is a moving history, but an incomplete story. As time passes and those involved in the battles die and pass on, and as the United States becomes embroiled in less clear-cut engagements, it is thought that reactions to the displays will become in their turn more complex. This chapter is no empirical dataset but rather, it should be noted, a personal reaction to a visit made by me and my son, then aged 16, in February 2006. In the initial book proposal there was no mention of including this chapter but, on reflection, it appeared pertinent to include a museum of naval and air engagements — especially that of the Pacific in World War Two.

The chapter contains three main sections. First, and most briefly, an outline of the Pacific naval engagements of the Second World War as it was these battles and the experiences of those involved that were the primary motives for the establishment of the museum. Second, it describes the museum, its ships and exhibits, and then the nature of the visitor experience is assessed. Finally, it describes a mixed reaction to the interpretations that the museum offers.

The Context of Pacific Naval Warfare: 1941–1945

The battles of the Pacific Ocean in the Second World War involved the largest maritime forces ever seen, with battles occurring out of the commander's sight in air and over land and water as the respective aircraft carrier-based planes sought to destroy bases and offensive armaments. After the outbreak of war in 1941, Japanese plans were to seize Malaysia, Singapore, the Dutch East Indies, the Philippines and various island groups in the central and western Pacific. This was completed by March 1942. The next stage was to isolate Australia, and in March initial attacks were made against the north coast of Papua New Guinea. However, attacks by the Japanese on Port Moresby were delayed because of action by American forces. In May 1942, the first carrier action of the Coral Sea took place, wherein the *USS Lexington* and the Japanese light carrier, the *Shoho* were lost. The Japanese identified the Midway Island as an important base behind which to strengthen their lines and, on 5 May, Imperial General Headquarters issued 'Navy Order No. 18'. This directed Admiral Yamamoto to carry out the occupation of Midway Island and key points in the western Aleutians in cooperation with the Army. Unknown to the Japanese however, the US Intelligence officers had cracked the Japanese codes and Admiral Nimitz was able to plan countermeasures. On 3rd June, with both fleets having major carriers, the preliminary stages of the Battle of the Midway started. The last air attacks of the battle took place on 6 June when dive bombers from *Enterprise* and *Hornet* bombed and sank the heavy cruiser *Mikuma*, and damaged destroyers *Asashio* and *Arashio*, as well as the cruiser *Mogami*. In return, however, the Japanese had severely damaged the *Yorktown*, and on June 7th a Japanese submarine was able to sink both the *Yorktown* and the destroyer USS *Hammann*.

The battle was important because it halted Japanese expansion and the balance of power began to swing towards the American forces. In August 1942 the 1st Marine Division invaded Tulagi and Guadalcanal in the Solomon Islands. From that time Guadalcanal was the scene of bloody fighting as the US forces repulsed Japanese efforts to retake the region until in December 1942 Japanese troops were ordered to retreat. In February 1943 Japanese resistance ended in Guadalcanal.

By late 1943, the US forces increasingly took the offensive and carrier forces, including a new *USS Yorktown* that began to destroy Japanese naval bases on the Marshall Islands and, in February 1944, the major one at Truk in the Caroline Islands. By mid-1944, the Japanese were increasingly dependent upon untested forces and on 19 June 1944, the 'Marianas Turkey Shoot' took place as the US carrier-based fighters shot down 220 Japanese planes for a loss of only 20 American planes. A month later, Guam was taken by American forces, while later naval battles in the Leyte Gulf in October also ended in Japanese defeat. However, such victories were bought at significant costs, and off Okinawa, for example, the destroyer *Laffey* was badly mauled.

It is these events that motivated the finding of the National Naval Museum in Charleston — which features ships involved in these battles.

The Museum, Ships and Exhibits

In 1975 the first ship at the National Naval Museum was opened to the public at Patriots Point, Charleston, South Carolina. Today, visitors are able to explore many of the nooks and crannies of four vessels: (a) the Coast Guard Cutter, the *Ingham*, (b) the submarine *Clamagore*, commissioned in 1945, (c) the destroyer *Laffey*, commissioned in 1944 and involved in the Normandy landings in World War II and (d) most specifically of all the *Yorktown* — an aircraft carrier commissioned in 1943 to replace its namesake lost in the battle of the Midway a year earlier. The 888 ft Yorktown, familiarly known as *The Fighting Lady*, saw significant action in the Pacific offensive when it carried a crew of 380 officers, 3,088 enlisted men and 90 aircraft. The carrier also served in the Vietnam War when she was modified with an angled deck to take jet aircraft. In 1968 the vessel was nominated to recover the Apollo 8 space capsule, and then 2 years later, in 1970, the ship was decommissioned to become the centrepiece of the museum in 1975.

However, each of the other vessels has a distinguished history. The *Laffey* saw significant action in the closing part of the Pacific operations in 1945, being attacked by a strike force of 22 Japanese bombers and kamikaze pilots off Okinawa in April 1945. The ship's defenders lost 32 killed and 71 wounded, but in return shot down 11 enemy planes. So badly damaged was the vessel that it had to be towed to safety and the boat was subsequently refitted at Seattle before re-entering active service. The ship was then later engaged in the Korean War, and finally served in the Atlantic and Pacific oceans before being decommissioned in 1975.

Although specifically commissioned as a Coastal Foot Cutter for the American Coast Guard in September 1936, the *Ingham* also saw war service as a convoy escort in the North Atlantic, and in this capacity sank the enemy submarine *U-626* in December 1942. From the spring of 1943 to the summer of 1944, the *Ingham* had convoy duty in the Mediterranean before sailing to the Pacific, where it became the flagship for the Mariveles-Corregidor Attack Group. The boat was later involved in the Vietnam War for blockade duties. After the war it returned to customs duties including the interception of drug runners to be finally decommissioned in May 1988 after 52 years of active service.

The submarine *Clamagore* missed active duty in World War II and for most of her active period served in the Caribbean being based at Key West in Florida. As such the submarine is believed to have carried out surveillance duties during the Cuba missile crisis, but such is the sensitivity still of this period that information is incomplete. This silence serves in stark contrast to the other stories told by the museum. However, the *Clamagore* is symbolic of the tremendous loss of life and actions of the US submarines in the Second World War. Those submarines accounted for 30 percent of Japanese warships, but of the 288 US submarines serving in the War, 52 were lost. Of these, 38 were lost with all hands, over 3,400 personnel. On the other hand, it is also recorded that US submarines sank 55 percent of Japan's merchant ships, again with considerable loss of life on the part of the then enemy.

Accompanying the vessels can be found other paraphernalia of war. Foremost among these are different aircraft within the bay of the *Yorktown* and on its flight deck. Notable among these are the aircraft from the Second World War that flew from the US aircraft carriers. The exhibits include a F4F-3A Wildcat, dedicated to the memory of Commander Edward Henry 'Butch' O'Hare. On 20 February 1942, O'Hare engaged, alone, 8 Japanese bombers and effectively broke up the attack on the aircraft carrier *USS Lexington*. He was to lose his life in action in November 1943. The F6F-5 Hellcat is also on display, a tribute to its popularity and the fact that 45 Hellcat pilots from the *Yorktown* were lost in different actions during the war. Representing the period of the Korean War, the AD-4N Skyraider dedicated to Lt. Commander Harold 'Swede' Carlson and Rear Admiral Arthur K. Knoizen sits within the main hangar bay with folded wings. Both these pilots were foremost pilots of the Korean campaign. From the period of the Vietnam War, there is a F-8K Crusader, while bridging the period from Vietnam to the first Gulf War, in 1991, there is a F-4J Phantom, which model of aircraft was in active service in both campaigns.

The Visitor Experience

Until 2004 the advertising for the *Yorktown* was based upon the slogan 'The greatest generation's greatest weapon' — a slogan that encapsulates what was seen as the attraction's target market. But as observed above, time moves and successive generations with no direct link to the events of the 1940s have no personal experiences of those times. Visitor numbers declined in the early 2000s, but some of this may well have been due to a 'September 11th' effect, as a decline in visitor numbers hit many of Charleston's attractions. In 2005 a 2 percent increase in visitor numbers was recorded. The advertising of the site can be said to be 'low key' and advertising budgets are small. In an unpublished report for the Charleston Convention and Visitor Bureau based on a sample of 351 visitors, Crotts and Litvin (2004) found that only 22.9 percent of visitors to Charleston interviewed had actually been to Patriots Point. Of these, 49 percent were over the age of 41 years; yet this was an under-representation of that age group as these ages formed about two-thirds of the total sample. This finding implies a failure to reach even the market segment seen as the base of potential demand. A subsequent small sample undertaken by Epps, Ernst, Henry and Johnson (2005) of actual visitors to the *Yorktown* found that 70 percent of visitors were actually from within the state of South Carolina, and only 6 percent of visitors were international. Projects on the marketing of the *Yorktown* undertaken by students at the College of Charleston in 2005 were made available to the author. This revealed a general lack of knowledge about the site by visitors. Second, all indicated a younger age group's perspective that the nature of the exhibits was not only static, but also aesthetically unappealing to a generation familiar with the interactive nature of the internet and other museums. For the most part, the exhibit is the vessels themselves, while commemorative displays are consistent with the norms of the 1940s, being generally 'severe' comprising of citations of bravery and photographs in some instances. The overall light level is low, sombre and respectful.

Consequently, for the most part, the visitor experience comprises reactions to being aboard the vessels; an experience of stark contrasts between the restricted space of the submarine and the vast aircraft hangars of the aircraft carrier. The remnants of a different life surround one — a life dominated by metal, of machinery and what would have been the close proximity of other men and the robustness of an electro-mechanical age where levers were pulled and sweat involved in contrast to a modern navy where buttons are pushed and computers control weapons fixed on targets many miles away. Today the caverns of the aircraft carrier and the close confines of the submarine lie still, clean and devoid of noise and spaces pervaded by smells of engines, cooking, and unwashed bodies. Yet, in spite of these absences, the spaces are far from sterile. The artefacts of war lie around. The submarine's torpedo bays lie open to inspection, the destroyer's chart rooms can be seen, there are aircrafts within the hold of the carrier with wings folded. There is a feeling that men who served on these vessels could return and be immediately familiar with layout and purpose, even as the vessels remain tethered to the ground to such an extent that on low tide they rest on the bottom of the river, and barnacles and mussels are evident on their sides.

But further emotions exist, for the ships contain a series of exhibits devoted to those who lost their lives in different campaigns. Indeed, this is possibly the main purpose of the whole museum. It is here worth citing at length Ewing's introduction to the guide *Patriot's Point — In Remembrance*.

> First sights and natural questions aside, all that is immediately apparent to the visitor does not begin to convey the essence of the Naval and Maritime Museum's primary reason in being. For the most part, contemporary Americans cannot understand or appreciate the depth of feeling some other societies have for war as no recent war has been fought on American soil. With the meaning of duty, honor, sacrifice, deprivation and the horror of war not fully comprehensible, Patriots Point's mission is — in part — to educate visitors to the axiom that 'freedom isn't free'. To underscore this reality the museum, in a setting of historic ships and planes, presents remembrance of sailors, marines and airmen who met earlier challenges to America's freedom.
>
> In sum, Patriot's Point is a memorial museum (Ewing, 1999, p. 1).

For myself, a poignant display was that devoted to the US Navy carrier torpedo squadron (VT) attacks on 4 June 1942, at the Battle of the Midway. Facing Japanese Zero fighters superior in speed, and impeded by a need to slow to the 'sitting duck' speed required for dropping their torpedoes, all their crew sought to fulfil their duty in sinking enemy ships. Of the 12 flying from the original carrier *Yorktown*, only 2 returned. In total, of the 43 air-craft involved, just 3 returned. The photographs of these young men stare out at the visitor who gazes upon them in return. A question forms — how is it that men could face such odds knowing that death was almost certain? Throughout the carrier there exist similar memorials — nearly everywhere there are names. In total over 8,000 names are recorded in the *Yorktown* of those who lost their lives in action while serving on aircraft carriers.

As stated above, for the most part, the exhibits are static — names, photographs, a few words to describe an action, often not even that. In some instances, just fragments exist: a letter penned by an airman to his wife prior to action, and death; a piece of painted fuse-lage taken from a disabled plane before it was jettisoned. All, in their isolation and silence, are symbolic of past human emotion, and bravery. There remains one further, graphic exhibit, and that is the film *The Fighting Lady*. The film was originally made in 1944, and released in American cinemas as part of a morale-boosting programme at a time when the war against Japan was at its height. Filmed on the *Yorktown*, the identity of the ship and the men featured in it was not then made public, and it was not until 1986 in a re-release of the Academy Award winning film that the ship and its crew were identified.

Today the film, with a length of about one and quarter hours that includes an addendum made in 1986, is shown four or more times a day in the Smokey Stover Memorial Theatre.

The theatre is named after one of the *Yorktown's* pilots. At the age of 24 years, 'Smokey' had a distinguished career in action, while he had also served as operations commander for a number of missions. With others, in February 1944, Smokey flew his F6F Hellcat to attack the main Japanese base at Truk. Eyewitnesses among those who returned indicated that Smokey had been shot down, had landed alive, but it was surmised that he was subsequently captured and executed. Smokey became symbolic of the many young men who had given their lives, and in 1952 the veteran's association presented to his parents a small plaque in his memory. From that gesture there grew a determination to provide a better memorial to the sailors and airmen of the various fleets who had served their country. When the *Yorktown* was decommissioned, one of the first things that was done in 1975 was to transform the ship's elevator into a theatre for the holding of commemorative events, and the showing of the film. This became the Smokey Stover Memorial Theatre. The film itself traces events from the period soon after the commissioning of the *Yorktown* to the attacks on Marcus Island, the Marshall Islands and the Battle of the Philippine Sea. In the 1986 version, being able to identify the personnel shown on film, details are provided of interests, home and attitudes. The images gain a life, and make the commitment of colleagues to the establishment of the memorial all the more understandable. For me, filmed as it was on action and with the stirring military music of its period, the film had an integrity as representation of that time: for my 16-year-old son, it appeared old fashioned and in need of an updated telling of the story.

The story of the *Yorktown* and the Museum is not, however, solely a story of past stirring deeds, of gallantry and bravery, but also of a commitment to remember and a devotion to keep alive that memory. In the film could be seen personnel such as Jim Bryan, the aviation ordnance officer of the *Yorktown* during its World War II campaign, and Dick Tripp, the Landing Signal officer. It was Jim Bryan who organised the first re-union for veterans of the *Fighting Lady* in 1948, and with the decommissioning of the *Yorktown*, he spearheaded the fund-raising to secure the ship for Charleston. He later did much to obtain funding for other purchases and remained active in the Yorktown Association until suffering a debilitating stroke in 1996.

The visitor is thus surrounded by this naval memorabilia and the plaques to the dead. This is the naval equivalent to the Arlington Cemetery. A further feature of the carrier is The National Congressional Medal of Honour Museum. The museum has eight displays that record the recipients by major campaigns: The Civil War, Indian campaigns, Wars of American Expansion, Peace time, World War I, World War II, Korea and Vietnam. As at 1999, there were 3,418 recipients. Not all displays are of war and the dead. As the *Yorktown* was the recovery vessel for the *Apollo 8* mission, there is a replica of that capsule, and of the Gemini capsule in which John Glenn became the first American to orbit the earth. By the side of these two exhibits can be found a flight simulator. Outside the Smokey Stover Theatre when I visited the ship there was also a replica of the Wright's first aircraft, the *Kitty Hawk*. Additionally, because it was Black History Month, there was a display which is brought especially to the main hangar deck in February every year to commemorate the contribution made by black Americans (at other times of the year the exhibit can be found in the second deck compartment). It records the number of black Americans who served in various campaigns, the fact that prior to 1948 there were separate all-black units, and it also commemorates individuals such as Brigadier General Hazel Winifred Johnson, who became the first black female general in the US Army in 1979 in the Nursing Corps. It is one of the few notes of a wider social history to be found in the exhibition. A second is the exhibition of entitled 'Women in the U.S. Military'.

Personal Reactions to Interpretation

The record that is being presented throughout the museum is primarily a factual record — of ships' commanders, of the (mainly) men who fought under them and the actions in which they engaged. The story that is constructed is one of devotion to duty and anyone seeking an explanation of why these events occurred would have to search elsewhere. It is accepting of a military ethic that requires acceptance of duty, a patriotic defence of American interests and the support of comrades. The museum and its displays emanate from a desire by those who were comrades of the fallen to remember the individuals and the times shared. But the years have passed, and the world is different to that of the 1940s. Some of the wars, in which the United States has since engaged, do not possess some of the terrible simplicities of an earlier epoch. American engagement in the Pacific in the 1940s was a reaction to an unprovoked attack on the American fleet at Pearl Harbour. It ended with the dropping of atomic bombs at Hiroshima and Nagasaki There is no record of this on the *Yorktown*. The Korean War saw intercession by the United States with other nations under a mandate from the United Nations in response to an attack by Communist North Korea on South Korea. Subsequent wars with American involvement have required no less a sacrifice of young men and a devotion to duty and comradeship even while the political imperatives of those wars are less certain.

The main emphasis of the Museum is on the period of the 1940s by reason of the history of the engagements entered into by the vessels on display. Nor, however, should it be thought that Vietnam goes unrecorded. There is, in fact, on the shore near the ships, a representation of a Vietnam base camp of the type used by the US Navy in their patrols of Vietnamese waterways. In the student reports referred to above, it is described as 'tatty' — almost as an embarrassment. Yet a soldier or a sailor exhibits no more or less bravery when seeking to destroy an enemy post or save a comrade in one war as against another — but perhaps the poignancy of sacrifice is all the more when one believes a war to be unjustified. The ethos of the armed services is such that personnel have little choice as to which engagement they serve — rather there is an expectation of the performance of a duty to honour and support comrades. There is a brutal fact that war is dangerous, bloody and deadly. Any soldier, aviator or sailor is very dependent upon friends and colleagues with whom they serve. One of the problems facing the United States in 2006 is that its armed forces in Iraq exhibit that same devotion even when the reasons for their presence are controversial. Those merits deserve respect, but arguably that respect was utilised by a political regime that argues that opposition to the war is a lack of support for 'our troops' even when it appears the Bush government over-rode military objections to the nature of the engagement it was asked to undertake. The fault arguably lies not with an army, but with its political masters. Yet at Nuremburg, the defence of simply following orders was not perceived to be a legitimate defence — at least for those high up the command structure. By its very nature the museum becomes constrained in its considerations — and for myself, reading of the engagements, watching *The Fighting Lady* I could not help but be moved by the sacrifices made in defence of freedoms that I now enjoy. There might well have been alternative histories whereby possibly a Japanese military autocracy collapsed within itself to end with situations akin to that which exist today, but such thoughts are mere speculations and certainly Americans in the 1940s could not compensate themselves with such thoughts. Similarly, in the 1960s and Vietnam, as in the period of American occupation of Iraq, the thoughts that these engagements are mistaken do not lessen respect for the men or women who sought to do their duty.

But such interpretations are bound to be controversial and the context and times of the exhibits need to be recognised. Not only were those who established the museum remembering the 1940s, but the museum being located in South Carolina exists in a State with strong Republican tendencies. Both predisposition and political necessity might limit the nature of the interpretations being offered. The brochure handed to visitors states that "our goal is to tell the personal stories of the men, women and families who made their sacrifices to preserve our freedoms". Elsewhere the brochure notes that the Congressional Medal of Honor Exhibit "features displays focused on significant eras and events in America's history that generated the circumstance for individual acts of valor" — but the emphasis and memorabilia relate to the individual acts, not the social and political forces that gave rise to the combats. Most of the other material in the brochure provides figures of men lost in engagements, of sizes of ships and lists of aircraft on display.

Yet, even while recognising that the interpretation is constrained, it does not fail to move — partly because of the authenticity of the surroundings. These ships are no replicas, no mock ups or still fabrications — the starkness of the bunks, the ease with which sound echoes around the hulls, the sight of emerging from a hold to come on deck and see other ships, guns and aircraft standing in mute honour to their respective pasts lends an integrity to the museum and its values. Standing on the deck of the *Laffey* in one direction I could see the bulk of the aircraft carrier beyond the *Ingham* and it could not be denied that it was impressive. On the starboard side of the destroyer, lay a marina full of yachts under a blue sky. The juxtaposition of past war for the freedom to enjoy a relaxing sail under a peaceful sky lay strong in my mind. It seemed both incongruous and also fitting. Perhaps one purpose of museums such as these is to leave one in a state of disquiet. It is possibly easy to feel total horror at a holocaust museum, but is it so easy to leave a museum with respect for the bravery and gallantry shown in past wars where, in one case, the end was through the atomic bombing of numerous women and children, and in other cases engagement was through a policy of supporting governments simply because they opposed a communist regime, which today happily does business with the United States. And what of a future museum for the Second Gulf War — how will that come to be honoured and interpreted? Museums through their silences can be as articulate in the prompting of thought as through the things they choose to exhibit. Patriots Point thus represents many nuances and complexities in both its pride and silence.

Finally, it should be noted that the above text relates to circumstances as they existed in early 2006. The Museum is aware of passing time and the need to address new generations without direct experiences of the events recorded. In 2002 it commissioned Seaman, Whitesides and Associates to establish a new Conceptual Masterplan and a redesigned site lies waiting to be achieved. The plan calls for, among other things, a strengthening of local naval tradition with a display devoted to the submarine *Hunley* and an updated and new Vietnam Exhibition moved to a new site and given greater prominence. A new visitor centre with new interpretations is envisaged and the changing of the site with reference to the location of car parking incorporates more into the site the memorial to those who served in the forces during the cold war — currently it lies isolated and rarely visited. A greater use of interactive displays is also envisaged and an unprecedented fundraising campaign has been launched to achieve these goals. Additionally in April 2006, a fund raising drive for US$8–10 million was announced by the Patriots Point Naval and Maritime Museum Foundation to develop a facility that could be rented by veterans, visitors and the community. This building, currently named 'Patriots Hall' would accommodate the offices of the Foundation and include banqueting and catering facilities capable of accommodating 1,000 people. Executive Director David Burnette was also reported (White, 2006) as saying that new demographics required an updating of displays, and that yet there was still a need to renovate and paint the flight deck — activities that require US$7 million. Corporate support was thus a necessity to ensure the future of the centre. White (2006) notes that the centre receives no funding from any level of government, and thus the centre is dependent upon revenues derived from visitors, members and sponsorship. Yet through this, the future displays will remain true to the *Yorktown's* basic themes and tenets, for as the Charter Membership brochure notes: "Join us in our mission of making sure the American story of courage, valor and patriotism lives on at Patriots Point Naval and Maritime Museum". That message epitomises the story constructed at this Museum. As a final comment it is perhaps worth noting that James Bradley, the author of *Flags of our Fathers* and *Fly Boys*, stated in an interview on Public National Radio on 29 March 2006 prior to his talk at the College of Charleston on April 5 of that year, that in interviewing over a 1,000 veterans of the Pacific War, none used the word 'patriotism' and for the most part emphasised not the extraordinary nature of the deeds and their heroism, but rather that they were normal people caught up in events where they did as anyone would have done. In some ways it is these comments that captured my own feelings as I looked at the photographs of the flyers and sailors — many of whom were little older than my son who stood by my side. Ordinary people can do extraordinary things, and that too is part of the story of the *Yorktown*.

Chapter 17

Romanticising Tragedy: Culloden Battle Site in Scotland

Fiona McLean, Mary-Catherine Garden and Gordon Urquhart

Introduction

"The evocative scene of the last major battle fought on mainland Britain" (website), Culloden, according to the National Trust for Scotland (NTS) which manages the site, represents "a turning point in Scottish history" (leaflet). Already a significant tourism attraction in the Highlands of Scotland, in 2007 it opened a new visitor centre, which is destined to become one of the major Scottish tourist attractions. What is it about Culloden that is so 'evocative', and how does its significance extend beyond Scotland to become a major tourism player? How does Culloden compare with other battlefield sites, and how can it capitalise on its inherent qualities as a tourist destination? These were some of the questions posed in the initial stages of a longitudinal study of the heritage of Culloden.

The Significance of Culloden

The Battle of Culloden, which was fought in 1746, is regarded as being one of the most contentious events in Scottish history, both amongst historians and the general public. Since the publication, in 1961, of John Prebble's book *Culloden*, which brought the battle, its causes and aftermath into the contemporary literary and public eye, opinion has raged about the significance of the battle to Highlanders, Scots and the British government. Such a historiography is beyond the scope of this paper, although an attempt will be made to summarise the most pertinent issues.

A popular understanding of the battle dictates that it was a battle between 'the Scots and the English', which the Scots lost, a gross over-simplification which is used, often as a justification for nationalist and anti-English feeling (Urquhart, forthcoming). As such it has become conflated with Mel Gibson's Oscar winning film *Braveheart*, itself the subject of much debate, as a key cultural symbol in the awakening of a twenty-first century

Battlefield Tourism: History, Place and Interpretation
Copyright © 2007 by Elsevier Ltd.
All rights of reproduction in any form reserved.
ISBN: 0-08-045362-7

consciousness of Scottishness (http://www.macbraveheart.co.uk/messages/bhapp-01.htm). Whilst Gibson's film has, in purpose at least, some justification, dealing as it does with the War of Independence and the rise of the Scottish nation in the fourteenth century, Culloden is at once more limited and more general.

Taking its origin in the Glorious Revolution of 1688, Culloden should be seen, firstly in the context of the rise of Jacobitism and the desire of the Stuart dynasty to reclaim their alleged right to the British throne. The Catholic King James VII was supplanted by the protestant William of Orange on the throne of Great Britain, precipitating a series of risings to reinstate the Stuarts, the traditional god-kings of the Scots, to their rightful throne (Duff, 2003). The risings in 1715 and 1719 had been put down at no great cost, but it was The Young Pretender, the grandson of James, who pressed for a rising in 1745. It is in the context of 'The 45' that Culloden should be understood, to fully appreciate its importance.

The Highlands of Scotland had been subdued for some time, with the British army fighting on the continent, and the French government, unwilling hosts to the Stuart Court in exile, wishing to maintain the status quo. Despite this, a cartel of Jacobite supporters, mainly Scots and Irish bankers in exile, encouraged Charles Edward Stuart, the Bonnie Prince Charlie of legend, to force a rising of Scottish Jacobites.

Charles set sail in June 1745, before eventually landing in the Western Isles of Scotland. Here he set to rally his supporters, many of whom were initially reluctant to commit themselves to the venture. Yet the Prince raised his standard at Glenfinnan and set about to take the nation's capital, Edinburgh. He met an ill-equipped army at Prestonpans, where the Highland Charge proved too strong for young recruits, unused to hand-to-hand fighting. Word had reached the government that the clansmen had risen again and mobilisation of civic defence and militia forces began both in London and in the North, amongst Presbyterian clans, and those loyal to the Hanoverian king, George II.

The Jacobites did not attract as much rolling recruitment as they would have liked and used some coercive measures to boost their numbers. Charles also perpetrated the hope that the French King Louis XV, impressed by his progress, would send substantial forces to assist him. This proved a false hope right to the end. Yet the Prince had a charm which would, at this stage at least, see that his expedition was funded. At this point the rifts in Charles' war cabinet became apparent. Many of his officers, most particularly the Clan Chiefs, advised staying in Scotland and consolidating his victory, whilst others, those he had sailed over to Scotland with, favoured heading South and taking London, gathering recruits and funding as they went.

Meanwhile, the government's militias began to assemble in order to defend London, and the main British Army was called back from the Continent. The lack of any substantial support, either in terms of recruitment or finance, began to seem ominous for the Jacobite leadership. At Derby the Jacobite War Cabinet took the decision to retreat. This further divided the leadership. Though it is a matter of much speculation amongst historians as to what would have happened had the army decided to march on to London, suffice to say that they were tired, disorganised and surrounded by Government forces. However, some contemporary accounts evoke a London in panic and threatened by the advance (Duff, 2003).

Despite victories at Clifton Moor and Falkirk, the Jacobite leadership advocated returning to the Highlands and scattering, awaiting another chance. The army had been hit by desertions, the distance and weather taking its toll on the Highland soldiers. In their retreat up north, the Jacobites hoped to destroy government forces who got in their way and to leave the east coast ports clear for the longed for French forces. The Government forces under the Duke of Cumberland sailed up the east coast and began to march west at some speed, hoping to arrest the Jacobite force before it had a chance to disperse. The government forces camped at Nairn, some 12 miles from the Jacobite encampment. A Jacobite raiding party attempted to surprise that camp at night but was forced to retire to Culloden, tired, hungry and demoralised. That was how the government forces found them the next day. The battle lasted 40 minutes and resulted in the slaughter of the Prince's army (Reid, 2005). No quarter was given and reprisals carried on for several months throughout what was seen to be the Prince's main recruiting ground — the area around Inverness and the Great Glen.

Unlike previous risings, the government wanted to rid itself of Jacobitism for once and for all. Attempts were made to destroy the fabric of Highland life and economy. Weapons were surrendered on pain of death; Highland dress, the badge of the outlaw was banned; the Gaelic language was forbidden and the system of Clanship, heritable jurisdictions, was abolished. The Highlands were changed forever and it is this, perhaps, rather than the battle itself that is the true significance of Culloden (Lenman, 1986).

As the link between the Highlander and his chief was severed, so was the link from the Highlander to the land. Whilst Culloden itself did not precipitate great waves of emigration — many of those captured after the battle were sent overseas — it was a necessary, if not sufficient, cause for the redevelopments in agricultural practice, called the Highland Clearances, which was the catalyst for the departures to North America, Canada and Australasia. The fact that 83 million people from these nations now look to the Highlands of Scotland as their ancestral home is due, at least partly, to the events and aftermath of the battle of Culloden (Hunter, 1999).

Culloden as a Tourist Destination

It was only after Culloden, in the latter half of the eighteenth century, that travellers began to make the long and exceedingly difficult journey through what was at that time an impenetrable Scottish Highlands and Islands, accessible only by horse and boat. Thomas Pennant's *Tour in Scotland* was written in 1769, followed by Samuel Johnson's *Journey to the Western Islands of Scotland*, first published in 1775, on which he was accompanied by James Boswell, who in 1785, published his account of the journey in *Journal of a Tour to the Hebrides*. Inspired by Martin Martin's *Description of the Western Islands of Scotland*, published in 1703, Johnson was especially seeking a wild and primitive Scotland, which he considered to be rapidly disappearing in the aftermath of the 1745 uprising. These writings were to be influential in opening up Scotland as a destination for travellers, which with the creation of General Wade's military roads and the advent of the railway, was to become a significant tourist destination. It is interesting to note, that Boswell, a patriotic Scot, and a Catholic, "wept over the memorials of 1745" (Levi, 1984, p. 11).

At the same time as Johnson and Boswell were travelling came the Romantic movement, which through the writings in particular of 'Ossian' and later, Sir Walter Scott, was to unleash a nostalgia for a Scotland that never existed and which was to become bound up with the conflation of the Highlands and Scotland in the tourist imagination. The publication of Ossian's poetry in 1760, which was to be rejected by Johnson himself as fake, nevertheless, spread representations of Scotland throughout western Europe, which established Scotland as "a special place, close to ancient virtues long lost elsewhere, with a history that merited a pilgrimage, even if the pilgrims had only the vaguest ideas about it" (Scott, 1994, p. 366). Sir Walter Scott was implicit in the invention of representations of Scotland, both through his literary works which recounted tales of chivalry against a backdrop of border and Highland settings, and through his influence as "pageant-master for George IV's visit to Scotland" (Gold & Gold, 2003, p. 195), where the King of Britain was persuaded to wear the tartan kilt, the wearing of which had originally been banned after 1746. It was Scott who "wrote the script for the promotion of Scottish tourism in the years to come" (Gold & Gold, 2003, p. 83).

By the time Queen Victoria bought Balmoral Castle in the Scottish Highlands as a holiday retreat, the Highlands had become a holiday destination. Traditions were being 'invented' (Hobsbawm & Ranger, 1983) to create an 'authentic' Scotland, a portrayal of tartan, mountain scenery and castles, a Highland distillation, which to this day is the dominant discourse representing Scotland. Visit Scotland, which is charged by Scotland's government, the Scottish Executive, with the promotion of Scotland retains what has proved to be a highly successful portrayal of Scotland in attracting tourists both from within the British Isles and internationally. Culloden has become a signifier for Scotland within this romantic, invented tradition. This is perhaps particularly apt given that, as we pointed out earlier, Culloden was not a battle for nationalist ideologies. Bannockburn, the other battlefield, which retains significance in the Scottish imagination, as the field where 'Braveheart' or William Wallace defeated the English, does have nationalist credentials. However, it does not have the 'authentic' landscape of Culloden, resembling a park in a housing estate, and certainly does not have the romance of the destruction of a people and their culture that is resonant in Culloden. Bannockburn was a victory; Culloden was a defeat, which touches the Celtic imagination, which glorifies sorrow (Morton, quoted in McArthur 1994, p. 97).

McArthur (1994) has traced the history of the memorialising of Culloden to its present position as an elegiac site, equating the romantic view of Scotland with Culloden. Culloden is bound up with the romanticisation of 'Bonnie Prince Charlie' and his protracted escape from Scotland after the battle, with the various stories and legends surrounding his flight, including his escape with the assistance of Flora MacDonald. It is also a symbol of the events which were to follow, most notably the clearances of Highlanders from their homes. Culloden has become an emblem, of a romantic re-invention of tradition, while at the same time symbolising a Scottish tragedy. As McCrone and his colleagues have observed:

> What was a military defeat has been turned into a moral victory, overcoming contrary historical evidence that whatever else it was about, it was not a Scottish-English battle. Now it has come to stand for Scotland, especially as it has acquired the patina of heritage. Its power as an icon derives from its contemporary cultural-political meaning rather than from its eighteenth century significance. (McCrone, Morris & Kiely, 1995, p. 195).

Since McCrone and his colleagues were writing, the Highlands of Scotland have witnessed a revival both economically and culturally. As Scotland's First Minister has claimed:

> The Highlands and Islands are leading the way … We are increasingly looking at the region as an examplar for the rest of Scotland. That might not sound like much. But it was unthinkable, over the last three centuries, that the Highlands and Islands would [one day] be held up as an exemplar to others — that a lead would be taken from the north of Scotland (Jack McConnell, quoted in Hunter, 2006).

Culturally, this is paralleled in the 2007 celebrations of the Highland Year of Culture, which originally was a response to the Highland failure in their bid to become European City of Culture, and has now become a major event that showcases a revival in the fortunes of Highland culture and in central government support for the Gaelic language. The opening of the new visitor centre at Culloden is one of the centrepieces of this celebration.

Culloden as a Battlefield

After many years of focussing on the battlefield from the perspective of the battle event, scholars are more often turning their attention to battlefields not just as a moment of conflict but rather for their enduring role as a place and as key elements in identity construction (cf. Carman, 2006, Gatewood & Cameron, 2004). Increasingly, scholars are realising that to "understand the underlying attitudes towards battlefields held by different people at different times requires an investigation of the places itself as well as the battle as an event" (Carman, 2006, p. 1). As a preserved battlefield, Culloden sits in a particular set of sites that in contemporary society have strong roles as both a tourist destination — an historic site — and as a site of memory.

Around the world, battlefields are marked in a variety of ways: with or without visitor centres, with or without interpretative signage, and some remembered vividly whilst others are only recalled. This is important as the preservation of battlefield sites has much to do with the role that they will have in memory making.

Visiting battlefields is not new; for over a century people have made tours, come as pilgrims or have simply stopped by sites of battles. This phenomenon is widely acknowledged to have taken hold in the years after the Battle of Waterloo (Holguín, 2005) and Lloyd (1998), among others, makes mention advertisements and other notices that appear in the 1830s promoting these tours. Paralleling the rise in travel and the advent of travel as a commercial activity battlefield visits increased through the later nineteenth century. Lloyd (1998, p. 21) notes that by the time of the Boer War there appears to be 'active encouragement' (if not full-fledged 'selling') of visits to the very new battlefields. The nineteenth-century visits to Culloden would fall into this growing trend of battlefield visits and, indeed, of commemoration.

Some scholars (e.g. Gatewood & Cameron, 2004), acknowledging the very draw of battlefields, provide them with their own category of visit, locating them within a 'subset of commemorative activities'; however, within this categorisation lies a danger of conflating what are very different spaces (both in the past and in the present) into a more seamless group. The battle event, the individuals or groups involved and the contemporary role that conflict may or may not play in today's society, all influence the way in which the site is marked and its role as a contemporary tourist destination.

The preservation of a site tells much about the commemoration and the role of the site within the identity and memory making of its visitors. Despite the profusion of battlefields around the world, not all are marked (tangibly) and among those that are, there exists considerable variation (Carman, 2006). From the monuments of the Great War (e.g. the Canadian monuments at Vimy Ridge) to small roadside signs marking a site, battlefields as contemporary spaces may be very different. Carman (2006) distinguishes between battlefield sites that exist as (largely) empty spaces and those that include dedicated facilities for tourists (e.g. visitors centres and other amenities). Culloden with its visitor centre, reconstructed cottage and interpretative signs and activities would fall into the second group. The visitor experience offered at each of these two types of site is quite different. Carman (2006) notes that, in general, there are very few of these battlefields-as-tourist-destination sites in the United Kingdom and identifies only one English site — Bosworth — as having been established with visitors in mind.

Among battlefields found throughout the world, Culloden occupies a position amongst other sites that are overtly marked and offer a highly interpreted and managed visit. In this way, Culloden has parallels with a number of the nineteenth-century American Civil War sites. Like Culloden some of these — notably Gettysburg 1863 — are both battleground and burial site and also like Culloden there is strong evidence that the ground itself has been imbued with sacred qualities and has, over time, become hallowed (e.g. Gatewood & Cameron, 2004). While clearly this has much to do with the role of the place as both a battlefield and as a shrine to the fallen, this issue no doubt can also be linked to the 'fallout' of these battles; in each instance, the American Civil War and at Culloden, the sites held specific roles as sites for the construction of identity in the face of a loss of both a tangible and intangible heritage.

In Smith's (1996) typology of war attractions, Culloden firmly sits in the 'remember the fallen' category, where lives were lost in defence of national principles and personal freedoms, despite the fact that the National Trust for Scotland have endeavoured not to adopt what Ashworth (1991) would describe as a nationalist narrative in their representative approach, but to set the record straight. This will be made more explicit in the new visitor centre, where they intend to portray it as the end of the Stuart bid for the throne, since "It wasn't a Scottish defeat, not at all. And that's the story we're going to try and get over. And emphasise this as much as possible. Now clearly we're up against the popular myths here, and that's very difficult to dislodge" (interview with NTS manager).

The Culloden Site

The site has long been a place of pilgrimage and tourism, although there was little interest in preserving the authenticity of the site throughout the nineteenth and twentieth centuries. The track through the site, secondary to the main road to the East, became a full road in 1835. Later it became a forestry plantation, the trees of which were cleared when the NTS took over management of the site.

In a process starting in 1858, the clan gravestones, the monument to the Irish Picquets, The Keppoch Stone and most particularly the Memorial Cairn (1881) date from a period when there was a revived interest in all things Celtic. In 1963 and 1994, the Military History Society of Ireland and the White Cockade Society installed their own permanent memorials after negotiations with the NTS. These are however memorials of loss, and there is no sense that the Culloden site is perceived, by Government forces or any contemporaries involved, as a victory to be celebrated. Whilst these monuments and the graves to the clans are later additions, and their provenance may be doubtful, it will be argued that they add to the sense of place and that any 'restoration' must come second place in these occasions.

Leanach Farm was gifted to the Trust by Alexander Munro in 1937, and more land by his son, John Munro, in 1959. The Graves, Memorial Cairn and King's Stables were presented by Hector Forbes of Culloden, in 1944. The Trust purchased the field in which the Cumberland Stone stands in 1945. Further land purchases took place in 1981, 1989 and 1998.

The NTS opened its first visitor centre in 1959, amidst much furore about tourism and sacrilege. What the current visit entails is dependent both on the time of the visit and the individual choice of the visitor. The Visitor Centre, sitting in typical fashion between the car park and the site, is accessed via a short path bordered by native plants and National Trust for Scotland 'branded' signs. Within the Centre may be found a bookshop and a café (with large windows and a vista outwards away from the main site towards the distant hills), and subject to an entrance fee, a theatre, a small museum and a number of interpretative signs. In 2006 these included a number of storyboards detailing plans for the new visitor centre. While the visitor centre's interpretative devices offer a sound, if perhaps dated, introduction to the site, it is not always guaranteed that a visitor will make his or her way through these areas. Neither the theatre nor the museum lie on the natural pathway through the visitor centre. There is another exit, leading to the Leanach Cottage. However, this door lies beyond the admissions desk and the museum and theatre. Perhaps the most natural and obvious pathway is via the bookshop and toilets offering a route to the door leading onto the battlefield. Moreover, as it is easy (and less costly) to simply enter the battlefield via the marked path leading off the main path (from the car park), it is very likely that a large number of visitors may not even enter the visitor centre.

Once on the site, visitors are faced with a largely empty landscape through which gravel paths wind, guiding visitors across the moor. Along the way wooden markers note the position of clans and weapons on the field. More obviously red and yellow flags dot the landscape marking the position of the two sides.

The Leanach cottage, the stone grave markers and the 1881 Memorial Cairn are all located in areas that lie near the visitor centre with the Cairn in clear sight from the centre itself. The nature of the site, the layout of the markers/monuments and much more mundane factors such as inclement weather often mean that visitors only see part of the site and, thus, the site visit may include those areas immediately surrounding the entrance and the visitor centre. Whilst it is unlikely that this diminishes the visit to Culloden, it does mean that within the established interpretative plan, there are any number of different visitor experiences that relate directly to the parts of the site visited.

At present more than 200,000 visitors visit the battlefield each year, with half that number visiting the visitor centre. Many of these visitors come in coach parties, since

Culloden falls within the Inverness coach tour attractions. In 2001 22% of visitors came in groups of 5 or more. Most visitors are from England and Wales (41%), with 35% originating from Scotland and 18% from overseas. As a NTS manager has suggested, "I would say that Scots visitors are quite a minority, in all honesty. The vast majority of our visitors are probably English …. Oh, it's probably seen as an English victory you see. That's the perception".

This centre will be demolished and replaced by a new visitor centre in 2007, the Scottish Year of Highland Culture. The NTS has long been keen to work with the Clan Societies, both in Scotland and overseas, in what it sees as its trustee role in maintaining the site in a manner suitably respectful to the manner in which these societies see the site. Rightly or wrongly, the iconography of Highland loss has Culloden at the top. Much more calendar worthy than the sailing of a ship of economic migrants, it was on the battlefield that the start of the exodus from the Highlands began. Current historiographic thought, however, is keen to separate Culloden from the Clearances, though this is arguably a discrepancy over the difference between necessary and sufficient causes.

Interpretation of the site remains similarly a matter of some compromise. On the field, there is the desire to offer full interpretation, whilst being as non-intrusive as possible. Handheld learning devices (e.g. PDAs or mobile phones) are probably going to be the mainstay of this area, with some costumed living history interpreters, but it should be noted that the NTS has never allowed any re-enactment to take place on the battlefield, no doubt out of respect for the fallen.

Inside a large walkthrough exhibition is planned, offering multi-sensory stimulation, whilst still opening access as fully as possible. The story will be told as factually as possible in line with current historiographic thought, and situated in the international political and military context of the time. Old myths will be addressed, most particularly that it was not a Scottish versus English battle and that both causes and ramifications were much more complex. Multi-media elements will also be implemented in order to fully enhance the experience. First person narratives will encourage empathy with protagonists, both innocent and guilty, from both sides. In addition, the exhibition will address archaeological procedures as they apply to the site. The concluding area will pay due homage to the fallen of both sides.

Accordingly the role of Gaelic in the interpretation is a matter of some ongoing debate at the time of writing. The reduction of its presence in the exhibition seems a matter of contingency. Events after Culloden saw the outlawing of the language, and it is only now, centuries later, that it is experiencing a minor resurgence. Whilst Gaelic has returned to the educational and cultural agenda, there are no monoglot Gaels still extant, and only 1.9% of Scots speaking the language (Scottish Census, 2001), current linguistic thought has tied culture to language in an inextricable way. Thus, enshrined in the priorities of the new Scottish government, the organisation has a civic responsibility to provide Gaelic interpretation under its diversity mandate.

The fieldwork that we undertook at Culloden during 2005–2006 needs to be set within these dominant discourses and the historiography of the site. We have undertaken in depth interviews with the key personnel within NTS and at the Culloden visitor centre and reviewed any relevant documentation, which they made available to us. At Easter weekend 2006, we conducted 24 sets of interviews with a total of 32 visitors in the visitor centre café for between 15 and 30 minutes. We have analysed the results separately and subsequently as a team. The following discussion is based on this fieldwork and relates specifically to two of our objectives, to better understand the significance of Culloden as a tourist destination, and to compare Culloden to other battlefield sites in order to ascertain the inherent qualities of Culloden. All but one of the interviewees was on holiday, nine of them referenced themselves as Scottish, eight were international visitors, with the rest referencing themselves as English, Welsh and British.

Discussion

The following considers the themes that emerged from our analysis of the fieldwork data: Culloden as an icon; Culloden as an international battlefield; Culloden as a visitor attraction and Culloden as a spiritual place.

Culloden as an Icon

One of the first questions we asked each visitor was 'Why did you decide to visit Culloden?' As anticipated, a few mentioned that they came merely because it was part of their tour's itinerary. Some had an educational purpose in their visit, for example, "To try and stimulate some interest in history in my children" (British female, 45). A substantial number of the visitors came 'as a pilgrimage'. Interestingly, the international tourists almost without exception came for this purpose. For example:

> Well it was this good reputation about its great history, about the highlands. We would like to, wanted to see the battle, the battlefield. We've been told it's a very important place for the Scottish people (Greek male, 30).

> We have decided we have read very much about the battle and so we said, ok, if we visit Scotland and don't visit Culloden then it won't go together, so we decided to come over here (German female, 35–59).

> My Mom had mentioned it and she said that it was just a very sacred place for her. It was beautiful and I like the history of it so (American female, 18–34).

By contrast, most of the Scottish visitors were visiting for much more mundane reasons, because they were passing or to go to the café, with a few indicating that they were repeat visitors. The site was more likely to be regarded as a visitor attraction by the Scottish visitors than as a place of pilgrimage. Despite being considered a Scottish icon, it was not actively being used by Scots as a place to "experience a deep sense of nationhood and increased level of patriotism" (Timothy, 1997) although, as we see later, the site was reinforcing their sense of identity. It was, however, being used by international tourists as a site to read off national characteristics of the Scottish nation. Fed on a diet of Scottish Romanticism and the links with the Scottish diaspora, this finding is not surprising. What is intriguing, though, is the emphasis that is placed by the international tourists on Culloden as a totem for a Scotland of the past. This is particularly significant for the NTS in giving Culloden its place on the world stage as an international tourist attraction.

Culloden as an International Battlefield

Nine of the visitors had not visited any other battlefield. Of those who had, Bannockburn was the most visited (six visitors) followed by French battlefields (five visitors) and Glencoe (two visitors). Of these visitors, we asked the question, 'How does Culloden compare with the other battlefields that you have visited?' The results for this question were fairly inconclusive, although some reference was made to the comparative authenticity of Culloden, which also presaged a later question on the emotions aroused by the site, such as:

> Funnily enough, maybe cos it's my first time here and as I say I grew up round Prestonpans and Pinkie. [other Jacobite battle sites] There's an eeriness here, a different feel for some strange reason. Maybe it's the openness of the moor and just the actual fact you being aware of the history and all the mystique that goes around with it (Scottish female, 35–59).

We also attempted to gauge Culloden's importance both at an individual level and at national and international levels, so we asked the questions, 'Is Culloden important to you and why?' and 'Do you think Culloden is important to Scotland/Britain/internationally?' On a personal level, Culloden was particularly important to those with family connections and Scottish lineage,

> As a historical event that directly impacted on my family, yes it is (British female, 35–59).

> Yes, because I have an interest in Scottish history, and it's a key part of Scottish history (Scottish male, 35–59).

> Yes, because I'm a Scot. Both sides of my family and in fact my great, great, great, grandfather was actually born in Beauly. So generations back we're back to where we started. So, yes, I think Scottish history is important to any clansmen (Scottish male, 35–59).

> It's one of the most important things in Scottish history ... it's just part of our history, part of who we are I suppose, aye, who we are (Scottish female, 35–59).

Although the Scottish visitors had indicated that they were visiting on a more casual basis than their non-Scottish counterparts, it nevertheless seems that the visit was reinforcing their sense of identity.

We had anticipated that there may have been a sense, particularly amongst English visitors that the site was important because it was an 'English victory', but this was not apparent in any of the responses. Instead, when asked of its importance to Scotland, the response was emphatic, 'absolutely'. Interestingly, an understanding of the aftermath of Culloden helped one English visitor who lives in Scotland,

> You do tend to get some hostility still, but in the history of Culloden and what went on here you can sometimes make allowances for that by

understanding what's gone on in the past and why some people still hate the English, but it does happen (British female, 35–59).

In the interviews, the visitors repeatedly referenced the aftermath of the battle. It appeared that in many ways this was as significant to them as the events which actually took place on the day. Its significance within various discourses, such as the history of the Gael, the Clearances, and Scottish identity, had more resonance with the visitors than any detail on the battle formation. For example, when asked 'What did you think of the battlefield?', one respondent replied:

> Well, it's not so much the battle but the aftermath of the battle (Scottish male, 35–59).

Others remarked:

> If you remember that so many people died out there, and what came after Culloden. I think the tartans were forbidden after this … (German female, 35–59)

> I feel that coming here you get the feeling of the tragedy that it was just the change of the whole way of life in the north (Scottish male, 70+).

> Really interested. I'm certainly not involved because I'm not Scottish, but I think that Scottish people should really try to give their heritage and I feel sad that they don't mention their language any more. It gives me that feeling. It's a nation that has been defeated and they just now have only some exhibition, some tourist guide (Greek male, 18–34).

This was not just a Scottish response but was articulated by visitors from all origins. This has implications for the representation of Culloden, and suggests that the emphasis is placed on the subsequent 'tragedy' as much, if not more, than the 'tragedy' of the day of battle. As David Lloyd rightly indicates, each battle site is different, and we cannot generalise from one to another. People come to a specific battlefield for specific reasons, and it does not seem to matter if they have not visited other battlefields previously. Many of the visitors are not necessarily 'prepared' for their visit, in that they have no previous experience of battlefields. The fact that their response is so palpable at Culloden, despite their lack of experience, and that they place emphasis on the aftermath of the battle, indicates that the experience of visiting the site of the battle is bound up with its cultural significance.

Culloden as a Visitor Attraction

The response to Culloden as a visitor attraction was generally positive. For example, when asked about the visitor centre, the responses were typically,

> Fantastic, we love it. If you want to learn it makes learning fun (English female, 35–59).

> Superb, absolutely excellent (British female, 35–59).

Some visitors, though, were somewhat more critical of the visitor centre,

> I didn't like it very much. I found it was really old fashioned (Welsh female, 18–34).

> Well, the history could be made more interesting, to be honest (British female, 35–59).

Reference was made to the living history aspect of the attraction adding to the overall experience. For example,

> It was good. It's really nice to be able to go to something that makes you feel a part of the age (British female, 18–34).

There were mixed feelings about the content of the exhibition, and the visitors were not always clear about what happened on the battlefield. One of our questions attempted to ascertain if the exhibition was getting the message across that Culloden was not simply a battle of two nations pitted against each other. In some instances it was successful, but in others this belief seemed so ingrained that the visit had made little impact on the visitor's understanding.

> One thing I did learn today which I didn't realise before I came today. I thought it was between the English and the Scots, but we learned today that it wasn't just about the English and Scots, was it? Yes, it was about politics and about systems as well. What I learned today, which I didn't realise before, I just thought it was the idea that English and the Scots just hated each other (British male, 35–59).

This compared with another typical response:

> She's interested isn't she when she knows it's a Scottish English thing (English female, 35–59, referring to her daughter).

In the new visitor centre, the NTS are keen to give a balanced portrayal of the battle, which, in particular, is emphatic that this was not a battle between the Scots and the English. It will be interesting to examine how the visitors respond to this, particularly those who clearly have an ingrained impression that it was a nationhood struggle. The site has long been appropriated as a national symbol, not least through the organisations that gather there to commemorate the anniversary of the battle.

Spiritual Culloden

For many of the visitors Culloden offered a spiritual experience, which for some was almost otherworldly. When asked, 'Can you describe your feelings about the battlefield?', typical responses were:

> I think it's a sacred place, a special place, I really do, and all the people who go round it seem to respect that it's a graveyard … a haunting feeling, very sombre (British female, 35–59).

> Now in English that's difficult for me … it's a very strong impression I think, if you remember that so many people died out there and even … what came after Culloden … it's a strange feeling standing on such historical ground (German female, 35–59).

> there was like an atmosphere, like you feel as though you're actually there at the battle of Culloden.… Yes, I feel sadness, really. The first question you asked us, had we Scottish relatives, I wished I'd had, cos I would have fought for the Jacobites (British, 35–59, couple from England, with no Scottish connection).

> I think it's an eerie place/ It's really strange, it makes you feel really cold, doesn't it? (Scottish/English couple, 35–59).

> I'll tell you, it's very eerie, you can just about visualise what it must have been like when it happened … you do get a sense of realism … there's a sadness about it you know (British male, 35–59).

> When we were standing at the viewpoint, it got really quite blustery, and we were saying actually that it was quite appropriate … it just made it all the more poignant … you were reading it was a blustery day and everything, and so it really did make it just a bit more poignant … it gave it a bit more atmosphere … not that you need more atmosphere. It just gave you goose-pimples (Scottish female, 18–34).

This sense of eeriness was not merely because Culloden is a burial ground. Less than half of the respondents realised that the site was also a burial ground. Of those who did, it augmented their sense of the spiritual:

> When you tread ground where people have died. Scapa Flow is like that. I remember going to the beach where some of the Americans died practising for D-Day and the sands, they were trapped in the sands. I felt a prickle at the back every time I went through it and then I saw it about how many people died (Scottish male, 35–59).

The tragic ambiance of the site is filtered through those who fought and died there and those who were left behind and came after them, in what has been termed the 'ethnic cleansing' of the Highlands and Islands. It is the combination of these two tragedies, which evoke a tragic past.

The perceived authenticity of the site is also relevant here. As a place, Culloden has a naturalness and is seen as 'real' rather than being a constructed site. Rather than being frozen in time isolated from both its historical context and from its physical surroundings, Culloden instead appears to be at once distinct and yet also integrated into the larger landscape. There is a strong sense of place at this site. Culloden is not merely a static display, but is a changing landscape, both in the physical and interpretive senses. This notion of Culloden as a landscape in which change plays an ongoing role contributes significantly to the strong sense of place evident at the site. The refurbishment of the Visitor Centre gives the NTS opportunities in portraying the battlefield within its landscape, in its tangible role and its historical and intangible roles, as a site of contemporary significance.

Conclusions

Culloden is the perfect icon for the tourist who seeks a culture of Scottish romance. It also fulfils the need to appropriate a site for national mourning both for Scots and for the Scottish diaspora. Culloden has become a site for an authentic Scotland, operating as a signifier of and for that country. It has become a spiritual place, which is a combination of the relative authenticity of the site and of the double tragedy that took place on the day of battle and in its aftermath.

There is a need to contextualise the battle and its contemporary understandings within the resurgence of the Highlands and Islands. The increased interest in the Gaelic language and culture is not merely a romantic response, although it cannot easily be unravelled from what has gone before. There is a radical shift in Highland identity at the local and national levels, which resonate with the proposed changes within the new NTS visitor centre. It remains to be seen the extent to which this shift is portrayed.

The interpretation of Culloden has largely represented Culloden as a one-time event, a battle, which took place on this site. It could be argued that this is, in fact, much less interesting than the memory making and the construction of identities that has occurred, and continues to occur, since 1746. What seems to resonate with visitors is Culloden as a physical space through which its meanings are continually evolving. It is a site of contemporary significance because of this evolution, its representation as a site of contemporary as well as historical significance. In re-evaluating its role as a signifier, NTS has an opportunity in its new visitor centre to portray Culloden in all its complexity. Many other international battlefield sites, which are set up as visitor attractions, tend to be in need of refurbishment, having been established at least 20 years ago. Some of these (e.g. Gettysburg) are also using this opportunity to re-assess their role not only as a site of a battle but, perhaps more importantly, as a tourist attraction, which figures highly in the way that its visitors interpret and locate themselves within the past. The findings of our research indicate that interpreting a battle site as an event does not sufficiently resonate with visitors, who are also seeking the contemporary significance of the battle's heritage. Culloden, though, as are all battle sites (Lloyd, 1998) is unique, not least because it resonates with the Scottish sense of tragedy,

> Grief locks the English heart but it opens the Scottish. The Celt has a genius
> for the glorification of sorrow(Morton, quoted in McArthur, 1994, p. 97).

Acknowledgement

The authors would like to thank the National Trust for Scotland for their support and assistance in undertaking this research.

Chapter 18

Forts Sumter and Moultrie: Summer Cruise into a Catalyst for War

Chris Ryan

Introduction

This chapter describes the tours offered to Fort Sumter in the harbour of Charleston, South Carolina, USA. Four sections follow, these being, first, the historical importance of Forts Sumter and Moultrie and their role in the American Civil War. Second, observations are made about the boat trip, information provided to passengers at the time of ticket purchase and the nature of the harbour cruise. Third, reference is made to the actual interpretation offered at the Forts. Finally, a conclusion comments on the nature of the interpretation and the messages it contains.

The Historical Importance of Forts Sumter and Moultrie

There are many causes for the American Civil War, and the stresses caused by those causes did not appear suddenly, but rather grew until secession became attractive to the southern States as a means of protecting their heritage and way of life. Yet, even almost to the last moment, there were various searches for compromise and a wish to avoid war. Even after Lincoln's election, John J. Crittendon, a member of the powerful Senate 'Committee of Thirteen' as it was named, proposed a number of amendments to the Constitution that would have guaranteed slavery against future interference by a Federal government while prohibiting slavery north of latitude 36° 30' — amendments that were designed not to be overridden at any future time. Lincoln, however, advised senior Republicans to vote against the proposals, which were lost 7–6 in the Senate Committee of Thirteen, to be later rejected in the Senate by a vote of 23–25, with all of the 25 vote majority coming from Republican party members. McPherson (1988), however, is of the opinion that by that time the die had been cast and no compromise could have stopped secession; the catalyst being the victory of Lincoln in the previous election. This is a view endorsed by guides at

Battlefield Tourism: History, Place and Interpretation
Copyright © 2007 by Elsevier Ltd.
All rights of reproduction in any form reserved.
ISBN: 0-08-045362-7

Fort Sumter when the author visited it in April 2006. The election of Lincoln, who at that time was of a view that slavery should be circumscribed within those states that currently practiced it, was counter to the interests of a southern economy for whom growth meant an extension of slavery into states yet to join the Union. Thus Lincoln's election was the catalyst for the secession of South Carolina on 20 December 1860.

The period from the Louisiana purchase of 1803 to the mid-nineteenth century was remarkable in many ways for the United States. At the beginning of the nineteenth century, the United States featured comparatively little in European affairs — other than perhaps in the concerns of the British and their Canadian interests. Its population was about the same as that of Ireland. But the pre-industrial world of that era quickly gave way to a revolution in transportation, the implementation of the division of labour in factories and the special-isation of production for overseas markets. By the 1860s, the embryo of mass consumption, mass production and capital-intensive methods had become visible. In the 1851 Great Exhibition at Crystal Palace, American products not only attracted attention because of their ingenuity or quality, but also because American industry had quickly seized upon the advantages of standardisation across producers to the point where many machine compo-nents were interchangeable. One such example was in the American production of small arms, and indeed the British imported American gun-making equipment to permit Enfield to manufacture guns and gun parts for the Crimean War. In part, the adoption of deskilling work, standardisation and mass production was a response to a comparative shortage of labour, in spite of an emergent trend of immigration; not that immigration was a simple economic answer to problems of both production and consumption. Depressed wages for much of the period, harsh working conditions and national differences among migrant groups led to extreme violence as shown in the New York riots of 1863, and these bouts of nihilism at various stages played an important role in national and state elections right up to the commencement of the Civil War.

Initially, the factory system became established in the northern part of the States. Burlingame (1938) notes that of 143 important patents registered between 1790 and 1860, 93 percent came from the free states, and indeed almost 50 percent came from New England alone. The geography of fast flowing rivers provided easily harnessed sources of power — and most of these rivers were to be found in the north. Geography, however, accounted for another economic fact, and that was the cultivation of raw cotton (which doubled in every decade after 1800) that was grown primarily in the south. Southern staples provided 60 percent of all American exports in the mid-part of the nineteenth century, and cotton grown by slave labour was the source of about 60 percent of the world supply of cotton — an important crop in the heady days of the textile manufacturing revolution of that time.

The concerns over the extension of slavery beyond the southern states as they existed at the mid-point of the nineteenth century lay in the growth of the United States both west-wards and southwards in the 1840s. The Californian Gold Rush of 1848 attracted not only gold diggers, merchants and entrepreneurs but also politicians concerned by issues of good governance, good relationships with other states and political aspirations at both state and federal levels. A little earlier, in September 1847, Generals Scott and Taylor brought the Mexican War to a successful conclusion to complete a linkage of states from Louisiana to California. That war brought to the fore men who were to become even more famous in the conflict that was to follow — Lee, Grant, Beauregard, McClellan, Hooker, Bragg and others had fought side by side and became well known to each other. Writing of the Mexican War, McPherson (1988, p. 51) comments "Jefferson's Empire of Liberty had become mostly an empire of slavery. Territorial acquisitions since the Revolution had added the slave states of Louisiana, Missouri, Arkansas, Florida and Texas to the republic, while only Iowa, just admitted in 1846, had increased the ranks of the free states". Many northerners thus condemned the Mexican War as being a means of extending a slave owning class. Further, talk of an invasion of Cuba as an extension of the Mexican War was simply seen by many in the north as an extension of an economic power of a slave owning class.

Slave labour attracted growing criticism from several quarters and for several reasons in the early nineteenth century. In 1807 the African slave trade had been abolished, meaning that the structure of black slave families in the United States became important, and controversial. In 1839 Theodore Weld published *American Slavery as It Is* and documented the break up of families through forced sales of parents and children. Harriet Beecher Stowe was to use Weld's book to even greater effect in causing a moral storm with the publication of *Uncle Tom's Cabin* in 1852. Not that all in the north shared the sentiments expressed in Stowe's book, or the moral outrage into which it fed. Some were opposed to any extension of slavery on economic grounds. The 'Free-Soil' movement of the 1840s saw slavery as an impediment to the spread of free labour, which was deemed to be more efficient. Additionally, its very presence was seen to prejudice the spread of education, and create poverty through the depressing of wages. Therefore, the spread of slavery was perceived to be inimical to longer term American interests. For their part, southerners criticised the conditions of factories as being inhumane, of there being a wage slavery that was worse than any slavery experienced in southern states, and logically extended their arguments to challenge constitutional niceties that appeared to (a) deny slave holding to new states and (b) deny the return of property to rightful owners — which principle was perceived as an obstacle to owners pursuing run away slaves. This issue of ownership and repossession of slaves was to create, at various times, two sets of competing 'governments' in states such as Kansas. (See Figure 18.1 and Table 18.1 for data relating to the slave economy.)

The institution of slavery was itself, no simple social structure. Kroger (1985) studied census records in South Carolina from 1790 to 1860 and found that in 1830 there were 450 black slave owners who possessed 2412 slaves but, by 1860, these numbers had been reduced to 171 and 766, respectively. Indeed, by the 1850s, it was very much an urban phenomenon based almost entirely in the city of Charleston, a centre of Confederate resistance to Federal government. Kroger (1985, p. 197) also notes that "Unlike the freedmen of South Carolina, the coloured slave owners of Charleston City entered the post-war era with property, education, and status, which contributed to their success during the Reconstruction and the post-Reconstruction periods". While, however, black slave owning diminished in the 1850s, based on data collected by Soltow (1975) and Philips (2004), white slave owners increased their wealth holdings in land and slaves — although some of this reflected price changes whereby the price of slaves increased by 70 percent in the decade, and land by 72 percent. Much of this price movement was a derived demand fed by increasing demand and prices for cotton. In the same decade, cotton prices rose by 50 percent, and production more than doubled. Similar movements were also occurring in

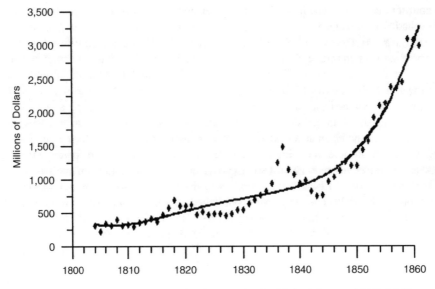

Figure 18.1 : The value of stock of slaves in the United States, 1805–1860.

Table 18.1: The fraction of Whites' incomes from slavery.

State	Percent of the population that were slaves	Per dapita earnings of free Whites (in dollars)	Slave earnings per free White (in dollars)	Fraction of earnings due to slavery
Alabama	45	120	50	41.7
South Carolina	57	159	57	35.8
Florida	44	143	48	33.6
Georgia	44	136	40	29.4
Mississippi	55	253	74	29.2
Louisiana	47	229	54	23.6
Texas	30	134	26	19.4
Seven Cotton States	46	163	50	30.6
North Carolina	33	108	21	19.4
Tennessee	25	93	17	18.3
Arkansas	26	121	21	17.4
Virginia	32	121	21	17.4
All 11 States	38	135	35	25.9

Source: Gunderson (1974, p. 922, Table 1).

sugar and tobacco — to the point that the amount of land devoted to food crops in the south declined in this period.

The causes of the Civil War are thus based upon a mixture of economics and differing fortunes, moral certainties on both sides, and differing views as to the right of states to determine their own policies free from federal intervention, and the right of the federal government to intervene in order to circumscribe policies perceived as anti-social and inimical to the wider interests of the country as a whole.

Yet, in any political crisis that precedes war, there comes a point where attitudes sufficiently harden whereby one side feels impelled to take action. In the case of the American Civil War, the site was Fort Sumter. The Fort still stands on its man-made granite island, located at a point where it dominates shipping making its way to Charleston 4 miles further within the bay. With walls 40–50 ft high and 8–12 ft thick, the Fort had space for 146 big guns. However, in December 1860, the Fort was largely unmanned except for workmen undertaking maintenance on the interior. Most of the garrison, then only 80 strong, were based at Fort Moultrie on Sullivan's Island, close to the mainland and a mile from Fort Sumter. After declaring independence, South Carolina sent representatives to Washington seeking ownership of the forts and their garrisons. In the last days of his Presidency, President Buchanan procrastinated, and while not surrendering the forts, neither did he reinforce them. Concerned for the well-being of his men and being sensitive to their vulnerability in the case of attack, which seemed to him to be increasingly likely, the fort commander, a Kentuckian, Major Robert Anderson, took advantage of ambiguous orders and night time conditions to move his garrison to Fort Sumter on the night of 26 December 1860. This action made him a hero in the northern press and a villain to the southern papers. It also led to the resignation of pro-southern sympathisers from the Buchanan cabinet, leading the President to adopt the suggestion made by General-in-Chief Scott and order reinforcements to Fort Sumter.

In an attempt to do this without making it an act of war, a civilian ship, *Star of the West*, was entrusted with a force of 200 soldiers, but the movements quickly became an open secret and when the ship reached Charleston Bay it was fired upon and the civilian captain quickly returned to port. By March 1861 Buchanan had been succeeded by Lincoln, who again refused negotiations with commissioners sent by Jefferson Davis on the part of the Confederacy. But Davis had not relied upon diplomacy alone, and had ordered General Beauregard to take command of troops and artillery to surround the fort, which had been done. By the first week of March, Anderson got word out that he was beginning to run out of supplies and he estimated he had approximately six weeks of provisions at most.

Lincoln was faced with conflicting advice. Of his then cabinet only Montgomery Blair supported holding the fort whatever the risk (McPherson, 1988). Both were reinforced in their views by a northern groundswell of public opinion that wanted no concession to be made to the secessionist states. Faced with a divided cabinet and a wish to avoid, if possible, war, Lincoln hit upon the strategy of sending a message to Jefferson Davis that he would send solely provisions, and no attempt would be made to send ammunition, armaments or men. Davis himself had political problems. The lower south required the upper south's men and resources if it was to hold together in conflict; likewise the upper south would not aid the lower south if it felt that its own claims would not be supported. The *Charleston Mercury,* however, made clear the opinion of many with leaders and letters voicing the view that the future of the south hung upon the claiming of Fort Sumter (e.g., see, *Charleston Mercury* of 24 January 1861). Davis thus ordered Beauregard to reduce the fort before help arrived. On April 12th at 4.30 am Beauregard commenced firing. The relieving fleet was scattered by a gale and played no part in the siege. Within 33 hours a bombardment of more than 4,000 shot and shells reduced a significant part of the Fort, and Anderson surrendered.

The impact in the northern states was electric. On 15 April 1861, Lincoln ordered a mobilisation of 75,000 militiamen to be pressed into national service for a period of 90 days. It unified, at least for time, northern Democrat support behind the Republican president, and state governors petitioned Washington to increase the troops being asked for. In the south, the upper southern states of Kentucky, Tennessee, Missouri, Virginia, North Carolina and Arkansas sent specific rejections of Lincoln's call to Washington. The Confederate cause was now concentrated upon a rejection of coercion, a need to maintain state sovereignty and honour, and a sense of brotherhood between the states. The Confederacy moved quickly and the ordinance factory at Harper's Ferry was taken, as was the Gosport navy yard. The Rubicon had been crossed.

The Cruise, Warnings and More Information

Located as it is in the approaches to Charleston Harbour, Fort Sumter can only be approached by sea. Today the Fort lies on the same New York granite that was imported in the 1830s to be loaded onto the shoal that then existed. The shifting sands of the Low Country sea coast and dredging mean that today a spit of land extends north-west from the Fort's foundations, and trees and grasses are taking root. Passengers can embark from one of two locations. The first is at Patriot's Point where the vessels operated by SpiritLine Cruises depart from a small jetty under the shadow of the aircraft carrier *Yorktown*. This is the subject of many photographs. At the side of the gift shop a small display and frieze tells the story of Fort Sumter, and in the gift shop various memorabilia can be purchased. However, from observation, because of the layout of the car park and access points to the jetty, few passengers see this, and in any case most of the information it contains is duplicated in greater detail by the National Parks rangers who provide commentary on the vessel and at the Fort. The second embarkation point is from the Fort Sumter National Monument located next to the South Carolina Aquarium in Liberty Square fronting Charleston Harbour. A new facility, the Monument, contains a detailed telling of the events of that period.

The cruise differs little regardless of the point of embarkation as the vessels swing round the harbour in the clockwise direction so that Patriot's Point and the harbour frontage of Charleston with its graceful frontage of houses and the church spires beyond can be viewed and photographed. In spring, summer and early fall, the waters sparkle and many sea birds can be seen including pelican and gulls and, if lucky, an osprey, while the author has also seen dolphins. In total the trip takes approximately 2 hours and 15 minutes, of which 1 hour is spent at the Fort itself.

As passengers embark, family and group photographs are taken underneath a sign — which photos can be purchased upon disembarkation as souvenirs. Passengers might also be asked to open their bags by Park Rangers as a security measure. The commentary commences just prior to leaving the jetty with a series of messages about safety and where life jackets can be found. Additionally, a detailed brochure is provided to passengers at the point of ticket purchase, and while this provides an account of the events of 1861, a fuller perspective of the Fort's history is provided. For example, it is stated that Fort withstood one of the longest sieges in military history. Having lost the Fort, Union Forces sought to regain the Fort to tighten a blockade on Charleston. On 7 April 1863 nine armoured vessels attacked the Fort in an artillery duel. By this time the Fort had been reinforced with a complement of 95 fully working guns. Following the failure of the sea attack, Union forces effected a landing on Morris Island and after some early desultory rounds a bombardment commenced in all seriousness on 17 August 1863. It is stated that on the first day alone about 1,000 shells were directed at the Fort. Confederate held Forts at Moultrie and elsewhere plus the guns of Fort Sumter were directed at Federal positions (National Park Service, U.S. Department of the Interior, 2005a). The period just prior to this was also notable for the attack of 54th Massachusetts Infantry on Fort Wagner, held by Confederate forces — an attack not so much notable for the outcome as for the fact that the 54th was a showcase black American regiment that did, indeed, distinguish itself for its bravery. McPherson (1988) notes that the regiment lost almost half its numbers in the attack. While the brochure omits mention of this action, the recorded commentary on the boat does mention the battle. The brochure does note that Union action against the Fort continued for almost the whole period from August 1863 to January 1865, when Confederate forces finally withdrew from the Fort to avoid being isolated due to the advance made by Sherman through South Carolina and Grant's campaign against Richmond. In that period it is estimated that Federal guns hurled over one million pounds of metal at the Fort which, although reduced almost to rubble, nonetheless continued to be held at a cost of 52 killed and 267 wounded.

In addition to these facts being noted, the brochure also provides a brief history of the Fort in the period after the Civil War. In the period up to 1876, the rubble was cleared, some reclamation was carried out and a lighthouse was constructed. For the next 21 years the Fort was not garrisoned and little was done until the outbreak of the hostilities of the Spanish-American War. Much of the current structure of the Fort owes to this period with the construction of the Battery Isaac Huger that dominates the middle part of the Fort. The guns were never fired and a small garrison remained, including during the years of World War One. In the 1930s some tourism commenced, but the outbreak of the Second World War saw the installation of antiaircraft guns to protect the naval base at Charleston from enemy attack. In 1948 the Fort was transferred to the National Park Service.

This history is, as stated above, explained in detail on the second side of the brochure. The first side, entitled *Fort Sumter*, concentrated on the period 1860–1865. The second side, entitled *Fort Sumter Today*, provides the later history and details a walking tour. The tourist is thus provided with sufficient information for their one hour stay at the Fort, while the brochure also explains why passengers will not see the Fort in its 'full glory' of 50-ft high walls and multiple guns pointing seaward.

As the boat nears the Fort commentary continues providing details of the surrounding land, pointing out landmarks such as Fort Moultrie, Fort Johnston and the story of Major Anderson. However, for many passengers it is suspected that their attention is distracted by children, taking photographs, enjoying the trip and the views and talking to friends and relatives. As the vessel nears the jetty at the Fort, the Ranger reinforces a message of care that is provided in a second brochure that is also given to passengers at the time of ticket purchase (National Park Service, US Department of the Interior, 2005b). It is reinforced that it is a Federal Offence to take any bricks from the Fort, that if one goes beyond the chain a 30 ft drop awaits you and you might therefore miss the boat — for ever — for humour is employed. One is told that there are big cannons, but it is not a good idea to stuff children, parents or mothers-in-law in the cannon, for if they get stuck they will be left behind for, in this particular case, the boat will leave at 12.20 pm. One is also told that two rangers await you to provide a guided tour, and in this instance special arrangements have been made for the parties of junior school children.

Interpretation on the Fort is provided through primarily seven means. At the Fort itself it is provided by the spoken word by rangers providing a welcome. Second, there are illustrated signposts. Third, there is a museum. Fourth, there is a small bookshop that contains for sale written material and items relating to the Civil War. On the way to the Fort by boat there is the commentary provided by a ranger over a loudspeaker system. Prior to embarkation there are the displays at or near the jetties, of which the Visitor Education Centre at Liberty Square is the main one. Finally, Fort Moultrie is also open to the public and that too has an interpretative centre.

The welcome to the Fort commences with a brief history of the Fort prior to 1860 — which explains its importance in controlling the access to the port and the irony of it being built on Union granite. The guide comments that "Of course, the main reason you are here is because of the Civil War", but goes on to use the other terms by which the conflict is known — The War of the States, The War of Northern Aggression. A recognition of the fact that even at the commencement of the twenty-first century these terms are still used in the South. But the fact that it was a civil war is quickly established by the allusion to the relationship between Major Anderson and General Beauregard. Not only was the latter the pupil of the former at West Point, but they had also become close friends and indeed had often dined at each others' homes, with General Beauregard being a not infrequent visitor to the Anderson's New York home. It is explained that both were artillerymen, and both felt honour bound to obey their orders. It is noted that after secession Buchanan and then Lincoln felt it important that a federal presence should be maintained to symbolise disapproval of an illegal act of secession — while the opposing view is also presented, namely that apart from any issue of potential control over vessel movement, the continued occupation of the Fort symbolised the presence of an external power in a newly declared sovereign state. The original size of the Fort is described by reference to the visual markers of the five flag poles found at the Fort, and the height of the walls is referenced by the height of the poles. The significance of the five flags is explained and questions asked of the audience. The conditions of the Fort are explained, the buckled wall is pointed out — bent by a blaze when red hot cannon balls were lobbed into the Fort on the second day of the siege to spread fire that threatened the Fort and which enforced Major Anderson to dump some of his own explosives for fear that they would destroy the fortifications if the fire spread to them. A story is told of the meagre rations upon which the garrison depended. The oral interpretation takes approximately 20 minutes and ends with a final story of the surrender of the Fort to Beauregard. The defenders left with a 100 gun salute and until that point no-one had in fact been killed in the 1861 bombardment. But, in the salute a gun exploded, killing a soldier, the first victim in a conflict that went on to claim over 620,000 casualties, more in total than any of the other wars in which the United States has been involved. At this point visitors are then left to explore the fort for themselves, and are able to ask questions of the rangers should they wish.

The signposts make reference to the subsequent siege by the Federal troops. For many visitors on a spring, summer or early fall day, the scene is far removed from those days of embattled conditions. The flags flutter in the wind, birds fly overhead, passing freight carriers and sailboats sail through the waters. The visitors mill about, children run from one point to another: on one visit the author was able to photograph a group of cheer leaders from Dallas undertaking a routine to be photographed by parents and high school colleagues in front of the flags and memorial to Major Anderson.

However, arguably the museum begins to detach the visitor from the contemporary. Within the walls of the Fort, away from the sunlight, in a dimly lit room (dimly lit to help protect the contents), the visitor is faced not simply with the panels that record the events, but also artefacts of the day, and the flag that flew above the Fort in 1861 which Anderson was able to bring back to the Fort when it was recaptured in 1865. Perhaps it is here, away from the shouts of children, from the wind, sun and sea, that reflection on those events and what they meant to the participants of the day becomes that more poignant. As in any museum, the visitor gaze is held and becomes a focused one an artefact, photograph, statement that for the visitor encapsulates a meaning, however brief perhaps is the stay in front of an exhibit (Pearce, 1988).

However, many of the passengers will also derive information from one and possibly two other sites as part of their total tour. Many will leave from downtown Charleston and will have visited the Fort Sumter National Monument in Liberty Square. The first detailed display facing the visitor as they enter the Monument is one that outlines the constitutional issues and predates them to the Missouri Declaration over 40 years prior to the war whereby, while not abolishing slavery, the Declaration sought to impose constraints on the spread of slavery to the west. There is also a display relating to the Dred Scott case in 1857 where the Supreme Court declared the 1820 Missouri Declaration unconstitutional. In short, the visitor is given the initial view that slavery was a secondary issue and it is not until one enters further into the exhibition that information about the importance of slavery to the Charleston economy can be found. Differing contemporary views about slavery are also cited. Certainly, there are statements about the importance of slavery as a means of sustaining a pattern of life and, interestingly, while there is reference to *Uncle Tom's Cabin*, it is in reference to a letter by a southern lady expressing the view that the author of that work had obviously no knowledge of the institution of slavery. In short, there is an attempt to contextualise the war within constitutional argument and move away from the war as being simply about a single issue over the morality of slavery. Of interest to the author is the selection of a quotation of Abraham Lincoln's, in 1857, where he does not seek to abolish slavery, but simply sustain the constitution. It is true that Lincoln was not initially an abolitionist, but it is a view to which he increasingly gravitated over time for both principled and pragmatic reasons. Given the emphasis on the southern perspective that the war was about state's rights, there is a relative silence about the actual events at Fort Sumter, with most of the interpretation being devoted to the siege in 1861. In the whole of the exhibition there is comparatively little about the subsequent siege of the Confederate forces that held the fort, and what is contextualised within a wider story of the Federal bombing and siege of Charleston – with a note that more about 'The City Under Siege' could be found at the Charleston Museum. The author also found it of interest that while there a visitor viewing this exhibition could exclaim, 'Those dammed Yankees — sons of bitches!', a single incident but one confirming a sense acquired in interviews that the story of Northern Aggression is still felt in some quarters in the South.

The Monument itself exists in a state of interpretative hybridity. Outside the Centre is flown the Star Spangled banner — a not uncommon feature in the United States. Yet it flies by a commemorative plaque to Septima Clark, an Afro-American teacher born in 1898 and who died in 1987, honoured by President Carter as a living heritage. A teacher in adult literacy, she was fired from her post in Charleston on the grounds of her membership of the NAACP (National Association for the Advancement of Colored People) in 1947, but undeterred in 1957, she returned to St John's Island outside Charleston to find the first of many 'Citizenship Schools'. There seemed to this author an appropriate irony that outside a display of constitutional issues there flies the American flag to honour a black school teacher who challenged the State to correct the disadvantages under which black Americans lived long after the Civil War.

In the story of the events of 1861 and the subsequent siege of Fort Sumter, it has been noted that Fort Moultrie also played a role. Many tourists will visit both forts, but the interpretation at Fort Moultrie is based upon a theme of America's coastal defences, and both the static displays and the 22 minute film shown to visitors concentrate upon a story of the fort responding to and then being bypassed by changing technologies. It traces the history from the first fort and its defiance of the British in the Revolutionary War, to its being washed away in a hurricane, its re-establishment, its role in 1861–1865, and subsequent reinforcement in 1895 for the Spanish War. Its role as a command centre in the Second World War is also explained and the view is given that at the time of its closure the fort had gone through many changes in responses to changing conditions, only now to be no longer required in the defence of America. The interpretation is certainly valid and presents a different perspective to inform the visitor, but in selecting this story to be constructed, the events that initially may draw the curious are de-emphasised and to a large extent by-passed, even though the second display within the centre has two sides to it — the first being the story of Anderson's defence and a Federal view, the second, presenting a Confederate perspective. But these panels come after the defeat of the British in the Battle of Sullivan's Island — the first victory of significance for the fledging United States. It should also be noted that the interpretation is consistent with the 1998 Management Plan for the site, which plan emerges naturally from the configuration of the site that owes most to the period since 1895 rather than the previous eras. (One irony is that the Management Plan notes that the exact location of the first Fort and the Battle site of 1776 is in fact unknown.) Consequently, while the interpretation may not wholly meet the needs of a visitor drawn by the significance of the period 1861–1865, it is to a significant extent determined by the nature of what the visitor can actually see. Yet, as shown in Table 18.2, the National Parks Service recognises that much of the significance of these Forts exist for reasons that account for but a few years of long history.

Table 18.2: Statements drawn from the Management Plan for Forts Sumter and Moultrie.

SIGNIFICANCE STATEMENTS
Significance statements are derived from identifying the park's exceptional resources and values that must be preserved to accomplish the park purpose.

Fort Sumter:
◆ For Sumter is where one of our Nation's most critical defining moments, the Americal Civil War, began.

◆ For Sumter is the most heavily bombarded site in the western hemisphere as a result of the Union forces' attempt to gain control of Charleston Harbor.

◆ For Sumter was and is a powerful symbol to both the North and the South, and it remains a memorial to all who fought to hold it.

Fort Moultrie:
◆ Fort Moultrie is the site of the first patriot defeat of the British navy in the Revolutionary War and contributed to British reluctance to invade the South.

◆ Fort Moultrie served as the Charleston operational headquarters of the Confederate Army during the opening battle of the Civil War and the siege of Charleston.

Source: National Parks Service: US Department of the Interior.

The 1998 Management Plan, which in 2006 still dictates policy, also indicated that trips to Fort Sumter would leave solely for the new development by the Fort Sumter Monument, but local political action meant that the Park Service had to retain the departure point at Patriot's Point near the *Yorktown* (which is described in chapter 16). Visitors departing from that point will, for the most part, bypass a small display by the side of the gift shop, but that display also possesses interest for its content. In many ways, small though it is, it provides the most comprehensive history of all of the locations. In a series of small paintings accompanied by text it tells the story of the initial siege in 1861, the escape of Robert Smalls, an Afro-American, on the coastal steamer, *The Planter* in 1862, the landing on Morris Island by Federal troops and the Battle of Secessionville, the attack on Fort Sumter by the iron clad USS Keokok in April 1863 (piloted by Robert Smalls), the capture of Morris Island in 1863 after the assault on Battery Wagner by the 54th Massachusetts, the siege of Charleston and the eventual withdrawl of Confederate troops. But it will be noted that this is purely a military history, the displays behind the panel are of a military nature.

Conclusions

Forts Sumter and Moultrie are comparatively small spaces, but they possess significant historical interest. They became the focus of attention in the last months of 1860 and early 1861, for the exigencies of the time meant that they became the site of the initial hostilities of the American Civil War. Writing in the *Charleston Post and Courier* of Thursday, 6 April 2006, Greenberg refers to John C. Calhoun,"patron saint of nullification, interposition and eventually secession and devastation" who was "much enamoured of anything Athenian, believing that only a slave society could afford its citizens the leisure to be truly free". Greenberg (2006, p. 13A) notes that this view is tenable, but only when you look at society from the top downwards. He goes on to observe that "The old houses of Charleston may not represent the way we really were, but certainly symbolize the way we wish we had been. Never underestimate the formative influence of the wish, the myth, the dream. Certainly not in these latitudes, where the Lost Cause may have molded the Southern consciousness far more than the actual cause did".

In these words, Greenberg catches a southern consciousness that in part explains current ambivalences that can be found about the 'Northern War of Aggression' and which are also explored in chapter 15. The interesting thing about the interpretations being offered at Forts Sumter and Moultrie is that they are every much the outcome of a professional interpretative service of a National Parks Commission. The tone is generally respectful, except for comments that relate to visitor behaviour as described above. The material relates to factual events and the care to address a silence not, one suspects, appreciated by many prior to their trip, that Fort Sumter suffered two sieges in the war of 1860–1865. There is a care to ensure balance. Yet, one wonders, does the commentary perhaps vary a little from site to site. The ranger welcoming guests at Fort Sumter asks from whence they come. As, for the most part, the visitors are Americans from other states, often including northern states, the balance between northern and southern views as to the symbolism of the act of occupation of the Forts in the 1860s becomes itself an act of harmonisation, of bringing together descendants of past combatants into a current Union. In a sense neither the old south nor old federalism survived the Civil War. In its place emerged a nation and a union born of fire, and a romanticism of a lost pattern of life. As the rangers note, the South fought to preserve a way of life in face of the increased industrialisation of the North — it lost and its way of life changed in the period of reconstruction. Throughout the perorations at the Fort there is a further silence. It is reiterated that the war was because the election of Lincoln compromised the spread of slavery, but what slavery meant is not explained. The 54th Massachusetts regiment gets a mention on a notice, but the emphasis is on Major Anderson and General Beauregard. There are silences. There were some women and children on the Fort, members of the civilian families of some of those constructing the Fort at the time when Major Anderson arrived in December 1860. While the names of the garrison at Fort Sumter for the period April 12–14, 1861 are recorded on a memorial zone, which includes the name of one female, the matron Ann Amelia Wenfield, at the very bottom of the right-hand column there is a silence as to the names of the civilian workforce who were present on the Fort. They are not part of the formal history: a tension exits between the symbolism and actions of power brokers complete of a personalisation of who they were, but other actors are, in the main, unnamed and unknown.

The visitor to Forts Moultrie and Sumter will have experienced vistas of the sea, a boat journey through the harbour which is alive with yachts, sea birds, dolphins and large freighters, they will have views of the *Yorktown* aircraft carrier and the frontage of Charleston known as Charleston Battery, and an explanation of not only the events of 1861, but a wider context. For the most part the trips will be ones of leisure, but there is also a careful allocation and selection of story construction — construction that is as sensitive to the demands of today as to the histories of the past.

Chapter 19

Synthesis and Antithesis

Chris Ryan

In Chapter 1 it was argued that battlefield sites may be classified based upon dimensions of site specific (narrow) to social context (wide), and from the 'factual' to the mythic. In many ways this is a pre-modern definition in the sense that it primarily refers to a specific location where past conflict has taken place. However, the different examples in the book have identified changing technologies of warfare. In Piekarz's chapter of English battle-fields, and equally in other chapters such as those about Rangiriri, Batoche or Culloden, specific places of fighting between opposing forces can be identified with varying degrees of certitude. However, it is evident, starting with the chapter on Fort Sumter, that improv-ing technologies increasingly meant that forces could be subjected to bombardment from growing distances, and by the time of the Second World War an aircraft carrier such as the *Yorktown* was able to strike several miles and several times over considerable distances, even whilst being subjected to attacks from far-flung enemy bases. Subsequently, the abil-ity to sustain and endure even more prolonged attack is evidenced by the example of Kinmen. Such developments then mean that the commemoration of those involved in war-fare becomes increasingly less geographically certain in the sense of being tied to a spe-cific site of conflict — rather the commemorative sites increasingly can be distant from the place of battle, especially when the fighting engaged very mobile forces over large dis-tances. Often these same technical developments mean that at a place characterized by skirmishing, the actual remnants of battle may be comparatively few. There are no large constructions, no myriad of trenches or tunnels, and perhaps relatively few remains of bul-lets or other signs of warfare. Such an example is arguably provided by the text associated with the battle of Aicken.

Consequently, the site of commemoration may shift from the theatres of war to places of more military permanence, or indeed of memory of engagement. This is illustrated by Prideaux and, to a lesser extent, by Wight in their respective chapters. Prideaux provides examples of Australian sites of memory where no real engagement occurred, and in many ways the Australian War Memorial in Canberra exemplifies this approach. From the view-point of interpretation, this represents a significant difference to the interpretation being offered at, say, a Culloden or Hastings. The interpreter has to replace place with artifacts of war and additional contextualisation as the visitor needs to envisage more without the prompts of terrain, scenery or possibly mood inducing weather as noted in the case of Culloden. Equally, the stories can become more complex, as the contextualization begins to range beyond the narrow confines of an actual battle to, for example, the consequences of fighting. For example, one of the more emotive displays within the Australian War Memorial might be said to be that on the Australian prisoners of war held by the Japanese after the fall of Singapore and elsewhere. A further consequence of the widening physical range of engagement is the increasing involvement of non-combatants and civilians. To some extent this is evidenced by the example of Quemoy in this book, but of course more significant examples would include the sites at Nagasaki and Hiroshima. Such examples begin to stretch the definition of a battlefield. If by a battlefield is meant a place of the fallen, where people lie dead and dying, or suffering from wounds derived from an enemy action directed by a need to overcome a foe and achieve victory, then such a definition could well include Hiroshima.

Indeed, extensions of the definition imply further constructions of the nature of warfare. Traditionally it might be stated, a battle was an encounter between opposing forces where it is implied or understood that each force is specially trained and equipped in the arts, skills and technologies of military manoeuvres. Under these circumstances the distinction between the military and the civilian is maintained, and under such a definition the sites of massacre or killing of civilians would not be defined as a battlefield. However, with increasing technologies it became evident, as in the American Civil War, that the civilian population was itself involved in war as a producer of weapons, clothing, supplies and transport, so that by the time of the Second World War whole populations become mobilized, and indeed in the Third Reich slave labour was engaged in addition to a 'home front'. From the involvement of home populations in war labour it becomes a relatively small step to begin to legitimize onslaught upon civilian populations as being militarily necessary. This was exemplified by the steps taken by British Bomber Command for a period commencing February 1942 on German industrial targets, and then on Dresden and Cologne — attacks motivated in part as revenge for the Blitz and in a mistaken belief that an invasion of Europe by land-based forces could be avoided. Controversial at the time, and undertaken with significant misgivings by Churchill, actual bombings varied with differing intensities over the period 1943–1944 dependent on interpretations of what was required and reactions to such things as the V1 and V2 bombs.

Recognizing the moral dilemmas involved in such bombings, and the dropping of the atom bombs in Japan, it might be said that at least such events occurred within a context of formal declarations of hostilities by nation states. As the twentieth century progressed, the concept of the battlefield became increasingly questionable. While there were staged battles in Vietnam in the 1960s, much of the daily regime was of aerial strikes, mortar fire at positions that were not directly visible to the soldiers firing the rounds and continuous skirmishing with hit and run Vietnamese forces. Increasingly frustrated, American commanders in 1967 authorised bombing raids on Hanoi — meaning that civilians were again perceived as legitimate targets in terms of a need to undermine a will to continue fighting. By the last few decades of the twentieth century, increasingly hostilities began to involve attacks upon states by non-national organizations. Whether Mau Mau, the IRA or Al Queda, all organizations share a commonality of attacking national governments without formal declarations of war, and without possessing national status of being governments. In return, it can be observed that national governments have not always seen it necessary to regularize their own military adventures, sometimes with almost bizarre results where high-level government officials are unknowing, or wish to remain unknowing, of what is practical policy. One such infamous example is perhaps the Iran-Contra affair where the Central Intelligence Agency, or at least that part of it influenced by Lieutenant-Colonel Oliver North, was illegally selling arms to the Iranian government to finance support of the Contras opposed to the Sandinista Government of Nicaragua. In the early years of the twenty-first century, it can be argued that the logical development of the nature of the battlefield site was demonstrated by the attack on the World Trade Center in September 2001.

In short, in a post-modern period the site of conflict is arguably less well defined even allowing for the fact that past ages are not without examples of cities being sacked and their citizens subjected to the sword and pillage. War has arguably not always recognized the confines of participation being restricted to organized groups of military. However, recognizing these issues, and the complexities noted by Prideaux with reference to the potential for cyber warfare and other forms where the terrain of battle may well have little traditional geography, the question begins to arise as to whether battlefield tourism is not simply some variant of human atrocity to the point where it is caught by Foley and Lennon's (1996) definition of 'dark tourism', or is it simply an extension of 'the heritage of atrocity' as described by Tunbridge and Ashworth (1996). Inasmuch as some define 'dark tourism' as including natural disaster (e.g. Smith & Croy, 2005), it can be argued that the events described in this book stand aside from these actions as being created *by* people and done *to* other people. Dunkley (2006) specifies seven forms of thanatourism, of which warfare-based tourism is but one. She suggests 11 possible motives for engaging in this form of tourism, and these are primarily motives for visitation and include:

Special interest. An interest emerging from sustained commitment associated with serious leisure, an interest in history or personal and/or family association with an event;

Thrill/risk seeking. Which motive might be associated with re-enactors who wish to have a sense of what it is to be involved in battle but which, in the view of this author, is not wholly tenable, given the strict controls and constraints under which many battle re-enactments are staged. However, it cannot be denied that the opportunity to, say, take part in a cavalry charge is not without its thrill and its risks, and injuries can and do occur;

Validation. This motive relates to the legitimization of action and engages social approval and recognition of an event. However, it is perhaps worth noting the comments of Slayton (2006) in writing of Gettysburg, namely:

> Edward Everett's Gettysburg Oration on November 19, 1863 carries little significance in history, but the words might well be contemplated as we visit the sacred ground 'no lapse of time, no distance of space, shall cause you to be forgotten.' A pilgrimage to Gettysburg seems to be a part of the American way of life, a powerful ritual that must be observed. The fascination of Gettysburg lies not so much in its historical significance, but in its

escapism and excessive commercialism. While historians and writers examine and reconstruct the battle scene and others reenact the events in elaborate period costumes, tourists arrive by the carload for a chance to 'play' at war. In this curious compulsion and fanfare of tourism, we can only hope that this battlefield will be remembered, as it should be, as a sacred 'sepulchre of illustrious men'.

The process of validation as a social process thus, in her view, potentially runs the risk of commodification and commercialism;

Authenticity. The search for authenticity is complicated by the obvious response — whose authenticity, and for what purposes are interpretations held to be authentic? Probably, a better motive to replace this classification is that of educational attainment: the visitor comes to a site to learn, and arguably the best form of learning is that which elicits questioning. Thus the questions as to why a site is interpreted the way it is, who has interpreted, what is omitted are probably better ways of approaching the battlefield site than to engage in a quest for authenticity — a will of the wisp it might be said given the previous text and the observations made by Tunbridge and Ashworth (1996, p. 11), *viz*:

> although logically the intrinsic definition of authenticity can be dismissed here as the concern of historians while heritage planners define authenticity ... in terms of the consumer, these two quite different approaches become intertwined in practice. This occurs in part through the organizational structure of heritage production .... Consequently frictions are almost inevitable in the selection and management of heritage products and accusations of overinterpretation, triviality, dishonesty and distortion from one side, and elitism, rigidity, obscurantism and irrelevance from the other.

Self-discovery. This motive might be said to exist in terms of developing a sense of sharing and understanding with past family members. The sentiment was found to be common among re-enactors, as evidenced in this book by comments made in the case of the Armistice Day celebrations in Cambridge, New Zealand or Charleston, South Carolina. The need to identify with reference to ancestors is perhaps particularly strong where other sources of a sense of 'rootedness' to place becomes difficult in an age when fields disappear under housing estates and buildings are demolished to make way for shopping malls;

Iconic sites. Some battlefield sites have arguably attained this status. In this book, Culloden is one such. Gettysburg may be another. What is of interest is how others fail to become iconic in spite of historical significance — one such being the site of the Battle of Waterloo. Others become both general and divisive. The Battles of the Ypres (Ieper) salient from 1914 to 1918 are remembered for their awful causalities, including over 5,900 Canadians in April 1915 alone, but Tunbridge and Ashworth (1996) note that for Flemish nationalist groups the site represents one of oppression by a French-speaking officer class. Interestingly, the Diksmuide monument now attracts neo-Nazi groups and Flemish nationalists, while a museum also opened in 1998;

Convenience. Battlefield sites may simply be near to an itinerary and thus be seen as a possibly interesting place to visit. Parents with young boys may see such sites as an opportunity to pander to the interests of their male offspring in the hope of acquiring a little peace: in short, not all visitors to battlefield sites are necessarily motivated by seemingly higher motives;

Morbid curiosity. This motive is often associated with 'dark tourism' or 'thanatourism'. Interestingly in the research for this book and in various discussions all that may be noted, albeit at an anecdotal level, is that little evidence of this motive was apparent. Rather significant evidence seemed to exist for the next three related motives;

Pilgrimage. Hall (2002) and Slade (2003) have noted the growing sense of pilgrimage on the part of the young of Australia and New Zealand to Gallipoli, while a growing participation of the young at Cenotaphs in services or remembrance has been remarked upon in various journalistic accounts (e.g. Oliver, 2003);

Remembrance and empathy. This motive is so closely associated with the previous one that one might question whether they are the same. Certainly, as noted in the case of the chapter on Cambridge's Armistice Day, participants do experience a questioning of 'what was it like' and are able to recall family stories. There is, it might be said, a realization that many of those who fell were young people, which in itself is a motive for a sense of loss;

Contemplation. This follows from the previous statement — the realization of past sacrifice and the consequence of that sacrifice for self is, arguably, specifically engineered at an Armistice Day celebration and, to some extent, in the patterns of interpretation currently (in 2006) on offer at the *Yorktown*.

To these motives for visitation might be added motives for preservation, recording and memory. These can include:

Legitimization. Such motives include the state patronage of sites to engender feelings of national pride, establish and reinforce policies the state wishes to enforce, and in short to help sustain feelings of national identity. In this book one can look to the example of red tourism, but other examples come to mind such as the representations of the demilitarized zone between North and South Korea where, on the southern side, the messages are one of reconciliation and kinship mediated through the lens of ecological rebirth on the zone itself;

Economic resurgence. In this sense the battlefield is simply akin to many other tourist resources. It is seen as a means of engendering visitation that will, in turn, create employment and income flows. The battle zone may therefore become the prime attraction, or simply part of a portfolio of products that may be incorporated into some wider theme based upon history, culture or heritage;

Discovery of heritage. This equates with Dunkley's motive of self-discover but, as noted, the acts of self-discovery may initiate the creation of product and many examples exist whereby local communities discover a sense of identity through past histories, or where history enthusiasts such as those involved in re-enactment societies create product. As illustrated within this book, such product can be spatially displaced, as shown by the example of the Cambridge Armistice Day celebrations, or they may be very place specific. As in many instances, questions of identity and interpretation are written large;

Acts of remembrance. A key motive for product supply is a genuine wish to remember past sacrifice, the loss of life and the disruption of family lives. There is often associated with this a need by those involved to recall the past, to remember comrades, to associate with those chosen few who, through having been there, can fully understand the past pain as no other person can. Thus veteran's societies are formed, and at times establish a special place of remembrance. In this book, the *Yorktown* serves as such an example. Often, at least initially, unsupported by official institutions, over time such sites gain legitimacy, and thereby advance the claims of survivors for not only acts of remembrance but also more explicit means of support such as compensation for poor health or family support;

Personal aspirations. Given that many sites are sponsored by individuals, personal aspirations also need to be considered. These motives for product supply may emanate from a desire to remember as just noted, but other motives can also play a role, including those of seeking political and or social prestige. Groups seeking to establish community goals can be attractive to those seeking support for political office, and a mutual synergy can be created between those altruistically motivated and others wishing to obtain profile and support for their own ends. This is understandable, and need not be injurious to the longer term aims of community groups, but implicit in this is the need for the community group to secure a strong and separate identity that can subsequently sustain the loss of a political supporter.

Given all of these motives and the changing nature of sites as identified at the commencement of this chapter, it becomes obvious why battlefield sites are complex places of not only past conflict but continuing differences even whilst they may seek to achieve reconciliation between past warring parties. However, such differences are those of a post-conflict era and thus, hopefully, are more pacific in their nature. Battlefield sites are thus worthy of attention and research for they represent not only memories of the past, but also statements of the present and aspirations for the future. They seek to remind, educate, create sombre reflection; they are places to pause and consider the means by which contemporary societies came into being. They are places where the visitor can exercise empathy, be repelled by violence that shattered peoples' lives and re-confirm a wish to avoid future conflict. They are also reminders that at times ordinary people are required to do extraordinary things; that some values are worth defending with the final sacrifice, even while they pose questions as to how those values are to be defined. They may well be challenging places to visit — and so they should. They thus become challenging places to interpret and manage visitor experiences, balanced as some may be between a wish to conserve and a need to be financially secure. In some ways battlefield sites are treacherous places ready to catch the unwary with thoughts not looked for when a visit is planned, and that too is no bad thing in a post-modern world that displaces history, time and space with compressions of hybridity. As stark reminders of what men saw fit to fight over, battlefield sites represent a special type of tourist place.

References

Adreano, R. (1962). *The economic impact of the American Civil War.* Cambridge, MA: MIT Press.

Agrusa, J. Tanner, J., & Dupuis, J. (2006). Determining the potential of American Vietnam veterans returning to Vietnam as tourists. *International Journal of Tourism Research,* 8(3), 223–234.

Ahmad, S. (2004). Japanese invaders in the East Coast. *New Straits Times,* April 23.

Akin, D. (1989). World War II and the evolution of Pacific Art. *Pacific Arts, 27,* 5–11.

Alpert, M. (2004). *A new international history of the Spanish Civil War* (2nd ed.). Basingstoke: Palgrave Macmillan.

Ames, K. L., Franco, B., & Frye, L. T. (1997). *Ideas and images: Developing interpretive history exhibits.* London: Sage Publications.

Anon. (1998). No apologies for any unanswered questions. *Ballarat Courier,* Eureka Stockade Centre: Birthplace of the Australian Spirit (supplement). 27 March, p. 4.

Anon. (2004). As Eureka flag flies, Hick's role sparks a flutter. *The Age,* News, 3 December, p. 1.

Arun, N. (2004). Outsourcing the war. *BBC News,* 2 April, http://news.bbc.co.uk/1/hi/world/middle_east/3591701.stm (accessed 6 August 2004).

Asahi Shimbun. (2004). *Takenaka enters the ring.* Unattributed, Tokyo: Asahi Shimbun.

Ashworth, G. J. (1991). *War and the city.* Routledge: London.

Ashworth, G., & Hartmann, R. (Eds). (2005). *Horror and human tragedy revisited: The management of sites of atrocities for tourism.* New York: Cognizant Communication Corporation.

Australian War Memorial (2006). www.awm.gov.au (accessed 10 April 2006).

Ballard, R. D. (1993). *The lost ships of Guadalcanal.* Toronto: Warner/Madison Press.

Bates, S. (1994). Old wounds, new pains. *The Guardian,* 24 August.

Battle of Vinegar Hill (2006). http://www.battleofvinegarhill.com.au/ (accessed 14 March 2006).

Bauman, Z. (2000). *Liquid modernity.* Cambridge: Polity.

BBC (2005). Analysis: Defining genocide. *BBC News,* http://news.bbc.co.uk/2/hi/africa/3853157.stm (accessed 13 February 2006).

BBC Mundo (2005). *No mas estatuas de Franco en Madrid. BBC World* at http://news.bbc.co.uk/hi/spanish/international/newsid_4357000/4357593.stm.

Beck, L., & Cable, T. (2002). *Interpretation for the 21st century — Fifteen guiding principles for interpreting nature and culture.* Champaign, IL: Sagamore Publishing.

Bedall, J. (1871). Personal report to Thomas Cook on the ending of the Paris Siege. Thomas Cook Archive, Peterborough.

Bedford, R. D. (1973). *New Hebridean mobility: A study of circular migration.* Canberra: ANU.

Beech, J. (2000). The enigma of holocaust sites as tourist attractions: The case of Buchenwald. *Managing Leisure,* 5(1), 29–41.

Beevor, A. (1982). *The Spanish Civil War.* London: Cassell Military Paperbacks.

Beevor, A. (2006). *The battle for Spain: The Spanish Civil War 1936–1939.* London: Weidenfeld and Nicolson.

Beggs Sunter, A. (2001). Remembering Eureka. *Journal of Australian Studies,* December (70), 49–59.

Beggs Sunter, A. (2004). Contesting the flag: The mixed messages of the Eureka flag. Unpublished paper presented at Eureka 1854–2004: Reappraising an Australian legend. Seminar at University of Melbourne, 1 December.

Belich, J. (1988). *The New Zealand wars and the Victorian interpretation of racial conflict.* Auckland, New Zealand: Penguin.

Belich, J. (1996). *Making peoples.* Auckland, New Zealand: Allen Lane/Penguin.

Bellam, M. E. P. (1970). The colonial city: Honiara, a case study. *Pacific View Point, 11*, 66–96.

Bennett, J. A. (1987). *Wealth of the Solomons: A history of a Pacific Archipelago, 1800–1978.* Honolulu: University of Hawaii Press.

Biao, Y. (2005). Historical memory in Australia and Japan. In: S. Alomes, (Ed.), *Islands in the stream: Australia and Japan face globalisation* (pp. 115–124). Hawthorn: Maribyrnong Press.

Black, J. (1992). *The grand tour in the eighteenth century.* Stroud: Sutton Publishing Ltd.

Black, J. (2000). *War: Past, present and future.* Stroud: Sutton Publishing Ltd.

Blainey, G. (2004). Victoria's bloody Sunday. *Royal Auto, 72*(4), 16–20.

Blumer, H. (1969). *Symbolic interactionism.* Englewood Cliffs, NJ: Prentice Hall.

Boyd, S. W. (1999). North-south divide: The role of the border in tourism to Northern Ireland. *Visions in Leisure and Business, 17*(4), 50–71.

Brendon, P. (1991). *Thomas Cook: 150 years of popular tourism.* London: Secker & Warburg.

British Solomon Islands Protectorate (BSIP) (1962). *News Sheet,* 12 July February, Honiara.

British Solomon Islands Protectorate (BSIP) (1964). *News Sheet,* June, Honiara.

Bryne, C. (1997). Terror tourists queue for trips to war zones. *The Sunday Times,* 16 March.

Burlingame, R. (1938). *March of the iron men: A social history of union through invention.* New York: Charles Scribner's Sons.

Buruma, I. (1994). *The wages of guilt.* London: Phoenix.

Butler, R. (1980). The concept of a tourism area cycle of evolution. *Canadian Geographer, 24*(1), 5–12.

Butler, R. W. (1996). The development of tourism in frontier regions: Issues and approaches. In: Y. Gradus & H. Lithwick (Eds), *Frontiers in regional development* (pp. 213–229). Lanham, MD: Rowman & Littlefield.

Butler, R. W., & Mao, B. (1996). Conceptual and theoretical implications of tourism between partitioned states. *Asia Pacific Journal of Tourism Research, 1*(1), 25–34.

Button, J. (2004a). The Eureka myth. *The Age,* Insight section, 23 October, p. 3.

Button, J. (2004b). Eureka the 150 year war: How children of the rebellion maintain the rage. *The Age,* News, 27 November, pp. 1, 10.

Cahill, R. (1987). *Border towns of the southwest: Shopping, dining, fun and adventure from Tijuana to Fuarez.* Boulder, CO: Pruett Publishing Co.

Calder, S. (2000). Bermuda shorts and battle dress. *High Life,* June.

Cardow, A., & Wiltshier, P. (2003). Collective amnesia and the elevation of heritage tourism. In: C. Ryan, & M. Aicken (Eds), *Proceedings of the tourism at the limits conference.* University of Waikato: Department of Tourism Management. December.

Carlton, C. (1992). *Going to the wars.* London: Routledge.

Carr, R. (1986). *The Spanish tragedy: The Civil War in perspective.* London: Phoenix Press.

Carter, S. (1998). Tourists and traveller's social construction of Africa and Asia as risky locations. *Tourism Management, 19,* 349–358.

Casodo, M. (1999). Observations on the effects of terrorism. *Journal of Hospitality and Tourism Education, 10*(4), 57–59.

Centro de Desarrollo de Monearos (2006). *La Guerra Civil en Aragon Visitor leaflet for La Guerra Civil en los Monegros. Ruta Orwell.* Centro de Desarrollo de Monegros. Spain: Grañén.

Chapple, G. (2006). Te Araroa — the long pathway. A hiking trail the length of New Zealand. http://www.teararoa.org.nz/trail_stories.php?story_id=26.

Chen, L., Lu, L., & Lin, S. (2004). The development and utilization of the Jinggangshan tourist resources. *Tourism Tribune, 19*(6), 19–20.

China Tourism Newspaper (2004). The cooperative agreement signed by China National Tourism Administration and State Development Bank to jointly promote the development of the Red Tourism. *China Tourism Newspaper,* March 14.

Chronis, A. (2005). Coconstructing heritage at the Gettysburg storyscape. *Annals of Tourism Research, 32*(2), 386–406.

Clark, D. (1998). The current growth of Jewish museums in Europe. In: N. Ravenscroft, D. Philips, & M. Bennett (Eds), *Tourism and visitor attractions — leisure, culture and commerce.* Leisure Studies Association, na. (pages — Leopold's citation). Loughborough, UK.

Clough, P. T. (1991). *The end(s) of ethnography.* Newbury Park, Calif: Sage.

Cohen, E. (1973). Nomads from affluence: Notes on the phenomenon of drifter tourism. *International Journal of Comparative Sociology, XIV*, 1–2.

Cole, T. (2003). Turning the places of holocaust history into places of holocaust memory. In: S. Hornstein, & F. Jacobowitz (Eds), *Image and remembrance: representation and the holocaust,* Bloomington: Indiana University Press (pages — Leopold's citation).

Conde, C. H. (2005). Long afterward, war still wears on Filipinos. *International Herald Tribune,* August 13, p. 1.

Cook, T. J. (1871). Re-opening of Paris. *Travel Excursionist,* Thomas Cook Archive, Peterborough, 15 May.

Cooper, M. (2006). The Pacific War battlefields: Tourist attractions or war memorials? *International Journal Of Tourism Research, 8*(3), 213–222.

Cooper, M., Jankowska, R., & Eades, J (2006). The politics of exclusion? Japanese cultural reactions and the government's desire to double inbound tourism. In: P. Burns, & M. Novelli (Eds), *Tourism and politics: Global frameworks and local realities.* London: Elsevier Advances in Tourism Research Series (In Press).

Conrad, S. (2003). Entangled memories: Versions of the past in Germany and Japan, 1945–2000. *Journal of Contemporary History, 38*(1), 85–99.

Creveld, M. (1994). Why men fight. In: L. Freedman (Ed.), *War.* Oxford: Oxford University Press.

Crompton, J. L. (1979). Motivations for pleasure vacation. *Annals of Tourism Research, 6*, 408–424.

Crooke, E. (2001). Confronting a troubled history: Which past in Northern Ireland's museums? *International Journal of Heritage Studies, 7*(2), 119–136.

Crotts, J., & Litvin, S. (2004). *Survey of visitors to Charleston.* Unpublished survey for the Charleston Conference and Visitor Bureau. Department of Hospitality and Tourism, College of Charleston, Charleston, SC, USA.

Crow, J. A. (1985). *Spain: The root and the flower.* London: University of California Press.

Csiksentmihalyi, M. (1990). *Flow: The psychology of optimal experience.* New York: Harper & Row.

D'Amore, L. (1989). Tourism — the world's peace industry. *Annals of Tourism Research, 27*, 35–40.

Dang, N. (2005). Jinggangshan Mountain: Leading the Red Tourism. *Town Tourism, 2*, 10–13.

Dann, G. (1977). Anomie, ego-enhancement and tourism. *Annals of Tourism Research, 4*, 184–194.

Dann, G. M. S. (1996). *The language of tourism: A sociolinguistic perspective.* Wallingford, Oxon, UK: CAB International.

Davis, J. B. (2001). Commentary. Tourism research and social theory: Expanding the focus. *Tourism Geographies, 3*(2), 125–134.

Davis, W. C. (1999). *Three roads to the Alamo: the lives and fortunes of David Crockett, James Bowie and William Barret Travis.* New York: Harper.

de Burlo, C. (1984). *Indigenous response and participation in tourism in a south west Pacific nation, Vanuatu.* Ph.D. dissertation, Syracuse University.

de Meneses, F. R. (2001). *Franco and the Spanish Civil War.* London: Routledge.

Denzin, N. K. (1989). *Interpretive interactionism.* Newbury Park, CA: Sage.

Denzin, N. K. (1992). *Symbolic interactionism and cultural studies — The politics of interpretation.* Oxford: Blackwell.

Deutschlander, S., & Miller, L. J. (2004). A discursive analysis of cultural resistance: Indigenous constructions of blackfoot superiority. *Tourism, Culture and Communication, 5*, 59–68.

Dickason, O. P. (1986). Frontiers in transition: Nova Scotia 1713–1763 compared to the north-west 1869–1885. In: F. L. Barron, & J. B. Waldram (Eds). *1885 and after: Native society in transition* (pp. 23–38). Regina, Saskatchewan: Canadian Plains Research Center, University of Regina.

Douglas, N., Douglas, N., & Derrett, R. (Eds). (2001). *Special interest tourism: Context and cases.* Milton, Queensland: J. Wiley & Sons Australia.

Duff, C. (2003). *The '45.* London: Cassell.

Duffy, T. M. (2001). Museums of human suffering and the struggle for human rights. *Museum International, 53*, 1.

Duncan, A., & Opatowski, M. (2000). *Trouble spots: The world atlas of strategic information.* Stroud: Sutton Publishing.

Duncan, A., & Opatowski, M. (2002). *The essential guide to the world's trouble spots.* Stroud: Sutton Publishing.

Dunkley, R. A. (2006). The thanatourist: A fascination with death and atrocity. Powerpoint presentation for the tourism society.

Dwan, R., & Homqvist, (2005). Major armed conflicts. *SIPRI yearbook 2005.* Oxford: Oxford University Press.

Dyer, G. (1998). On with the war. *The Guardian,* 20 August.

El País, (2004). 8.000 personas conmemoran en el Valle de los caídos la muerte de Franco, *El País,* 21 November 2004.

El País, (2005). 30 asociaciones dan ideas al Gobierno para transformar el Valle de los Caidos, *El País,* http://www.elpais.es/articulo/elpepiautmad/20050329elpmad_10/Tes (accessed 12 May 2005).

El País, (2006). La Futura Ley de la Memoria: 90.000 fusilados, 900 desenterrados', *El País,* 13 August, 24.

Elsrud, T. (2001). Risk creation in travelling. *Annals of Tourism Research, 28*(3), 597–617.

Engel, M. (2001). Born in the USA. *Guardian,* 4 December.

Epps, B., Ernst, H., Henry, A., & Johnson, R. (2005). *Marketing plan for Patriot's point.* Unpublished project. Department of Hospitality and Tourism, College of Charleston, Charleston, SC, USA.

Ersavci, M. (2006). Brutal battles that created legends. *The Sunday Mail,* 23 April, 40–41.

Essex, S. J., & Gibb, R. A. (1989). Tourism in the Anglo-French frontier zone. *Geography, 74*(3), 222–231.

Eureka 150 (2004). *Eureka 150: Diversity, dissent, democracy.* Melbourne: State Government of Victoria.

Fieguth, M., & Christensen, D. (1986). *Historic Saskatchewan.* Saskatoon: Western Producer Prairie Books.

Figal, G. (2002). Censoring history: Citizenship and memory in Japan, Germany, and the United States. *The Journal of Japanese Studies, 28*(1), 166.

Foley, M., & Lennon, J. (1996). JFK and dark tourism: A fascination with assassination. *International Journal of Heritage Studies, 2*(4), 198–211.

Foley, M., & Lennon, J. (1997). Dark tourism — An ethical dilemma. In: M. Foley, J. Lennon, & G. Maxwell (Eds), *Hospitality, tourism and leisure management.* Oxford: Cassel (Leopold citation).

Frank, R. B. (1990). *Guadalcanal: The definitive account of the land battle.* Middlesex, England: Penguin Books Ltd.

Frangialli, F. (2001). Tourism: The enhancement of respect. *UN Chronicle, 38*(2), 51–54.

Franklin, A. (2003). *Tourism: An introduction.* London: Sage Publications.

Friedmann, J. (1966). *Regional development policy: A case of Venezuela.* Cambridge, MA: MIT Press.

Frost, W. (2005). Making an edgier interpretation of the Gold Rushes: Contrasting perspectives from Australia and New Zealand. *International Journal of Heritage Studies, 11*(3), 235–250.

Frost, W. (2006a). Braveheart-ed Ned Kelly: Historic films, heritage tourism and destination image. *Tourism Management, 27*(2), 247–254.

Frost, W. (2006b). From Diggers to Baristas: Tourist shopping villages in the Victorian goldfields. *Journal of Hospitality and Tourism Management, 13*(2), 136–143.

Frost, W. (2007). Refighting the Eureka Stockade: Managing a dissonant battlefield. In: C. Ryan (Ed.), *Battlefield tourism: History, place and interpretation* (pp. 187–194). Oxford: Elsevier.

Garrison, R. (1983). *Task force 9156 and 111 islands command: A story of a South Pacific advanced base during World War II*. Efate, New Hebrides. Boston: Nimrod Press.

Gatewood, J., & Cameron, C. M. (2004). Battlefield pilgrims at Gettysburg National Military Park. *Ethnology, 43*(2), 193–216.

Gibbons, J. D., & Fish, M. (1987). Market sensitivity of U.S. and Mexican border travel. *Journal of Travel Research, 26*(1), 2–6.

Glosserman, B. (2004). Fog of politics obscures war. *The Japan Times*, January 27, 19.

Goffman, E. (1959). *The presentation of self in everyday life*. Garden City, NY: Doubleday.

Gold, J. R., & Gold, M. M. (2003). Representing Culloden: Social memory, battlefield, heritage, and landscapes of regret. In: S. P. Hanna, & V. J. Del Casino (Eds), *Mapping Tourism* (pp. 108–131). Minneapolis: University of Minnesota Press.

Goldin, C., & Lewis, F. (1975). The economic costs of the American Civil War: Estimates and implications. *Journal of Economic History, 35*, 299–326.

Goldin, C., & Lewis, F. (1978). The Post-Bellum Recovery of the South and the cost of the Civil War: Comment. *Journal of Economic History, 38*, 487–492.

Goodheart, A. (2005). Hallowed ground, US Civil War battlefields see new conflicts. *National Geographic, 207*(4), 62–85.

Goodman, D. (1998). Eureka stockade. In: G. Davison, J. Hirst, & S.MacIntyre (Eds). *The Oxford companion to Australian history* (pp. 227–228). Melbourne: Oxford University Press.

Gordon, B. M. (1998). Warfare and tourism: Paris in World War II. *Annals of Tourism Research, 25*(3), 616–638.

Goulding, C. (2000). The commodification of the past, postmodern pastiche, and the search for authentic experiences at contemporary heritage attractions. *European Journal of Marketing, 34*(7), 835–853.

Graham, B. (1996). The contested interpretation of heritage landscapes in Northern Ireland. *International Journal of Heritage Studies, 2*(1), 10–22.

Graham, B. (2002). Heritage as knowledge: Capital or culture? *Urban Studies, 39*(5/6), 1003–1017.

Graham, B., Ashworth, G., & Tunbridge, J. (2000). *A geography of heritage: Power, culture and economy*. London: Arnold Publishers.

Graham, H. (2005). *The Spanish Civil War*. Oxford: Oxford University Press.

Grattan, C. H. (1963). *The southwest Pacific since 1900*. Ann Arbor: University of Michigan Press.

Greenberg, P. (2006). Even with change, Charleston is never a 'No South'. *Charleston Post and Courier*, April 6, 13A.

Griffiths (1993). Down with the cult of monument. *Battlefield Trust Newsletter*, July.

GRM International (2006). *Invitation to tender: Profile and marketing plan for a tourism niche, WWII history of the Solomon Islands*. Sydney: GRM International.

Gu, H., Ryan, C., & Zhang, W. (2007). Jinggangshan Mountain – a paradigm of China's Red tourism. In: C. Ryan (Ed.), *Battlefield tourism: History, place and interpretation*. Oxford: Elsevier.

Guest, D., & Guest, K. (1996). *British Battles*. Fulham: Harper Collins.

Guest, K., & Guest, D. (1996). *British battlefields*. London: Harper Collins.

Gunderson, G. (1974). The origin of the American Civil War. *Journal of Economic History, 34*, 915–950.

Hall, C. M. (2002). ANZAC day and secular pilgrimage. *Tourism Recreation Research, 27*(2), 83–87.

Hall, C. M., & McArthur, S. (1998). *Integrated heritage management.* London: The Stationery Office.

Hannam, K. (2006). Contested discourses of war and heritage at the British residency, Lucknow, India. *International Journal Of Tourism Research, 8*(3), 199–212.

Harris, P. (1998). Testosterone tourism: The ultimate war zone adventure holiday. *Combat and Survival, 12*(8).

Harrison, D. (2005). Contested narratives in the domain of heritage. In: D. Harrison, & M. Hitchcock (Eds), *The politics of world heritage: Negotiating tourism and conservation* (pp. 1–10). Clevedon: Channel View Publications.

Harvey, J. (1994). *Eureka rediscovered: In search of the site of the historic stockade.* Ballarat: University of Ballarat Press.

Hastings, M. (1984). *Overlord: D-day and the battle for Normandy.* London: Pan Books.

Hellyer, R. (2002). Historical and contemporary perspectives on the Sakoku theme in Japanese foreign relations 1600–2000. *Social Science Japan Journal, 5*(2), 255–259.

Henderson, J. (2000). War as a tourist attraction: the case of Vietnam. *International Journal of Tourism Research, 2*(4), 269–280.

Hendry, J. (2000). *The orient strikes back. A global view of cultural display.* Oxford: Berg.

Herzog, L. A. (1990). *Where north meets south: Cities, space, and politics on the U.S.-Mexico border.* Austin: Center for Mexican American Studies, University of Texas.

Hewison, R. (1987). *The heritage industry: Britain in a climate of decline.* London: Metheun.

Hewison, R. (1989). *The heritage industry: Britain in a climate of decline.* London: Methuen.

Hobsbawm, & Ranger (Eds). (1983). *The invention of tradition.* Cambridge: Cambridge University Press.

Hocking, G. (2000). *To the diggings! A celebration of the 150th anniversary of the discovery of gold in Australia, 1851–2001.* Melbourne: Lothian.

Holguín, S. (2005). National Spain invites you: Battlefield tourism during the Spanish Civil War. *The American Historical Review, 10*(5), 1399–1426.

Hollinshead, K. (1999). Tourism as public culture: Horne's ideological commentary on the legerdemain of tourism. *The International Journal of Tourism Research, 1,* 267–292.

Holmes, R. (1997). *War Walks 2.* London: BBC Books.

Hornstein, S. (2003). Invisible topographies. In: S. Hornstein, & F. Jacobowitz (Eds), *Image and remembrance: Representation and the Holocaust.* Bloomington: Indiana University Press.

Hornstein, S. & Jacobowitz, F. (2003). *Image and remembrance: Representation and the Holocaust.* Bloomington: Indiana University Press.

Howard, P. (2003). *Heritage: Management, interpretation, identity.* London: Continuum.

Huber, J. (1974). The emergency of emergent theory. *American Sociological Review, 38,* 274–284.

Hunter, J. (1999). *Last of the free.* Edinburgh: Mainstream.

Hunter, J. (2006). Inaugural speech for the UHI Centre for History, Dornoch, 19th May 2006, www.heritagenorth.org.uk/Prof_Jim_Hunter_Inaugural_Speech.html.

Husbands, W. (1981). Centres, peripheries, tourism and socio-spatial development. *Ontario Geography, 17,* 37–59.

Imperial War Museum (2005). www.iwm.org.uk (accessed 13 August 2005).

Imperial War Museum (2006). *Imperial war museum,* http://www.iwm.org.uk/ (accessed 1 July 2006).

Inder, S. (1966). New cash, new owners – but the same old policy for Honiara Mendana. *Pacific Islands Monthly,* March, 125–127.

Inglis, K. S. (1998). *Sacred places: War memorials in the Australian landscape.* Melbourne: University of Melbourne Press.

International Council of Museums (2001). *ICOM code of ethics for museums.* International Council of Museums, http://icom.museum/ethics_rev_engl.html (accessed 23 October 2003).

Jia, H., Zhang, Y., & Fang, S. (2005). The development of the red tourism in the Jinggangshan Mountain and the increase of the farmers' income. *Journal of Jiangxi Normal University, 8*, 60–62.

Johnson, D. G., Sullivan, J. (1993). Economic impacts of Civil War battlefield preservation: An ex-ante evaluation. *Journal of Travel Research, 32*(1), 21–29.

Kawakatsu, H. (2000). *Opening Sakoku*. Tokyo: Dobunkan.

Kegley, C. W., & Wittkopff, E. R. (2001). *World politics* (8th ed.). Basingstoke: Macmillan Press Ltd.

Kemp, A. (1998). Satisfying the spirit of adventure in a world without war. *The Observer*, 15 November.

Kennett, J. (1998). Cherish the past, look to the future. *Ballarat Courier*, Eureka Stockade Centre: Birthplace of the Australian Spirit (supplement), 27 March, p. 2.

Kibata, Y. (2005). Unfinished decolonisation and conflicts over historical memory. In: S. Alomes (Ed.), *Islands in the stream: Australia and Japan face globalisation* (pp. 103–114). Hawthorn: Maribyrnong Press.

Kim, Y. K., & Crompton, J. L. (1990). Role of tourism in unifying the two Koreas. *Annals of Tourism Research, 17*, 353–366.

Kinross, J. (1979). *Discovering battlefields of England*. Aylesbury: Shire Publications Ltd.

Kinross, J. (1988b). *Walking and exploring the battlefields of Britain*. London: David & Charles.

Knox, D. (2006). The sacralized landscapes of Glencoe: From massacre to mass tourism, and back again. *International Journal Of Tourism Research, 8*(3), 185–197.

Koenig, H. (1981). The two Berlins. *Travel Holiday, 156*(4), 58–63, 79–80.

Kogure, S. (2004). Casualty of war. *The Japan Times*, June 16, Community, 14.

Koppel, B. M., & Orr, R. M (Eds). (1993). *Japan's foreign aid*. New York: Westview Press.

Kroger, L. (1985). *Black slave owners: Free black slave masters in South Carolina, 1790–1860*. Columbia, SC: University of South Carolina Press.

Kupiananen, J. (2000). *Tradition, trade and wood carving in Solomon Islands*. The Finish Anthropological Society TAFAS45, Helsinki. HojBergm Denmark: Intervention Press.

Landwehr, A. (2006). An important seat at the global table. *Bangkok Post*, 8 September, Section 1, p. 8.

Laracy, H. (1988). War comes to the Solomon Islands. In: H. Laracy & G. White (Eds), *Taem Blong Faet: World War in Melanesia. 'O' O. A. Journal of Solomon Islands Studies, 4*, 4–26.

Lee, Y-S. (2006). Tourism for peace? Legacy of Korean War on the tourism industry and its people in South Korea. *International Journal Of Tourism Research, 8*(3), 157–170.

Lenman, B. (1986). *The Jacobite cause*. Glasgow: NTS/Richard Drew.

Lennon, J. J., & Foley, M. (2000). *Dark tourism: The attraction of death and disaster*. London: Continuum.

Leopold, T., & Ritchie, B. W. (2003). Former Nazi concentration camps in Germany: Memorials or tourist attractions? In: B. W. Ritchie (Ed.), *Managing educational tourism* (pp. 78–82). Clevedon: Channel View Publications.

Levi, P. (1984). Introduction. In: S. Johnson, & J. Boswell, *A journey to the western islands of Scotland and the journal of a tour to the Hebrides*. Harmondsworth: Penguin Edition.

Light, D. (2000). Gazing on communism: Heritage tourism and post-communist identities in Germany, Hungary and Romania. *Tourism Geographies, 2*(2), 157–176.

Lintner, B. (1991). Forgotten frontiers: Peace brings investors to notorious border region. *Far Eastern Economic Review*, 16 May, 23–24.

Lister, D., McGregory, D., & Beeston, R. (2004). Briton shot dead in Iraq was on leave from army. *The Times,* 30 March.

Lloyd, D. (1998). *Battlefield tourism: pilgrimage and the commemoration of the Great War in Britain, Australia, and Canada, 1919–1939*. Oxford: Berg.

Loewen, J. W. (1999). *Lies across America: What our historic sites get wrong*. New York: New Press.

Lonely Planet (2004). *Madrid: City guide*. London: Lonely Plant Publications.

Lowenthal, R. (1981). *Our past before us: Why do we need to do it*. USA: Temple Smith.

Lutz, T. (1994). *Making historical sites visible — holocaust memorials in Germany.* Berlin: Topography of Terror Foundation.

MacCannell, D. (1989). *The tourist: A new theory of the leisure class.* New York: Schocken Books.

MacCannell, D. (1999). *The tourist: A new theory of the leisure class.* London: University of California Press.

Maier, C. (1994). A surfeit of memory? Reflections of history, melancholy and denial. *History and Memory, 5,* 136–152.

Malvar, A. (2005). Belchite, Parque Tematico? *El Mundo,* http://www.elmundo.es/cronica/2005/494/1112479206.html (accessed 15 February 2006).

Mason, R. H. P., & Caiger, J. (1997). *A history of Japan.* Boston: Tuttle.

Mayor de la Torre, J. A. (2005). La Verdad del Valle, *El País,* http://elpais.es/articulo Completo.html?d_date=&xref=20050508elpepiopi_11&t (accessed 12 May 2005).

McArthur, C. (1994). Culloden: A pre-emptive strike. *Scottish Affairs, 9,* 97–126.

McBride, P. (2006). Brothers? Well, maybe cousins. *Camp Chase Gazette, XXXIII*(5), 30–31.

McCabe, E. (2000). They shall not pass. *Guardian,* 10 November.

McCrone, D., Morris, A., & Kiely, R. (1995). *Scotland the brand: The making of Scottish heritage.* Edinburgh: Edinburgh University Press.

McLean, D. (1986). 1885: Métis rebellion or government conspiracy? In: F. L. Barron, & J. B. Waldram (Eds), *1885 and after: Native society in transition* (pp. 79–104). Regina, Saskatchewan: Canadian Plains Research Center, University of Regina.

McGahey, S. Tourism development in Iraq needs support of international academia. *International Journal Of Tourism Research, 8*(3), 235–239.

McPhail, C. (1991). *Far from the madding crowd.* New York: Aldine de Gruyter.

McPherson, J. (1988). *Battle cry of freedom: The Civil War era.* Oxford: Oxford University Press.

Meo, N. (2001). Backpackers risk all for the thrills of Kabul. *The Sunday Telegraph,* 26 August.

Merridale, C. (1999). War, death, and remembrance in Soviet Union. In: J. Winter, & E. Sivan (Eds), *War and remembrance in the twentieth century* (pp. 61–83). Cambridge: Cambridge University Press.

Midas Tours (2005). *Midas tours: Battlefield and historical tours 2005.* Gliingham: Midas Tours.

Midas Tours (2006). The Spanish Civil War, http://www.midastours.co.uk/t078a.html (accessed 21 July 2006).

Mihalic, T. (1996). Tourism and warfare — the case of Slovenia. In: A. Pizam, & Y. Mansfeld (Eds), *Tourism, crime and international security issues* (pp. 89–104). Chichester: John Wiley & Sons.

Miles, W. F .S. (2002). Auschwitz: Museum interpretation and darker tourism. *Annals of Tourism Research, 29*(4).

Mintel International Group (2002). Alternative destinations — global. February, available at http://reports.mintel.com/sinatra/mintel/searchexec/ (accessed 22 February 2005).

Mintel International Group (2004). Emerging destinations — international — September 2004, http://reports.mintel.com/sinatra/mintel/searchexec/ (accessed 22 February 2005).

Mohs, M. & Dunn, J. (1982). Guadalcanal: 40 years after. *Time,* 30 August.

Moir, R. (1991). Battlefields as national treasures. Battlefields as national treasures conference. Leicester University, 11 April.

Molinero, C., Sala, M., & Sobreques, J. (2003). *Una imensa prision.* Barcelona: Critica.

Molony, J. (1984). *Eureka.* Melbourne: Viking.

Molony, J. (2004). Dawn of a democracy. *The Age,* Review section, 27 November, 1–2.

Morris-Suzuki, T. (1998). *Re-inventing Japan: Time, space, nation.* New York: M. E. Sharpe.

Moscardo, G. (1996). Mindful visitors: Heritage and tourism. *Annals of Tourism Research, 23*(2), 376–397.

Museu d'Historia de Catalunya (2003). *Les Presons de Franco.* Barcelona: Generalitat de Catalunya.

Nash, E. (2005). Monument to Franco may be converted into memorial to his victims. *The Independent*, 29 March.

National Park Service, U.S. Department of the Interior (2005a). *Fort Sumter national monument South Carolina*. U.S. Government Printing Office 310-394/00301.

National Park Service, U.S. Department of the Interior (2005b). *History can hurt*. U.S. Government Printing Office 530-398.

Newark, T. (2001). *In heroes' footsteps: A walker's guide to battlefields of the world*. New York: Barrons Hauppauge.

Niigata Prefectural Board of Education (1997). *Preserving peace: Beyond the tragedy of Naoetsu POW camp (Heiwa wo Mamoru: Naoetsu Horyo Shuyojo no Higeki wo Koete)*. Niigata: Niigata Prefectural Board of Education.

Noakes, L. (1997). Making histories: Experiencing the blitz in London's museums in the 1990s. In: M. Evans, & K. Lunn (Eds), *War and memory in the twentieth century* (pp. 89–104). Oxford: Berg.

O'Connor, J. (2002). Where's the new Prague? *Observer*, 15 December.

Oliver, D. (1961). *The Pacific Islands* (rev. ed.). New York: Anchor Books.

Oliver, M. (2003). Parade of 10,000 pays tribute to the fallen. Centenarian veterans lead Cenotaph march past. *The Guardian*, 10 November, 1.

Osborn, A. (2006). Club Gulag: Tourists are offered prison camp experience. *The Independent*, 4 August.

Osifelo, Sir Fredrick (1985). *Kanaka boy. An autobiography*. Suva: Institute of Pacific Studies and Solomon Islands Extension Centre of the University of South Pacific.

Ospina, G. (2006). War and ecotourism in the national parks of Colombia. Some reflections on the public risk and adventure. *International Journal Of Tourism Research*, 8(3), 241–246.

Pacific Islands Monthly (1949). Honiara now has a hotel. June, 64, Sydney (PIM).

Pacific Islands Monthly (1971). Forever upwards! The hotel boom. June, 113–114, Sydney (PIM).

Page, S. J. (1994). Perspectives on tourism and peripherality: Review of tourism in the Republic of Ireland. *Progress in Tourism, Recreation and Hospitality Management*, 5, 26–53.

Paris, R. (2004). *At war's end: Building peace after civil conflict*. Cambridge: Cambridge University Press.

PATA (1985a). *Solomons Islands, advisory mission report*. PATA South Pacific Region Office, Sydney 25.

Patrimonio Nacional (2004). *Santa Cruz del Valle de los Caidos (Guidebook)*. Madrid: Patrimonio Nacional.

Patrimonio Nacional (2005). www.patrimonionacional.es (accessed 22 August 2005).

Patterson, J. S. (1989). From battle ground to pleasure ground: Gettysburg as a historic site. In: W. Leon, & R. Rosenzweig (Eds), *History museums in the United States: a critical assessment* (pp. 129–157). Urbana, IL: University of Illinois Press.

Payne, D., & Dimanche, F. (1996). Towards a code of conduct for the tourism industry: An ethics model. *Journal of Business Ethics*, 15(9), 997–1008.

Peattie, M. R. (1988). Nanyo. *Pacific Islands Monograph Series No. 4*, Center for Pacific Island Studies. Honolulu: University of Hawaii Press.

Pelton, R. Y. (2005). *The world's most dangerous places* (5th ed.). New York: Collins.

Pelton, R. Y., Aral, C., & Dulles, W. (1998). *The world's most dangerous places* (3rd ed.). New York: TemboLLC/Fielding Worldwide, USA.

Philibert, J. M. (1976). *La Bonne Vie: Lève et la Réalité*. Ph.D. dissertation, University of British Columbia, Vancouver.

Philips, U. B. (2004) *American Negro slavery*. New York: Kessinger Publishing Rare Reprints.

Piekarz, M. (2007). It's just a bloody field! Approaches, opportunities and dilemmas of interpreting English battlefields. In: C. Ryan (Ed.), *Battlefield sites as tourism attractions: History, heritage and interpretation*. Oxford: Pergamon Press.

Pinto, M., & Fleta, C. (2005). Que hacer con el panteón del franquismo? *El País,* http://www.elpais.es/ articulo/elpdomrpj/20050403elpdmgrep_2/Tes/Qu%C3%A9/hacer/pante%C3%B3n/franquismo (accessed 12 May 2005).

Plog, S. (1973). Why destinations rise and fall in popularity. *Cornell Hotel and Restaurant Quarterly,* November, 13–16.

Port Down Publishing (2006). Expeditionary Force by Ken Brittian. http://www. porttownpublishing.com/sciencefiction.htm (accessed 16 January 2007).

Powell, G. (2001). Napoleon is coming. *Wartime Magazine, 13,* 4–11.

Preston, P. (1996). *A concise history of the Spanish Civil War.* London: Fontana Press.

Preston, P. (2006). *The Spanish Civil War: Reaction, revolution & revenge.* London: Harper Perennial.

Pryer, M. (1997). The traveller as a destination pioneer. *Progress in Tourism and Hospitality Research, 3,* 225–237.

Ransom, R. L. (1998). The economic consequences of the American Civil War. In: M. Wolfson (Ed.), *The political economy of war and peace* (pp. 49–74). Norwell, MA: Kluwer Academic Publishers.

Raynor, M. (2004). *English battlefields.* Stroud: Tempus.

Red Tourism. http://www.crt.com.cn/news/Html/quanwei/00008640.html.

Reid, S. (2005). *Culloden 1746 — A battlefield guide.* Barnsley: Pen and Sword.

Reisinger, Y., & Turner, L. W. (2003). *Cross-cultural behaviour in tourism: Concepts and analysis.* Oxford: Butterworth Heinemann.

Restall, H. (2005). Opposing the sun: Japan alienates Asia. *Far Eastern Economic Review, 168*(4), 8–17.

Richards, M. (2002). From war culture to civil society: Francoism, social change and memories of the Spanish Civil War. *History and Memory, 14*(1/2), 93–120.

Richter, L. K. (1999). The politics of heritage tourism development. In: D. G. Pearce, & R. Butler (Eds), *Contemporary issues in tourism development* (pp. 108–126). London: Routledge.

Rigdon, J. (2001). *The battle of Aiken — February 11, 1865.* Augusat: GA Eastern Digital Resources.

Risi, M. (2005). Espana, un caso insolito de impunidad. *BBC World,* http://news.bbc.co.uk/hi/spanish/ international/newsid_4696000/4696473.stm (accessed 20 July 2005).

Roberts, D. (2003). A moment in time archives: The valley of the fallen. http://ehistory.osu.edu/world/ amit/display.cfm?amit_id=2392 (accessed 6 June 2005).

Roosevelt, M. (2001). Greetings from Zapatista land. *Time,* 3 September.

Ruiz, B. R. (2001). Las Rutas de guerra y los periodistas portugueses. *Historia y Comunicación Social, 6,* 123–134.

Ryan, C. (2006). The impact of China on tourism research: An outsider's perspective. Keynote paper. Tourism and the New Asia: Implications for Research, Policy and Practice. Peking University, Beijing. August 9–12.

Ryan, C., & Trauer, B. (2005). Adventure tourism and sport — an introduction. In: C. Ryan, S. J. Page, & M. Aicken (Eds), *Taking tourism to the limits — issues, concepts and managerial perspectives* (pp. 143–148). Oxford: Elsevier.

Ryan, C. (2006a). Trends in tourism research – Keynote Presentation. *12th Asia Pacific Tourism Association and 4th Asian Pacific Chrie Conference.* Taiwan Hospitality and Tourism Conference, Hualien, Taiwan.

Ryan, C. (2006b). The Impact of China on Tourism Research: An outsider's perspective. Keynote paper. Tourism and the New Asia: Implications for Research, Policy and Practice. Peking University, Beijing, August 9–12.

Sakai, K. (2004). Sampugita Holidays Sdn Bhd. 15 January.

Salamone, F. A. (1997). Authenticity in tourism: The San Angel inns. *Annals of Tourism Research, 24*(2), 305–321.

Salazar, N. B. (2004). Developmental tourists vs. developmental tourism: A case study. In: A. Raj (Ed.), *Tourism behaviour* (pp. 85–107).

Scates, B. (2006). Returning to Gallipoli. *Wartime, 34*, 8–10.

Schouten, F. F. J. (1995). Heritage as historical reality. In: D. T. Herbert (Ed.), *Heritage tourism and society*. London: Mansell.

Scotland's Census (2001). General Register for Scotland, www.gro-scotland.gov.uk/census/censushm/index.html.

Scott, P. H. (1994). The image of Scotland in literature. In: J. M. Fladmark (Ed.), *Cultural tourism* (pp. 362–373). Wimbledon: Donhead.

Seaton, A. (1999). War and thanatourism: Waterloo, 1815–1914. *Annals of Tourism Research, 26*(1), 130–158.

Seaton, A. (2000). Another weekend away looking for dead bodies: Battlefield tourism on the Somme and in Flanders. *Tourism Recreation Research, 25*(1), 63–77.

Seaton, A. V., & Bennett, M. M. (1996). *The marketing of tourism products: concepts, issues and cases*. London: International Thomson Business Press.

Sengupta, K., & Marbeau, L. (2003). Have war and terror made the planet too hot for tourism? *Independent,* 5 February.

Seymour (1997). *Battles in Britain: 1066–1746*. Chatham, Kent: Wordsworth Military Library.

Shillingsburg, M. J. (1988). *At home abroad: Mark Twain in Australasia*. Jackson, MI: University Press of Mississippi.

Short, V. (2002). Spain: Socialist Party demands opening of Franco's Mass Graves, *World Socialist,* www.wsws.org/articles/2002/oct2002/fran-o31.shtml (accessed 30 April 2004).

Siddle, R. & Hook, B. (Eds). (2003). Contested memories. In: *Japan and Okinawa: Structure and Subjectivity*. New York: Routledge.

Siegenthaler, P. (2002). Hiroshima and Nagasaki in Japanese Guide Books. *Annals of Tourism, 29*(4), 1111–1137.

Silver, L. (1989). *The battle of Vinegar Hill*. Sydney: Doubleday.

Simpson, J. (2002). *News from no man's land*. Basingstoke: Macmillan.

Singh, T. V. (2004). *New horizons in tourism: Strange experiences and stranger practices*. Wallingford, CT: CAB International.

Slade, P. (2003). Gallipoli Thanatourism: The meaning of ANZAC. *Annals of Tourism Research, 30*(4), 779–794.

Slayton, S. L. (2006). Gettysburg – the sacred ground. In: J. Trotta (Ed.), *Grief tourism*, www.grief-tourism.com.

Slowe, P. M. (1991). The geography of borderlands: The case of the Quebec-US borderlands. *Geographical Journal, 157*(2), 191–198.

Smith, L. J. (1993). *Tourism analysis: A handbook* (2nd ed.). Edinburgh: Longman.

Smith, N., & Croy, W. G. (2005). Presentation of dark tourism: Te Wairoa, the buried village. In: C. Ryan, S. Page, & M. Aicken (Eds), *Taking Tourism to the limits: Issues, concepts and managerial perspectives* (pp. 199–214). Oxford: Elsevier.

Smith, V. (1998). War and tourism: An American ethnography. *Annals of Tourism Research, 25*(1), 202–227.

Smith, V. L. (1996). War and its tourist attractions. In: A. Pizam, & Y. Mansfeld (Eds), *Tourism, crime and international security issues* (pp. 247–264). Chichester: John Wiley & Sons.

Smurthwaite, D. (1984). *The ordnance survey complete guide to the battlefields of Britain*. London: Webb & Bower.

Sofield, T. (1993). Indigenous tourism development. *Annals of Tourism Research, 20*, 729–750.

Soltow, L. (1975). Men and wealth in the United States 1850–1870 — Yale series in history. Yale: Yale University Press.

Sontag, S. (2004). The photos are us. *The Guardian,* 25 May.

Squires, N. (2003). War nearly destroyed the Solomons — now it can save them. *South China Morning Post,* August 3, 12.

Staiff, R. (no date). Contemporary tourism issues, Venice: A case study. *Tourism Geography,* www.hsc.edu.au/geography/activity/local/tourism/venicep.pdf (accessed 15 June 2006).

Stanley, G. F. G. (1986). The last word on Louis Riel — The man of several faces. In: F. L. Barron, & J. B. Waldram (Eds), *1885 and after: Native society in transition* (pp. 1–22). Regina, Saskatchewan: Canadian Plains Research Center, University of Regina.

Stevens, T. (1989). War and peace: Tourism's dilemma. *Leisure Management,* 9 (Nov.).

Swarbrooke, J. (1994). The future of the past: Heritage tourism into the 21st century. In: Seaton (Ed.), *Tourism: State of art* (pp. 222–229). Chichester: John Wiley & Sons.

Swarbrooke, J., & Horner, S. (2000). *Business tourism.* Oxford: Butterworth-Heinemann.

Talmadge, E. (2004). Echoes of war haunt Iwojima. *The Japan Times,* March 18, 3.

The Economist (2004a). Democracy's low-level equilibrium. *The Economist,* 14 August.

The Economist (2004b). Reporting from the edge. *The Economist,* 14 August.

The Economist (2006). Viva Zapatero. *The Economist,* 29 July, 15.

Thomas, H. (2003). *The Spanish Civil War.* London: Penguin.

Tilden, F. (1977). *Interpreting our heritage* (3rd ed.). Chapel Hill, North Carolina: The University of North Carolina Press.

Timmo, W. (2005). Armistice big bang doesn't come easy. *Cambridge Edition.* 2 November, 12.

Timothy, D. J. (1995a). International boundaries: New frontiers for tourism research. *Progress in Tourism and Hospitality Research, 1*(2), 141–152.

Timothy, D. J. (1995b). Political boundaries and tourism: Borders as tourist attractions. *Tourism Management, 16,* 525–532.

Timothy, D. J. (1997). Tourism and the personal heritage experience. *Annals of Tourism Research, 34,* 751–754.

Timothy, D. J. (2000). Borderlands: An unlikely tourist destination? *Boundary and Security Bulletin, 8*(1), 57–65.

Timothy, D. J. (2001). Tourism in the borderlands: Competition, complementarity and cross-frontier cooperateon. In: S. Krakover & Y. Gradus (Eds), *Tourism in frontier areas* (pp. 233–258). Baltimore, MD: Lexington Books.

Timothy, D. J., & Boyd, S. (2003). *Heritage tourism.* Harlow: Pearson Education Limited.

Toby, R. P. (1984). *State and diplomacy in early modern Japan: Asia in the development of the Tokugawa Bakufu.* Princeton, N.J.: Princeton University Press.

Tokyo Shimbun, (2004). Reading Koizumi. Unattributed, Tokyo: Tokyo Shimbun, 8 April.

Torres, F. (1988). *Belchite/South Bronx: A trans-cultural and trans-historical landscape.* Amherst, MA: University of Massachusetts.

Traynor, I. (2003). The privatisation of war. *The Guardian,* 10 December.

Trefalt, B. (2002). War, commemoration and national identity in modern Japan, 1868–1975. In: S. Wilson (Ed.), *Nation and nationalism in Japan.* London: RoutledgeCurzon.

Tunbridge, J. E., & Ashworth, G. J. (1996). *Dissonant heritage: The management of the past as a resource in conflict.* Chichester: Wiley.

Tusa, E. (1986). Silas Eto of New Georgia. In: G. Trompf (Ed.), *Prophets of Melanesia. Six essays.* Institute of Papua New Guinea Studies, Port Moresby and Institute of Pacific Studies, Suva, Fiji.

Twain, M. (1897). *Following the equator: A journey around the world, Vol. 1.* New York: Ecco, republished ©1996.

Ulmer, G. L. (1989). *Teletheory.* New York: Routledge.

United Nations (2004). *United Nations peacekeeping operations,* http://www.un.org/Depts/dpko/dpko/index.asp (accessed 27 November 2004).

US Department of Education, Institute of Education Sciences (2004). *National assessment of education progress — US history*. Washington: US Department of Education.

Uzzell, D. L. (1989). The hot interpretation of war and conflict. In: D. L. Uzzell (Ed.), *Heritage interpretation: The Natural and built environment* (pp. 33–46). London: Belhaven Press.

Vass, J. (1996). Culloden — 250 years on. http://www.highlanderweb.co.uk/culloden/inmemory.htm (accessed 25 September 2006).

Virr, C., Paterson, H., & Calder, S. (2001). Spanish Civil War journeys. *The Independent*, at http://travel.independent.co.uk/themes/culture/article163157.ece (accessed 20 July 2005).

Vogt, J. W. (1976). Wandering: Youth and travel behaviour. *The Annals of Tourism Research, 4*(2), 74–105.

Wakling, C. (2005) Rubbernecking in hell: Why do people holiday in war zones? *Adventure Travel Magazine*, Issue 59, September.

Walsh, K. (2001). Collective amnesia and the mediation of painful pasts: The representation of France in the Second World War. *International Journal of Heritage Studies, 7*(1), 83–98.

Wanhill, S. (1997). Peripheral area tourism: A European perspective. *Progress in Tourism and Hospitality Research, 3*(1), 47–70.

Weaver, D. B. (1998). Peripheries of the periphery: Tourism in Tobago and Barbuda. *Annals of Tourism Research, 25*, 292–313.

Weaver, D. B. (2000). The exploratory war-distorted destination life cycle. *The International Journal of Tourism Research, 2*(2), 151–161.

Weaver, D., & Lawton, L. (2002). *Tourism management*. Milton, Queensland: J. Wiley & Sons Australia.

Weiner, A. (1982). Ten years in the life of an Islander: The anthropology of development policies in the Trobriands, an anthropological view. *Bikmaus, 3*(4), 64–75.

Weld, T. (1839). *American Slavery as it is: Testimony of a thousand witnesses*. New York.

Whitacre, C., & Greene, J. A. (2005). From tragedy to symbol: The efforts to designate the Sand Creek Massacre Site as a national historic site. In: G. Ashworth, & R. Hartmann (Eds), *Horror and human tragedy revisited: The management of sites of atrocities for tourism* (pp. 60–69). New York: Cognizant.

White, G.M. (1995). Remembering Guadalcanal: National identity and transnational memory-making. *Public Culture, 7*, 529–555.

White, S. (2006). Patriots Point Museum Foundation gearing up for major capital campaign. *Moultrie News*. P. 1. Section B. April 12, *42*(15).

Whitmarsh, A. (2000) We will remember them: Memory and commemoration in war museums. *Journal Of Conservation and Museum Studies*, November, 1–15.

Wight, M. (1994). Wars of gain, fear and doctrine. In: L. Freedman (Ed.), *War*. Oxford: Oxford University Press.

Wight, A. C., & Lennon, J. J. (2005). Towards an understanding of visitor perceptions of 'dark' attractions: The case of the Imperial War Museum of the North, Manchester. *Journal of Hospitality and Tourism, 2*(2).

Wilkinson, P. (2001) *Terrorism versus democracy*. London: Frank Cass Publishers.

World Bank (1993). *Pacific Islands transport sector study, Vol. II: Solomon Islands*. Transport Survey; Report No. 10543-EAP, March 1993.

World Tourism Organisation (1998). *Tourism 2020 vision*. Madrid, Spain: World Tourism Organisation.

World Tourism Organisation (1999a). *Changes in leisure time: The impact of tourism*, Madrid, Spain: WTO.

World Tourism Organisation (1999b). *Approval of the global code of ethics for tourism*, http://www.world-tourism.org/projects/ethics/preamble.htm (accessed 23 September 2003).

World Tourism Organisation (2003). *Tourism highlights 2003,* http://reports.mintel.com/sinatra/mintel/searchexec (accessed 22 February 2005).

Worsley, P. (1968). *The trumpet shell sound: A study of cargo cults in Melanesia.* (Second Augment edn). New York: Schocken Books.

Wright, C. (2004). Sisters in arms. *The Sunday Age,* Agenda section, 28 November, 19.

www.jgstour.com (2006). Jinggangshan tour.

Yale, P. (1991). *From tourist attractions to heritage tourism.* UK: Elm Publications.

Yao, S., & Wang, F. (2005). The probe into the red tourism. *Journal of Beijing International Studies University, 2005*(5), 83–86.

Yoneyama, L. (1999). *Hiroshima traces: Time, space and the dialectics of memory* (213–214). Berkeley: University of California Press.

Young, L. (1998). *Japan's total empire.* Berkeley: University of California Press.

Yu, F., & Lu, L. (2005). The diagnosis and solution of the problems in the development of the red tourism. *Tourism Tribune, 20*(4), 56–61.

Yu, L. (1997). Travel between politically divided China and Taiwan. *Asia Pacific Journal of Tourism Research, 2*(1), 19–30.

Zoleveke, G. (1980). Zoleveke. In: J. Chick (Ed.), *A man from Choiseul. An Autobiography.* Suva: Institute of Pacific Studies, University of the South Pacific.

Further Reading

Akin, D. (1999). Compensation and the Melanesian State: Why the Kwaio keep claiming. *The Contemporary Pacific*, *11*, 35–67.

Alasia, S. (1989a). Population movement. In: H. Larcy (Ed.), *Ples Blong iumi. Solomon Islands the four thousand years*. Suva: Institute of Pacific Studies, University of the South Pacific.

Ballalae Eco-tourism Development Project (2005). *Chief concern for war wrecks*, 30 October, 2005—9:01pm. TokTime, *Solomon Star*, http://www.solomonstarnews.com/?q=node/5578 (accessed 4 June 2006).

Bantin, J. (1999). Diving war wrecks of the Solomon. *Diver*, http://www.divernet.com/travel/supp199/solomons.htm.

Barker, E. T. (1933). *Holiday trip to the Solomons*. Sydney.

Beattie, J. W. (1909). Catalogue of a series of photographs illustrating the scenery and peoples of the islands in the South and Western Pacific. Hobart.

Boutileir, J. (1989). Kennedy's army: Solomon islanders at war, 1942–1943. In: G. White & L. Lindstrom (Eds), *The Pacific Theater: Islands Representation of World War II*. Honolulu: University of Hawaii Press (Pacific Theater: Islands Representative).

British Solomon Islands Protectorate (BSIP) (1966). *News Sheet*, December, Honiara.

British Solomon Islands Protectorate (BSIP) (1968). *Annual Report*, Honiara.

Burt, B. (1994). *Tradition and Christianity: The colonial transformation of a Solomon Islands society*. Langhorne, PA: Harwood Academic Publishers.

Clement, W. F. M. (1942). *District officers diary, Guadalcanal*. Suva: Central Archives of Fiji (microfilm).

Collin, C. W. (1926). *Life and laughter 'mist the cannibals*. London: Hurst & Blackett.

Coombe, J. D. (1991). *Derailing the Tokyo express: The naval battles for the Solomon Islands that sealed Japan's fate*. Harrisburg, PA: Stackpole Books.

Dann, G. (1996). *The language of tourism: A sociolinguistic perspective*. Wallingford, Oxon: CAB International.

Danielsson, Marie Therese, & Danielsson, B. (1986). New light on JFK and PT109. *Pacific Islands Monthly*, *57*(1), 24–6.

de Burlo, C. (1990). Islanders, soldiers and tourist: The war and the shaping of tourism in Melanesia. In: G. White & L. Lindstrong (Eds), *The Pacific Theater: Islands representation of World War II*. Honolulu: University of Hawaii Press.

Douglas, N. (1996). *They came for savages: One hundred years of tourism in Melanesia*. Lismore, NSW: Southern Cross University Press.

Douglas, N. (2004). Towards history of tourism in Solomon Islands. *Journal of Pacific Studies*, *26*(1), 29–49.

Douglas, N., & Douglas, N. (1996). P & O's Pacific. *Journal of Tourism Studies*, *7*(1), 1–14.

Douglas, N., & Douglas, N. (1999). Towards a history of tourism in Sarawak. *Asia Pacific Journal of Tourism Research*, *4*(1), 77–86.

FiFi'i, J., & Akin, D. (1988). World War II and the origin of Maasina rule: One Kwaio view. In: White et al. (Eds), *The big death: Solomon islanders remember World War II* (pp. 216–226). Suva: Institute of Pacific Studies.

Frank, R. B. (1990). *Guadalcanal: The definitive account of the land battle*. Middlesex, England: Penguin Books Ltd.

Gegeo, D., & Watson-Gegeo, K. A. (1989). World War II experience and life history two cases from Malaita (Solomon Islands). In: G. White and L. Lindstrom (Eds), *The Pacific Theater: Islands representation of World War II*. Honolulu: University of Hawaii Press.

Harwood, F. (1978). Intercultural communication in the western Solomons: The Methodist mission and the emergence of the Christian fellowship church. In: J. A. Boutilier, D. B. Hughes & W. T. Sharon (Eds), *Mission, church and sect in Oceania*. University Press of America.

Hook, D. (1981). Battlefields of the South Pacific, the Solomon Islands. In: *Fodor's Australian, New Zealand and the South Pacific* (pp. 493–497). New York: David Mckay.

Hviding, E. (1995a). Maritime travel, present and past, in Marovo, western Solomon Islands. In: R. Feingberg (Ed.), *Seafaring in contemporary Pacific Islands studies in continuity and change.* DeKalb: Northern Illinois University Press.

Iso-Ahola, S.E., & Weissinger, E. (1990). Perceptions of boredom in leisure: Conceptualization, reliability and validity of the leisure boredom scale. *Journal of Leisure Research, 22*, 1–17.

Keesing, R. (1982). Kastom in Melanesia: An overview. In: R. Keesing & R. Tonkinson (Eds), *Reinventing Traditional Culture: The Politics of Kastom in Island Melanesia.* Special issue of *Mankind, 13*(4), 297–301.

Keesing, R. (1989). Creating the past: Custom and identity in the contemporary Pacific. *The Contemporary Pacific, 1*, 12–42.

Kenilorea, P. (1976). Cultural values versus the acquisitiveness of man. *Pacific Perspectives, 5*(2), 3–8.

Kupiananen, J. (1997c). The colonial transformation of woodcarving in Bellona and Gatokae in the Solomon Islands. *Journal of the Finnish Anthropological Society, 22*(1), 18–30.

Lennon, J. & Foley, M. (2000). *Dark tourism: The attraction of death and disaster.* London: Continuum.

Lindstrom, L., & White, G. (1990). *Island encounters: Black and white memories of the Pacific war.* Washington, DC: Smithsonian Institution Press.

Lindstrom, L., & White, G. M. (Eds). (1994). *Culture, kastom, tradition: Developing cultural policy in Melanesia.* Suva, Fiji: Institute of Pacific Studies.

Lloyd, D. (1998). Battlefield tourism, pilgrimage and the commemoration of the Great War in Britain, Australia and Canada, 1919–1939. Library of Congress cataloging-in-publication data. UK: Oxford International Publishers Ltd.

Lowenthal, D. (1986). Introduction. In: E. C. Penning-Rowsell & D. Lowenthal (Eds), *Landscape meanings and values* (pp. 1–3). London: Allen and Unwin.

Nelson, H. (1980). Taim bilong pait: The impact of the Second World War on Papua New Guinea. In: A. W. McCoy (Ed.), *South east Asia under Japanese occupation. Transition and transformation.* New Haven: Yale University Press.

Nelson, H. (1982). Taim bilong masta: The Australian involvement in Papua New Guinea. Australian Broadcasting Commission, Sydney.

Otter, M. (2002). *Solomon Islands human development report 2002: Building a nation.* Solomon Islands Government, University of Queensland, Australia.

Pacific Islands Monthly (1934). Non-spending tourists. October, 44, Sydney (PIM).

Pacific Islands Monthly (1966). Letters to editor. July, 51, Sydney (PIM).

Pacific Islands Yearbook (1932). *Pacific shipping services* (1st ed.), Sydney: Pacific Publications.

Parr, T. (1985). *Solomon Islands. Advisory mission report.* Sydney: PATA Pacific Regional Office.

Philibert, J.-M. (1986). The politics of tradition: Toward a generic culture in Vanuatu. *Mankind, 16*, 1–12.

PT BOAT 109: The rescue of Kennedy, http://news.nationalgeographic.com/news/2002/07/0709_020710_kennedyPT109.html (accessed June 2006).

Rusa, D. (2006). Solomon star. Defacing of World War wrecks stun tourist, *Solomon Star*, http://www.solomonstarnews.com/?q=node/6662.

Russel, D., & Stabile, J. (2003). Ecotourism in practice: Trekking the highlands of Makira Island, Solomon Islands. In: D. Harrison (Ed.), *Pacific Island tourism*. London: Cognizant Communication Corporation.

Smith, V. L. (1996). War and its tourist attractions. In: A. Pizam & Y. Mansfeld (Eds), *Tourism, crime and international security issues* (pp. 247–264). Brisbane: John Wiley and Sons Ltd.

Solomon Islands Ministry of Finance (1979). *Statistical yearbook (December)*. Honiara: Solomon Islands.

Solomon Islands Tourism Authority (1990). *Solomon Islands tourism development plan 1991–2000*. Honiara: Solomon Islands Tourist Authority.

Solomon Islands Visitor Survey (1999). *A survey report*. Suva, Fiji: Tourism Council of the South Pacific.

Solomon Star (2005a). WWII provides historical link between SI and Japan 9 December, 2005–10:29am. Nation, http://www.solomonstarnews.com/?q=node/6334 (accessed 6 May 2006).

Solomon Star (2005b). Melanesian block on tourism drive 29th June 2005: http://www.solomon-starnews.com/?q=node/3427 (accessed 10 March 2006).

Solomon Star (2005c). Government committed to tourism development. 21 April, 2005, http://wwhttp://www.solomonstarnews.com/?q=node/2094w.solomonstarnews.com/?q=node/2100 (accessed 21 March 2006).

Solomon Star (2006a). Lawrence Foanaotoa, Director of National Museum War Wrecks (Solomon Star 19th January 2006), http://www.solomonstarnews.com/?q=node/6647 (accessed 4 June 2006).

Solomon Star (2006b). Tourist arrogancy, 25 January, 2006. Letters, http://www.solomonstarnews.com/?q=node/6720 (accessed 6 May 2006).

Solomon Star (2006c). Radio operator visits battleground, http://www.solomonstarnews.com/?q=node/5555 (accessed 6 May 2006).

Solomon Star. A review of Solomon Islands' 1991–2000 tourism development plans is currently underway to improve the country's tourism sector, http://www.solomonstarnews.com/?q=node/5112 (accessed 2 February 2006).

South Pacific Regional Tourism Marketing Plan (1998–2002). *The Dawning of a New Millennium*. TCSP Publication.

South Pacific Tourism Organisation (SPTO) (2002). *2002 Annual summary of regional tourism statistic*. Suva: SPTO.

Spennemann, D. H. R. (1992). Apocalypse now? – the fate of World War II sites on the Central Pacific Islands. *Cultural Resources Management,* (U.S.National Park Service, Washington), *15*(2), 15–16, 22.

Steinbauer, F. (1979). *Melanesian cargo cults*. Brisbane: University of Queensland Press.

Technical Report, AusAID (2004). *Pacific regional transport study, volume 2, country action plan*. Honiara: Solomon Islands Government Printer.

Terkel, S. (1984). The good war. An oral history of World War II. New York: Pantheon.

Uzzel, D. L. (1989). The hot interpretation of war and conflict. In: D. L. Uzzel (Ed.), *Heritage interpretation: The natural and built environment* (pp. 33–46), London: Belhaven.

White, G. M., Gegeo, D., Akin, D., & Watson-Gegeo, K. (Eds.), (1988). *The big death: Solomon islanders remember World War II*. Suva: Institute of Pacific Studies.

Unpublished Sources

BSIP 1/111, F 14/9. Solomon Islands National Archives, Honiara.

BSIP 1/111, F 14/19. Solomon Islands National Archives, Honiara.

BSIP 1/111, F 14/34. Solomon Islands National Archives, Honiara.

BSIP 1/111, F 14/45. Solomon Islands National Archives, Honiara.

BSIP 1/111, F 14/9 Part 1: Solomon Islands National Archives, Honiara.

BSIP 1/111, F 14/51. Solomon Islands National Archives, Honiara.

BSIP 1/111, F 14/56. Solomon Islands National Archives, Honiara.

BSIP 1/111, F 14/32. Solomon Islands National Archives, Honiara.

Gasa, Biuku Nebuchadnezar and Aaron Kumana, n.d. (1980) The PT10-9 Crew.

Rescue: The Scouts stories. Unpublished ms 8pp. Gizo, Western Province Information Office.

Subject Index